Public Real Estate Markets and Investments

FINANCIAL MARKETS AND INVESTMENTS SERIES
H. Kent Baker and Greg Filbeck, Series Editors

Portfolio Theory and Management
H. Kent Baker and Greg Filbeck (Co-Editors)

Public Real Estate Markets and Investments
H. Kent Baker and Peter Chinloy (Co-Editors)

Private Real Estate Markets and Investments
H. Kent Baker and Peter Chinloy (Co-Editors)

Public Real Estate Markets and Investments

EDITED BY H. KENT BAKER

and

PETER CHINLOY

OXFORD
UNIVERSITY PRESS

OXFORD
UNIVERSITY PRESS

Oxford University Press is a department of the University of Oxford.
It furthers the University's objective of excellence in research, scholarship,
and education by publishing worldwide.

Oxford New York
Auckland Cape Town Dar es Salaam Hong Kong Karachi
Kuala Lumpur Madrid Melbourne Mexico City Nairobi
New Delhi Shanghai Taipei Toronto

With offices in
Argentina Austria Brazil Chile Czech Republic France Greece
Guatemala Hungary Italy Japan Poland Portugal Singapore
South Korea Switzerland Thailand Turkey Ukraine Vietnam

Oxford is a registered trade mark of Oxford University Press
in the UK and certain other countries.

Published in the United States of America by
Oxford University Press
198 Madison Avenue, New York, NY 10016

Library of Congress Cataloging-in-Publication Data
Public real estate markets and investments / edited by H. Kent Baker and Peter Chinloy.
p. cm. — (Financial markets and investments series)
Includes bibliographical references and index.
ISBN 978–0–19–999327–7 (alk. paper)
1. Real estate investment trusts. 2. Real estate investment. I. Baker, H. Kent (Harold Kent),
1944– II. Chinloy, Peter, 1950–
HG5095.P83 2014
332.63'24—dc23

2014003348

Contents

Acknowledgments

Editing is like pruning the rose bush you thought was so perfect and beautiful until it overgrew the garden.
—Larry Enright

Public Real Estate Markets and Investments required the efforts of many people. The chapter authors deserve special recognition for their substantial efforts writing highly informative chapters. Without their chapters, there literally would be no book. As co-editors, we appreciate the latitude they gave us to prune their work so the beauty of each word stood out. Our expert team at Oxford University Press deserves thanks for exhibiting a high degree of professionalism throughout the process. We also thank Claudie Peterfreund, Cover-to-Cover Indexing Services, for developing the index. The list of those contributing to this book is long and their efforts added substantially to the quality of the book. We also want to recognize the support provided by the Kogod School of Business at American University. The authors dedicate this book to Linda Baker, Chris Chinloy, and Diana Hancock for their ongoing support.

About the Editors

H. Kent Baker, CFA, CMA, is University Professor of Finance in the Kogod School of Business at American University. Professor Baker has authored or edited 23 books. Among his most recent books with Oxford University Press are *Portfolio Theory and Management* (2013), *International Finance: A Survey* (2013), and *Survey Research in Corporate Finance* (2011). His most current books with John Wiley & Sons, Inc. are *Investor Behavior—The Psychology of Financial Planning and Investing* (2014), *Market Microstructure in Emerging and Developed Markets* (2013), *Alternative Investments—Balancing Opportunity and Risk* (2012), and *Socially Responsible Finance and Investing* (2012). As one of the most prolific finance academics, he has published more than 150 refereed articles in such journals as the *Journal of Finance, Journal of Financial and Quantitative Analysis, Financial Management, Financial Analysts Journal, Journal of Portfolio Management,* and *Harvard Business Review.* He has consulting and training experience with more than 100 organizations, serves on six editorial boards, and is the past president of the Southern Finance Association. Professor Baker holds a BSBA from Georgetown University; MEd, MBA, and DBA degrees from the University of Maryland; and an MA, MS, and two PhDs from American University.

Peter Chinloy is Professor of Finance and Real Estate in the Kogod School of Business at American University. His teaching experience includes managerial economics and corporate finance, as well as all types of real estate courses at the graduate and undergraduate levels including income properties, mortgage securities, development, residential, and commercial real estate. Professor Chinloy serves on the editorial boards of *Real Estate Economics, Journal of Real Estate Finance and Economics,* and *Journal of Real Estate Research.* He has also served on the board of directors of business firms, including for the entity that operates the MRIS multiple listing service in the Washington, DC area and two organizations in the San Francisco Bay Area. He received a BA in commerce from McGill University and an MA and PhD in economics from Harvard University.

About the Contributors

Xudong An is an Associate Professor of Finance and the Endowed Professor of Real Estate at San Diego State University. He is also a visiting scholar at the UCLA Anderson School of Management and the NUS Institute of Real Estate Studies. Professor An's research mainly focuses on mortgage default risk, but he has wide interests in real estate finance, risk management, financial markets, and housing economics. He has developed an expertise in using econometric models to analyze, predict, and price default risk. Professor An conducts research on securitization, mortgage lending, real estate valuation, house price dynamics, and corporate bankruptcy. He has published in such academic journals as the *Journal of Financial Economics, Journal of Policy Analysis and Management, Journal of Real Estate Finance and Economics,* and *Real Estate Economics.* Professor An received a PhD from the University of Southern California.

Eric S. Belsky is Managing Director of the Joint Center for Housing Studies of Harvard University and Lecturer in Urban Planning and Design at the Harvard Graduate School of Design. Before his Harvard appointments, Professor Belsky held positions with Price Waterhouse LLP, Fannie Mae, the National Association of Home Builders, and the University of Massachusetts at Amherst. In 2001 and 2002, he served as Research Director for the bipartisan Millennial Housing Commission established by the Congress of the United States. Professor Belsky has co-edited five books and authored numerous articles and book chapters. He earned a BA, MA, and PhD from Clark University.

Walter I. Boudry is an Assistant Professor of Real Estate in the School of Hotel Administration at Cornell University. Previously, he taught undergraduate and graduate real estate courses at the University of North Carolina at Chapel Hill's Kenan-Flagler Business School and New York University's Leonard N. Stern School of Business. His research interests include real estate and general finance. His most recent works focus on REITs and examine their repurchase decisions, dividend payout policy, security issuance decisions, and price dynamics. He is a regular presenter and discussant at the annual meetings of the American Real Estate and Urban Economics Association (AREUEA). He has published in *Real Estate Economics, Journal of Real Estate Finance and Economics,* and *Journal of Business Finance and Accounting.* He received his bachelor of commerce with first class honors and bachelor of economics from the University of Queensland, Australia, and his MPhil and PhD from New York University.

Stephen L. Buschbom is a graduate assistant and PhD student at the University of Georgia. His previous experience includes commercial real estate underwriting and CMBS modeling for ING Investment Management in Atlanta. He earned a BBA in real estate at the University of Georgia.

Stephen A. Buser is Emeritus Professor of Finance at Ohio State University (OSU), where he has been a member of the faculty since 1975. While at OSU, Professor Buser served terms as Chair of the Department of Finance and Associate Dean for the Fisher College of Business. During sabbaticals from OSU, he was a visiting professor at the University of Chicago and MIT. Professor Buser has also served on editorial boards for academic journals including a term as co-editor of the *Journal of Finance* and has provided consulting services to many companies. The Treasurer of the State of Ohio appointed him to serve on the Board of Directors for the State Teachers Retirement of Ohio. Professor Buser served on the Obama-Biden transition team and currently serves as the official historian for the American Finance Association. He received a bachelors degree in economics from Princeton University and a PhD in economics from Boston College.

Brad Case is Senior Vice President, Research and Industry Information for the National Association of Real Estate Investment Trusts (NAREIT). His research has been published in *Review of Economics and Statistics, Real Estate Economics, Journal of Real Estate Finance and Economics,* and *Journal of Portfolio Management.* He is the co-inventor of both PureProperty indexes and "backward-forward" trading contracts (both patented) and sole inventor of a method for producing investable indexes (patent-pending). Dr. Case earned his BA at Williams College, MPP at the University of California at Berkeley, and PhD in economics at Yale University. He also holds the CFA and CAIA designations.

K. W. Chau is Chair Professor of Real Estate and Construction and Director of the Ronald Coase Centre for Property Rights Research at the University of Hong Kong. His main areas of research include real estate finance and economics, real estate price indexes, and urban analysis. His research typically involves empirical studies with implications for policymakers and practitioners. He has published more than 100 articles in such journals as the *Building and Environment, Energy Policy, Environment and Planning B, Habitat International, Journal of Law and Economics, Journal of Real Estate Finance and Economics,* and *Urban Studies.* He received the International Real Estate Society Achievement Award in 1999. In 1996, Professor Chau became the founding president of the Asian Real Estate Society. He was elected president of the International Real Estate Society in 2000. He serves on the editorial boards of more than 10 peer-reviewed journals. He obtained his BSc and PhD degrees from the University of Hong Kong.

Man Cho is Professor of Public Policy and Management at the KDI (Korea Development Institute) School of Public Policy and Management where he teaches real estate finance, asset securitization, and other related courses. He also has a joint appointment as Director of the Real Asset Research Team at KDI and is currently managing various research projects on real estate markets and policy issues in Korea and other countries. Before joining the KDI School he worked at Fannie Mae, hold both research and management positions. His other professional appointments include being a consultant at the World Bank and an adjunct professor at the Johns

Hopkins University. He holds a PhD in applied economics and managerial science from the Wharton School, University of Pennsylvania.

Jarl G. Kallberg is the Alvin C. Wolff Distinguished Professor of Real Estate at Washington State University (WSU) in Pullman, Washington and Research Professor in the Finance Department at Arizona State University. Before joining WSU in 2013, he was Director of Research and Professor of Global Finance at the Thunderbird School of Global Management. From 1978 to 2006 he was a member of the finance faculty at New York University's Stern School of Business and for several years was the director of the finance PhD program. His research interests are in corporate finance, financial engineering, real estate, and financial contagion. He was a visiting professor at Bilkent University, the University of British Columbia, and Princeton University. He has published in such journals as the *Journal of Business*, *Journal of Financial and Quantitative Analysis*, *Journal of Law and Economics*, *Journal of Real Estate Economics*, and *Journal of Real Estate Finance and Economics*. He received a BSc in mathematics from the University of British Columbia, an MSc in mathematics from Simon Fraser University, and a PhD in business administration from the University of British Columbia.

James B. Kau is a Professor Emeritus of Real Estate and C. Herman and Mary Virginia Terry Distinguished Chair in Business Administration at the University of Georgia. Professor Kau's research concentration includes option theory and mortgage valuation as well as the pricing of mortgage backed securities and insurance pricing using option theory. He is the recipient of the Terry College of Business Outstanding Research Award and recipient of the George Bloom Award for outstanding contributions to the field of real estate academics by the American Real Estate and Urban Economics Association. He is also the recipient of the ARES Graaskamp Award for lifetime achievement in real estate. Professor Kau is the co-editor of the *Journal of Real Estate Finance and Economics* and also served as editor for *Real Estate Economics* from 1983 to 1987. He earned a BA in mathematics and an MA and PhD in economics at the University of Washington.

Donald C. Keenan is a Professor of Economics at Université de Cergy-Pontoise. Professor Keenan's research includes microeconomic applications, uncertainty and financial economics, and general equilibrium and dynamic systems. Previously, he was a Professor of Economics at the University of Georgia. He is a recipient of the Terry College of Business Outstanding Research Award and Kamerschen/Hampton Research Award. Professor Keenan earned a BA in economics at Carnegie Mellon University, an MA in economics at the University of Kansas, an MS in systems science and mathematics and a DSc in economics at the University of Washington.

Kyung-Hwan Kim is President of Korea Research Institute for Human Settlements (KRIHS). He is on leave from Sogang University where he is a Professor of Economics. He is also a research affiliate of the Center for Asset Securitisation and Management in Asia at the Sim Kee Boon Institute for Financial Economics at Singapore Management University. Professor Kim is a member of the board of directors of AREUEA and serves on the editorial board of the *Journal of Housing Economics* and the management board of *Housing Studies*. Previously, he taught at Syracuse University, University of Wisconsin-Madison, and Singapore Management University. He also served as an urban finance advisor at the UN Habitat, and president of the

Asian Real Estate Society. His research areas include land and housing markets, government regulations, and local public finance. He has published in the *Journal of Urban Economics, Journal of Real Estate Finance and Economics, Journal of Housing Economics,* and *Urban Studies*. Professor Kim received a PhD in economics from Princeton University.

John J. McConnell is the Weiler Distinguished Professor of Management (in Finance) at the Krannert Graduate School of Management at Purdue University. He has also taught at Ohio State University, University of Minnesota, Stanford University, and University of North Carolina. Professor McConnell has received numerous teaching awards including the Salgo-Noren Outstanding Teacher Award at Purdue. He served on the Boards of Directors of the Federal Home Loan Bank of Indianapolis, Harrington Financial Group, Los Padres Bank, and the American Finance Association, and as a consultant to numerous government agencies, investment banks, and law firms on various aspects of financial markets and securities. He has published more than 75 articles in peer-reviewed finance, economics, and management journals. He has been recognized as the Distinguished Scholar of the Eastern Finance Association and as a Fellow of the Financial Management Association. Professor McConnell has served on the editorial boards of the *Journal of Finance, Financial Management, Journal of Real Estate Finance and Economics, Pacific Basin Finance Journal, Journal of Financial and Quantitative Analysis, Journal of Fixed Income,* and *Journal of Real Estate Research*. He earned a BA in economics from Denison University, an MBA from the University of Pittsburgh, and a PhD in finance from Purdue University.

Ehsan Nikbakht, CFA, FRM, is Professor of Finance at Hofstra University and previously was a department chair and associate dean. He served on the Advisory Board of the International Association of Financial Engineers and Chair of Derivatives Committee of New York Society of Security Analysts. Professor Nikbakht currently serves on the editorial board of *Global Finance Journal*. He authored *Finance* published by Barron's and *Foreign Loans and Economic Performance* published by Praeger Scientific CBS as well as articles appearing in such journals as the *Journal of Applied Finance, Financial Decisions, Global Finance Journal,* and *International Journal of Business*. He received the Stessin Prize for an "Outstanding Scholarly Publication" for his manuscript on external debt. Professor Nikbakht received a BA from the Tehran School of Business, an MBA from the Iran Center for Management Studies, and a DBA in finance from the George Washington University.

Stephen E. Roulac heads Roulac Global Places LLC, a firm that advises on business decisions primarily concerning real estate involvements. Dr. Roulac has made presentations and speeches to some 400 organizations and has been the keynote speaker or featured instructor at many professional forums throughout the country and abroad. Dr. Roulac has written more than 350 articles and authored or edited a dozen books. *Modern Real Estate Investment: An Institutional Approach* has been recognized as the authoritative treatise on contemporary real estate investment practice. He received a BA in economics from Pomona College, an MBA with distinction from Harvard University, a JD from the University of California at Berkeley, and a PhD in finance and strategic management from Stanford University. Dr. Roulac holds the CPA and CMC designations and pursues extensive continuing education.

Anthony B. Sanders is Professor of Finance in the School of Management at George Mason University. He has previously taught at the University of Chicago (Graduate School of Business), University of Texas at Austin (McCombs School of Business), and The Ohio State University (Fisher College of Business). Professor Sanders also served as Director and Head of Asset-backed and Mortgage-backed Securities Research at Deutsche Bank in New York City. His research and teaching focuses on financial institutions, securitization, capital markets, and real estate finance and investments. He has published in the *Journal of Finance, Journal of Financial and Quantitative Analysis, Journal of Business, Journal of Financial Services Research, Real Estate Economics, Journal of Housing Economics,* and other journals. Professor Sanders has received six teaching awards and three research awards. He serves as associate editor for several leading journals. He has given presentations to the European Central Bank, Bank of Japan, U.S. Department of Treasury, and has testified on housing and mortgage markets in the U.S. Senate and House of Representatives. He has a master's degree and a PhD in real estate and urban economics from the University of Georgia.

Garrett Smith is a third year PhD student at Florida Atlantic University. Mr. Smith held management positions with Capital One Bank and Toronto Dominion Bank. He received an award for the best research paper in the Florida Atlantic University College of Business and participated in the State of Florida University System research competition. His current research focuses on real estate prices, firm diversification effects, and the effects of cash holdings on firm returns. He received a BSE in biomedical engineering from the University of Pittsburgh and an MBA with distinction from Hofstra University.

Andrew Spieler, CFA, FRM, CAIA, is a Professor of Finance in the Frank G. Zarb School of Business at Hofstra University. His research has been published in *Real Estate Economics, Journal of Real Estate Finance and Economics, Journal of Real Estate Portfolio Management,* and other journals. He served as Chair of the Derivatives Committee at New York Society of Security Analysts. Professor Spieler also serves as Co-Director of the annual real estate conference sponsored by the Wilbur F. Breslin Center for Real Estate Studies. He received undergraduate degrees in math and economics, an MS in finance from Indiana University, and an MBA and PhD from SUNY Binghamton.

Kerry D. Vandell is the Dean's Professor of Finance and Director of the Center for Real Estate at the Paul Merage School of Business, University of California-Irvine. He has served as President of the American Real Estate and Urban Economics Association and co-editor of the Association's journal *Real Estate Economics,* and currently is a member of the Board of Directors of the Asian Real Estate Society. He serves on the editorial board of six academic journals. He has researched and consulted extensively in the areas of real estate investment, urban real estate environmental economics, mortgage finance, housing economics and policy, and valuation theory and is a principal in the consulting firm KDV Associates, which is actively involved in expert witness assignments for litigation matters in the above areas. Professor Vandell received a BA and M Mech E degrees from Rice University, a MCP from Harvard, and a PhD from the Massachusetts Institute of Technology.

S. K. Wong is an Associate Professor in the Department of Real Estate and Construction at the University of Hong Kong. He is also a Senior Fulbright Scholar at the University of Connecticut, Post-doctoral Honoree at the Homer Hoyt Institute, Visiting Fellow at the University of Cambridge, and Research Fellow at the University of Melbourne. His research interest is in real estate economics, with works published in the *Journal of Real Estate Finance and Economics, Regional Science and Urban Economics, Journal of Real Estate Portfolio Management,* among others. As a core committee member of the Ronald Coase Centre for Property Rights Research, he is expanding his research to the area of institutional economics. He obtained his BSc and PhD degrees from the University of Hong Kong.

Zhonghua Wu is an Associate Professor of Real Estate and Tibor and Sheila Hollo Research Fellow at Florida International University. Professor Wu studies the broad areas of real estate finance and investments with a focus on REITs and commercial property markets. He has published in *Real Estate Economics, Journal of Real Estate Finance and Economics,* and *Journal of Real Estate Research.* He has served as session chair, program committee member, and discussant at conferences including those of the American Real Estate and Urban Economics Association and the American Real Estate Society . Professor Wu has also been a referee for *Real Estate Economics, Journal of Real Estate Finance and Economics,* and *Journal of Real Estate Research.* He received a PhD in business administration from the University of Wisconsin-Madison.

C. Y. Yiu is an active researcher in real estate economics and finance. He was an Assistant Professor of the Department of Real Estate and Construction at the University of Hong Kong, and is now running his own research center: REDBRIC. He has published in the *Journal of Financial Management of Property and Construction* and written a chapter appearing in *Challenges of the Housing Economy: An International Perspective.* He obtained his BSc, MPhil, and PhD degrees from the University of Hong Kong.

Peter Zabierek, CFA, is the Chief Executive Officer of Presima, Inc. in Montreal, Canada. He has more than 23 years of professional experience, including the last 15 years working exclusively in the global real estate securities space. Before joining Presima, Mr. Zabierek was Managing Director and Co-Head of Global Real Estate Securities at Urdang Capital Management. In that role, he served as Senior Portfolio Manager for $4.5 billion of global real estate securities and served on the firm's management committee. He has also held real estate investment roles at Morgan Stanley and Salomon Smith Barney in New York. Before his tenure on Wall Street, Mr. Zabierek worked as a consulting engineer in California, serving real estate developers and public agencies. He holds master's degrees in both business administration and civil engineering from the University of California at Berkeley and is a CFA charterholder and registered professional engineer.

Public Real Estate Markets and Investments

Part One

FOUNDATIONS OF PUBLIC REAL ESTATE

1

Public Real Estate Markets and Investments: An Overview

H. KENT BAKER
University Professor of Finance, Kogod School of Business, American University

PETER CHINLOY
Professor of Finance and Real Estate, Kogod School of Business, American University

Introduction

Real estate investing involves the purchase, ownership, management, rental, or sale of real estate for an expected gain from income or higher price. This investment entails either an *ownership interest* or a *leasehold interest*. An investor with an ownership interest such as in a home is entitled to the full rights of land ownership and also assumes the risks and responsibilities of a landowner. With a leasehold interest, the landowner agrees to pass some of the rights to a tenant in exchange for a payment of rent. For example, an investor has a leasehold interest when renting a commercial or multifamily residential property.

Investors may participate in real estate directly or indirectly. Direct ownership involves investment in residences, commercial real estate, and agricultural land. Indirect investment includes investing in companies engaged in real estate ownership, development, or management. These investments include real estate investment trusts (REITs), commingled real estate funds (CREFs), and infrastructure funds.

Both individuals and institutions invest in real estate. Many people have investments in real estate through owing their home. A home is one of the single largest investments that the average investor makes as part of an overall portfolio. However, individuals rarely pay the entire price of a property in cash. Instead, they finance a large proportion of the purchase price with debt. Houses or any real estate property are expensive relative to income and traditional investments such as stocks and bonds. Investors can participate with relatively small amounts of cash when buying debt or equity securities in public real estate markets. The core focus of this volume is on how investors can hold a diversified, scalable and complete portfolio of real estate equity and debt through financial instruments.

The proportion of the price that is debt is the *leverage* as reflected in the *loan-to-value (LTV) ratio*. The property's *net operating income (NOI)* is the rent collected less operating expenses and capital expenses. The ratio of NOI to the debt payment is the *debt service coverage ratio (DSCR)*. By comparison, non-taxable institutional investors receive no intrinsic benefit from leverage other than increasing portfolio size. These investors include sovereign wealth funds, endowments, and pension funds.

Real estate investment trusts offer this investment opportunity in equity financial markets. With the exception of REITs, real estate investors often follow a strategy of seeking to reduce their equity (i.e., the amount financed by the investor's own capital) and increase their leverage in order to enhance their return on investment (ROI). As with any investment, the return to real estate is the sum of a dividend yield and a capital gain. The *dividend yield* or the *income capitalization (cap) rate* is the ratio of NOI to the property price. Because the price is the ratio of NOI to the cap rate, the capital gain or growth in prices is the growth rate of NOI minus the growth rate of the cap rate.

REIT strategies differ because they are not taxable entities and receive no shield from an interest deduction. The amount that investors can borrow (leverage) to acquire real estate is much greater than that available to stock investors buying on margin. Without derivatives, margin requirements on securities are 50 percent, but LTV ratios on commercial properties typically exceed 60 percent on newly originated loans. Leveraging the purchase of an investment property requires periodic payments to service the debt and meet the DSCR targets in the initial underwriting. When properties are highly occupied, these are core or core-plus strategies. Alternative strategies involve investing in underutilized property in order to add value or to be opportunistic, but these often require successive equity infusions. Successful real estate investors must manage their cash flows to generate enough positive income from a property to offset the debt service. Thus, any successful real estate investment strategy involves managing and evaluating risk not only from leverage but also from other sources such as an economic downturn, market decline, cash shortfall (such as where the actual DSCR declines below one), and unexpected events such as fires or natural disasters.

TYPES OF REAL ESTATE

Real estate investments include income-producing and non-income-producing investments. The most common types of income-producing real estate are offices, retail, industrial, and leased residential properties including apartments. Offices tend to be the largest and highest profile property type but often has highly variable returns because the market is sensitive to economic factors. Retail covers a range of properties from shopping malls to single tenant buildings. Compared to offices, the returns from some tenants with high credit ratings tend to be more stable because of longer leases. Retailers are less inclined to relocate than office tenants. Industrial properties vary depending on the use of the building (e.g., manufacturing, warehousing, distribution, and research and development). Relative to their office and retail counterparts, industrial properties often require smaller investments, less management, and have lower operating costs. Leased residential properties provide the most stable returns because people need a place to live regardless of the state of the economy. Many other types of income-producing properties are available including hotels, healthcare (e.g., hospitals and senior care housing), parking lots, mini-storage, and infrastructure such as highways, airports, and ports. Non-income-producing investments include construction of houses for resale, vacation properties, vacant commercial buildings, and land.

ADVANTAGES AND DISADVANTAGES OF REAL ESTATE INVESTMENTS

Within a portfolio context, real estate is generally considered an alternative asset class. Real estate is a supplementary investment used to diversify a primary portfolio consisting of stocks, bonds, and other securities or assets. In a period of low interest rates but highly expansionary monetary policy, a risk exists of future rising rates and inflation. In this case, real estate can be a potential substitute for part of a bond portfolio by hedging the inflation risk while locking in interest costs. Thus, a major benefit of having real estate in a portfolio is its diversification value because real estate returns have relatively low correlations with other asset classes. Building a diversified real estate portfolio could be a challenge for many investors because this would involve buying real estate in different geographical locations and across types of real estate. Investors can buy units in a more divisible private pool or a public security such as REITs, which are generally backed by a diverse portfolio. Investors can purchase residential or commercial mortgage-backed securities (CMBS) or mortgage REITs to invest in securitized real estate debt.

Real estate can lead to enhanced yields by producing returns in rents and capital appreciation and can offer tax shelter offsets from depreciation, tax credits and exchanges, and carryover losses that reduce tax liability. Real estate permits achieving higher returns for a given level of portfolio risk. Real estate can also be an inflation hedge especially when returns are linked to rising rents from tenants. Nominal rents are expected to rise with inflation, but nominal payments on fixed-rate mortgage debt are constant. Another benefit of real estate entities is an ability to influence performance. Because real estate is a highly tangible asset, the investor can take steps to increase its value or performance such as improving the interior or exterior of a building. Unlike other types of investment, investors have greater control over the performance of a real estate investment.

When investing in real estate, other characteristics are relevant. For example, real estate requires management, has high transaction costs in private markets, has low liquidity with the exception of real estate securities, and varies among regions. Real estate is cyclical but the leasing and investment markets have potentially uncorrelated cycles. Measuring real estate performance can be challenging especially in private markets lacking good benchmarks for comparing portfolio results.

In most countries, real estate markets are less organized and efficient than traditional markets for stocks and bonds. Individual properties are unique and not directly interchangeable. This can create challenges for investors who want to evaluate prices and investment opportunities. Yet, market inefficiency is not necessarily a drawback. An *inefficient market* means that information asymmetry exists among market participants. Although real estate markets have information asymmetries, this enables informed investors to achieve profit opportunities by obtaining properties at bargain prices. Furthermore, emerging markets have limited securities markets. In developed countries, inflationary pressure, restricted land, and specific zoning and regulatory rules create investment opportunities.

PRIVATE VERSUS PUBLIC MARKETS

Real estate investors must decide whether to participate in private or public markets. This decision produces different exposures to risk and return. A *private market* is one in which an investor buys a direct interest in one or more properties. For example, an investor could buy a commercial building that was leased to one or more tenants paying rent. The investor could join a pool or syndicate such as a limited partnership or limited liability company to buy the property. Another option is to invest in public real estate markets. A *public market* is one in which an investor purchases a share or unit in a publicly traded real estate company such as a REIT. Because the company owns and manages the property on behalf of its shareholders or unit holders, investor exposure to the real estate market is indirect.

DEBT VERSUS EQUITY INVESTMENTS

Besides choosing between private or public markets, real estate investors can invest in debt or equity. *Private debt* involves lending directly to an owner of real estate, thereby investing in mortgages. Examples of investing in private debt are holding individual loans and a private mortgage pool. A mortgage pool accumulates capital that is invested in various mortgages. *Public debt* includes investing in mortgage REITs, residential mortgage-backed securities (RMBS), or CMBS. A *CMBS* is a pool of mortgage loans that a lender assembles on income-producing properties and then sells in tranches to the public market. Each tranche has a different set of risks, maturity, and sensitivity to changes in interest rates and return. Investors receive periodic interest payments and repayment of principal. Such real estate mortgage investments are similar to investing in bonds.

The tranche structure offers low returns to investors holding senior or A-piece securities within the pool in exchange for priority of payment from cash flows received. The subordinate or B-piece securities offer higher returns in exchange for a lower payment priority behind the senior A-piece issues. This is a conventional risk-return trade-off, but two agency issues inherent in the senior-subordinate structure lead to conflicts and potential disaster.

First, regulators permit banks to hold any mortgage debt as an asset without necessarily reserving capital, provided insurance is in place. Banks buy subordinate tranches and use some of the higher rate margin to buy insurance, which fails to completely price the risk of default. This insurance includes explicit products such as mortgage insurance as well as securitized issues such as credit default swaps (CDS). These contracts pay off when property prices decline, notionally hedging the risk from owning the B-piece securities supposed to take initial losses from default.

Second, servicers collect the payments from borrowers and are required to buy subordinate B-pieces. On default, servicers have an incentive to extend defaulted loans to protect their subordinate position at a cost to the senior holders. The fees for servicing are paid by all pool members, so senior holders further subsidize subordinate investors.

Alternatively, equity investments represent a residual interest in the property after payment of all debt and its service. Equity investors benefit if the property value appreciates or through rents. An equity position in real estate involves similar risks to owning stock. Not surprisingly, investing in equity is riskier than investing in debt but also offers the possibility of greater return.

Equity investments can be in either private or public markets. Private equity real estate investing is the traditional ownership method of owning a home or an investment property. Engaging in a private equity transaction requires due diligence of the prospective investment and involves various costs including brokerage and legal fees, financing fees, appraisal costs, and other administrative fees. Public equity real estate investing includes such securities as equity REITs and publicly traded real estate operating companies (REOCs). The major benefits of investing in public equity involve the relative ease of acquisition and their liquidity due to trading on a stock exchange. Both REITs and REOCs exhibit return patterns that are similar to some types of equities, despite the underlying assets being real estate.

REITs began in the United States after the REIT Act of 1960. An entity holding at least 75 percent of assets in property or mortgages, earning at least 75 percent of income from rent, and distributing at least 90 percent of income after reserves is exempt from paying corporate income tax. REITs have created an ability to invest in real estate through the stock market as individual securities. REITs have also emerged in developed economies including the United Kingdom, France, and Japan.

REITs offer other advantages. First, REITs are immediate candidates for dividend or yield-oriented investors. Consequently, income-oriented funds have been increasing their portfolio holdings in REITs. Second, some REITs are almost the mirror image of conventional corporate entities. Other firms hold cash in tax-avoidance strategies because of high and varying corporate tax rates. Because REITs worldwide have similar zero corporate income tax rates, no incentive exists to hold retained earnings or cash. REIT dividends are taxed as ordinary income and do not qualify for a lower preferential rate because the REIT pays no corporate income tax. Thus, less incentive exists to hold the stock for capital gains as opposed to dividends. Because investors treat REITs differently from other stocks, some view REITs as a separate asset class.

In summary, real estate investors need to select a market (private or public) and determine whether debt or equity investing is appropriate for achieving their objectives. As figure 1.1 shows, real estate is basically classified into four segments: private debt, private equity, public debt, and public equity.

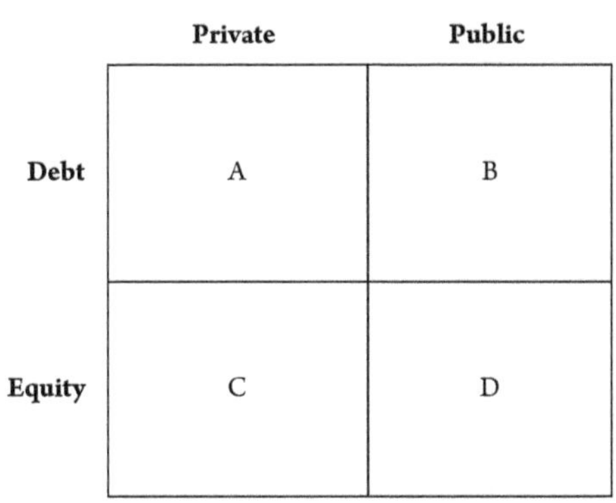

Figure 1.1 Types of Real Estate Markets and Investments. This figure shows two types of real estate markets (private and public) and two types of investments (debt and equity) where quadrant A is private debt, quadrant B is public debt, quadrant C is private equity, and quadrant D is public equity.

Purpose and Key Topics

The purpose of this book is to provide an overview and synthesis of public real estate markets and investments. This book is a companion to *Private Real Estate Markets and Investments,* which is also part of the Financial Markets and Investments Series from Oxford University Press. Readers can gain an understanding of the major types and the latest trends within this public real estate markets. The book also presents evidence from relevant research studies in a clear and concise manner.

This chapter has three sections: (1) foundations of public real estate, (2) public debt markets and investments, and (3) public equity markets and investments.

- *Foundations of public real estate.* The first section discusses the rationale for investing in real estate including diversification effects, examines international real estate markets, and presents strategies for improving returns and managing risk in a global context. Evidence indicates that adding real estate to a portfolio can increase risk-adjusted returns.
- *Public debt markets and investments.* The second section focuses on mortgages both in the United States and globally. Mortgage debt has become investable through mortgage REITs, mortgage-backed securities (MBS), and CMBS. This section also discusses the subprime mortgage crisis.
- *Public equity markets and investments.* The third section examines public equity markets including investing in REITs and REOCs both domestically and internationally.

Distinctive Features

This book has several prominent features.

- The book provides a detailed discussion of public real estate markets and investments in a global context.
- It offers a synthesis of important, recent, and relevant research studies in a straightforward manner.
- The book contains contributions from a diverse array of academics and practitioners, which helps to ensure different viewpoints.
- Chapters 2 through 14 each contain discussion questions that reinforce key issues and concepts. Guideline answers are presented at the end of the book.

Intended Audience

The book's distinctive features should be of interest to various groups including academics, practitioners, investors, students, and others interested in public real estate markets and investments. Academics can use this book in both their real estate and finance courses and to understand the various strands of research emerging from this area. Practitioners can use this book to navigate through topics involving public real estate markets and investments. Individual and institutional investors can benefit as they attempt to expand their knowledge base and apply the concepts to manage their portfolios.

Organization of the Book

The remaining 13 chapters are organized into three parts. A brief synopsis of each chapter by part follows.

PART 1 FOUNDATIONS OF PUBLIC REAL ESTATE

Chapters 2 through 4 examine the foundations of public real estate. Chapter 2 discusses the diversification benefits of including real estate in a portfolio. Chapter 3 extends this discussion of diversification to an international context. Chapter 4 examines investment strategies involving real estate to realize superior risk-adjusted returns.

Chapter 2 Diversification Benefits of Real Estate (Brad Case)

This chapter discusses diversification in the context of real estate investments. Real estate has historically provided strong risk-adjusted returns and low correlations relative to other assets and has therefore delivered diversification benefits to existing portfolios of stocks, bonds, and other asset classes. An understanding of the diversification benefits of real estate requires attention to how correlations and therefore diversification benefits of real estate have changed over time, as well as how they differ for investors with differing time horizons. Moreover, returns differ substantially across segments of the real estate asset class including real estate debt and equity, public and private real estate (listing status), investment strategies (core, value-added, and opportunistic), property types, domestic and international assets, and geographic submarkets within the United States.

Chapter 3 International Real Estate Markets (K. W. Chau, S. K. Wong, and C. Y. Yiu)

This chapter reviews the arguments for and against diversification using international real estate. Based on direct and indirect real estate price indexes, it also examines from 2007Q1 to 2012Q2 the medium-term performance for the following 17 real estate markets: Australia, Austria, Canada, China, Finland, France, Germany, Hong Kong, Italy, Japan, the Netherlands, Norway, Singapore, Sweden, Switzerland, the United Kingdom, and the United States. The direct and indirect real estate data are based on residential and REIT markets, respectively. The direct and indirect real estate performances in these markets differ in terms of average returns and volatilities, but they are generally positively correlated with each other. The chapter ends with a summary of the institutional barriers to foreign real estate investment including market transparency, capital gains taxes, agency commissions, access to mortgage loans, and features of REITs.

Chapter 4 Strategy: Seeking Alpha Opportunities and Managing Risks in Global Markets (Stephen E. Roulac)

Investing strategy for real estate is complex, daunting, and nuanced. To realize superior risk-adjusted returns or alpha, investors must be highly skilled and pursue strategies that diverge from the market norms. This chapter focuses on seeking alpha opportunities in real estate. These alpha-seeking property investing strategies may embrace more active rather than passive styles and involve investing in different places. Among the important landmarks on the path to alpha returns are a commitment to a policy orientation and recognition of the implications of change. Investors should be global in their investing outlook. This global orientation leads to reconciliation between the challenges of emerging markets and the blurring of that distinction relative to established markets.

PART 2 PUBLIC DEBT MARKETS AND INVESTMENTS

This section consists of six chapters. Chapter 5 examines public debt markets in the United States while chapter 6 extends this discussion to include mortgage markets internationally. Chapter 7 focuses on mortgaged-backed securities (MBS). Chapter 8 discusses prepayment and default risk, and chapter 9 looks at commercial mortgages and CMBS. Chapter 10 provides a probing analysis of the subprime mortgage crisis.

Chapter 5 Mortgage Markets: The United States (Eric S. Belsky)

This chapter examines the evolution of the structure, conduct, and performance of mortgage markets in the United States. It traces federal interventions in the mortgage markets from the 1930s to the present. These interventions dramatically shaped mortgage markets. The failure of regulators to contain private risk-taking in mortgage markets during the 2000s led to excessive leverage and risk. The financial crisis that ensued prompted the federal government to bailout the housing finance system. The chapter concludes with a set of issues raised by the near collapse of mortgage markets. These issues include how to: (1) regulate originators and securitizers; (2) protect claim hierarchies in first and second mortgages to allow debt restructuring, (3) construct pooling and servicing agreements; (4) regulate credit default swaps (CDS) so that sellers are monitored to ensure they have the capital to honor their commitments; and (5) provide adequate disclosures and protection against interest rate risk as markets soak up low-yielding debt obligations.

Chapter 6 Mortgage Markets: International (Kyung-Hwan Kim and Man Cho)

Mortgage markets differ across countries in terms of size, institutional and legal structures, and the extent and modality of government intervention. This chapter begins by briefly reviewing international comparative studies of mortgage markets. It then provides an overview of mortgage finance systems and describes the key features of mortgage markets of 21 countries. Next, the chapter offers an empirical analysis of mortgage markets using a data set comprising a maximum number of countries for which reliable data are available. It also characterizes ideal housing finance systems and presents a classification of countries based on a set of criteria. The last section summarizes the main findings and provides suggestions on future research.

Chapter 7 Development of the Market for Mortgage-Backed Securities (Stephen A. Buser and John J. McConnell)

The market for securities backed by mortgages was formally launched in 1970 when the Government National Mortgage Association made an initial public offering with a face value of $70 million. By 1996, the combined face value for mortgage-backed securities still less than $500 million. The value of new offerings reached $3 trillion in 2003. In response to a subsequent decline in real estate markets, new offerings fell to $1 trillion by 2006. The market recovered, at least partially, and for 2009 the combined face value for MBS was $2 trillion. This chapter provides a summary of economic and political factors that contributed to the development of MBS introduced by government and private sector entities. The chapter also summarizes studies that examine the effects of the MBS market on mortgage rates, the availability of mortgage credit, and the broader economy.

Chapter 8 Prepayment and Default Risk (Stephen Buschbom, James B. Kau, and Donald C. Keenan)

This chapter provides an introduction to structural and reduced form modeling of mortgage termination. The theory and functional form for each model is discussed as well as empirical results. Structural models, also known as option-pricing models, have long been the standard for estimating default and prepayment in relation to mortgage valuation, but they often project terminations that deviate from empirical observations. The recent literature has alternatively adopted a reduced form approach where default and prepayment are derived from past observations, allowing researchers to avoid rigid assumptions about when and why a borrower terminates a mortgage. The chapter also provides a brief overview of other recent topics in the mortgage termination literature.

Chapter 9 Commercial Mortgages and Commercial Mortgage-Backed Securities (Xudong An and Kerry D. Vandell)

This chapter provides a review of commercial mortgages and CMBS. The chapter begins by using a historical perspective to provide an understanding of commercial mortgages and CMBS as an asset class. Next, it provides a detailed discussion of the important issues related to commercial mortgage underwriting and recent perspectives. The following two sections focus on default risk and address CMBS structuring, theoretical foundations, subordination, ratings, and pricing. The final section concludes with a reflection on the future of commercial mortgage and CMBS markets. Commercial mortgage and CMBS markets are suffering from adverse reputational effects from the recent financial crisis. Over time, innovations in technology and capital market instruments and institutional structures for the delivery of capital will provide further opportunities to render the market for commercial property more efficient and complete.

Chapter 10 The Subprime Mortgage Crisis (Anthony B. Sanders)

The subprime mortgage crisis was a confluence of a burst of the housing bubble and rising unemployment resulting partly from extraordinary intervention by the government in terms of encouraging credit expansion. This crisis involved a housing bubble, surge in unemployment, and credit expansion all rolled into one super storm. Subprime borrowers tended to use adjustable rate mortgages with low down payments, creating the potential for problems if either housing prices fell or unemployment rose. Unfortunately, house prices declined and unemployment rose, leading to a spike in defaults for subprime borrowers far higher than for prime borrowers. The subprime crisis was more prevalent in the Southwest, Florida, and the northeast United States. Prime mortgages also suffered an increase in defaults, but the effect was not as large. Besides the other mentioned factors, the Federal Reserve enacted low-rate policies that helped create a housing bubble and then helped burst the bubble with rapidly increasing rate policies.

PART 3 PUBLIC EQUITY MARKETS AND INVESTMENTS

The final sections consist of four chapters. Chapters 11 through 13 examine various aspects of REITs both in the United States and internationally. Chapter 14 focuses on REOCs.

Chapter 11 REITs: Structure and Performance (Walter I. Boudry and Jarl G. Kallberg)

This chapter evaluates the recent performance of REITs versus more traditional equity and debt investments. It shows that REIT returns are very closely linked to mid-cap equity returns but are only very weakly correlated to returns on bonds and returns on the underlying real estate markets. Sharpe ratios indicate that REITs have underperformed both bonds and mid-cap equities over the period 1978 to 2012. The chapter also surveys the academic literature addressing the key determinants of REIT returns: corporate governance, dividend policy, institutional ownership, and the returns on the underlying real estate market. In general, strong corporate governance and higher levels of institutional ownership positively influence REIT returns. REITs are an important class of investments for institutional investors. The data show that in the largest size decile, institutional ownership is 93.1 percent of the total.

Chapter 12 REITs: International Dimensions (Ehsan Nikbakht, Garrett Smith, and Andrew Spieler)

This chapter focuses on the globalization of REITs, the overall composition of the global market for REITs, the advantages of international REIT (I-REIT) diversification, transmission of volatility between international real estate markets, and future trends. Real estate is a localized business. Despite the rapid growth of REITs worldwide, this tenet remains unchanged. International REITs allow both institutional and retail investors access to the real estate and, by extension, economic exposure to different countries or specific regions. Syndicating transactions increases liquidity in the property markets and gives investors direct access to different types of real estate markets. If markets are internationally integrated, some of the benefits of diversification are removed. Empirical research studies show that risk-adjusted returns for REITs have internationally outperformed their bond and equity counterparts. This outperformance may explain why investors have shifted asset allocations to REITs despite the financial crisis of 2007–2009 and after.

Chapter 13 REITs: Capital Structure (Zhonghua Wu)

This chapter discusses theories and empirical findings related to the capital structure of REITs based on recent research. REITs are capital-intensive firms. The consequence is that capital structure policies play an important role in REIT operations and management. Understanding capital structure is crucial for investors to analyze risks and returns of REITs. Because REITs have several unique features, they provide an interesting laboratory to examine issues related to capital structure. The discussion of REIT issues includes topics such as determinants of capital structure, security issuance decisions, financial liquidity management for cash policy and bank lines of credit as well as the impact of financing on investment. In summary, REIT capital structure is likely to continue to be a topic of interest for both practitioners and academics in the future.

Chapter 14 Real Estate Operating Companies (Peter Zabierek)
This chapter focuses on real estate operating companies (REOCs). With the passage of REIT legislation around the world, companies have more choices to organize as a REOC or a REIT. The advantages of REOCs over REITs include the benefits of using debt, growth potential, ability to time the market, fewer restrictions on investor base, more permissible activities, and greater financial flexibility including in times of distress. The characteristics of REOCs differ from those of REITs including higher yields, lower liquidity, and higher leverage. In the market environment, REOCs have higher systematic risk and greater volatility. They outperform REITs in up markets and underperform REITs in down markets.

Summary and Conclusions

Real estate is typically classified as an alternative investment to more traditional assets such as stocks and bonds. Real estate investments can be income-producing or non-income-producing. Although real estate can produce income like a bond and appreciate like a stock, this tangible asset has several unique characteristics as well as advantages and disadvantages relative to other investment alternatives. Some benefits of including real estate in a portfolio include diversification, yield enhancement, risk reduction, tax management, and inflation-hedging capabilities. The tax management feature arises because REITs are treated differently from all other traded stocks. They pay no corporate tax, but are required to pay out nearly all their free cash flow to shareholders, reversing many of the findings of corporate finance. Unlike other firms, REITs hold little cash, issue stock rather than engage in buybacks, and hold virtually no retained earnings. In exchange, shareholders do not receive preferential low individual tax rates on REIT dividends, which are taxed as ordinary income. This high dividend tax rate makes REITs preferable for retirement or other deferred accounts.

Unlike traditional investments, investors in real estate have the ability to influence performance. Real estate has drawbacks in that it requires management, is costly and difficult to buy, sell, and operate, and sometimes has lower liquidity. Additionally, measuring the relative performance of real estate can be challenging.

Both private and public real estate markets are available for investing in debt and equity. The choice between private and public markets and debt and equity investments depends on the type of exposure that investors see for their portfolios. This book focuses on public debt and equity real estate markets. Its companion *Private Real Estate Markets and Investments* complements the current volume. Investing in real estate offers opportunities for substantial returns but also involves numerous risks. Real estate investing requires due diligence to ensure that the risk-return trade-off meets expectations. Readers of this book should gain a greater appreciation of what is needed to be successful when investing in public real estate markets.

2

Diversification Benefits of Real Estate

BRAD CASE
Senior Vice President, Research and Industry Information,
National Association of Real Estate Investment Trusts (NAREIT)

Introduction

Real estate is generally classified among alternative assets, but the term is not carefully defined. An *alternative asset* is any asset other than publicly listed stocks or bonds and the risk-free asset (cash). Some use the term "alternative" as shorthand for any assets that are not listed. This is inappropriate because the underlying return pattern, not listing status, should define an asset class. Others use "alternative" to denote "optional," but this is certainly inadequate. Malkiel (2003, 11) notes that "basically, there are only four types of investment categories that you need to consider: cash, bonds, common stocks and real estate." Anson (2006, 7–8) states "real estate is not an alternative to stocks and bonds—it is a fundamental asset class that should be included within every diversified portfolio. Equity, fixed income, cash, and real estate . . . are the basic asset classes that must be held within a diversified portfolio."

This chapter focuses on real estate as an "alternative" to stocks, bonds, and cash exactly in the sense that its underlying return pattern offers diversification benefits. The chapter starts by examining the diversifying characteristics of real estate relative to stocks and bonds. Special attention is on how correlations with other assets change over time as well as the importance of the investment horizon. The chapter then turns to diversification within the broad real estate asset class, noting interactions between real estate debt and equity; between public and private forms of real estate investment; among real estate investment strategies (core, value-added, and opportunistic); among different property types; between U.S. and non-U.S. assets; and finally geographically within the United States. The final section provides a summary and conclusions.

Asset Class Diversification: Real Estate and Other Assets

The diversification benefits of real estate rest ultimately on the fact that the real estate market cycle differs from the stock market and bond market cycles, so that bull and bear phases in real estate tend not to coincide with those in other asset classes. Some note that stock market cycles often last about four years, but real estate cycles are typically about 18 years from peak to peak or trough to trough (Hoyt 1933). Indeed, the two most recent real estate market cycles lasted 17 and 17½ years, defined by peaks in 1972Q3, 1989Q3, and 2007Q1. Kaiser (1997) argued for a typical duration of 50–60 years with a pre-1989 cyclical peak in 1930, but noted that "perhaps the 18-year cycle still persists" and that intermediate downturns had simply been obscured.

The fundamental measure of the benefits of diversification is contained in the inequality

$$\frac{E(R_{new})-E(R_F)}{\sigma_{new}} > \left(\frac{E(R_p)-E(R_F)}{\sigma_p}\right)\rho_{R_{new},R_p}. \tag{2.1}$$

Equation 2.1 states that adding a new asset to an existing portfolio will improve the risk-adjusted returns of the combined portfolio if the Sharpe ratio of the new asset exceeds the Sharpe ratio of the existing portfolio multiplied by the return correlation between the new asset and the existing portfolio. For the added asset, the Sharpe ratio (which measures risk-adjusted returns) is $S_{new} = \frac{E(R_{new})-E(R_F)}{\sigma_{new}}$ where $E(R_F)$ is the expected risk-free rate and $E(R_{new})$ is the expected return on an added asset with standard deviation σ_{new}. The current portfolio without the new asset has an expected return $E(R_P)$ and standard deviation σ_P, so its Sharpe ratio is $S_P = \frac{E(R_P)-E(R_F)}{\sigma_P}$. The correlation coefficient between the new asset and the current portfolio is ρ_{R_{new},R_p}.

From January 1978 through April 2013, the Sharpe ratio of the stock market as measured using one-month returns of the Standard and Poor's 500 Index (S&P 500) was 0.475. The Sharpe ratio of the bond market as measured using one-month returns of the Barclays Capital U.S. Aggregate Bond Market Index was 0.553. A portfolio arbitrarily allocated 60 percent to stocks and 40 percent to bonds had a Sharpe ratio of 0.565. Real estate returns as measured by the monthly FTSE NAREIT All U.S. Equity REIT index produced a Sharpe ratio of 0.521 over the same period and had correlations of 0.580 with the stock market, 0.158 with the bond market, and 0.574 with the stock-bond portfolio. Thus, real estate would have provided diversification benefits relative to a stock-only holding (0.521 > 0.475(0.580) = 0.275), a bond-only holding (0.521 > 0.553(0.158) = 0.088), and the stock-bond portfolio (0.521 > 0.565(0.574) = 0.324).

Sa-Aadu, Shilling, and Tiwari (2010) find that listed equity REITs provide a diversification benefit even when the existing portfolio already includes U.S. large-, medium-, and small-cap stocks, U.S. Treasury and corporate bonds, commodities, and international stocks. Huang and Zhong (2013) reach the same conclusion regarding the diversification benefit of REITs even when U.S. and international stocks, U.S. and international bonds, commodities, and Treasury inflation-protected securities (TIPS) are already in the portfolio. These and other findings suggest that the REIT diversification benefit arises because of a set of return drivers—exposure to the real estate asset class—that cannot be accessed through non-real-estate investments.

Each relevant value—expected returns, volatilities, and correlations—may change over time, meaning that the diversification benefit of real estate relative to other assets may vary as well. Less widely recognized is that the investor's horizon is also critical in determining the diversification benefit of any asset.

DYNAMIC CORRELATIONS

Case, Yang, and Yildirim (2012) use the dynamic conditional correlation with generalized autoregressive conditional heteroskedasticity (DCC-GARCH) model developed by Engle (2002) to examine how the return correlations among the real estate, stock, bond, and cash asset classes vary over time. The authors find that the correlation between real estate and stocks fluctuated narrowly between January 1978 and August 1991 around an average value of 0.687 with no trend. From August 1991 through September 2001, however, the real estate-stock correlation trended downward to a low of 0.300, perhaps reflecting the entrance of new and relatively sophisticated investors into the listed equity real estate asset class. With the inclusion of REITs into the S&P 500 in October 2001 (Ambrose, Lee, and Peek 2007), the real estate-stock correlation reversed its trend, reaching 0.590 in July 2008. Figure 2.1, which depicts an update of the Case et al. analysis (thereby modifying the estimated REIT-stock correlation in every month), indicates that the DCC-GARCH correlation spiked as high as 0.787 in the aftermath of the 2008–2009 liquidity crisis before beginning to subside. This suggests

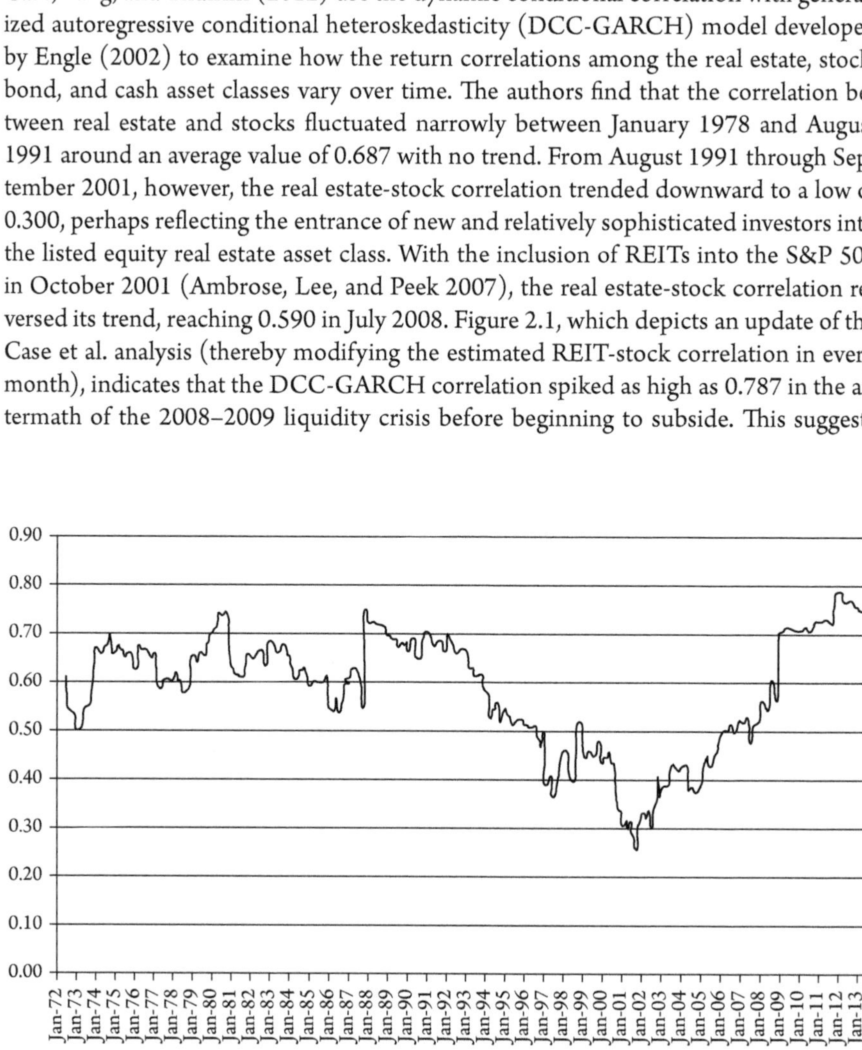

Figure 2.1 Time Variation in One Month Return Correlation between Listed Equity Real Estate and Listed Stocks. This figure shows the correlation of monthly total returns between listed REITs (FTSE NAREIT All U.S. Equity REITs Index) and the stock market (S&P 500), estimated using the Dynamic Conditional Correlation—Generalized Autoregressive Conditional Heteroskedasticity (DCC-GARCH) model described in Case et al. (2012) between January 1972 and April 2013.

that real estate provides less diversification benefit during market crises, a finding that is echoed by Hoesli and Reka (2013).

Case, Guidolin, and Yildirim (2014) use a Markov regime switching approach to evaluate dynamic correlations among listed equity, listed long-term government bonds, and listed real estate in the United States. They determine that returns among the three assets seem to be characterized by four regimes, with different correlations in each regime. The first regime is a "normal" bull market state with strong returns and nearly identical Sharpe ratios for stocks and REITs but weak returns and negative Sharpe ratios for bonds. Correlation coefficients are 0.655 for REITs with stocks, 0.413 for REITs with bonds, and 0.495 for stocks with bonds. The authors interpret the second regime as a "REIT premium" environment of higher returns and Sharpe ratios for REITs than for stocks. Correlation coefficients are 0.483 for REITs with stocks, –0.206 for REITs with bonds, and very close to zero for stocks with bonds. The third regime identified is a short-lived "surge" or "dream" environment of spectacularly high returns in all three assets along with very low correlations of 0.278 for REITs with stocks, zero for REITs with bonds, and 0.249 for stocks with bonds. Finally, the fourth regime is an equally short-lived but also infrequent "nightmare." The liquidity crisis of late 2008 and early 2009 is the longest example on record. There are strongly negative returns for REITs and stocks, very low positive returns for bonds, a REIT-stock correlation coefficient spiking to 0.807 illustrating the observation that "when markets fall, they tend all to fall together," and REIT-bond and stock-bond correlations not significantly different from zero illustrating the protection afforded by government bonds during equity market crises.

Diversification benefits depend not only on correlations but also on relative risk-adjusted returns. During the five-year period from January 2008 through December 2012, which encompassed the liquidity crisis of late 2008 and early 2009, the average (non-DCC-GARCH) correlation was abnormally high at 0.824 for real estate with stocks and 0.832 for real estate with the portfolio comprised of stocks and bonds. Given the relatively strong real estate Sharpe ratio (0.333), however, the correlations were low enough to provide diversification benefits in both cases ($0.333 > 0.166(0.824) = 0.137$ and $0.333 > 0.354(0.832) = 0.294$).

IMPORTANCE OF THE INVESTMENT HORIZON

Studies of asset return characteristics including Case et al. (2012) frequently use returns measured over one-month periods because monthly data are readily available. However, investors, particularly those for whom diversification benefits are important, generally do not have one-month investment horizons. Endowments, for example, have infinite lives, as do pension funds, particularly those that are not closed to new members, and most foundations, while individuals often have investment horizons of years or decades. Many investors do not recognize that investment return attributes including volatility and correlation depend on the investment horizon over which returns are measured. As a result, diversification benefits can vary dramatically over different investment horizons even if they do not vary over time.

Figure 2.2 demonstrates the importance of the investment horizon by depicting the correlation between broad stock market returns (S&P 500) and the returns for 10

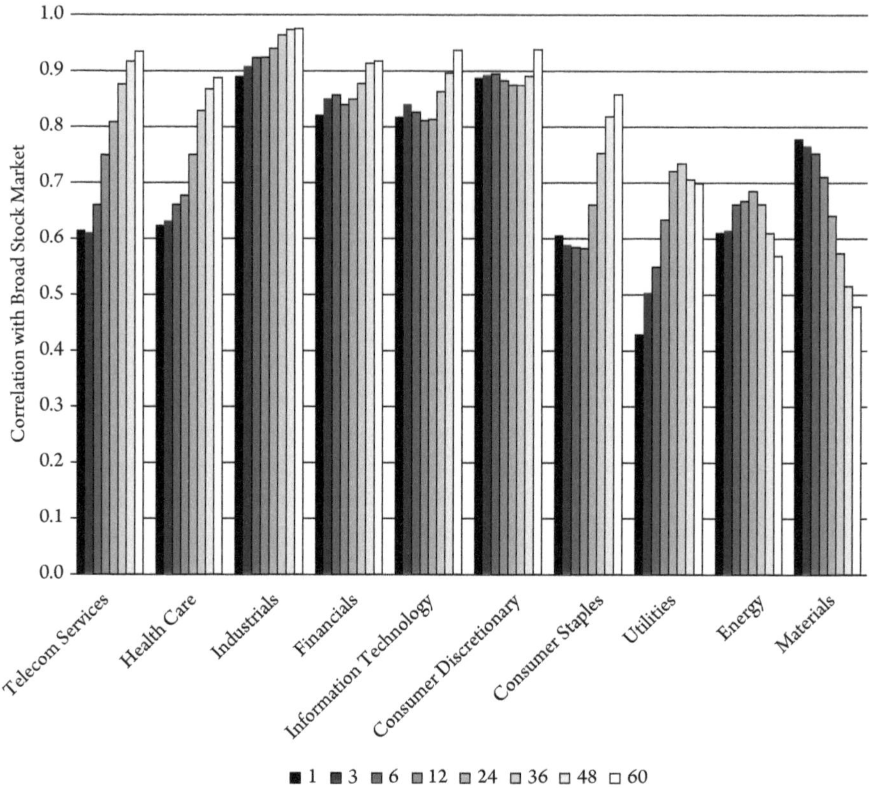

Figure 2.2 Term Structure of Correlations between Sector Returns and Broad Stock Market Returns. This figure shows the correlations between 10 sectors of the stock market (S&P 500 Sector index series) and the broad stock market (S&P 500) using total returns computed for investment horizons ranging from 1 month to 60 months between January 1990 and April 2013.

sectors of the stock market. Investors are likely to enjoy sector diversification benefits if the correlation between sector and market returns is low, as indeed they are when measured over one-month horizons. However, the graphs also show that the correlations over longer investment horizons are larger, in some cases dramatically so. Returns in the telecommunications sector, for example, show a correlation of just 0.649 when measured using one-month returns as opposed to 0.936 over a five-year period. The five-year correlation suggests that investors with longer investment horizons enjoy essentially no diversification benefit from investing in the telecommunications (telecom) sector relative to other parts of the stock market.

The reason for this phenomenon, which may be termed an "upward-sloping term structure of correlations," is that while short-term events may cause the returns of telecom companies to differ from those of companies in other sectors, longer-term earnings drivers are common to practically all sectors. That is, the stock market exposes investors to the stock market cycle, regardless of whether that cycle is accessed through telecom companies or companies in most other segments of the stock market. The only sectors that are exceptions as shown in figure 2.2 are energy and materials, which expose investors to a different market cycle in which commodity prices drive company earnings. That is, while short-term events may affect all companies in the stock market,

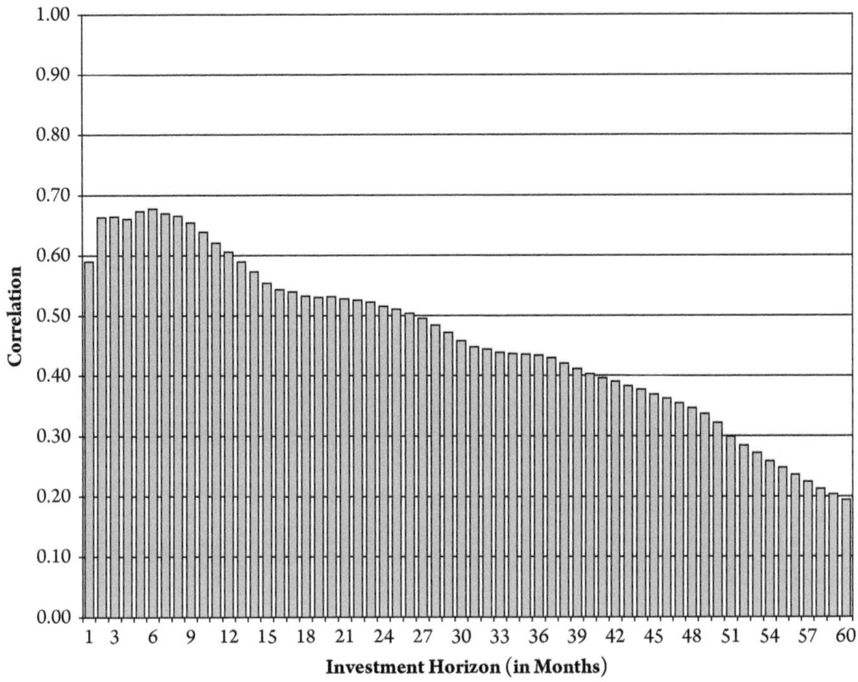

Figure 2.3 Term Structure of Correlations between Listed Real Estate Returns and Broad Stock Market Returns. This figure shows the correlations between listed equity REITs (FTSE NAREIT All U.S. Equity REITs Index) and the broad stock market (S&P 500) using total returns computed for investment horizons ranging from 1 month to 60 months between January 1990 and April 2013.

over longer horizons the commodity market cycle rather than the stock market cycle drives the returns of energy and materials companies.

Figure 2.3 shows another marked exception: listed REITs. Although listed REITs trade in the stock market, they expose investors to the real estate market cycle. The average correlation between REITs and the S&P 500 between January 1990 and April 2013 was 0.565 when measured using one-month returns (and 0.658 using six-month returns), but only 0.138 when measured using five-year returns. This "downward-sloping term structure of correlations" reveals that the diversification benefits of real estate are much greater for investors with long investment horizons than is apparent from correlation coefficients measured using monthly return data. In fact, for investors with longer horizons, real estate provides diversification benefits even relative to holdings in the financial sector, the sector into which listed REITs are classified (inappropriately, at least in the case of equity REITs). The correlation coefficient between the financial sector and REITs is just 0.343 based on five-year returns.

Figure 2.4 shows the term structure of correlations between real estate and the bond asset class. The correlation is quite low even using one-month return horizons (0.150) but, as with the real estate-stock correlation, the real estate-bond correlation shows a

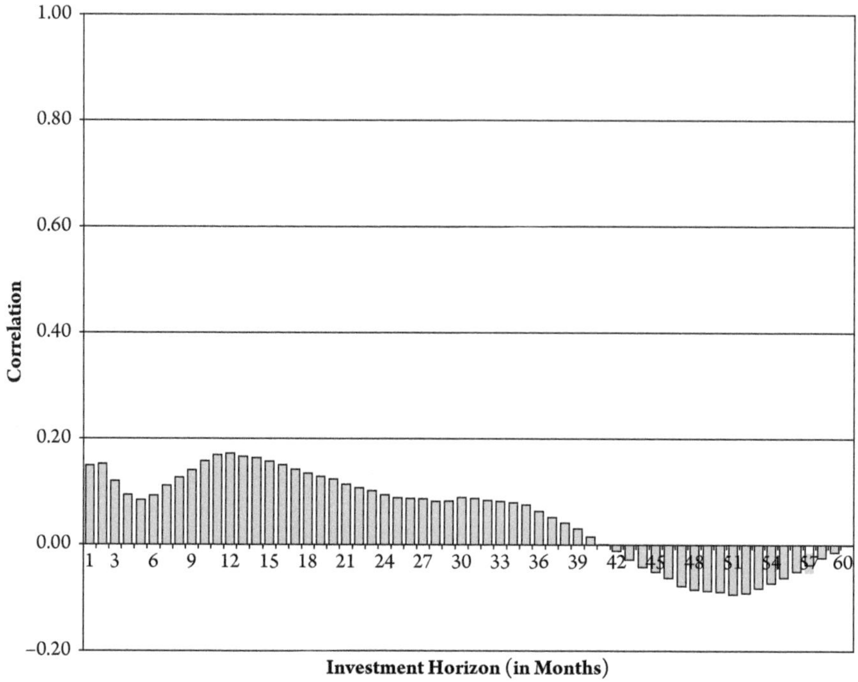

Figure 2.4 Term Structure or Correlations between Listed Equity Real Estate Returns and Broad Bond Market Returns. This figure shows the correlations between listed equity REITs (FTSE NAREIT All U.S. Equity REITs Index) and the broad bond market (Barclays Capital U.S. Aggregate Bond Index) using total returns computed for investment horizons ranging from 1 month to 60 months between January 1990 and April 2013.

downward-sloping term structure. In fact, the correlation of five-year returns is virtually zero (−0.001), indicating that, in terms of risk-adjusted returns, investors with long horizons can benefit very strongly from diversification among stocks, bonds, and real estate due to low correlations between these asset classes.

Diversification within the Real Estate Asset Class

Many investors may be attracted to real estate due to the diversification benefits of real estate relative to other asset classes in a strategic portfolio allocation. However, real estate also provides diversification benefits within the asset class.

When two assets have the same expected return patterns, investors can still benefit by holding both of them, but this benefit is not diversification. Instead, dividing the overall holding among a larger number of individual assets—all of them with the same expected return pattern—instead of consolidating the holding in one asset achieves *granularity,* which protects the investor against having an unexpected loss affect too large a portion of the overall portfolio. This section focuses on diversification (i.e., different expected return patterns) among various segments of the real estate market. For example, an investor can deploy capital into real estate equity or debt, as well as into private or public real estate holdings. Capital can be deployed to follow different investment strategies such as core, value-added, and opportunistic. Investors can choose investments in different property types or in domestic and foreign markets. Finally, investors in domestic real estate can seek further diversification through investing in properties in different areas within their home country (e.g., Boston and San Francisco) as well as submarkets of a particular area (e.g., Midtown versus the Upper East Side of Manhattan).

REAL ESTATE DEBT AND EQUITY

The three main categories of real estate debt are mortgages, MBS, and unsecured debt of real estate companies. Some include common equity shares of mortgage REITs, which are companies whose assets consist entirely or mostly of mortgages and MBS, as well as preferred equity shares of equity and mortgage REITs, because preferred stock has certain fixed-income characteristics.

The value of a mortgage is driven by the discounted value of a contracted stream of principal and interest payments on that mortgage as well as the probability of default or prepayment of the mortgage. Valuation of mortgage investments is affected by changes in interest rates (which influence prepayment behavior, as well as payment streams on variable rate instruments). Valuation of mortgages is also affected by changes in property values because mortgage holders are more likely to default if their equity position is reduced. MBS and unsecured debt of real estate companies are valued using the same general framework, except that a default on the security or bond would generally arise because of a decline in property values on multiple assets as opposed to a single asset. That is, a high degree of correlation in asset values might cause many of the mortgages underlying an MBS to default, or might cause a decline in the overall financial condition of the owners of the underlying collateral.

The two main categories of real estate equity are ownership shares in properties themselves (direct equity) and common equity shares of equity REITs, which are companies whose assets consist entirely or mostly of properties (indirect equity). Property values primarily drive the value of real estate equity. Property values can be represented as the stream of future net earnings generated by the real estate asset discounted at the appropriate capitalization (cap) rate, which itself is a function of prevailing interest rates.

Because the underlying return drivers—property values and interest rates—are the same for real estate debt and equity, they are generally considered two segments of the same real estate asset class rather than two separate asset classes. Yet, their return patterns differ substantially, offering the opportunity for diversification within the real estate asset class. As Figure 2.5 shows, the correlation of one-month returns to equity REIT stocks (FTSE NAREIT All U.S. Equity REITs Index) and REIT bonds (Barclays Capital U.S. Corporate Credit: Investment Grade: REIT Sector) between September 1997 and April 2013 was just 0.416, indicating very substantial potential benefits of diversification between real estate equity and debt investments. Interestingly, the term structure of correlations is initially increasing. This may reflect that information affecting values of both types of real estate is processed more quickly and efficiently through

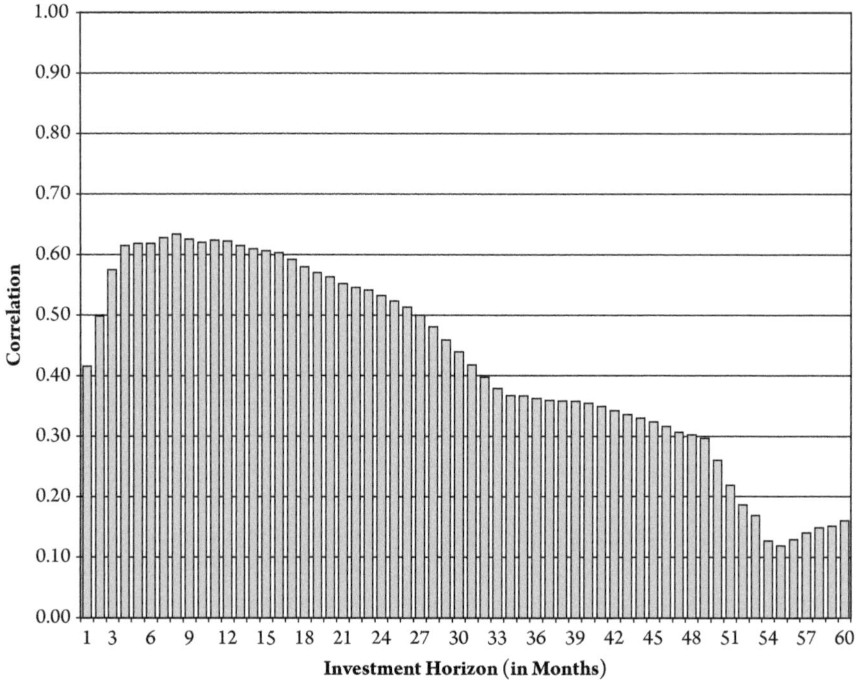

Figure 2.5 Term Structure or Correlations between Listed Real Estate Equity Returns and Listed Real Estate Debt Returns. This figure shows the correlations between equity REIT stocks (FTSE NAREIT All U.S. Equity REITs Index) and REIT bonds (Barclays Capital U.S. Corporate Credit: Investment Grade: REIT Sector Index) using total returns computed for investment horizons ranging from 1 month to 60 months between September 1997 and April 2013.

one market (presumably the equity market, which is substantially more liquid) than through the other. After reaching a maximum value of 0.634 for eight-month returns, however, the correlation declines over longer investment horizons and is just 0.161 when measured over a five-year period.

PUBLIC AND PRIVATE REAL ESTATE

The real estate return data cited to this point has come from the listed equity REIT market, where liquid trading in homogeneous assets (shares of any given REIT) efficiently reveals the effects of new information on asset values. Listed REITs, however, control only about 15 percent of investment-quality commercial property in the United States, meaning that the large majority of the equity real estate asset class is owned in the relatively illiquid private side of the market. While the return drivers and therefore the expected movements in value of public and private real estate are the same, private real estate is characterized by two factors (extreme illiquidity and heterogeneity) that make measuring returns extraordinarily difficult.

Illiquidity Lag, Appraisal Lag, and Temporal Diversification

Consider the effect of new information suggesting that future demand for office space will be stronger than previously expected. Other factors remaining equal, an increase in expected future demand should translate into an immediate increase in office property values because the present value of any asset can be modeled as the present discounted value of its future stream of earnings. Such an increase in office property values will be revealed right away in the stock prices of listed REITs that own office properties, because equity shares in office REITs (representing indirect ownership of their underlying portfolios) trade in a liquid, informationally efficient market. The same increase will also be revealed in measurements of returns on the private (unlisted) side of the real estate market, but appraisal data may not show the change until (1) transactions are closed at the new higher price (a process that requires about two quarters on average), and (2) appraisals on non-transacting properties incorporate the information revealed in completed comparable transactions (a process that requires two to three additional quarters on average). The result is that transaction-based measurement of property returns on the private side of the market lags measurement on the public side by about two quarters, while appraisal-based measurement lags by four to five quarters.

This private market valuation lag results in what can be called *temporal diversification,* which reduces the measured volatility of a combined public/private real estate portfolio even if no difference exists in actual return patterns between public and private real estate holdings. To see how temporal diversification works, consider the same asset whose returns are reported twice: once contemporaneously and again with a two-quarter lag or a four-quarter lag. For example, the correlation between real estate returns (the FTSE NAREIT All U.S. Equity REITs Index, January 1972–April 2013) and their own lagged values is –0.137 with a two-quarter lag (the average for transaction-based measurement of private real estate) and +0.160 with a four-quarter lag (the average for appraisal-based measurement of private real estate). If public and private real estate have the same returns and volatilities and differ only in the private-side measurement lag, then combining them in a portfolio provides substantial diversification benefits because

$$\frac{E(R_{RE})-E(R_F)}{\sigma_{RE}} > \frac{E(R_{RE})-E(R_F)}{\sigma_{RE}}(-0.137) \text{ and}$$
$$\frac{E(R_{RE})-E(R_F)}{\sigma_{RE}} > \frac{E(R_{RE})-E(R_F)}{\sigma_{RE}}(0.160)\,. \tag{2.2}$$

Specifically, the combined portfolio with one half unlagged and one half lagged returns would have the same average return (13 percent per year) but annualized volatility of only 11 percent (using a two-quarter lag) or 13 percent (using a four-quarter lag) compared to 17 percent for a temporally undiversified portfolio. This reduction in volatility would improve the measured Sharpe ratio of a portfolio comprised of public real estate measured with and without a lag.

In the same way, if public and private real estate returns are identical except for the effects of illiquidity lag and appraisal lag, then combining them in the real estate portfolio produces a temporal diversification benefit, at least for reporting purposes. The question then is whether the assets exhibit the same return patterns.

Illiquidity Smoothing, Appraisal Smoothing, and Non-Appraisal Smoothing

As noted, private real estate is characterized by two problems that make evaluating returns extraordinarily difficult: illiquidity and heterogeneity. Returns can be measured using data on property transactions, but because transactions are infrequent and assets are heterogeneous, individual transactions must be aggregated to produce summary measures with tolerable statistical properties. This process results in *illiquidity smoothing* (also called *aggregation bias*). For example, transaction-based quarterly price indices for the private real estate market reflect the average prices of all properties sold during that quarter, while a quarterly price index for the public real estate market typically reflects the prices of only the last shares of REIT stock sold on the last day of that quarter.

Similarly, appraisal-based quarterly price indices for the private real estate market reflect the average appraised values of all properties appraised during that quarter. Appraisals, however, involve two additional sources of smoothing. First, appraisers display the behavioral bias known as *anchoring*, in which "people make estimates by starting from an initial value that is adjusted to yield the final answer" but "adjustments are typically insufficient," so answers "are biased toward the initial values" (Tversky and Kahneman 1974, 1128). Diaz and Wolverton (1998) and Clayton, Geltner, and Hamilton (2001) provide evidence that anchoring plays an important role in commercial property appraisals. Specifically, the stated appraised value for a given property in a given quarter tends to be a weighted average of the actual value of that property and the previous appraised value of that property

$$R_t^{\text{reported}} = (1-\alpha) R_t^{\text{actual}} + \alpha\, R_{t-1}^{\text{reported}}. \tag{2.3}$$

Empirical analysis of the NCREIF Property Index (NPI) published by the National Council of Real Estate Investment Fiduciaries suggests that the value of α, called the *first-order autocorrelation parameter,* is about 0.85, indicating that the NPI suffers from very considerable *appraisal smoothing,* which causes the volatility of untraded real estate to be underestimated.

Second, appraisal is a costly process. Standard industry practice is to appraise the value of a given property just once each year and, between appraisals, to update stated property values through a simple process of extrapolation. In fact, until recently the industry norm was appraisal once every three years. This practice of extrapolating the stated values of unappraised properties may be termed *non-appraisal smoothing* because new information that affects the actual values of unappraised properties will generally not be reflected in their stated values.

The combined effects of illiquidity smoothing, appraisal smoothing, and non-appraisal smoothing are to reduce the measured but not the actual volatility of returns on private real estate assets, thereby artificially inflating their reported Sharpe ratio. Moreover, the three sources of smoothing along with illiquidity lag and appraisal lag reduce the measured but not the actual correlations between private real estate returns and the returns of other assets. The result is an artificial increase in their reported diversification benefits.

Geltner (1989) and others suggest methods to "de-smooth" private real estate returns, but they do not eliminate the problem. Table 2.1 compares the volatility of unlevered returns measured using the NCREIF Transaction Based Indexes (NTBI) of

Table 2.1 **Volatility of Unlevered Private and Public Equity Real Estate Returns**

	NCREIF TBI	*PureProperty End-of-Quarter*	*PureProperty Average-in-Quarter*
By property type			
Apartment	10.91	10.47	8.60
Industrial	10.71	12.82	11.81
Office	10.88	10.72	9.00
Retail	11.16	11.52	9.28
Health care	Unavailable	14.32	10.79
Hotel	Unavailable	14.48	11.95
By region			
East	11.19	11.65	9.53
Midwest	10.20	10.17	8.52
South	10.46	10.74	9.11
West	10.93	11.88	9.78
Total	10.78	10.74	8.88

Note: This table compares the annualized volatility of quarterly capital appreciation for private real estate equity (NCREIF Transaction Based Index Series) and public real estate equity (FTSE NAREIT PureProperty Index Series). The second data column shows volatility when quarterly public returns are computed using end-of-quarter index values. The third data column shows volatility when quarterly public returns are computed by averaging across all index values during that quarter, an approach that imitates the illiquidity smoothing (or aggregation bias) of the NCREIF Transaction Based Index methodology.

private real estate and the FTSE NAREIT PureProperty Indexes of public real estate. The second column shows public real estate volatility measured in the standard way, using the last REIT stock transactions on the last day of each quarter. Strikingly, volatility measured in this way is nearly identical to private real estate volatility. As noted, however, even a transaction-based index of private real estate suffers from *illiquidity smoothing* because all transactions occurring during a given quarter must be aggregated to produce the index. To correct for this difference in measurement, the third column shows the volatility implied by an alternative set of quarterly returns computed by averaging all daily values of the PureProperty index during each quarter. The volatility of these alternative quarterly returns is substantially less than reported private real estate volatility. In fact, a theoretical basis exists for expecting this result. If the same assets are traded through markets that differ in informational efficiency, volatility should generally be less in the more informationally efficient public market.

Figure 2.6 shows the term structure of correlations between public and private real estate, with the investment horizon increasing from one quarter (the frequency of the NTBI and NPI) to 20 quarters (five years). As the graph shows, returns measured at the one-quarter horizon suggest a correlation very close to zero, which is unreasonably low

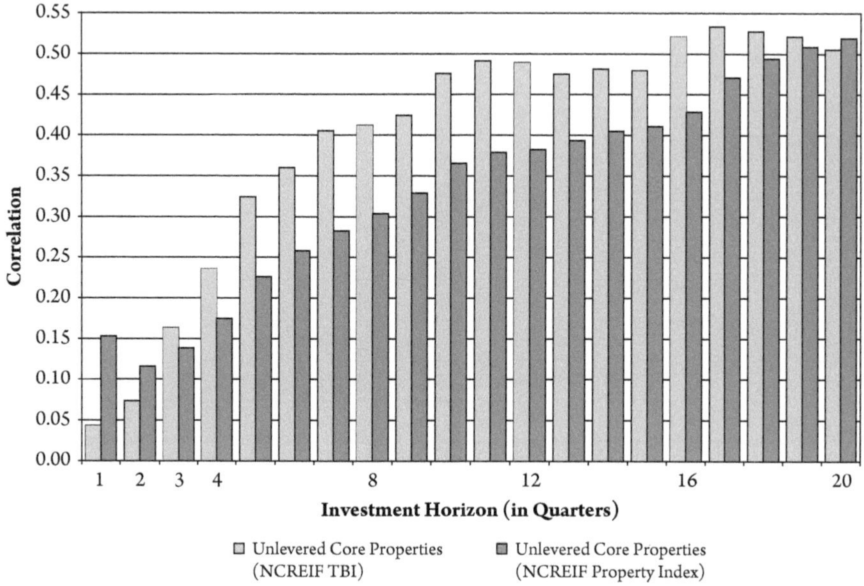

Figure 2.6 Return Correlation between Listed Real Estate Equity Returns and Listed Real Estate Debt Returns by investment Horizon. This figure shows the correlations between equity REIT stocks (FTSE NAREIT All U.S. Equity REITs Index) and REIT bonds (Barclays Capital U.S. Corporate Credit: Investment Grade: REIT Sector Index) using total returns computed for investment horizons ranging from 1 month to 60 months between September 1997 and April 2013.

given that the two sides of the market respond to the same earnings drivers. Yet, with an upward sloping term structure, the correlation reaches 0.505 using the NTBI and 0.519 using the NPI at the 20-quarter investment horizon. De-lagging increases the measured correlation at the 20-quarter horizon to 0.642 for the NTBI with a two-quarter lag and to 0.643 for the NPI with a four-quarter lag. This increased correlation between public and private real estate returns mimics several other studies including Boudry, Coulson, Kallberg, and Liu (2012) showing the public and private real estate markets are closely related.

To summarize, evaluating the true benefits of diversifying by listing status within the real estate asset class is difficult. This is because return measurement problems make knowing the true volatility and therefore the Sharpe ratio of private real estate difficult. With private real estate volatility subject to measurement error, correlations between private real estate and other assets including public real estate are similarly difficult to estimate.

In terms of average return, the PureProperty Index and the NTBI indicate that unlevered net total returns during 2000Q1–2013Q1 averaged 9.71 percent per year for public real estate and 7.29 percent per year for private real estate. If the volatility of public real estate is less than or the same as that of private real estate, this suggests that the former offers diversification benefits relative to the latter. Whether private real estate offers diversification benefits relative to public real estate holdings depends on the unknown actual correlation between them.

Without question, however, returns measured on the private side of the market lag behind returns produced by public REITs. This phenomenon produces a temporal diversification benefit that appears to be very substantial. There is a value, at least for reporting purposes, of constructing a portfolio that includes both private and public segments of the real estate asset class.

DIVERSIFICATION BY INVESTMENT STRATEGY

Investors typically apply any of three main strategies when investing in real estate equity: core, opportunistic, and value-added. The *core* strategy focuses on acquisition and long-term holding of high-quality, fully-leased properties in apartment, industrial, office, and retail property types. The strategy involves using little or no leverage. The goal is to generate total returns similar in terms of average and volatility to those of investment-grade bonds, with strong current income. The strategy involves limited attention to capital appreciation.

The *opportunistic* strategy focuses on acquiring and subsequently selling properties that embody substantial leasing risk, often because properties require major renovation or even completion. This strategy uses substantial leverage up to the ability of the properties or entities to sustain it. The hope is to generate high total returns composed mainly of capital appreciation with little attention to current income.

The *value-added* strategy represents a hybrid. It focuses on core investments using substantially more leverage, or on acquiring and selling properties requiring managerial change or minor renovation using less leverage than opportunistic investments.

Table 2.2 summarizes return data compiled by NCREIF for private real estate investment funds following core, value-added, and opportunistic strategies between 1988Q4 and 2012Q4. As the table indicates, correlations among the three strategies are surprisingly high: 0.904 for core with value-added, 0.806 for value-added with opportunistic, and 0.727 for core with opportunistic. This evidence suggests that different investment strategies offer little diversification benefit. This is consistent with the findings of Shilling and Wurtzebach (2012). They report that differences among core, value-added, and opportunistic returns to property investments tracked by NCREIF are attributable primarily to variations in using leverage. Leverage dominates property-level characteristics, geographic location, or other specific return drivers.

On the other hand, an examination of the income and capital appreciation components of total return, also shown in Table 2.2 (with listed equity REITs included for comparison), suggests that the opportunistic strategy differs from the core and value-added strategies. A larger share of total return from the opportunistic strategy comes from capital appreciation. Moreover, the correlations among investment strategies are higher in the capital appreciation component than in the income component: 0.900 versus 0.879 for core with value-added, 0.776 versus 0.235 for value-added with opportunistic, and 0.673 versus 0.213 for core with opportunistic.

The problems of appraisal-based measurement of private real estate returns may inflate the reported correlations among different strategies, especially in the capital appreciation component. This is because errors by any given appraiser are likely to be

Table 2.2 **Return Components and Correlations of Real Estate Returns by Investment Strategy**

Investment Strategy	*Net Total Return*	*Net Income Return*	*Capital Appreciation Return*
Compound average			
Core	5.48	6.26	−0.74
Value-added	5.06	5.35	−0.31
Opportunistic	8.14	4.43	3.55
Listed equity REIT	10.50	6.15	4.11
Correlations			
Core/Value-added	0.904	0.879	0.900
Core/Opportunistic	0.727	0.213	0.673
Value-added/Opportunistic	0.806	0.235	0.776

Note: This table compares the components of reported net total returns of private real estate investment funds following core, value-added, and opportunistic strategies between 1988Q4 and 2012Q4, along with reported return correlations.

positively correlated across holdings in different strategies. Taking this into account, investors are likely to benefit from diversification at least between core and opportunistic strategies in the real estate asset class.

PROPERTY TYPE DIVERSIFICATION

As noted, the four property types considered core are rental apartments, industrial facilities, office buildings, and retail properties. Yet, the investable commercial real estate asset class includes a wide variety of other property types. These types include health care facilities and hotels, both of which are nearing recognition as core property types. Other investable assets include self-storage facilities, manufactured housing communities, data centers, and infrastructure. Emerging investable real estate assets include agriculture and farms, timber, and even single-family rental housing. A common set of real estate market drivers including construction costs and the cost and availability of capital for asset acquisition or development affects returns to all property types. Other return drivers are specific to one or a few property types.

For example, single-family mortgage rates and availability, household formation, and employment growth in the younger age cohorts affect the demand for rental apartments. Employment growth in those occupations most likely to use offices, such as business services, affects the demand for office space. Growth in domestic and foreign trade in tangible goods affects the demand for industrial facilities. Return drivers specific to each property type suggest the likelihood of benefits to diversification.

Table 2.3 shows the average correlations among unlevered total returns of six major property types as measured using one-month returns of the FTSE NAREIT

Table 2.3 **Diversification Benefits by Property Type**

	Apartment	*Health Care*	*Hotel*	*Industrial*	*Office*	*Retail*
Average annualized total return	9.76	14.98	7.90	9.53	8.92	11.27
Annualized volatility	10.67	13.94	13.39	13.24	10.57	11.14
Sharpe ratio	0.727	0.931	0.441	0.569	0.654	0.833
Correlation	Apartment	0.692	0.687	0.741	0.851	0.816
	Health care		0.590	0.756	0.788	0.844
	Hotel			0.751	0.778	0.772
	Industrial				0.852	0.890
	Office					0.904

Note: This table presents the average annualized total returns, annualized volatilities, and correlations of unlevered real estate holdings in six major property types using monthly data from the FTSE NAREIT PureProperty Index Series between January 2000 and April 2013.

PureProperty Index Series between January 2000 and April 2013. The correlations range from 0.59 (health care with hotel) to 0.90 (office with retail), but most are between 0.74 and 0.85. Combined with the realized Sharpe ratios, the correlations suggest that adding apartment, health care, or retail holdings to an existing portfolio of any other type would have provided diversification benefits. Adding industrial or office holdings would have provided diversification benefits relative to each other as well as to apartment or hotel properties. Finally, adding hotel holdings would have increase the Sharpe ratio of an existing portfolio of industrial properties. However, the limited sample period may not be representative of other historical periods in terms of returns, volatilities, or correlations by property type.

DOMESTIC AND INTERNATIONAL REAL ESTATE

Many factors driving the real estate market cycle may differ across international borders even if they relate to global long-term real and financial cycles. These factors include demand drivers such as employment growth and retail activity or supply drivers such as construction costs, the cost and availability of development capital, and government permitting activity. These international differences suggest the likelihood of cross-border diversification benefits in the real estate asset class.

Table 2.4 summarizes returns, volatilities, and correlations among listed equity real estate returns in several countries and regions. The data are one-month total returns as measured by the FTSE EPRA/NAREIT Index Series of REIT and listed property company (LPC) return indexes. Most of the correlations are quite low, with the majority between 0.37 and 0.59, and most of the correlations specifically with U.S. returns are between 0.40 and 0.57. Real estate returns in the United States provide the strongest risk-adjusted returns with a Sharpe ratio of 0.575. Nevertheless, an

Table 2.4 **Diversification Benefits of Global and International Real Estate**

	Developed	*Ex-U.S.*	*Asia*	*Europe*	*North America*	*Australia*	*Belgium*	*Canada*	*France*	*Germany*	*Hong Kong*	*Italy*	*Japan*	*Netherlands*	*Singapore*	*Sweden*	*Switzerland*	*U.K.*	*U.S.*
Annualized Average Total Return	10.03	9.05	10.56	7.18	14.52	12.54	5.90	5.11	13.53	8.02	17.00	7.79	8.01	7.28	13.39	8.06	10.36	6.46	14.69
Annualized Volatility	19.35	20.44	25.73	18.53	20.86	19.67	16.88	23.45	20.63	28.00	35.49	32.01	32.11	18.66	38.90	33.70	17.77	19.99	20.16
Sharpe Ratio	0.359	0.292	0.290	0.220	0.548	0.480	0.166	0.086	0.506	0.176	0.392	0.147	0.153	0.224	0.265	0.147	0.409	0.169	0.575
Correlation																			
Developed	1	0.890	0.876	0.796	0.786	0.682	0.538	0.549	0.658	0.441	0.684	0.457	0.473	0.692	0.626	0.532	0.466	0.637	0.735
Ex-U.S.	0.890	1	0.921	0.724	0.506	0.695	0.473	0.495	0.621	0.432	0.814	0.414	0.566	0.636	0.748	0.507	0.491	0.665	0.542
Asia	0.876	0.921	1	0.567	0.484	0.599	0.381	0.431	0.471	0.303	0.864	0.324	0.543	0.511	0.758	0.378	0.330	0.431	0.425
Europe	0.796	0.724	0.567	1	0.667	0.649	0.701	0.500	0.873	0.596	0.392	0.595	0.357	0.846	0.446	0.675	0.589	0.846	0.641
North Am	0.786	0.506	0.484	0.667	1	0.529	0.461	0.569	0.530	0.404	0.304	0.395	0.240	0.583	0.343	0.392	0.354	0.534	0.944
Australia	0.682	0.695	0.599	0.649	0.529	1	0.474	0.487	0.576	0.389	0.429	0.433	0.330	0.623	0.439	0.454	0.426	0.601	0.551
Belgium	0.538	0.473	0.381	0.701	0.461	0.474	1	0.342	0.690	0.437	0.268	0.483	0.169	0.660	0.308	0.508	0.464	0.523	0.420

Table 2.4 **continued**

	Developed	*Ex-U.S.*	*Asia*	*Europe*	*North America*	*Australia*	*Belgium*	*Canada*	*France*	*Germany*	*Hong Kong*	*Italy*	*Japan*	*Netherlands*	*Singapore*	*Sweden*	*Switzerland*	*U.K.*	*U.S.*
Canada	0.549	0.495	0.431	0.500	0.569	0.487	0.342	1	0.395	0.283	0.313	0.352	0.285	0.474	0.392	0.252	0.333	0.436	0.541
France	0.658	0.621	0.471	0.873	0.530	0.576	0.690	0.395	1	0.560	0.319	0.563	0.318	0.814	0.370	0.580	0.569	0.729	0.517
Germany	0.441	0.432	0.303	0.596	0.404	0.389	0.437	0.283	0.560	1	0.259	0.470	0.184	0.569	0.325	0.380	0.444	0.521	0.432
Hong Kong	0.684	0.814	0.864	0.392	0.304	0.429	0.268	0.313	0.319	0.259	1	0.232	0.238	0.356	0.747	0.281	0.280	0.323	0.304
Italy	0.457	0.414	0.324	0.595	0.395	0.433	0.483	0.352	0.563	0.470	0.232	1	0.193	0.580	0.303	0.393	0.390	0.457	0.376
Japan	0.473	0.566	0.543	0.357	0.240	0.330	0.169	0.285	0.318	0.184	0.238	0.193	1	0.282	0.321	0.278	0.230	0.377	0.283
Netherlands	0.692	0.636	0.511	0.846	0.583	0.623	0.660	0.474	0.814	0.569	0.356	0.580	0.282	1	0.402	0.530	0.549	0.697	0.560
Singapore	0.626	0.748	0.758	0.446	0.343	0.439	0.308	0.392	0.370	0.325	0.747	0.303	0.321	0.402	1	0.320	0.293	0.394	0.353
Sweden	0.532	0.507	0.378	0.675	0.392	0.454	0.508	0.252	0.580	0.380	0.281	0.393	0.278	0.530	0.320	1	0.341	0.478	0.400
Switzerland	0.466	0.491	0.330	0.589	0.354	0.426	0.464	0.333	0.569	0.444	0.280	0.390	0.230	0.549	0.293	0.341	1	0.537	0.409
UK	0.637	0.665	0.431	0.846	0.534	0.523	0.523	0.436	0.729	0.521	0.323	0.457	0.377	0.697	0.394	0.478	0.537	1	0.619
US	0.735	0.542	0.425	0.641	0.944	0.420	0.420	0.541	0.517	0.432	0.304	0.376	0.283	0.560	0.353	0.400	0.409	0.619	1

Note: This table presents the average annualized total returns, annualized volatilities, and correlations of unlevered real estate holdings in global and international markets using monthly data from the FTSE EPRA/NAREIT index series during January 1990–April 2013.

Table 2.5 **Diversification Benefits of Global and International Investments Relative to U.S. Stock Portfolios**

	Stock Market Indexes	*Listed Real Estate Indexes*
Total number of indexes	1,247	18
Correlation with U.S. stocks is greater than U.S. REIT correlation with U.S. stocks	992 (80 percent)	5 (28 percent)
Provides diversification benefits relative to existing portfolio of U.S. stocks	716 (58 percent)	12 (67 percent)
Provides greater diversification benefits relative to U.S. stocks than U.S. REITs provide	23 (2 percent)	3 (17 percent)

Note: This table summarizes the diversification benefits of global, ex-U.S., regional, and non-U.S. country-specific investments in stocks and listed real estate between January 1990 and April 2013 relative to an existing portfolio of U.S. stock holdings (S&P 500 Stock Index).

investor with existing holdings in U.S. real estate would still have realized diversification benefits by adding holdings in Asia or in Australia, France, Hong Kong, Singapore, or Switzerland.

Table 2.5 summarizes correlations between the one-month returns to the S&P 500 and 1,247 other indexes for which monthly data are available between January 1990 and April 2013. The indexes measure returns to investments in global, ex-U.S., regional, and non-U.S. country-specific stock markets, including style (value, growth, and blend) and market capitalization (small, mid, and large) focuses. Perhaps surprisingly, 80 percent of the indexes of non-U.S. stock market returns are more highly correlated with the U.S. stock market than are U.S. listed equity REITs. This occurs even though U.S. REITs are traded through the U.S. stock market and 17 REITs are constituents of the S&P 500. Moreover, only 58 percent of the non-U.S. stock market indexes would have offered diversification benefits to an existing portfolio matching the S&P 500. Fewer than 2 percent of them would have offered greater diversification benefits than an allocation to U.S. listed equity REITs. This suggests that diversification into non-U.S. stock markets is less important than diversification, through the U.S. stock market, into the separate real estate asset class.

Table 2.5 also summarizes correlations between the U.S. stock market and listed real estate returns in every country and region shown in Table 2.4. Perhaps surprisingly again, listed real estate returns in five of the 18 non-U.S. countries and regions are more highly correlated with the U.S. stock market than are U.S. listed real estate returns. Although listed real estate in 12 countries and regions would have provided diversification benefits to an existing S&P 500 portfolio, only France and Switzerland plus the North American region would have provided greater diversification benefits than U.S. REITs.

U.S. listed equity REITs provide better diversification benefits relative to the U.S. stock market, despite being traded through that market, than listed real estate in most foreign countries. Several possible reasons may explain this result.

First, LPCs in many other countries, notably in Asia, differ markedly from the equity REITs included in the FTSE NAREIT All U.S. Equity REITs Index. U.S. REITs are required to hold qualifying real estate constituting at least 75 percent of their assets and to derive at least 75 percent of their income from such holdings. Several non-U.S. indexes include homebuilding and other companies whose earnings do not derive primarily from the ownership and management of income-producing properties.

Second, even in those countries where LPCs tend to be most like U.S. REITs, the real estate markets themselves are less highly developed outside the United States. The maturity of the market could affect the relationship between real estate returns and their underlying drivers. These reasons may cause LPC returns outside the United States to be more highly correlated with their own domestic stock markets than are REIT returns in the United States. Thus, relatively high correlations among global stock markets may cause non-U.S. LPC returns to be relatively highly correlated with U.S. stock market returns.

GEOGRAPHIC DIVERSIFICATION

As noted, the main drivers affecting real estate returns are property values and interest rates. While efficient capital markets in the United States minimize regional differences in interest rates, the factors affecting demand for and supply of commercial properties may well differ geographically. Because of this, investors may gain geographic diversification benefits within the domestic market. Table 2.6 summarizes returns, volatilities, and correlations among unlevered total returns to commercial real estate in four regions of the United States as measured by the FTSE NAREIT PureProperty Index Series. Risk-adjusted returns have been similar across the four regions, with Sharpe ratios ranging only between 0.736 (South) and 0.780 (West). Correlations are relatively high at 0.81 for the Midwest region with any of the other three, 0.89 for the South region with either the East or the West, and 0.94 between the East and West regions. Notwithstanding relatively high correlations, the data indicate that adding a portfolio of holdings from any region would offer diversification benefits to an existing portfolio of holdings from any other region.

Table 2.6 **Diversification Benefits by Geographic Region**

	East	*Midwest*	*South*	*West*
Average annualized total return	10.41	9.40	10.24	11.12
Annualized volatility	11.34	9.70	11.19	11.68
Sharpe ratio	0.741	0.763	0.736	0.780
Correlation	East	0.821	0.889	0.943
	Midwest		0.812	0.814
	South			0.882

Note: This table presents the average annualized total returns, annualized volatilities, and correlations of unlevered real estate holdings in four major regions of the United States using monthly data from the FTSE NAREIT PureProperty Index Series between January 2000 and April 2013.

The four broad regions shown in Table 2.6 do not represent the only way of pursuing geographic diversification within the United States. For example, differentiating returns of properties in the central business district (CBD) of major cities from those of properties in suburban portions of major cities or in smaller cities is common. Another common approach is to distinguish between properties located in cities with high *barriers to entry* or constraints on new commercial property construction and those located in cities with few barriers to new construction activity. To date, however, total returns are not measured with enough accuracy to evaluate the diversification benefits of such submarket distinctions.

Summary and Conclusions

For most investors, real estate investments offer their most important diversification benefits because real estate is separate from the other fundamental asset classes of stocks, bonds, and cash. Real estate has different return drivers and low correlations, along with strong risk-adjusted returns. The correlations between real estate and other assets have changed over time. For example, the correlation of monthly returns between listed equity REITs and stocks remained uniformly high at around 0.69 until about August 1991, then declined sharply to about 0.30 by September 2001 before increasing to about 0.59 before the market-wide liquidity crisis of 2008.

For most investors, correlations based on monthly data can be misleading because diversification benefits over more realistic investment horizons can be very different from those evaluated on the basis of one-month returns. The REIT-stock correlation declines to very low levels at longer investment horizons. It is just 0.14, for example, over five-year investment horizons. This suggests that the diversification benefits of real estate may be much greater for long-term investors than they realize.

Segments of the real estate asset class offer possibilities for diversification between real estate debt and equity, between public and private real estate, by investment strategy, by property type, between U.S. and non-U.S. assets, and geographically within the domestic market. Real estate debt and equity respond very differently to the same fundamental earnings drivers. The term structure of correlations declines from around 0.60 for investors with relatively short horizons to less than 0.20 for longer-term investors.

Both public and private equity real estate respond to the same drivers and exhibit an upward-sloping term structure of correlations. Yet, the diversification benefits of private real estate cannot be evaluated fully. Existing indexes of private real estate returns fail to measure volatility fully, and therefore fail to accurately measure risk-adjusted returns or correlation with other assets. Private real estate returns are measured with a substantial lag. This lag is about two quarters when measured using completed transactions and four to five quarters when measured using appraisals. The lag gives rise to *temporal diversification* that can provide important benefits at least for reporting purposes.

Real estate investment strategies (core, value-added, and opportunistic) appear to provide surprisingly little diversification benefit, but this may be attributable to measurement problems that are themselves correlated across strategies. Correlations among returns for different property types are generally low. Substantial variation in risk-adjusted returns over the available historical period suggests that some property types offer important diversification benefits. Correlations among returns in different regions of the United States have generally been much higher. Despite little regional difference in risk-adjusted returns, they still offer diversification benefits to regionally concentrated portfolios.

Correlations of non-U.S. with U.S. real estate returns are generally quite low, mostly between 0.40 and 0.57, but historical risk-adjusted returns have generally been much weaker than in the United States. As a result, non-U.S. real estate has not generally offered diversification benefits in spite of low correlations. Most non-U.S. markets in both real estate and stock asset classes have failed historically to offer as substantial a diversification benefit to an existing U.S. stock portfolio as U.S. REITs have. This absence of a diversification benefit comes despite the fact that U.S. REITs are part of the U.S. stock market.

In short, the real estate asset class has historically offered very strong diversification benefits to investors with holdings in stocks, bonds, and other assets. The major segments of the real estate market have offered additional possibilities to benefit from diversification within the real estate asset class.

Discussion Questions

1. Discuss how the diversification benefits of real estate relative to other asset classes have changed over time.
2. What effect does the investor's horizon have on the diversification benefits of real estate?
3. What problems arise when evaluating the benefits of diversifying between public and private real estate, and what conclusions can be drawn?
4. Identify the benefits of diversifying among different real estate investment strategies.
5. Discuss whether property type diversification, international diversification, or geographic diversification in the United States provides greater diversification benefits.

References

Ambrose, Brent W., Dong Wook Lee, and Joe Peek. 2007. "Co-Movement after Joining an Index: Spillovers of Nonfundamental Effects." *Real Estate Economics* 35:1, 57–90.

Anson, Mark J. P. 2006. *Handbook of Alternative Assets*. Hoboken, NJ: John Wiley & Sons, Inc.

Boudry, Walter I., N. Edward Coulson, Jarl G. Kallberg, and Crocker H. Liu. 2012. "On the Hybrid Nature of REITs." *Journal of Real Estate Finance and Economics* 44:1–2, 230–249.

Case, Brad, Massimo Guidolin, and Yildiray Yildirim. 2014. "Markov Switching Dynamics in REIT Returns: Univariate and Multivariate Evidence on Forecasting Performance." *Real Estate Economics* 42:2, 279–342.

Case, Brad, Yawei Yang, and Yildiray Yildirim. 2012. "Dynamic Correlations among Asset Classes: REIT and Stock Returns." *Journal of Real Estate Finance and Economics* 44:3, 298–318.

Clayton, Jim, David Geltner, and Stanley W. Hamilton. 2001. "Smoothing in Commercial Property Valuations: Evidence from Individual Appraisals." *Real Estate Economics* 29:3, 337–360.

Diaz, Julian, III, and Marvin L. Wolverton. 1998. "A Longitudinal Examination of the Appraisal Smoothing Hypothesis." *Real Estate Economics* 26:2, 349–358.

Engle, Robert F. 2002. "Dynamic Conditional Correlation: A Simple Case of Multivariate Generalized Autoregressive Conditional Heteroskedasticity Models." *Journal of Business and Economic Statistics* 20:3, 339–350.

Geltner, David. 1989. "Estimating Real Estate's Systematic Risk from Aggregate Level Appraisal-Based Returns." *Real Estate Economics* 17:4, 463–481.

Hoesli, Martin, and Kustrim Reka. 2013. "Volatility Spillovers, Comovements and Contagion in Securitized Real Estate Markets." *Journal of Real Estate Finance and Economics* 47:1, 1–35.

Hoyt, Homer. 1933. *One Hundred Years of Land Values in Chicago*. Chicago: University of Chicago Press.

Huang, Jing-zhi, and Zhaodong (Ken) Zhong. 2013. "Time Variation in Diversification Benefits of Commodity, REITs, and TIPS." *Journal of Real Estate Finance and Economics* 46:1, 152–192.

Kaiser, Ronald W. 1997. "The Long Cycle in Real Estate." *Journal of Real Estate Research* 14:3, 233–256.

Malkiel, Burton G. 2003. *The Random Walk Guide to Investing*. New York: W. W. Norton & Company, Inc.

Sa-Aadu, J., James Shilling, and Ashish Tiwari. 2010. "On the Portfolio Properties of Real Estate in Good Times and Bad Times." *Real Estate Economics* 38:3, 529–565.

Shilling, James D., and Charles H. Wurtzebach. 2012. "Is Value-Added and Opportunistic Real Estate Investing Beneficial? If So, Why?" *Journal of Real Estate Research* 34:4, 429–461.

Tversky, Amos, and Daniel Kahneman. 1974. "Judgment under Uncertainty: Heuristics and Biases." *Science* 185:4157, 1124–1131.

3

International Real Estate Markets

K. W. CHAU

Chair Professor, Department of Real Estate and Construction and the Ronald Coase Centre for Property Rights Research, The University of Hong Kong

S. K. WONG

Associate Professor, Department of Real Estate and Construction and the Ronald Coase Centre for Property Rights Research, The University of Hong Kong

C. Y. YIU

Associate Professor, Department of Geography and Resource Management, The Chinese University of Hong Kong

Introduction

International real estate investment refers to any investment portfolios or strategies that include real estate from different countries. These portfolios can be mixed with other asset classes such as stocks and bonds, or invested only in real estate. Perhaps the most common reason for including international real estate assets in an investment portfolio is risk reduction through geographic diversification, although its viability and effectiveness are sometimes challenged. The chapter later provides a discussion of other arguments for and against diversification using real estate.

Another important issue is how to invest in foreign real estate markets. In general, real estate can be divided into direct real estate (DRE) and indirect real estate (IRE) investment. *Direct real estate* refers to the direct ownership and operation of real property assets such as houses, shopping centers, hotels, and offices. *Indirect real estate* refers to the use of public (listed) real estate companies, private (unlisted) real estate funds, REITs, MBS, and related investments. These investments offer exposure without direct involvement in the selection, creation, and management of physical real estate. Indirect real estate should be more convenient for international investors, but this involves costs. The section on international real estate performance shows that the correlation between DRE and IRE can differ significantly within the same market, so the choice of real estate investment vehicles becomes highly important. The section on institutional settings further examines different institutional costs and constraints in international real estate investment.

Although this chapter does not provide a review of all real estate markets in the world, it does cover major real estate markets. Specifically, it examines 17 real estate markets on four continents—North America, Europe, Asia, and Australia. The markets discussed are: (1) Australia, (2) Austria, (3) Canada, (4) China, (5) Finland, (6) France, (7) Germany, (8) Hong Kong, (9) Italy, (10) Japan, (11) The Netherlands, (12) Norway, (13) Singapore, (14) Sweden, (15) Switzerland, (16) the United Kingdom, and (17) the United States. The chapter excludes Spain because some data are unavailable. To make best use of available data for a consistent comparison across market, the time frame of study is 2007Q3 to 2012Q2. The Oxford Housing Indexes data available from Datastream serve as performance indicators for the DRE markets. The FTSE EPRA/NAREIT indexes represent the IRE markets, which include all types of listed real estate securities such as real estate companies and REITs. Because the FTSE EPRA/NAREIT index is unavailable in China, the Shanghai Stock Exchange Real Estate Index, which reflects the performance of major Chinese real estate companies, is used instead.

International Diversification

Diversification through international real estate has been a popular research topic, attracting more than 50 studies over the past decades. Three large-scale literature reviews on international real estate include Sirmans and Worzala (2003) on DRE investment, Worzala and Sirmans (2003) on IRE investment, and Wilson and Zurbruegg (2003) on both. This section begins by reviewing these three studies and examines more recent studies.

Sirmans and Worzala (2003) provide a comprehensive literature review of 31 papers on the international diversification of DRE investment published from 1985 to 2002. Early studies usually only took the U.S. and U.K. real estate markets into account when constructing international portfolios, while later ones also covered continental Europe and Asia Pacific. Geographic coverage is limited by data availability. Because not every country has data on DRE returns, an appraisal valuation is used in place of price in many cases. To assess diversification benefits, most studies compare correlations between DRE and other asset classes to identify risk reduction potential and employ the mean-variance framework to generate efficient portfolios. Despite using different countries, assets, and time periods in different studies, Sirmans and Worzala (2003, 1099) conclude that "international real estate did provide diversification benefits and investors should not ignore this asset class when making asset allocation decisions." However, they note that currency risk is an important issue for international DRE investors. Establishing feasible strategies for hedging exchange rate fluctuations over a long investment horizon requires further research.

Worzala and Sirmans (2003) study the same diversification problem with IRE, which some contend behaves more like stocks than DRE. After reviewing 33 papers on international IRE investment published from 1990 to 2002, they believe most findings support international real estate investment: portfolios diversified with international IRE generally outperform those without. However, diversification benefits vary with regions and could be reduced by currency risk. For instance, some studies show high correlations across Asian markets and across European markets, making diversification less effective within the same continent.

In fact, evidence for holding international real estate is not one-sided. In their review of more than 50 papers, Wilson and Zurbruegg (2003, 259) conclude that "there is no consensus on how much benefit can be derived from the global diversification of property . . . irrespective of whether direct or indirect property assets are being examined." Apart from the currency risk problem, they point out that correlations between countries were unstable. Some evidence suggests that global markets are becoming more integrated, thereby reducing international diversification benefits. More importantly, several studies, including a recent one covering the subprime crisis (Hoesli and Reka 2013), show that markets can become much more correlated at times of high volatility. Therefore, Wilson and Zurbruegg warn that international diversification may fail to reduce risk when investors need it most.

With better databases and advances in econometric tools, recent studies can go beyond correlation analysis and examine the underlying drivers of real estate returns in greater detail. For example, Ling and Naranjo (2002) use a multifactor model to study more than 600 real estate companies in 28 countries between 1984 and 1999 and find evidence of country-specific factors driving international real estate returns. In a follow-up study, Bond, Karolyi, and Sanders (2003) note that country-specific factors are more important for real estate markets in the Asia Pacific region than in Europe and North America. Both studies suggest that the presence of country-specific factors may imply diversification opportunities.

Regarding what these country factors are, the latest studies turn to examining the institutional differences across countries. Edelstein, Qian, and Tsang (2011), who examine the excess returns of real estate companies in 20 countries, find that the quality of a country's legal system, corporate governance, and accounting standards affect returns. Eichholtz, Gugler, and Kok (2011) suggest that the increased transparency of global real estate markets might have improved the performance of internationally diversified real estate companies relative to local peers. In the early part of a sample period from 1996 to 2007, international property companies underperform as compared with locals. The difference is attributable to politics and a lack of transparency. These differences largely disappear near the end of the sample period, suggesting that transparency of real estate markets has improved. However, the sample size is relatively small. In line with the direction of these two studies, the following sections examine the performance and institutional settings of 17 real estate markets.

The comparison is on direct real estate in houses and indirect investment in REITs. The regulation of housing markets differs and some countries have relatively low population density and target overseas investment. Notable among these countries are Australia and Canada. Both countries allow overseas investors to buy houses as part of an inbound immigration entitlement. These countries target immigration of wealthier and skilled residents. Hong Kong is another jurisdiction with similar targeting until 2010. Other countries either restrict their housing markets to offshore investment or are not targeting this explicitly, such as Japan and in Scandinavia. These institutional differences in immigration and tax parameters are capitalized in house prices. House prices are higher in countries using their housing markets explicitly as part of immigration packages and increase during the capitalization period. Countries with such immigration targeting end with high house prices relative to domestic incomes.

Conversely, investment in REITs is a more passive activity. Until recently, playing the housing market directly by investing in REITs has not been possible. Even where this is the case, the investor is singularly targeting returns as opposed to other benefits. REITs are typically holding commercial real estate properties as opposed to houses, so different demand and supply conditions may exist in making comparisons.

The sample window is between 2007 and 2012. Housing markets are cyclical, and the window captures some in downturns while others are in upturns. The return in the United States during this period is negative, but it was substantially positive before 2007.

International Real Estate Performance

With the Oxford Housing Indexes representing the DRE markets and the FTSE EPRA/NAREIT indexes representing the IRE markets, a global comparison of DRE and IRE performance is made across 17 markets: Australia, Austria, Canada, China, Finland, France, Germany, Hong Kong, Italy, Japan, The Netherlands, Norway, Singapore, Sweden, Switzerland, the United Kingdom, and the United States. This section begins by examining investment characteristics in terms of returns, volatilities, and correlations, and then highlights the risk of currency fluctuations and housing bubbles in some of the markets.

RETURN AND VOLATILITY

Table 3.1 summarizes the medium-term (five-year) capital returns in U.S. dollars of 17 pairs of DRE and IRE markets from 2007Q3 to 2012Q2. The table shows that 13 DRE markets have a positive average return with Hong Kong, Singapore, and Switzerland earning more than 10 percent a year. The four housing markets with negative average returns are Italy (–1.4 percent), The Netherlands (–2.2 percent), the United Kingdom (–3.2 percent), and the United States (–3.8 percent). A majority of the DRE markets show volatility, as measured by standard deviation (SD) of 10 to 20 percent a year, except China and the United States, which have less than 5 percent volatility. In terms of average return-to-volatility ratios (i.e., the mean-to-SD ratio), China and Hong Kong's housing markets are the top performers, whereas the United States ranks last.

One issue that concerns international real estate investors is whether using U.S. dollars as the currency denomination matters. To answer this, Table 3.2 shows the same information as Table 3.1 but in each market's local currency. Except for the United States and Hong Kong, most housing markets show a considerable reduction in average returns expressed in local currencies. This is expected because of the depreciation of the U.S. dollar against certain currencies after 2009. By the same token, using local currencies compresses the volatility of most DRE markets to below 6 percent a year. Changes in relative housing market performance as measured by average return-to-volatility ratios also occur. For example, Switzerland jumps from fifth to first, but Japan falls from fourth to thirteenth. This result suggests the choice of currencies matters when comparing international housing market performance.

Although most housing shows positive returns, the REIT markets tell a different story. Table 3.1, which is based on U.S. dollars, indicates that only six REIT markets

Table 3.1 **Global Direct and Indirect Real Estate Market Performance between 2007Q3 and 2012Q2 (in USD)**

Country/City	*Australia*		*Austria*		*Canada*		*China*		*Finland*		*France*	
Markets	***DRE***	***IRE***	***DRE***	***IRE***	***DRE***	***IRE***	***DRE***	***IRE***	***DRE***	***IRE***	***DRE***	***IRE***
Annual mean return	9.3	−10.4	3.2	−9.0	4.2	5.7	8.4	6.9	1.1	−6.9	0.6	−3.9
Annual SD of return	20.7	36.9	11.2	55.3	10.5	30.1	3.6	46.4	13.6	39.1	13.6	33.7
Mean-to-SD ratio	0.45	−0.28	0.29	−0.16	0.40	0.19	2.36	0.15	0.08	−0.18	0.04	−0.12
Country/City	*Germany*		*Hong Kong*		*Italy*		*Japan*		*Netherlands*		*Norway*	
Markets	***DRE***	***IRE***	***DRE***	***IRE***	***DRE***	***IRE***	***DRE***	***IRE***	***DRE***	***IRE***	***DRE***	***IRE***
Annual mean return	0.7	−10.3	14.6	6.3	−1.4	−25.8	9.0	−10.2	−2.2	−10.2	6.3	−20.4
Annual SD of return	11.9	39.7	10.1	40.0	12.4	46.1	12.2	26.4	12.0	32.7	17.2	66.8
Mean-to-SD ratio	0.06	−0.26	1.45	0.16	−0.12	−0.56	0.74	−0.39	0.18	−0.31	0.37	−0.30
Country/City	*Singapore*		*Sweden*		*Switzerland*		*United Kingdom*		*United States*			
Markets	***DRE***	***IRE***	***DRE***	***IRE***	***DRE***	***IRE***	***DRE***	***IRE***	***DRE***	***IRE***		
Annual mean return	11.7	−3.4	3.0	1.3	10.1	9.5	−3.2	−16.0	−3.8	2.3		
Annual SD of return	15.2	34.9	16.7	36.0	13.8	23.7	14.2	36.6	2.4	32.9		
Mean-to-SD ratio	0.77	−0.10	0.18	0.04	0.73	0.40	−0.23	−0.44	−1.59	0.07		

Note: This table gives the annual mean capital return, volatility, and mean-to-volatility ratio of 17 pairs of direct and indirect real estate markets in USD between 2007Q3 and 2012Q2. Means and standard deviations (SD) are in annual percentage points. The mean-to-SD ratio measures the risk-adjusted return under common zero riskless rates.

Table 3.2 **Global DRE and IRE Market Performance between 2007Q3 and 2012Q2 (in Local Currency)**

Country/City	*Australia*		*Austria*		*Canada*		*China*		*Finland*		*France*	
Markets	***DRE***	***IRE***	***DRE***	***IRE***	***DRE***	***IRE***	***DRE***	***IRE***	***DRE***	***IRE***	***DRE***	***IRE***
Annual mean return	3.6	–17.6	3.9	–11.8	1.7	1.8	4.4	3.3	1.4	–8.7	0.9	–5.5
Annual SD of return	4.8	26.9	5.5	50.1	1.9	24.4	2.9	46.7	4.6	32.1	3.9	25.4
Mean-to-SD ratio	0.73	–0.65	0.71	–0.24	0.92	0.07	1.51	0.07	0.31	–0.27	0.23	0.22
Correlation coefficient	0.422		–0.258		0.282		0.090		0.612		0.158	
Country/City	*Germany*		*Hong Kong*		*Italy*		*Japan*		*Netherlands*		*Norway*	
Markets	***DRE***	***IRE***	***DRE***	***IRE***	***DRE***	***IRE***	***DRE***	***IRE***	***DRE***	***IRE***	***DRE***	***IRE***
Annual mean return	1.2	–12.0	14.5	6.1	–1.1	–27.5	0.7	–16.8	–1.7	–11.8	4.6	–27.0
Annual SD of return	2.5	34.0	10.3	39.8	1.4	41.0	11.4	29.3	1.9	24.3	6.0	56.1
Mean-to-SD ratio	0.49	–0.35	1.41	0.15	–0.74	–0.67	0.06	–0.57	–0.89	–0.48	0.77	–0.48
Correlation coefficient	–0.630		0.612		–0.295		0.361		–0.184		0.346	
Country/City	*Singapore*		*Sweden*		*Switzerland*		*United Kingdom*		*United States*			
Markets	***DRE***	***IRE***	***DRE***	***IRE***	***DRE***	***IRE***	***DRE***	***IRE***	***DRE***	***IRE***		
Annual mean return	7.5	–8.5	2.5	–0.8	3.8	2.8	0.0	–15.1	–3.8	2.3		
Annual SD of return	11.9	31.1	4.0	28.8	1.3	16.4	4.1	28.4	2.4	32.9		
Mean-to-SD ratio	0.63	–0.27	0.62	–0.03	2.88	0.17	–0.01	–0.53	–1.59	0.07		
Correlation coefficient	0.297		–0.039		0.346		0.474		0.366			

Note: This table gives the annual mean capital return in percent, volatility, mean-to-volatility ratio, and correlation coefficient of 17 pairs of DRE and IRE markets in local currency between 2007Q3 and 2012Q2. SD stands for standard deviation.

receive a positive average return. These six positive-return REIT markets include the United States whose housing market has the lowest average return during this 2007 to 2012 window. Among the 11 IRE markets with negative average returns, the United Kingdom, Norway, and Italy drop the fastest, at a rate of more than –15 percent a year. The volatility of most IRE markets is between 20 and 40 percent, substantially higher than that of the DRE markets. Norway, Austria, China, and Italy's volatilities exceed 40 percent. In terms of average return-to-volatility ratios, Switzerland's REIT market performs the best, whereas Italy's is the worst. Using local currencies, as in Table 3.2, generally reduces average returns and volatilities, but to a lesser extent than in the DRE markets. As such, the choice of currencies does not much affect the ranking of international IRE performance based on average return-to-volatility ratios.

Because the international DRE and IRE markets appear to deliver different performances, checking how large or small the differences are within each country is worthwhile. Small differences may imply high substitutability between DRE and IRE, indicating that real estate is a single asset regardless of form. Here a non-traded housing asset is being compared with a traded commercial property. Large differences in performance suggest that housing and REIT markets provide investors with distinct real estate exposure. From Table 3.2, which is in local currencies, countries with the smallest average return differences are Canada (0.1 percent), Switzerland (1.1 percent), China (1.2 percent), and Sweden (3.3 percent), whereas those with the largest differences are Norway (31.6 percent), Italy (26.5 percent), and Australia (21.1 percent). Other countries' differences are within 6 to 18 percent. For volatilities, large differences occur ranging from 15 percent (Switzerland) to 50 percent (Norway). Taking these together, Switzerland seems to be the country with the most consistent DRE and IRE performance, whereas Norway is the least consistent.

CORRELATION

DRE and IRE performance could differ for many reasons. One is the institution governing how DRE and IRE are traded in their respective markets. Another is that the indexes used to capture performance represent different segments of a real estate market. The Oxford Housing Indexes represent the residential property segment, whereas the FTSE EPRA/NAREIT indexes represent REITs, whose underlying assets include all types of properties. However, in a competitive land market where land use is substitutable within a set of institutional constraints, the returns on residential and non-residential properties should be positively correlated in the long run. Held constant here is only the supply side with the land market and with entitlement restrictions being comparable for residential and nonresidential property.

A separate issue is the demand side. Technology and substitution along with relative prices determine demand for space. These demand conditions and implied subsidies can persist in housing markets and differ across countries.

Additionally, the residential sector is often the largest by total stock or market value; condominium units are particularly actively traded in some markets. These make the estimation of housing price indexes representative and reliable. Therefore, housing price indexes are used to measure and compare the performance of the DRE markets.

The last row of Table 3.2 reports the correlation coefficients between the DRE and IRE returns for each country in local currencies. The evidence shows positive correlations in 12 markets, with the largest ones in Finland (0.612) and Hong Kong (0.611). The United Kingdom (0.477) and Australia (0.422) came next, followed by the United States (0.366), Japan (0.361), Switzerland (0.346), and Norway (0.346). Although a majority of the markets have their DRE and IRE returns co-move with each other, five markets, namely Italy (−0.295), Austria (−0.258), The Netherlands (−0.184), Germany (−0.630), and Sweden (−0.390), have negative correlation coefficients.

CURRENCY RISK

The return and volatility analysis show that real estate performance can vary substantially depending on the currency used. Thus, currency risk is an important factor to consider because it can impose a strong or even opposite effect on the medium-term performance of an international real estate investment. If currency risk is not or cannot be hedged, picking a market for international real estate investment involves both real estate and currency skills.

Table 3.3 summarizes the exchange rates of the U.S. Dollar (USD) against 11 currencies from 2007Q3 to 2012Q2. Based on the coefficient of variation, the Australian Dollar (AUD) and Japanese Yen (JPY) are the most volatile, followed closely by the Swiss Franc (CHF) and British Pound (GBP). Other currencies, namely the Sweden Krona (SEK), Norwegian Krone (NOK), Canadian Dollar (CAD), Singapore Dollar (SGD), Euro (EUR), Chinese Renminbi (CNY), and Hong Kong Dollar (HKD), have a coefficient of variation below 10 percent. HKD had almost zero volatility because of the pegged exchange rate system between the HKD and the USD.

Some currencies exhibit sharp appreciation or depreciation against the USD. The JPY increased by 50.2 percent during the sample period. This increases the average return on Japan's DRE from 0.7 percent to 9.0 percent from the perspective of U.S. investors. In contrast, GPB drops by 19.0 percent, which drives the original zero percent average return on the U.K.'s DRE down to −3.2 percent, from the perspective of U.S. investors. These examples reinforce the importance of currency risk in international real estate investment.

REAL ESTATE BUBBLES

Bubbles are often difficult to detect until after they have occurred. Whether real estate prices are too high depends on what the right price should be, which has no universally accepted answer. A commonly used definition of *bubbles* is the deviation of the observed price from the estimated equilibrium price that reflects market fundamentals. The equilibrium price is a combination of a transaction price and a time to sell. In spot markets, the rent is adjusted by the rate of occupancy, which is one minus the rate of vacancy. The equilibrium price reflects (1) the level of rent and vacancy determined by demand and supply fundamentals and (2) the capitalization (cap) rate as a function of market discount rate and expected future growth. When deviations of the actual price are zero from equilibrium, then market participants are said to have expectations supported by market fundamentals.

Table 3.3 **Exchange Rate Fluctuations between 2007Q3 and 2012Q2**

	USD/ AUD	*USD/ CAD*	*USD/ EUR*	*USD/ HKD*	*USD/ JPY*	
Mean	1.10	1.10	0.70	7.80	93.60	
Standard deviation	0.17	0.08	0.04	0.02	13.18	
Coefficient of variation	14.60	7.30	6.00	0.30	14.10	
Cumulative appreciation against USD	19.90	10.20	–5.70	0.60	50.20	
	USD/ NOK	*USD/ SGD*	*USD/ SEK*	*USD/ CHF*	*USD/ GBP*	*USD/ CNY*
Mean	5.90	1.40	7.00	1.00	0.60	6.80
Standard deviation	0.47	0.10	0.63	0.11	0.060	0.38
Coefficient of variation	8.00	7.10	9.10	10.90	10.60	5.50
Cumulative appreciation against USD	1.20	20.40	–4.50	29.70	–19.00	21.60

Note: This table gives the mean, standard deviation, and coefficient of variation of the USD against 11 currencies used in the 17 markets. The last row shows the cumulative appreciation of the currencies against the USD.

Source: Calculated from the quarterly exchange rates provided by EPRA.

How the equilibrium price can be justified by market fundamentals becomes another unresolved problem. In the residential market, a bubble indicator is the price-to-household income ratio. The higher the ratio, the less affordable real estate is to local people.

An examination of the affordability of five housing markets using data from Demographia (2013) shows the following price-to-income ratios: Australia (6.5), Canada (4.7), Hong Kong (13.5), the United Kingdom (5.1), and the United States (3.2). These ratios are calculated from the median house price divided by gross annual median household income using data for the third quarter of 2012. Among the five markets, the most unaffordable place for housing for local residents is Hong Kong, with its median housing price amounting to 13.5 times its median annual household income. This ratio is at least twice that of the next highest market. The most affordable place for housing is the United States, where the median housing price was just 3.2 times higher than the median household income. Interestingly, Hong Kong and the United States also rank the first and last in terms of medium-term DRE returns, as shown in Table 3.1. This suggests that real estate prices heavily influence affordability, but whether affordability has any predictive power of future real estate prices is an open-ended question.

Institutional Settings

Institutional settings govern how real estate is traded in each market. They cover a wide range of issues including the legal framework, accounting and reporting standards, transaction costs, and regulation or policy on real estate ownership and operation. Different institutional settings can lead to different real estate performance, so this section examines the institutional costs and constraints in international real estate investment. Because information on some markets is not readily available, for some detailed comparisons, the analysis focuses on six markets: Australia, Canada, Hong Kong, Singapore, the United Kingdom, and the United States.

MARKET TRANSPARENCY

Jones Lang LaSalle (2012) introduced a transparency index to quantify and rank several institutional features of global real estate markets. The index, which is based on quantitative data and qualitative survey data, rates each market by examining five aspects: (1) performance measurement, (2) market fundamentals, (3) governance of listed vehicles, (4) regulatory and legal environment, and (5) transaction process. An index score between 1.0 and 1.7 is regarded as highly transparent, 1.7 and 2.6 as transparent, 2.6 and 3.76 as semi-transparent, 3.76 and 4.2 as low, and 4.2 and 5.0 as opaque.

Table 3.4 shows the transparency index of the 17 real estate markets in 2012. All the markets are regarded as highly transparent or transparent, except for China, which is deemed semi-transparent. The United States, the United Kingdom, and Australia are the top three transparent markets in the world. The United States has the world-best rating in market fundamentals (e.g., market data's quality and coverage) and governance of listed vehicles (e.g., corporate governance and financial disclosure). The United Kingdom has the world-best rating in performance measurement (e.g., availability of market benchmarks) and the best rating in transaction process (e.g., property agents' professional standard) among the 17 markets. Australia ranks third in performance measurement and second in market fundamentals. These three markets, however, are not as strong as some other markets in terms of the regulatory and legal environment (e.g., building codes and title registration). For example, Sweden receives the highest score in this aspect among the 17 markets.

Despite their lower rankings, some markets have made large improvements in transparency during the last decade. Table 3.5 shows the improvement of transparency of the 17 markets from 2004 to 2012. Eight markets improved their transparency (the score becomes smaller), while the transparency of nine markets deteriorated (the score becomes larger). The markets with the greatest improvement are China and Japan, whose indexes decreased from 3.71 to 2.83 and from 3.08 to 2.39, respectively. On the other hand, Singapore and Hong Kong show the most deterioration in transparency, although they remain the most transparent real estate markets in Asia.

TRADING COSTS IN THE DRE MARKET

A distinctive feature of DRE investment is its relatively high trading costs, which typically include taxes, agency commissions, and other professional fees such as for

Table 3.4 **Transparency Index of 17 Markets in 2012**

	Transparency Index		*Performance Measurement*	*Market Fundamentals*	*Governance of Listed Vehicles*	*Regulatory and Legal*	*Transaction Process*
Market	*Global Rank*	*Score*	*Sub-Index Rank*	*Sub-Index Rank*	*Sub-Index Rank*	*Sub-Index Rank*	*Sub-Index Rank*
Australia	3	1.36	3	2	4	10	9 tied
Austria	22	2.22	17	> 20	20	19	> 20
Canada	6	1.56	8	6	1 tied	8	15
China	32	2.83	> 20	19	> 20	> 20	> 20
Finland	8	1.57	9	10	8	5 tied	> 20
France	7	1.57	7	20	14	3	> 20
Germany	12	1.80	13	12	11	14	16
Hong Kong	11	1.76	11	5	18	17	> 20
Italy	20	2.16	15	18	10	> 20	> 20
Japan	25	2.39	10	> 20	> 20	> 20	> 20
Netherlands	4	1.38	4	4	6	12	> 20
Norway	18	2.08	16	> 20	> 20	> 20	13
Singapore	13	1.85	14	13	17	5 tied	> 20
Sweden	9	1.66	12	16	9	2	> 20
Switzerland	10	1.67	5	> 20	3	11	11
United Kingdom	2	1.33	1	8	5	9	7
United States	1	1.26	2	1	1 tied	7	9 tied

Note: This table gives the transparency index (in terms of global rank and score) of 17 real estate markets in 2012. The table also reports the ranks of five sub-indexes: performance measurement, market fundamentals, governance of listed vehicles, regulatory and legal environment, and transaction process.

Source: Jones Lang LaSalle (2012).

Table 3.5 **Improvement in Transparency of 17 Markets between 2004 and 2012**

Year	*Australia*	*Austria*	*Canada*	*China*	*Finland*	*France*
2004	1.19	2.08	1.37	3.71	1.64	1.62
2006	1.15	1.85	1.21	3.50	1.63	1.40
2008	1.20	1.72	1.17	3.33	1.56	1.34
2010	1.22	1.71	1.23	3.14	1.53	1.28
2012	1.36	2.22	1.56	2.83	1.57	1.57
Change (2012–2004)	0.17	0.14	0.19	–0.88	–0.07	-0.05
Year	*Germany*	*Hong Kong*	*Italy*	*Japan*	*Netherlands*	*Norway*
2004	1.60	1.50	2.73	3.08	1.37	2.15
2006	1.67	1.30	2.14	2.40	1.37	1.96
2008	1.58	1.55	1.82	2.39	1.33	1.78
2010	1.38	1.76	1.89	2.30	1.38	1.75
2012	1.8	1.76	2.16	2.39	1.38	2.08
change (2012–2004)	0.2	0.26	–0.57	–0.69	0.01	-0.07
Year	*Singapore*	*Sweden*	*Switzerland*	*United Kingdom*	*United States*	
2004	1.55	1.51	1.68	1.24	1.24	
2006	1.44	1.38	1.94	1.25	1.15	
2008	1.55	1.43	1.87	1.31	1.20	
2010	1.73	1.25	1.87	1.24	1.25	
2012	1.85	1.66	1.67	1.33	1.26	
change (2012–2004)	0.30	0.15	-0.01	0.09	0.02	

Note: This table shows the transparency index scores of 17 real estate markets in 2004, 2006, 2008, 2010, and 2012. The last row reports the overall change from 2004 to 2012.

Source: Jones Lang LaSalle (2004, 2006, 2008, 2010, 2012).

valuation, legal compliance, and building inspection. Investment involving land development and operations would incur even more costs. This section focuses on the two most typical trading costs: capital gains taxes and agency commissions. High trading costs may result in a longer investment period and hence a less liquid market.

Table 3.6 shows capital gains taxes levied in six selected markets. Some markets such as Hong Kong and Singapore have no capital gains tax. In Australia there is no capital gains tax on principal residences. In Canada half of the capital gains are excluded from taxation. Effectively, capital gains in Canada are taxed at half the rate on ordinary income such as from wages and interest.

Table 3.6 **Capital Gains Taxes in Six Markets**

Country	*Capital Gains Tax*
Australia	50 percent of capital gains are counted as personal income for the assessment of income tax
Canada	50 percent of the capital gain is taxable
Hong Kong	No capital gains tax
Singapore	No capital gains tax
United Kingdom	Capital gains tax is applied to U.K. citizens only. The rate is 18 percent and 28 percent for property priced below and above 20,000 pounds, respectively
United States	Capital gains on long-term holdings in excess of 12 months are taxed at preferential rates and can be deferred by exchanges

Note: This table summarizes the capital gains tax requirements in six markets.

Source: Global Property Guide (2012).

Delcour and Miller (2002) examine agency commissions in 14 markets: Australia, Canada, China, Finland, Germany, Hong Kong, Italy, Japan, The Netherlands, Norway, Singapore, Sweden, the United Kingdom, and the United States. Their results show that China has the highest commissions (7.5 percent). This was the case in 2000, but commissions dropped by 2010. The commission varies across cities in China but in general is less than 3 percent. Agency commissions in the United States are typically 6 percent. Hong Kong's agents charge the lowest commission (1 percent) but given that both the buyer and seller need to pay, the total commission is 2 percent. The commissions of other markets are between 2 and 5 percent.

MORTGAGE TERMS

Table 3.7 shows the characteristics of mortgage loans of international DRE investment in six selected markets. The maximum payment periods range from 25 years to 35 years and the maximum loan-to-value ratios range from 65 to 85 percent. However, mortgages in Hong Kong are *recourse loans,* which give the lender the right to recover any loss from the borrower's personal wealth in the case of default. Compared with a non-recourse mortgage, a recourse mortgage gives the lender more protection because the loan is backed by the mortgaged property and personal assets of the borrower. The 90-day delinquency ratio in Hong Kong has always been well below 2 percent even after the residential price declined by 70 percent during the period 1997–2003 (Hong Kong Monetary Authority 2011).

REIT MARKETS

To gain real estate exposure, REITs serve as an alternative to but not necessarily a substitute for DRE. The United States and Australia have the longest REIT history and

Table 3.7 **Characteristics of Mortgage Loans of Six Markets in 2012**

Country/City	*Maximum Payment Period*	*Loan-to-Value Ratio*	*Mortgage Rate 2011*	*Fixed or Floating Rate*
Australia	30 years	Maximum 70 to 80	≥ 5.5	Both
Canada	35 years	Maximum 65	5 to 8	Both and non-recourse
Hong Kong	25 years	Maximum 70	2.25	Mostly floating, recourse
Singapore	Based on ages and income	70 to 80	1.2 to 2.0	Both and non-recourse
United Kingdom	25 years	Maximum 85	2.5 to 5.5	Fixed
United States	≤ 30 years	Average 71.2	4.81	Mostly fixed and non-recourse

Note: This table summarizes the characteristics of mortgage loans, including maximum repayment period, loan-to-value ratio, mortgage rate, and fixed-or-floating rate, in six markets. Loan-to-value and mortgage rates are in percentages.

dominate the global REIT market. As Table 3.8 shows, the U.S. REIT market alone accounts for almost 60 percent of the REITs in the world. Australia's REIT market, being the second largest, accounts for another 10 percent. In the past decade, REIT markets developed quickly in other parts of the world. The largest REIT markets in Europe and Asia are France (6 percent of international market capitalization) and Japan (5 percent). The development of global REIT markets provides international investors with an additional channel of real estate investment. Trading REITs is generally more liquid and less costly than trading DRE. However, countries have different REIT requirements.

REITs are typically required to distribute most of their income to shareholders on a regular basis. Table 3.9 shows the profit distribution obligations of REITs in six markets. The minimum distribution ranges from 90 percent to 100 percent of operating income. However, different countries may define income differently, and the treatment of asset depreciation can substantially affect the calculation of income for distribution purposes.

REITs have various restrictions. Table 3.10 shows the restrictions on REITs activities and investments in six markets: Australia, Canada, Hong Kong, Singapore, the United Kingdom, and the United States. REITs are required to invest most of their funds in real estate. Some markets further restrict REITs to investing in income-producing property only. The restrictions may or may not allow land development. Although these restrictions give REITs less flexibility, they may give more confidence to investors who want to seek pure real estate exposure.

Table 3.11 shows the corporate and withholding tax of REITs from international IRE investment in six markets. It is comparable to the capital gains tax for DRE. Hong Kong and Singapore do not have capital gains taxes for either DRE or IRE. Some jurisdictions provide income tax exemptions for REIT investment.

Table 3.8 **REIT Market Size by Countries/Cities in 2012**

REITs	*Australia*	*Austria*	*Canada*	*China*	*Finland*	*France*
Market capitalization (Euro million)	71,764	NA	39,062	NA	NA	45,350
share of global REIT market	9.36	NA	5.09	NA	NA	5.91
Number of REITs	45	NA	37	NA	NA	40
REITs	***Germany***	***Hong Kong***	***Italy***	***Japan***	***Netherlands***	***Norway***
Market capitalization (Euro million)	1,115	15,294	472	37,423	6,712	NA
share of global REIT market	0.21	1.99	0.06	4.88	0.87	NA
Number of REITs	4	9	2	35	5	NA
REITs	***Singapore***	***Sweden***	***Switzerland***	***United Kingdom***	***United States***	
Market capitalization (Euro million)	28,977	NA	NA	33,865	454,789	
share of global REIT Market	3.78	NA	NA	4.41	59.31	
Number of REITs	26	NA	NA	21	189	

Note: This table summarizes the market size of REITS in 17 markets in terms of market capitalization, share of global REIT markets, and number of REITs.

Source: EPRA (2012).

Summary and Conclusions

This chapter discusses the medium-term performance and institutional arrangement of the DRE and IRE markets of 17 countries and cities. The performance is five-year rolling mean annual capital returns and standard deviations as a risk proxy. The chapter presents and compares performance in U.S. dollars and in local currency. This reflects the effects of currency risk in international real estate investment and discusses the substitutability between DRE and IRE investments in these markets.

A major conclusion is that geographic diversification can reduce country-specific risk. However, such a benefit has to be balanced against various costs, notably currency risks, an unstable correlation between markets, and institutional constraints in laws and

Table 3.9 **Profit Distribution Obligations of REITs of Six Markets in 2012**

Country/ City	*Operative Income*	*Capital Gains*	*Timing*
Australia	Typical distribution of 100 percent of trust's income as defined in the trust's constitution	To the extent included in the trust's income, any capital gains realized on disposal of property including interest held in other sub-trusts or other entities	Annually or semi-annually
Canada	All income of the mutual fund trusts (MFT) for a taxation year is paid or payable to unit holders in the year so that MFT does not incur tax	All capital gains are paid out and retain their character in the hands of unit holders, provided that the MFT makes a designation	All income must be paid or recognized as a payable in the taxation year of the MFT. If it is payable, the amount can be paid out later
Hong Kong	90 percent of audited annual net income after tax	Specified in the trust deed	Annually
Singapore	90 percent of taxable income	Not required	Annually, semi-annually, or quarterly
United Kingdom	90 percent of tax-exempt profits	Not included in the distribution obligation	Within 12 months of year end
United States	At least 90 percent of its taxable ordinary income	Not required to distribute	Annually

Note: This table lists the profit distribution obligations, including the proportion of operative income to be distributed, distribution from capital gains, and the timing of payments, in different REIT markets.

Source: EPRA (2012).

taxes that undermine real estate performance and liquidity. As long as currency risk cannot be effectively hedged, international real estate investment requires skills in both real estate and foreign exchange markets.

Another important insight is drawn by comparing the performance of DRE and IRE markets. These markets do not deliver similar performance in terms of average returns and volatilities. During 2007–2012, DRE markets typically had positive returns, whereas IRE markets generally experienced negative returns. The annual return differences between these two markets are up to 31.6 percent. The volatility of most IRE markets is between 20 and 40 percent, substantially higher than that of the DRE markets. However, the correlations show greater consistency. A majority of the countries or cities

Table 3.10 **Corporate Tax and Withholding Tax of REITs of Six Markets in 2012**

Country/City	*Current Income*	*Capital Gains*	*Withholding Tax*
Australia	Not taxable in the hands of the trustee provided the unit holders are presently entitled to the trust's income at the end of the income year, otherwise the trustee is taxed at the highest marginal rate	Tax treatment of capital gains is similar to that of ordinary income. The 50 percent capital gains tax discount may be available; however, it is proposed that the 50 percent discount will not apply to non-resident unit holders on capital gains accrued after May 8, 2012	N/A
Canada	A MFT is entitled to deduct in a year all income determined for purposes of the Income Tax Act (ITA) paid or payable to unit holders in the year so it may reduce its net taxable income to zero	Capital gains follow the same system for income, except only 50 percent of a 'taxable capital gain is included in income and 50 percent of a capital loss can be applied to offset taxable capital gains	Credit or refund of foreign withholding tax is possible
Hong Kong	REIT is exempt from profits tax. REIT may be subject to property tax. Special Purpose Vehicle (SPV) is subject to profits tax. Dividends from SPV are tax-exempt. Foreign sourced income is tax-exempt	N/A	N/A
Singapore	Eligible rental income is tax-exempt	No tax is imposed on capital gains	No foreign withholding tax refunds are allowed involving tax-exempt income

continued

Table 3.10 **continued**

Country/City	*Current Income*	*Capital Gains*	*Withholding Tax*
United Kingdom	Income from a property rental business is exempt from corporation tax. Residual business income is taxable at the highest rate of corporation tax (currently 26 percent)	Gains realized on disposals of assets used in the property rental business are not subject to tax	In principle, no withholding tax is levied on distributions that are made out of the residual business income. Distributions out of the property rental business profits (PIDs) are generally subject to a 20 percent withholding tax unless the recipient is a U.K. corporate, U.K. charity, or U.K. pension fund. Withholding tax on a U.K. REIT's property rental income from directly held non-U.K. real estate will be deducted in calculating the PID. Withholding taxes reduced by distributions in respect of shares will be part of the REIT's residual business and tax credit relief may be available
United States	Tax-exempt to extent distributed	Tax-exempt to extent distributed	No refund of foreign withholding tax. The REIT can use a foreign tax as a deduction

Note: This table lists the corporate tax and withholding tax requirements in relation to current income and capital gains in six REIT markets.

Source: EPRA (2012).

Table 3.11 **Restrictions on REITs Activities and Investments of Six Markets in 2012**

Country/City	*Restrictions on REITs Activities and Investments*
Australia	• Public unit trusts and managed investment trusts (MITs) investing in land must do so for the purpose, or primarily for the purpose, of deriving rent (eligible investment business).
	• Public unit trusts that carry on a *trading business* (i.e., a business that does not wholly consist of eligible investment business) are not accorded 'flow through' treatment and unit trusts that carry on a trading business will not qualify as a MIT.
	• May invest in a single property.
Canada	• Investing in property other than real property or an interest in real property is allowed.
	• The acquiring, holding, maintaining, improving, leasing, or managing of any real property (or interest in real property) that is capital property of the trust is allowed.
	• Any combination of the foregoing activities.
Hong Kong	• Must invest in real estate.
	• Must hold the real estate for at least two years.
	• Must not invest in vacant land or engage in property development activities.
	• Must not acquire any asset that involves the assumption of any unlimited liability.
	• May invest in real estate located in Hong Kong or overseas.
Singapore	• At least 75 percent of the REIT's deposited property should be invested in income-producing real estate.
	• No property development activities are allowed unless the REIT intends to hold the developed property upon completion.
	• May invest in foreign assets.
	• Should not derive more than 10 percent of its revenue from sources other than rental and other specified sources.

continued

Table 3.11 **continued**

Country/City	*Restrictions on REITs Activities and Investments*
United Kingdom	• At least 75 percent of a REIT's net profits must be derived from the property rental business as measured using financial statements.
	• At least 75 percent of a REIT's assets must be used in the property rental business as measured using financial statements.
	• The REIT must hold at least three separate assets.
	• No one asset may exceed 40 percent of the total assets.
	• May invest outside the United Kingdom in real estate wherever located.
United States	• At least 75 percent of its assets must be real estate, government securities, or cash.
	• At least 75 percent of the gross income must be derived from real estate property rental or from interest on mortgages on real estate property. And at least 95 percent of the gross income must come from a combination of real estate related sources and passive sources, such as dividends and interest.
	• Cannot own more than 10 percent of another corporation's stock, other than in another REIT or a taxable REIT subsidiary (ownership of a 100 percent owned 'qualified REIT' subsidiary is ignored).
	• No more than 5 percent of the value of its assets can be represented by securities of any one issuer, other than another REIT or a taxable subsidiary (ownership of a 100 percent owned 'qualified REIT' subsidiary is ignored).
	• Cannot own more than 25 percent of its assets in securities of one or more taxable REIT subsidiaries or receive more that 25 percent of annual income from capital gains.

Source: EPRA (2012).

studied have positive correlations between their DRE and IRE returns. Only five pairs of DRE and IRE markets have negative correlations.

Another comparison is between DRE investment in houses and IRE investment in REITs. The regulation of housing markets differs, and some of the countries have relatively low population density and are targeting overseas investment. Countries with such immigration targeting have high house prices relative to domestic incomes. Conversely, investment in REITs is a more passive activity. Until recently, playing the housing market directly by investing in REITs has not been possible. Even where this is the case, investors in IRE are singularly targeting returns as opposed to other benefits.

Finally, institutional settings, including capital gain taxes, agency commissions, legal frameworks, accounting and reporting standards, access to mortgage loans, information transparency, and regulation or policy on real estate ownership and REIT investment, varies substantially across markets. Understanding these settings helps investors better assess the risk-return characteristics of a foreign real estate market.

Discussion Questions

1. Provide the arguments for and against investing in international real estate.
2. Discuss the validity of the statement "international real estate investment requires skills in both real estate and foreign exchange markets."
3. Based on the 17 countries/cities examined in this chapter, discuss whether their DRE and IRE markets deliver similar performance in terms of average returns, volatilities, and correlations.
4. Identify the institutional barriers to investing in foreign real estate markets.

Acknowledgments

The authors would like to thank H. Kent Baker and Peter Chinloy for their helpful comments and suggestions. The quality and this chapter have been improved by their expertise and efforts in editing the original manuscript.

References

Bond, Shaun A., G. Andrew Karolyi, and Anthony B. Sanders. 2003. "International Real Estate Returns: A Multifactor, Multicountry Approach." *Real Estate Economics* 31:3, 481–500.

Delcour, Natalya, and Norman G. Miller. 2002. "International Residential Real Estate Brokerage Fees and Implications for the U.S. Brokerage Industry." *International Real Estate Review* 5:1, 12–39.

Demographia. 2013. "9th Annual Demographia International Housing Affordability Survey (2012: 3rd Quarter)." http://www.demographia.com/dhi.pdf.

Edelstein, Robert, Wenlan Qian, and Desmond Tsang. 2011. "How Do Institutional Factors Affect International Real Estate Returns?" *Journal of Real Estate Finance and Economics* 43:1, 130–151.

Eichholtz, Piet M. A., Nils Gugler, and Nils Kok. 2011. "Transparency, Integration, and the Cost of International Real Estate Investments." *Journal of Real Estate Finance and Economics* 43:1, 152–173.

EPRA. 2012. *Global REIT Survey 2012*. Belgium: European Public Real Estate Association. Global Property Guide. 2012. "Global Property Guide." http://www.globalpropertyguide.com/.

Hoesli, Martin, and Kustrim Reka. 2013. "Volatility Spillovers, Comovements and Contagion in Securitized Real Estate Markets." *Journal of Real Estate Finance and Economics* 47:1, 1–35.

Hong Kong Monetary Authority. 2011. "Loan-to-value Ratio as a Macroprudential Tool—Hong Kong SAR's Experience and Cross-country Evidence." *BIS Papers*, Bank for International Settlements, Number 57, October, 163–178. http://www.bis.org/publ/bppdf/bispap57k.pdf.

Jones Lang LaSalle. 2004, 2006, 2008, 2010, 2012. "A Global Transparency Index." http://www.joneslanglasalle.com/GRETI/en-gb.

Ling, David C., and Anthony Naranjo. 2002. "Commercial Real Estate Return Performance: A Cross Country Analysis." *Journal of Real Estate Finance and Economics* 24:1–2, 119–142.

Sirmans, C. F., and Elaine Worzala. 2003. "International Direct Real Estate Investment: A Review of the Literature." *Urban Studies* 40:5–6, 1081–1114.

Wilson, Patrick J., and Raif Zurbruegg. 2003. "International Diversification of Real Estate Assets: Is It Worth It? Evidence from the Literature." *Journal of Real Estate Literature* 11:3, 259–277.

Worzala, Elaine, and C. F. Sirmans. 2003. "Investing in International Real Estate Stocks: A Review of the Literature." *Urban Studies* 40:5–6, 1115–1149.

4

Strategy: Seeking Alpha Opportunities and Managing Risks in Global Markets

STEPHEN E. ROULAC
Chief Executive Officer, Roulac Global Places LLC

Introduction

If investors seek market returns, their investing strategy may seem to be easy, simple, and straightforward: invest in index funds. This decision is much more complex, daunting, and nuanced for investing in real estate. While index funds are available, other strategy questions potentially lead to higher returns.

To realize superior risk-adjusted returns or alpha, investors must be skilled and pursue strategies that diverge from the market norms. Alpha-seeking property investing strategies may embrace more active rather than passive styles and investing in different places. This chapter explores investing strategy considerations in search of alpha returns, involving pursuing opportunities that have more risk.

Among the important landmarks on the path to alpha returns are a commitment to a policy orientation and recognition of the implications of change. These strategies will lead to recognizing the appeal of and rationale for a global orientation. Investors are increasingly either explicitly or implicitly global in their investing outlook. This global orientation leads to reconciling the challenges of emerging markets and the blurring of that distinction relative to established markets.

This context sets the stage for addressing desired investing attributes, especially as applied to real estate investing. Among these factors explored are market structure and efficiency, investing in all real estate profit centers, and the influence of the relative status of real estate investing of the risks associated with certain markets. The chapter provides a brief discussion of future-proofing property investing strategy and consideration of investment implementation challenges.

Policy Primacy: Relatively Right, Absolutely Wrong

One of the challenges in crafting a real estate investing strategy is to match local and global priorities. The global rationale is both offensive and defensive. The offensive objective of global property investing is that extraordinary opportunities exist beyond one's hometown and native country. If investors do not venture beyond their local territory, they will miss out on extraordinarily rewarding property investing involvements. The defensive motivation for global property investing is the consideration that when domestic property involvements are in a downward phase of the cycle, properties in other places may be performing more positively. By investing globally, investors can achieve the diversification benefit of reduced volatility in their overall performance in ways that are not obtained locally.

Relative performance among economies is moving toward more parity, even as the outcomes within economies are reflecting greater disparity and inequality. Although certain global practice standards are becoming more accepted, cultural and other differences remain that entrepreneurs, executives, and investors should not ignore (Livermore 2010).

Because real estate demand follows population growth and absolute growing levels of prosperity, real estate demand in emerging economies is likely to be strong. That strength will be focused on economies where population and prosperity are growing. Emerging markets offer investors the prospect of returns superior to those in established, more mature economies. These superior returns come at the price of greater risks. Effective investing participation mandates acumen and sophistication that transcend what may previously have been appropriate for investing in established economies.

Notwithstanding evidence affirming the superiority of the top-down approach, the bottom-up fundamental analysis still appeals to many investors as the starting point. For example, Trahan and Krantz (2011) report the results of an investor survey in which a large percentage of investors favor a bottom-up, fundamental analysis as the most important aspect of the decision process.

Trahan and Krantz (2011) make several observations about a global investing strategy. They note that investors list globalization as the first of 10 major macro themes that are likely to affect investor portfolios in the future. A misinformed, overly aggressive pursuit of a trend can lead to speculative excesses, or an asset bubble, in which prices increase to levels that cannot be supported by underlying economic reality. Thus, prices plummet after recognizing the unsustainability of such speculative excesses. Six such asset bubbles in which tightened monetary policy triggered price declines include: (1) the building mania of the late 1950s, (2) conglomerates in the early 1970s, (3) commodities in the early 1980s, (4) biotech in the 1990s, (5) technology stocks in the late 1990s, and (6) housing from 1998 to 2006.

Central to investing strategy is the choice between a policy and a deal-making orientation. A policy orientation proceeds with a top-down perspective to identify opportunities that merit detailed consideration, while the deal-making approach is oriented to and commences with a bottom-up, fundamental analysis.

The perils of buying the best building in a weak market and thereby being relatively right but absolutely wrong are related by David Einhorn concerning the assessment of the home builder MDC Holdings. Einhorn was the renowned hedge fund investor whose Green Light Capital gained recognition for shorting Lehman Brothers in 2007.

"Some of my MDC analysis was quick. It was less risky than its peers and would hold up better in a down cycle because it had less leverage and held less land. But this just meant that almost half a decade later, anyone who listened to me would have lost about 40 percent of an investment instead of the 70 percent that the home building sector lost" (Trahan and Krantz 2011, 43–45). This shrewd investor observed that the cause of the loss was not bad luck but bad analysis. The lesson is that being agnostic about the big picture can be very expensive.

Strategy Importance

The investing approach that employs the discipline of strategy to guide the implementation of finance decisions may offer more rewarding outcomes than one that is innocent of strategic considerations and informed predominantly by the finance discipline. Investors' propensity to emphasize deal making and analysis over policy and strategy may result in relative innocence of the mindset and style necessary for an enterprise.

Effective real estate investing must be strategic in its approach. According to Goldsmith (2007), what was good enough in the past may not be good enough in the future. In the early 1990s, Dennis (1992) notes the importance and rapidity of change in real estate markets and the financing process. Arguably, the magnitude of change in the succeeding two decades has been of a substantially greater magnitude than what was recognized in the early 1990s. This means the emphasis must be on recognizing change, its implications for traditional practices, determining what may be threatened, identifying opportunities for differentiation, and innovating new approaches.

The adaptability style with its resilient, innovative, and inventive attributes is more often alien than familiar to the very nature and character of property investment. Given the accelerating pace of change, few individuals, companies, and investing programs are as adaptable today as they will need to be in the future (Hamel 2012). Investors, especially those with real estate involvements, face the challenge of adapting and adopting new strategies.

Global Investing Rationale

Established economies such as the United States, the United Kingdom, the Eurozone, and Japan face fundamental growth challenges. Yet, the *Financial Times* (2011, 12) reports "economic growth has practically vanished across the developed world." The paucity of growth in established markets makes emerging markets investing ever more important. According to Hughes (2011), emerging markets could be the last bastion of hope. The argument can be made that emerging countries are gaining substantial world economic market share, largely at the expense of European countries and Japan. This superior growth often is in spite of restrictive capital formation and direct foreign investment regulations. The result of the cumulative interactions of many forces is the inexorable and inevitable move to greater parity of economic outcomes in different regions of the world. Emerging countries will be major beneficiaries of this global move to economic and per capita gross domestic product (GDP) parity.

Should investors invest in a high-cost, low-growth company or a low-cost, high-growth company? Should they pay more for a company with a less productive workforce whose high-cost structure results in lower earnings and slower growth? Should they pay more for a company with a very capable workforce, whose cost structure is below the competition that delivers strong earnings and is growing very rapidly? Some would assert that the latter company should command a substantially higher price earnings (P/E) ratio than the former. Substituting established economies for the first company and emerging economies for the second company would show that the reverse relationship often holds true. Emerging market property companies can sell at substantially lower P/E ratios than property companies in established economies.

The talent, energy, and creativity of the people of emerging economies are being productively and profitably applied to global commerce at an accelerating pace. From a real estate investing perspective, the forces of outsourcing and off shoring transfer jobs and business activities to other places. They concurrently transfer real estate demand as jobs move from one place to another. Job losses in local economies, which reduce demand for real estate in the local economies, serve to create jobs and the associated real estate demand in other economies. These are likely to be emerging markets economies. Consequently, O'Sullivan (2011, 41) makes the following observation:

> For many finance chiefs, domestic bliss is not an option . . . emerging markets can't be ignored: their growing populations and rapid industrialization are giving rise to an increasingly sophisticated base of consumers who present a significant opportunity to expand business overseas . . . many companies now believe that the key to future growth is to think, and act, globally.

The ascendant role of Asia with China and India in particular is not a new development, but rather the return and reassertion of prior, long established leadership (Kennedy 1987; Roulac 2006). As Roulac (2001a) notes, some three-quarters of the world's new jobs are being created in Asia. Many emerging economies are growing much more strongly than the established economies of Europe, Japan, and the United States. The dramatic re-emergence of India and China, along with the rapid growth of Indonesia, Malaysia, South Korea, Vietnam, and other Asian countries, and the continuing presence of Japan, represent powerful economic growth engines. Strong economic growth is also being achieved in certain Eastern Europe and Latin American countries. The inevitable expanding global leadership role of the Pacific has profound implications for development in all regions and within regions.

Global Investing Challenge

With increasing emphasis on global considerations, conceiving that an effective real estate investment strategy would neglect global considerations is improbable, if not naive. It is daunting, as real estate investing can be difficult to implement in a place in which investors are familiar. This strategy is made much more difficult to implement on a global basis in places unfamiliar to these investors. Consider the difficulty of building a global portfolio of 50 residential condominiums, each located in different cities with the following activities required for each: (1) global market research, (2) local market research, (3) property research, (4) purchase negotiation and due diligence, (5) leasing, (6) tenant relations and property management, (7) asset management, (8) market monitoring and risk management, (9) sale decision, (10) buyer search, (11) sale negotiation and due diligence, (12) reinvestment decision, (13) portfolio management, and (14) property operations and management.

This effort requires substantial organization and might not even achieve exposure to attractive markets where foreign ownership is restricted or prohibited. This effort would only achieve exposure to one property, such as residential condominiums, and in one real estate profit center. This lack of diversification thereby misses potentially attractive opportunities in all the other profit centers in the real estate industry.

Venturing to new markets involves risks. Gordon (2011) observes that investors have made classic mistakes going across borders. For example, one mistake is assuming a group from New York, Tokyo, or London can parachute into a market over the weekend, tour a market, determine what to buy, buy it, and then go home and make money. The parachute approach to cross-border investing does not work.

This approach to cross-border investing parallels a person buying a house by traveling to a community, having never previously lived or spent any meaningful time there. The person looks at some houses and quickly buys one without knowing the culture of that place. Can an investor make an informed decision about a property without knowing the place in which the property is located?

The appeal of a property is strongly informed by its place context: communities, culture, micro climates, traffic patterns at different times of the year, recreation and entertainment, public services and government finance, and schools and libraries. Thus, an investor buying a property also buys a community. Consequently, the appeal and rewards of a property are the appeal and rewards of the community. Can these be reasonably, competently, and accurately discerned on a short visit?

Emerging Markets: Appeal and Challenge

Until recently, many companies, investment advisors, and investment professionals discounted and disregarded so-called emerging markets, preferring to concentrate on familiar established markets that traditionally had provided rewarding business and financial returns. Perceived as involving excessive risks and inadequate rewards, many investors shunned emerging markets. Given that emerging markets often deliver superior economic performance and investment returns relative to established ones, the strategy of concentrating exclusively on so-called established markets has limitations.

While investing in emerging markets can be rewarding, these investments are more daunting than are mature markets investments. For real estate, a successful investment requires an understanding of the culture of those who procure goods and services that indirectly involve property interests. An example is a retail purchase or a restaurant meal in which a property experience is bundled with the purchase. This knowledge of and competency in coping with the cultures of emerging markets will be increasingly important to major, mature established companies and therefore to investors in this era of increasing globalization both home and abroad.

While investing in emerging markets can be rewarding and arguably a prudently managed portfolio should include an emerging markets allocation. The very nature of these markets demands new ways of thinking, requires transformational innovation and resource shifts, and mandates rethinking and reconfiguring every element of existing business models (Prahalad and Lieberthal 1998). This rethinking embraces packaging, product design, brand management, and the price-performance expectation that connect product, price, and ambiance to local requirements and global expectations. Just as corporate management must employ very different thinking and strategies in implementing its emerging market involvements, so too must investment managers and investors employ very different strategies in their emerging markets involvements. The ideas, concepts, and strategies that may have contributed to success in established markets are not necessarily appropriate for emerging markets. Understanding differences in certain factors that influence investment returns and risks is a necessary precondition to effective emerging markets participation.

By their very nature, emerging markets investments are more daunting than those in mature markets. Especially for those more accustomed to participating in the familiar mainstream, local business and investing community, emerging markets are inherently less familiar and reflect greater complexity than established markets. Often emerging markets are characterized by a culture that differs from that familiar to professionals whose earlier involvements had primarily emphasized established markets.

Viewing real estate as the platform or stage on which life and the culture of a place are lived and experienced is essential to effective real estate involvements. Thus, understanding the culture of those who would procure property goods and services by purchasing property interests directly and engaging in transactions that indirectly involve property interests is a precondition to effective property involvement. If investors do not understand the culture of a place and integrate that understanding into their investing in the property goods and services of that place, they may not profitably and effectively realize desired rewards of the property involvement.

Changes in established markets lead to the cultures of places, especially major metros in developed economies of the Eurozone and the United States being characterized by cultural diversity. Many metros and countries, once culturally homogeneous, are increasingly becoming culturally heterogeneous. Consequently, a person might encounter references to as many as 15 different cultures on a given day in any one place in an established developed economy. One consequence of their cultural diversity is that awareness of the cultures of different places becomes increasingly important to function effectively in the primary chosen place or place of origin (Livermore 2010).

Knowledge of and competency in coping with the cultures of emerging markets will be increasingly important to major, mature established companies and therefore to investors. Consequently, members of the business and financial community necessarily will be more involved in emerging markets. This involvement is proactive in search of superior opportunities and rewards. The involvement is derivative, reactive, and defensive to function competently in their familiar market.

In response to competitors' initiatives, market share, and performance, business executives and investors need to possess the requisite cultural competence to participate effectively in emerging markets. Investors backing emerging market strategies as part of their due diligence may explicitly assess executives' and managers' cultural information (Livermore 2011).

Comprehending the Global Market

Established countries used to represent predictability, stability, and lower risk, while investors perceived emerging economies as unstable, uncertain, and risky. Many emerging economies have undertaken fiscal discipline even as policies in certain advanced economies border on fiscal irresponsibility. The realignment of relative financial position is evidenced by G20 advanced countries' escalating public debt, which in 2013 exceeded 100 percent of GDP. In the meantime emerging economies that are members of the G20 have declining public debt, projected by 2015 to be 25 percent of GDP. El-Erian (2008, 219) describes this relationship as a paradigm shift from the old days. This shift in relative position where established market countries have relatively high debt and the emerging economies relatively low debt is reflected in fundamental changes in the interest rates charged borrowers (Wirz and Phillips 2011).

Public debt is importantly connected to real estate in several ways. If more of an economy's production and resources are committed to servicing debt previously incurred, fewer funds are available for providing social services. These social services include healthcare and education delivered at a specific place. Limited funds are available for investing in infrastructure to enhance that same place. Inevitably, higher public debt requires higher taxes to service that debt and to deliver the relevant level of public services, absent that debt. Consequently, people and enterprises in places with high public debt inevitably receive lesser place experience value for money than do people in places with lower public debt. Then, real estate in places with higher public debt is less appealing and therefore less valuable than real estate in places with lower public debt.

A *muddle* or *hobble* baseline scenario (El-Erian 2008) is one in which sluggish growth and higher unemployment in advanced economies is paired with higher growth in emerging economies. In these emerging economies, income and wealth levels continue to converge to those of advanced economies. These relative increases reward prospects for real estate development and investment in the emerging economies rather than in the advanced countries. As Wirz and Phillips (2011) note, advanced country debt no longer involves just interest rate risk, but now also has meaningful credit risk. This credit risk once applied exclusively to emerging economies. Pointedly, this past pattern has been reversed; sovereign creditworthiness will continue to diverge, with the deterioration in advanced countries contrasting with a continued improvement in the emerging world as a whole.

As the world's economies have become more integrated, the differences in performance in any one economy relative to other economies are becoming blurred and less distinct. Companies increasingly source resources internationally, position their workforces globally, and sell to customers throughout the world. The economic performance of a company located in any one country may likely mirror the economic performance of all companies in the world. The features that previously distinguished emerging markets from established markets are becoming less unique. Consequently, the expansion and integration of global capital markets may diminish the relative advantages of emerging markets.

This idea of country economic and, therefore, investment performance homogenization overlooks the consideration that growth patterns in emerging markets are substantially greater than those in established, mature markets. The populations of many emerging markets are growing more rapidly than those of established markets. Faster population growth is especially important because more people lead to greater demand for property goods and services. Growth in incomes, population, and discretionary spending also leads to greater demand for property goods and services. This greater demand translates to higher rents, growing cash flows and property valuations, and higher investment returns.

Irrespective of whether economic performance is becoming less differentiated, the interdependency of the components economic elements of the global economy is unavoidable. As O'Sullivan (2011, 41) notes,

> From the earthquake and tsunami in Japan to political uprisings in Africa and the Middle East to the ongoing sovereign debt crisis in Europe, a seemingly unending series of dramatic global events has captured headlines in recent months. Many U.S. businesses have been directly affected by supply-chain disruptions, the loss of key customers, or damages to their foreign operations. Even for U.S. businesses without an overseas presence, the continuing turmoil in world markets has contributed to a feeling of unease, an anxiety that permeates the business world and dogs the recovery.

A local only mindset is no longer viable in the economy of the twenty-first century.

Desired Investment Attributes

Strategy is informed by considering attributes of investing alternatives, rather than starting with the different forms and types of investing options that investors might consider. Because real estate investing is a subset of the larger domain of investments, considering investing in general is worthwhile. The following are attributes of general investing:

- *Market structure and efficiency.* The structure of markets influences their efficiency. Participating in less than efficient markets offers less competition and is conducive to rewarding acumen and expertise.
- *Positive alpha.* This condition yields positive expected risk-adjusted returns.
- *Stability of investment performance.* Return volatility is asymmetrically cautious. Investors seeking to avoid large negative returns are willing to surrender substantial positive returns by engaging in low volatility strategies. Limiting the upside return is the price for protecting against excessive downside exposure.
- *Diversification.* Diversification accommodates risk protection and increases the likelihood of being exposed to extraordinary outcomes.
- *Liquidity.* Liquidity when employed astutely allows cash to be available when desired especially during unfavorable outcomes.
- *Inflation hedging.* Hedging against inflation protects the purchasing power of the invested funds.
- *Currency hedging.* Currency hedging protects the value of the money invested so that it is not diminished relative to other currencies.

- *Growth.* Growth allows participation in dynamic sectors and places in the global economy.
- *Income.* The investor determines the trade-off between income and growth consistent with needs, recognizing that a higher income may reduce expected capital gains.

The above attributes are appropriate standards against which to test an investment. But from a real estate perspective, investors should use other more nuanced and granulated criteria to design the real estate investing strategy.

Desired Real Estate Investment Attributes

Despite being an old asset class, real estate is less established, accepted, and mature than corporate securities such as stocks and bonds (Roulac 1994). Only since 1970 have institutions and individuals recognized and accepted real estate as a legitimate investment. Real estate is similar to an emerging market in that its institutions are not fully integrated with those for other assets. Investing in real estate in emerging economies involves an overlay of challenge and risk.

A viable real estate investment strategy should include the following attributes. In practice, developing and implementing a strategy that combines these attributes is likely to prove challenging because of barriers facing real estate investors.

- *Invest in the best markets.* Market selection is typically more important than selecting a specific property. Real estate investors find that gaining information about, tracking, and investing in the best of emerging markets can be difficult and expensive because of physical access to distant markets.
- *Benefit from access to insiders, local market connections, and expertise.* Because real estate is a local business, investors need to have local knowledge and connections. Investors often have difficulty obtaining local knowledge of many different markets in distant locations.
- *Partner with the best real estate professionals and companies.* While partnering with the best and brightest people and companies can offer advantages, individuals or companies often invest for their own account or partner with the largest, most sophisticated institutional investors.
- *Invest in partnerships with the best deals in which principals have their own money risk.* People who have their money at risk work harder and pay more attention than those who do not. Some investors expect to be entrepreneurs and to commit talent rather than money to ventures, and do not want to put their own money at risk. Others want to be passive investors, committing funds but not time.
- *Participate in the rewards of all property profit centers.* Access to multiple profit centers provides both diversification and the ability to realign the portfolio in response to changing market conditions. Yet, most property involvements are limited to a single profit center and only a few have multiple profit centers.
- *Retain flexibility to realign a portfolio to select property profit centers that best respond to changing marketing conditions.* Time and place are crucial in making property involvements. There is a time to buy, sell, build, provide services, be long, and be short. Most

real estate investing strategies are rigid, monolithic, and unresponsive to changing market conditions.

- *Gain access to the best strategic thinking on property investing and corporate property strategies.* Companies and investing programs with superior strategies outperform those with inferior strategies. By contrast, real estate investors generally emphasize deal making rather than strategy.
- *Emphasize top-down investment policy rather than building picking.* Investment policy has more impact on investment performance than does portfolio construction and securities analysis. In practice, most real estate investment managers emphasize deal making.
- *Adapt the capital structure to economic, property, and capital market conditions.* The capital structure should be appropriate to the current environment. Inappropriate capital structures such as extensive leverage can impose substantial risk. Too little leverage when interest rates are relatively low reduces returns. By contrast, most real estate investments employ a single financial position and risk structure irrespective of market conditions.
- *Benefit from diversification.* Diversification reduces risk and improves overall investment performance. Real estate investments often come in large units, making diversification difficult. Hence, real estate investors are typically under diversified.
- *Employ a forward-looking orientation and capitalize on opportunity.* In a dynamic economy characterized by accelerating change and discontinuity, having a forward-looking orientation concerning property investing is important. Yet, few real estate investments use a forward-looking perspective.
- *Employ the most advanced strategic portfolio risk management techniques.* The vast, unpredictable world of global securities markets offers opportunities for applying quantitative portfolio risk management techniques. Many market participants lack the knowledge of and advanced training in portfolio risk management. Implementing advanced portfolio risk management theories involves complex, highly sophisticated, resource-intensive technologies, requiring substantial financial and training investments to operate.
- *Lower overall portfolio risk by combining assets with low positive or negative correlations.* Physical real estate has relatively low positive correlations with other assets, while being highly positively correlated with inflation. The ideal real estate investment is meaningfully distinguished from corporate real estate investing. Unfortunately, this distinction is not always achieved because many real estate strategies are not meaningfully differentiated from certain types of corporate stock investing and other real estate investments.

Investors should consider several strategic considerations involving relative market efficiency and inefficiency, which varies materially by asset class. The variation is notable for subsets within that asset class. Investors should focus on how to benefit financially from real estate involvements. There are two tiers of asset investing. The first pertains to investing generally and concerns asset class selection and then choosing specialized segments within an asset class. The second tier pertains specifically to real estate.

Market Structuring and Efficiency

Emerging markets inherently are more inefficient than established markets. A greater likelihood exists of a transaction occurring at prices that diverge from what knowledgeable, informed, sophisticated professionals would conclude as representing fair value. The important implication of market inefficiency is that superior competence and expertise are more rewarded, while lesser capabilities or miscalculations are more severely penalized. Thus, the greater the market inefficiency, the greater is the reward for expertise and the greater the penalty for miscalculation. Emerging markets are less efficient and have greater variability and risk. The less efficient nature of real estate markets leads to greater rewards for superior expertise and to greater adverse consequences for miscalculation.

The relative levels of the following factors help to define the character, maturity, and efficiency of real estate markets:

- Transparency and accountability
- Quality and availability of information
- Competency, tools, and resources of professional services providers specializing in assisting and representing tenants
- Capital markets functions and maturity
- Occupiers' managerial sophistication and prioritization of the corporate real estate function
- Level and quality of scholarly and commercial research
- Academic societies' providing forums for the creation and dissemination of knowledge, through sponsoring journals publishing scholarly research and organizing meetings of thought leaders promoting knowledge.

These factors vary considerably between markets, reflecting their differing character, maturity, and efficiency. Additionally, these factors are more advanced in mature economies, such as the United States and the Eurozone, than in emerging markets such as in Africa (Oladokum 2010).

By virtue of their scale, rapid development pace, and capital-intensive expansion paths, emerging markets may be more dependent on substantial capital investment than established economies. Given the capital-intensive economic development priorities of emerging markets, these economies rely heavily on foreign direct investment (Froot, O'Connell, and Seasholes 2001). Consequently, capital flows loom large in influencing investment performance in emerging economies, both driving performance and influencing risk. While strong foreign capital flows drive economic expansion in emerging countries, abrupt shifts in the volume of capital flows can have adverse consequences. The consequences of abrupt capital flow changes were highly evident in the Asian currency crises during 1997 and 1998 as investors lost confidence and liquidated local investments, when substantial strong positive foreign capital flows abruptly reversed (Higgins and Klitbard 2000).

The differences in market attributes combined with the comparably lesser levels of real estate professionalism in emerging economies lead both to greater prospects of superior returns and to greater market risk. These market level risks may magnify or negate the gains to be realized from superior strategies and analytic sophistication, contributing a market synchronicity effect resulting in more common than differentiated performance of individual stocks (Morck and Yeung 2002).

Views about portfolio allocations to emerging markets differ. One approach is to select a modest allocation to minimize the consequences of adverse outcomes. Another is to select a large allocation to capture the rewards of outsized returns. Allocations can also be made to replicate the relative composition of the different types of assets that comprise that market. Still another approach is to design the composition of the portfolio not on the basis of existing assets but rather in terms of anticipated economic growth.

Profit Centers

Incorporating all real estate profit centers in crafting an informed investing strategy is likely to be difficult, except for very large portfolios. The reason is the large number of profit centers. The following are examples of real estate profit centers.

- Rental income
- Property appreciation
- Mortgage interest income
- Hotel related income
- Senior living services income
- Business space service income
- Serviced residential related income
- Sales of property related software and information products
- Development profit
- Service income from property operations
- Service income from the development process
- Financing and securitization fees
- Materials and supplies manufacturing, distribution, and sales
- Furniture manufacturing and sales
- Capturing unrecognized hidden real estate value
- Company appreciation.

Investors access these different profit centers through five primary real estate categories of activity,

- *Property investors.* Business properties, residential rental properties, retail and warehouse properties, diversified and other property portfolios, and mortgage portfolios.
- *Property development firms.* Homebuilders, commercial property developers, engineering and construction firms, cement companies, building steel manufacturers and suppliers, other building materials suppliers and furniture, and fixture and decorations suppliers.
- *Real estate service firms.* Hospitality related firms, real estate related healthcare and senior living services firms, real estate brokers, agents, property managers and other

Table 4.1 **Property Profit Center**

Traditional Property Investment	*Building Development*	*Business Services*
• Business property	• Homebuilders	• Leisure and tourism related firms
• Retail and warehouse	• Commercial property developers	• Business related service firms
• Diversified and other property	• Construction and civil engineering	• Real estate related information and software providers
• Hospitality	• Building materials	• Healthcare, senior living, and residential services
• Residential	• Cement manufacturers	
• Mortgage investment	• Building steel manufacturers	

Note: This table summarizes the five types of real estate firms: traditional property investment, building development, business services, property resources, and place strategy.

business space service providers, serviced apartment and other residential service providers, property and place related information and software providers.

- *Property resource firms.* Corporations without a real estate business model but which derive a substantial portion of firm value from land holdings. The ideal situation is that the land value exceeds the firm value as an operating business, thereby capturing hidden real estate value.
- *Place strategy firms.* Firms that create substantial value through a strategic use of place and space.

Table 4.1 depicts the intersection between these different property categories and the real estate profit centers.

Influence of Real Estate Professionalism

Real estate professionals implement investing strategy. The level of professionalism influences real estate investment performance. Factors leading to and reflecting higher levels of real estate professionalism are education programs, books, professional associations and designations, career guidance and resources, and licensing. The less developed status of real estate professionalism in emerging markets is a reflection on the status of all of these elements.

Real estate professional standards mirror the development status of that place: more advanced economies have higher levels of real estate professionalism than in emerging economies (Oladokum 2010). One consequence of real estate professionalism differences is the greater prospect of divergent outcomes at the transaction level. Another consequence is the greater prospect of miscalculation at the individual and company level and also by multiple companies. This can result in market dislocation or excess construction, leading to surplus supply inventory in excess of demand that diminishes the value of all properties in that market.

Historically, senior executives have de-emphasized the corporate real estate function (Manning and Roulac 2001). This has resulted in less senior management attention, managerial resources, and strategic analytic sophistication being applied to corporate real estate decisions than is warranted, given the financial and strategic importance of this function (Roulac 2001a). If the property owner applies more attention, invests managerial resources, and applies sophistication to the commercial real estate transaction, the negotiation outcomes are more likely to favor the property owner relative to tenants. Because real estate is their primary business, property owners necessarily tend to be more sophisticated in particular transactions than tenants for whom the real estate function is subordinate to their main business.

Tenants acting in this manner can lead to a corporation making suboptimal decisions. Property owners benefit from corporations lacking strategic priority and sophistication in implementing their commercial real estate transactions. Any given corporate tenancy negotiation may result in an outcome more advantageous to the property owner at the expense of the corporate tenant. Consequently, lesser levels of corporate real estate professionalism are conducive to property owners realizing alpha performance.

Beyond the inherent differences in real estate professionalism, circumstances, and motivation of market participants, other factors contribute to the relative differences in market efficiency between emerging and mature markets. As Choe, Kho, and Stulz (2005) note, transaction costs in emerging markets may be higher than those in established markets. While considerable parity exists concerning the liquidity of investments in mature developed markets, liquidity in emerging markets varies considerably (Lesmond 2005). Additionally, investor protection, including lower standards of corporate governance in emerging markets tends to compare less favorably to investor protection in mature markets (Shleifer and Vishny 1997). One consequence of diminished levels of investor protection is lesser analyst coverage (Lang, Lins, and Miller 2004), which also corresponds to lower company valuation (LaPorta, Lopez-de-Silanes, Shleifer, and Vishny 1997). These forces cumulatively lead to greater inefficiency in emerging markets.

Investors living in closer proximity to the companies and properties in which they invest may have distinct advantages over those who live far away for several reasons. First, they are more familiar with events surrounding the local economy. Second, they can more easily interact directly with people about an investment. Third, they experience lower costs, in terms of both time and direct expense, to evaluate and monitor the investment. Finally, investors have a greater likelihood of learning relevant material information in informal circumstances and through happenstance interaction.

Research evidence indicates that superior investment outcomes favoring domestic over foreign investors are attributable to informational asymmetry (Brennan and Cao 1997). Further, the information content of earnings forecasts by local analysts is superior to the earnings forecasts of foreign analysts (Bae, Stulz, and Tan 2005).

Coval and Moskowitz (2001) find that investors located in closer proximity to company headquarters realize superior returns than do investors located farther away. Proximity influences may be even more important in emerging markets. As Brennan and Cao (1997) find, local investors in emerging markets have a distinct advantage in terms of information access over foreign investors. Although local emerging market players have an inherent advantage, foreign investors have a competitive advantage in selecting from the collection of emerging markets. That is, they can choose from many different markets and have a more objective and less locally invested perspective. Although local investors having distinct advantages over those living far away, Seasholes and Feng (2004) finds that foreign investors sometimes outperform local investors. In those instances showing superior investment outcomes favoring domestic over foreign investors, informational asymmetry is often the major contributing factor. The information content of earnings forecasts by local analysts is superior to the earnings forecast of foreign analysts.

Investment Implementation Challenges

Investing in real estate within emerging markets presents a set of opportunities with limited prior history and inherent comfort level based on past experience in the market (Roulac 2001a, b, c). Comfort based on prior experience may be secondary to personal safety when investing in extreme emerging markets. As Farzad (2007) notes, such markets are appropriate only for investors with the patience and the capital to wait out the uncertainties and take the required risks.

Farzad (2007) discusses the challenge of investing in extreme emerging markets that is epitomized by the daunting circumstances foreign investors confront in Colombia. Even though the pace of Colombia's entrepreneurial expansion is impressive, traditional financial metrics are of much less priority than *confianza*, which translates into confidence and trust. Safety concerns discourage many from considering places such as Colombia for investing.

According to Haggarty and Lostaglio (1994), valuation assessments are essential to every investing involvement, but they are even more important in the higher risk emerging markets. Variable participant sophistication can cause perceptions of value that are either too conservative or too optimistic. Beyond variable participant sophistication leading to pricing distortions, major changes in institutional structures and political regimes, converting from public to private ownership and repositioning properties to serve a foreign clientele accustomed to the standards of a developed economy further complicate the valuation assessment. Transaction prices are unreliable indicators of value in future market conditions. The lack of sophistication of market participants leads to their emphasizing cost estimates, rather than prospective future income, resulting in an unrealistically low valuation assessment. Conversely, participants rely on so-called comparable transactions, reflecting unrealistically high prices that do not reflect reasonable development and investment economics.

While sector-based strategies are more relevant for developed countries, country allocations are more important for emerging markets (Chen, Bennett, and Zheng 2006). The investing strategies in an established economy involve a sector-based approach to portfolio construction. Investing in emerging markets involves addressing country allocation decisions. Implementing investing in emerging markets requires selecting between countries, metros within countries, and specific sectors and property types within and across metros and countries. This orientation differs from the approach used by the majority of investors, who are concerned with a single country and choose regions, metros, sectors, and property types within their countries.

Given the need to overcome the inherent obstacles to implement property transactions, securitization and fund-of-fund strategies offer advantages over private direct transactions. Securitization promises to accelerate the implementation of property involvements in emerging markets.

Addressing the role of private real estate fund-of-funds, also known as a *manager-of-managers* concept, Dohrmann (2005) writes:

> These funds of funds offer investors the ability to access unique investment managers and investment manager concepts that they otherwise might not feel comfortable accessing directly. It shifts the time-intensive work of identifying and underwriting these concepts and investment managers off the shoulders of the investment staff and onto the shoulders of the fund-of-funds manager. And, for smaller investors who otherwise might not meet the minimum investment requirements of these types of funds, it provides perhaps the only means by which they can participate in these funds. The rationale for the global fund-of-fund concept is even more compelling when investing globally and especially in emerging economies, for running an investment program that includes investments outside the United States has lots of challenges, including the additional costs associated with traveling around the world to underwrite investment management capabilities and deals, and monitor these investments.

Future Proofing Real Estate Investing

The adaptability challenges for real estate investors are especially great because of the inherent attributes of property intended to be long lasting to provide stability and security are contrary to the fundamentals of the new economy, which are dynamic, fluid, and intangible (Roulac 1994). As Hamel (2012, 120) notes, if business is "inherently conservative . . . management processes . . . built years ago with one goal in mind: efficiency . . . organizations that are focused, methodical, and rigorous . . . but not very inspired, proactive or experimental," then the challenge to property involvement is even greater.

Property investing strategy may be informed by considering lessons for future-proofing a company might be adapted to the investing process. To this end, Hamel (2012) suggests six critical factors to ensure company adaptability. Three of the factors concern various forms of flexibility—intellectual, strategic, and structural—and the other three focus on anticipation, variety, and resilience-friendly values.

Summary and Conclusions

A set of real estate attributes potentially generates positive alpha or risk-adjusted returns. These include targeting less efficient markets and considering higher volatility. Other attributes of real estate are diversification, liquidity, inflation, and currency hedging. Achieving positive alpha is likely to occur by carefully considering these characteristics.

The efficiency of real estate markets is defined by several factors. These include transparency, accounting information, competence of professionals, capital market maturity, managerial contracts, and real estate research including journal output. Markets where these features are less present are less efficient.

The high alpha propensity of the market depends on five types of real estate firms. Property investors operate existing assets including debt securities. Property developers carry out construction. Real estate service firms include management and brokerage. Property resource firms own assets including land. Place strategy firms target reallocation of assets.

Emerging markets and other areas that lack the market completion or the widespread availability of the real estate firms are those where markets are likely to be more inefficient. They provide returns to investors located nearby and higher alpha, or greater positive risk-adjusted returns.

Discussion Questions

1. Discuss whether real estate investing strategy is simple or complex.
2. Explain why investors should consider investing outside of their home country.
3. Identify the major challenges to investing in real estate on a global basis.
4. Discuss how market structure and relative market efficiency influence investing strategy.
5. Identify how investors can access different profit centers through five primary real estate categories of activity.
6. Discuss how the level of real estate professionalism of a place influences investing strategy.

References

Bae, Kee-Hong, René M. Stulz, and Hongping Tan. 2005. "Do Local Analysts Know More? A Cross-Country Study of the Performance of Local Analysts and Foreign Analysts." Working Paper 11697, National Bureau of Economic Research.

Brennan, Michael J., and H. Harry Cao. 1997. "International Portfolio Investment Flows." *Journal of Finance* 52:5, 1851–1880.

Chen, Jianguo, Andrea Bennett, and Ting Zheng. 2006. "Sector Effects in Developed vs. Emerging Markets." *Financial Analysts Journal* 62:6, 40–51.

Choe, Hyuk, Bong-Chan Kho, and René Stulz. 2005. "Do Domestic Investors Have an Edge? The Trading Experience of Foreign Investors in Korea." *Review of Financial Studies* 18: 3, 795–829.

Coval, Joshua D., and Tobias J. Moskowitz. 2001. "The Geography of Investment: Informed Trading and Asset Prices." *Journal of Political Economy* 109:4, 811–841.

Dennis, Marshall W. 1992. *Residential Mortgage Lending*. 3rd edn. Englewood Cliffs, NJ: Prentice Hall.

Dohrmann, Geoffrey. 2005. "Are We Having Funds Yet? Global Funds of Funds Make Sense." *Global Quarterly* 2, Fall. http://www.irei.com/publications/the-institutional-real-estate-letter-americas.

El-Erian, Mohamed. 2008. *When Markets Collide*. Noida, India: McGraw-Hill India.

Farzad, Robin. 2007. "Extreme Investing: Inside Columbia.". *Business Week*, May 28, 50. *Financial Times*. 2011. "Grow, Dammit!" August 12, 12.

Froot, Kenneth A., Paul G. J. O'Connell, and Mark S. Seasholes. 2001. "The Portfolio Flows of International Investors." *Journal of Financial Economics* 59:2, 151–193.

Goldsmith, Marshall. 2007. *What Got You Here Won't Get You There*. New York: Hyperion Books.

Gordon, Jacques. 2011. "Investing in Global Real Estate." Lecture at the University of Florida, November 30, 2011. http://www.youtube.com/watch?v=rVIZ2h7H7Lk.

Haggarty, Stephen G., and Keith L. Lostaglio. 1994. "Applying Western Valuation Techniques in Emerging Hospitality Markets." *Real Estate Finance Journal* 9:3, 4–7.
Hamel, Gary. 2012. What Matters Now: How to Win in a World of Relentless Change, Ferocious Competition, and Unstoppable Innovation. New York: Jossey-Bass.
Higgins, Matthew, and Thomas Klitbard. 2000. "Asia's Great Performance after the Currency Crisis." *FRBNY Economic Policy Review*, September, 37–49. Available at http://www.newyorkfed.org/research/epr/00v06n3/0009.higg.pdf.
Hughes, Jennifer. 2011. "The Short View." *Financial Times*, August 12, 13.
Kennedy, Paul. 1987. *The Rise and Fall of the Great Power Economic Changes and Military Conflict from 1500 to 2000*. New York: Random House.
Lang, Mark H., Karl V. Lins, and Darius P. Miller. 2004. "Concentrated Control, Analyst Following and Valuation: Do Analysts Matter Most When Investors Are Protected Least?" *Journal of Accounting Research* 42:3, 589–623.
La Porta, Rafael, Florencio Lopez-de-Silanes, Andrei Shleifer, and Robert W. Vishny. 1997. "Legal Determinants of External Finance." *Journal of Finance* 52:3, 1131–1150.
Lesmond, David A. 2005. "Liquidity of Emerging Markets." *Journal of Financial Economics* 77:2, 411–452.
Livermore, David. 2010. *Leading with Cultural Intelligence: The New Secret to Success*. New York: AMACOM.
Livermore, David. 2011. *The Cultural Intelligence Difference: Master the One Skill You Can't Do Without in Today's Global Economy*. New York: AMACOM.
Manning, Christopher, and Stephen E. Roulac. 2001. "Corporate Real Estate Research Thought Leadership Continues to Evolve." *Journal of Real Estate Research* 22:½, 1–6.
Morck, Randall, and Bernard Yeung. 2002. "The Puzzle of the Harmonious Stock Prices." *World Economics* 3:3, 105–119.
Oladokum, Timothy. 2010. "Towards Value-Creating Corporate Real Estate Asset Management in Emerging Economies." *Journal of Property Investment and Finance* 5:10, 354–360.
O'Sullivan, Kate. 2011. "Going Global." *CFO Magazine*, June, 1, 41. http://www.cfo.com/article.cfm/14578260/c_14577475.
Prahalad, C. K., and Kenneth Lieberthal. 1998. "The End of Corporate Imperialism." *Harvard Business Review* 69, July–August: 109–117.
Roulac, Stephen E. 1994. "Evolution of Real Estate Decisions." In James R. DeLisle and J. Sa-Aadu, eds., *Appraisal, Market Analysis and Public Policy in Real Estate: Essays in Honor of James A. Graaskamp*, 15–63. Boston: Kluwer Academic Publishers.
Roulac, Stephen E. 2001a. "Corporate Property Strategy Is Integral to Corporate Business Strategy." *Journal of Real Estate Research* 22:1–2, 129–152.
Roulac, Stephen E. 2001b. "Interview with Jacques Gordon." *Briefings in Real Estate Finance* 1:4, 376–382.
Roulac, Stephen E. 2001c. *Stephen Roulac on Place and Property Strategy*. San Francisco: Property Press.
Roulac, Stephen E. 2006. "India and the Property Discipline: Linked Legacy, Intertwined Future, Shared Destiny." *Financial Planning Journal* 8, October: 17–27.
Seasholes, Mark S., and Lei Feng. 2004. "Correlated Trading and Location." *Journal of Finance* 59:5, 2117–2144
Shleifer, Andrei, and Robert W. Vishny. 1997. "A Survey of Corporate Governance." *Journal of Finance* 52:2, 737–783.
Trahan, François, and Katherine Krantz. 2011. *The Era of Uncertainty: Global Investment Strategies for Inflation, Deflation and the Middle Ground*. Hoboken, NJ: John Wiley & Sons.
Wirz, Matthew, and Matt Phillips. 2011. "Sea Change in Map of Global Risk." *Wall Street Journal*, August 1, C1.

Part Two

PUBLIC DEBT MARKETS AND INVESTMENTS

5

Mortgage Markets: The United States

ERIC S. BELSKY

Managing Director, Joint Center for Housing Studies, Harvard University

Introduction

Mortgage markets in the United States are in a state of flux. During the 1990s, the United States had a system that could tap global capital markets to fund mortgage debt despite small loan sizes and heterogeneity of borrowers and collateral. This feat was accomplished by creating a broad secondary mortgage market in the form of MBS traded on an agency market. This is the market in which loans that carried either explicit or implicit federal guarantees were bought and sold.

With these backings, as well as standard documents and terms, the Securities Industry and Financial Markets Association established a deep and highly liquid "To-Be-Announced" (TBA) market. The TBA market facilitated interest rate commitment locks and widespread availability of fully amortizing, pre-payable, mostly fixed-rate loans with long loan terms. This in turn brought certain and low monthly mortgage payments to consumers.

Issuers structured MBS so that a range of securities tranches could be issued in a range of maturities off the underlying mortgages. This permitted investors to allocate and manage interest rate risk of long-term fixed-rate mortgages (FRMs). Outside this MBS market, adjustable rate mortgages (ARMs) were also readily available, allowing consumers to take advantage of the yield curve to receive lower interest rates. Explicit and implicit federal backstops in the agency market let global investors in agency MBS largely look past the specifics of the idiosyncratic mortgage borrowers and their situations, as well as specifics of the financial intermediaries involved in loan origination and servicing (Bipartisan Policy Center 2013).

Especially in 2004–2006, a dramatic shift occurred in the funding of mortgages, loan products offered, and underwriting standards and prudency. *Nontraditional mortgage products* (NTMs) in underwriting standards and product features and terms exploded onto the scene. These NTMs included the proliferation of loans to borrowers with weaker past credit histories than ever before (subprime loans) and borrowers who had stronger credit scores but wanted a range of variances of standard underwriting features and terms (Alt-A). NTMs included loans with higher debt-to-income ratios than were permissible in the agency markets, low or no documentation and verification of incomes and assets, and higher combined loan-to-value (CLTV) ratios. NTMs also included so-called "affordability" products designed to keep initial mortgage payments low through interest-only loans, pay-option loans where borrowers could opt to make less than required monthly payments and tack the difference onto the mortgage balance, and hybrid ARMs with a fixed short-term period that often offered a discounted interest rate (so called teaser-rate 2/28 mortgages).

Often lenders layered these risks one atop the other. A "non-agency" MBS market—referred to as the private-label securities (PLS) or asset-backed securities (ABS) market—largely funded these NTM products. Unlike the agency market, these securities and the mortgages backing them had no federal backstop, explicit or implicit. Whereas the agency market structured securities to address interest rate risk, the ABS market structured them primarily to manage credit risk.

From only a few percentage points of all originations in the early 1990s, subprime and Alt-A alone came to account for a third of mortgage volume in 2005 and 2006. Add in the share of jumbo and conforming prime loans without full documentation or affordability features and the share would be much higher still. For example, about one-quarter of the prime loans in those years had less than full documentation. NTMs turned in abysmal loan performance when rates climbed and home prices fell, throwing mortgage markets into turmoil and calling the safety, soundness, and wisdom of the whole mortgage lending system into question.

When loan performance eroded dramatically in late 2007, the ABS market shut down. In response to concerns over the financial soundness of the two giant corporations that had the special privilege of issuing guarantees with implicit federal backstops (Fannie Mae and Freddie Mac), the federal government took these entities into conservatorship. At the same time, the government dramatically expanded the volume of loan originations of the Federal Housing Administration (FHA)—a federal agency that offered explicit and 100 percent mortgage insurance on loans. These loans were pooled and issued as MBS through the Government National Mortgage Association (Ginnie Mae) that provided explicit guarantees of timely payment of principal and interest.

Private capital willing to absorb credit risk on U.S. mortgages was slow to return to the markets. As of 2012 Ginnie Mae, Fannie Mae, and Freddie Mac constituted virtually the entirety of new MBS issuances in the United States. Together they backstopped about 9 in 10 mortgages originated in the United States and 99 percent of the MBS.

Many people believe that having the government play such a dominant role in the market is undesirable. Others believe that moving precipitously to modify the system and reduce the federal footprint in mortgage markets could have dire consequences for the economy and the financial system if not done carefully and in the right sequence over a necessary transition period.

The Early Evolution of U.S. Mortgage Markets

Mortgage markets in the United States have gone through several relatively distinct phases. Before the Great Depression, savings and loan institutions (S&Ls) or thrifts provided the majority of mortgage loans. These loans had no government insurance against credit risk and the government made no effort to funnel funding to mortgage markets. Thrifts and banks decided how much of their deposit bases to allocate to mortgage loans and held mortgages on their balance sheets. Lenders typically offered loans with terms of five years or less that were not amortizing and thus required balloon payments (necessitating frequent refinancing) at the end of the term. Borrowers also had to put substantial amounts of money down—typically at least 50 percent.

During the 1930s, however, all this changed. This period ushered in various federal programs and agencies that innovated mortgage products that still dominate the market today. In one incarnation or another, most of the programs and agencies set up by the federal government during this decade are still operating today. In fact, these institutions and programs prevented mortgage markets from collapsing in 2008 and its aftermath. Thus, the 1930s can be thought of as the first important phase in the evolution of the mortgage markets.

Starting in the 1930s, the structure and conduct of the mortgage industry and markets became inextricably linked to federal agencies, special private but government-sponsored enterprises (GSEs), and the regulation of mortgage markets and financial institutions. Government involvement gave the country self-amortizing, pre-payable, 15- and 30-year FRMs. Many years later it produced the first MBS and allowed for the creation of the TBA market. Its interventions also fueled the growth of the secondary market for MBS and financial products that have helped manage mortgage interest rate and credit risk.

Federal direct intervention in the U.S. mortgage markets began with the Federal Home Loan Bank Act of 1932. The Act established 12 regional Federal Home Loan Banks (FHLBs). These 12 banks were the first GSEs. The FHLBs were cooperatives owned by their member banks. Their bonds had implicit federal backing, enticing investors to buy them and reducing their interest rates. The purpose of the FHLB system was to provide liquidity to banks to make home loans in the aftermath of bank runs. It created a specialized circuit of implicitly government-backstopped funding that was collateralized by loans to multiple banks.

Federal direct intervention expanded in three important ways in 1933 and 1934. In 1933 Congress created the Home Owners Loan Corporation (HOLC) to refinance private loans in default. HOLC replaced short-term bullet loans with government loans that had much longer terms, lower fixed interest rates and amortization. This short-lived program introduced products like long-term fixed rate mortgages that became staples of the housing market (Jackson 1987; Seidman and Jakabovics 2009).

In 1934, Congress created FHA under the National Housing Act. FHA insured 100 percent of unpaid principal balances. If the FHLB system was intended to supply its members with funds to lend for mortgages, FHA was intended to give them additional encouragement because at the time these thrifts were highly risk averse. In 1938, FHA chartered the Federal National Mortgage Association (Fannie Mae) to provide additional liquidity. Whereas the FHLB accomplished this through floating bonds and then advancing loans to its members, Fannie Mae provided funding by issuing bonds and buying FHA-insured mortgages from banks and thrifts.

With the Great Depression and then World War II, the mortgage lending supports put in place in the 1930s played important but limited roles because housing production remained depressed and the homeownership rate floundered. The Veterans Administration (VA) was created in1944 to offer more relaxed underwriting including no money down loans. After World War II, the volume of mortgage lending and home building increased sharply along with economic growth and federal spending on highways that opened up the suburbs for commuting.

With a mortgage finance system that could attract massive amounts of funding for mortgage credit with long fixed-rate terms and low rates, residential investment was unleashed and homeownership climbed dramatically. Owning a home was now within reach for Americans with moderate and middle incomes. As Figures 5.1a and 5.1b show, both residential construction and homeownership boomed between 1950 and 1970.

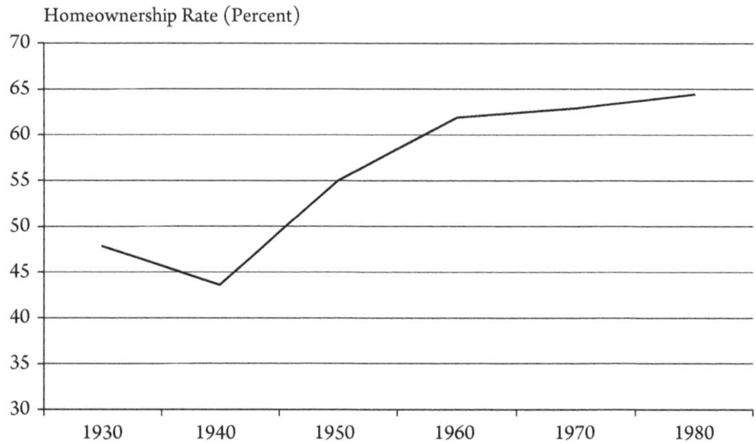

Figure 5.1a Homeownership Rates in the Decades after World War II. Homeownership rates rose sharply in the years after World War II. Source: *U.S. Census Bureau, Historical Census of Housing.* http://www.census.gov/hhes/www/housing/census/historic/owner.html.

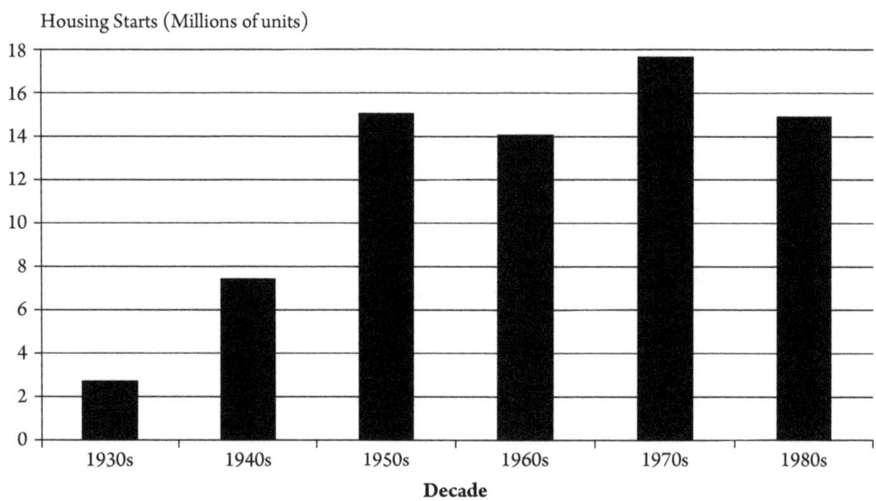

Figure 5.1b Construction of Housing Boomed between the 1950s and 1970s. Homebuilding accelerated in the 1950s and remained high for decades. Source: JCHS tabulations of data from the U.S. Census Bureau, New Residential Construction survey and *Historical Statistics of the United States: Colonial Times to 1970.*

MBS and Regulation of Markets

A series of events in 1968 marked the next major period in the evolution of U.S. mortgage markets: the passage of the Fair Housing Act and the Truth in Lending Act (TILA), the reconstitution of Fannie Mae as a publicly traded, shareholder-owned private company, and the creation of Ginnie Mae. These acts signaled the creation of an expanded role for GSEs, the launch of MBS, and the regulation of mortgage lending to better protect consumers, outlaw discrimination, and in the 1970s create an affirmative obligation to lend to underserved areas and disclose public information of mortgage lending patterns.

The Fair Housing Act outlawed discrimination based on race, national origin, religion, age, sex, familial status, disability, or veteran status. TILA compelled consumer disclosure of credit terms, such as the annual percentage rate to facilitate comparison-shopping. Other laws enacted included those on fair lending and the Real Estate Settlements and Procedures Act (RESPA—consumer disclosure of estimated closing costs). The Home Mortgage Disclosure Act (HMDA) required public disclosure initially of mortgage loans originated by census tract. The Community Reinvestment Act (CRA) involved affirmative obligations of banks and thrifts to meet the credit needs in low- and moderate-income communities where they have branches.

In 1968, Ginnie Mae issued the first MBS. Freddie Mac followed in 1971 and Fannie Mae 10 years later. These first MBS were simple pass-through structures in which the interest and principal payments on an underlying pool of mortgages were distributed to MBS investors on a pro rata basis. This allowed investors to buy into diversified loan pools with timely payment of principal and interest backed either explicitly (FHA/Ginnie Mae) or implicitly (Fannie Mae and Freddie Mac) by the federal government.

In the 1980s, Congress passed four laws that aimed to deregulate financial institutions and markets. The lifting of interest rate regulation occurred at a time when a spike in interest rates bankrupted many thrifts caught holding long-term FRMs with rates lower than prevailing deposit rates (Kane 1989; White 1991). Changes in accounting standards and insufficient attention to supervision of safety and soundness led S&Ls to take excessive risks in a desperate attempt to survive the run up in deposit interest rates or in a play to earn excessive compensation. It fueled securitization because Freddie Mac offered a guarantor program that allowed thrifts to swap mortgages for Freddie Mac MBS they could use as collateral to borrow against (Kling 2010).

Financial innovation and changes in tax law allowed the creation of structured MBS. In the agency markets, this took the form of separate tranches with different maturities and claims to principal and interest payments. These collateralized mortgage obligations (CMOs) allowed investors with different appetites for interest rate risk to purchase tranches with a wide range of maturities and rates across the yield curve. Agency CMOs allowed interest rate risk to be absorbed by those most able to handle it and supported a broad market for 30-year FRMs. The net result of the S&L crisis and CMOs was the deepening of the MBS market. Banks and thrifts sought to sell longer-term FRMs into the secondary market or to swap them for far more liquid MBS or CMBS. As a result, Fannie Mae and Freddie Mac increased their market share, expanded their portfolios, and created an immense agency MBS market.

The 1990s saw the extension of some trends begun in the 1980s. The Basel I accord of 1988 ushered in risk weights that provided powerful incentives for lenders to hold agency MBS rather than whole mortgage loans. Regulators required banks to hold no capital against Ginnie Mae MBS and only 1.6 percent of capital against Fannie Mae and Freddie Mac MBS, while whole mortgages required 4 percent. Congress also passed new laws that both further deregulated the financial industry and pressed the industry to better serve low-income and minority markets.

During the 1990s, Congress and the regulators strengthened and stepped up their enforcement of HMDA and CRA. Munnell, Tootell, Browne, and McEneaney (1996) presented evidence of mortgage discrimination. The Federal Housing Enterprises Financial Safety and Soundness Act of 1992 established goals for affordable and underserved area lending for Fannie Mae and Freddie Mac. This was an effort to ensure the secondary market, which had grown in importance during the 1980s, was supportive of the kind of lending that CRA encouraged in primary markets.

But the 1990s also saw the deployment of information technology and statistical risk assessment tools to better discern good risks from bad, and lower the costs of mortgage originations. Additionally, the 1990s saw the emergence of the PLS market for non-agency MBS that did not conform to the loan limits and, increasingly, the underwriting standards and product features demanded by FHA, Fannie Mae, and Freddie Mac.

During the 1990s the deployment of automated underwriting systems and statistical risk models allowed lending to underserved borrowers to expand by doing a far better job of discriminating good risks from bad and allowing one or more underwriting standards to be relaxed by compensating for one item with tighter application of others. Freddie Mac finds that automated underwriting expanded access to precisely the sorts of borrowers and areas that CRA targeted and without adding much or anything to the average risk of the book (Gates, Perry, and Zorn 2002).

During the 1990s, subprime lending also began to expand. Initially most subprime lending came from finance companies that issued bonds and held loans on their balance sheet. The business model involved extending credit at higher than prime interest rates to households with tarnished credit histories but ample home equity and reasons for missing past payments tied to events that appeared unlikely to be repeated. This allowed homeowners the ability to tap equity they otherwise would not have been able to borrow against.

Starting slowly at first, the subprime market began to expand more markedly around the mid-1990s with advent of a market for MBS backed by these loans. Non-agency MBS, or private label securities (PLS), backed by subprime mortgages started to be traded on the asset-backed securities (ABS) market. Powered by finance companies and investment banks and in some cases by banks that bought PLS during the early 2000s, the ABS market was only lightly regulated and supervised by federal agencies, apart from the Securities and Exchange Commission (SEC). By 2000 this PLS market reached 20 percent of all single-family MBS issuances, up from 15 percent in 1995 and 10 percent in 2000. This lightly regulated and supervised system became known as the "shadow banking system" (Pozsar 2008).

With this expansion of subprime came concerns that some of the lending taking place at much higher than prime mortgage interest rates was predatory. Several practices appeared designed to strip equity from unsuspecting homeowners, charge excessively high interest rates, and expose homeowners to excessive risk. In response, Congress enacted the Home Owners Equity Protection Act (HOEPA) of 1994 into law. An amendment to the Truth in Lending Act, it imposed heightened consumer disclosure requirements and restricted certain lending products and practices on refinance loans with interest rates, fees, and points above a high threshold. Because HOEPA emanated from concerns with certain subprime refinance and second mortgage installment loans, it did not cover home purchase loans. The safe harbor it created for mortgage interest rate spreads, points, and fees limited sharply the share of loans to which it applied. Deregulation continued with the landmark Financial Modernization Act of 1999. This bill undid many of the regulations put in place by the Depression-era Glass-Steagall Act. It lifted the firewalls from a single holding company structure owning banks, insurance companies, and investment companies.

Competitors argued that Fannie Mae and Freddie Mac had unfair and special advantages, exemption from securities registration requirements, and implicit guarantees of their corporate debt that allowed them to borrow at advantaged rates. Economists and some policy makers raised concerns that the two companies were not passing the full value of the implicit guarantee of their debt on to consumers (instead enriching management and shareholders) and exposing taxpayers to interest rate risk on their ballooning portfolios (Sanders 2002; White 2003; Pollock 2005).

2000–2007: Risk Layering

From 2000 to 2007 non-traditional mortgages proliferated, fueled by the ABS market as well as a decision by the depository regulators to allow those that received AA or AAA rating to receive the same risk weight as a Fannie Mae or Freddie Mac security (Hendershott, Hendershott, and Shilling 2010). Fannie Mae and Freddie Mac guaranteed or held in their portfolios very few loans that the industry considered subprime with borrower credit score of less than 620. Credit scores are usually based on a scale offered by Fair Isaac and Company (FICO). FICO scores range from 300 to 850 and 15 percent of borrowers score below 620 during mid-cycle economic conditions. The agencies purchased AAA-rated tranches of private label subprime securities, eventually holding $86 billion of them out of a $1.4 trillion portfolio. They became active in the Alt-A market for loans graded between prime eligible for agency purchase with credit scores of 620 or above or subprime. Pinto (2010) estimates that Fannie Mae and Freddie Mac issued only 11 percent of Alt-A MBS in 2005 and 12 percent in 2006. Their share of the subprime market was even less and nearly entirely in AAA tranches.

Non-traditional mortgages exposed borrowers and the financial system to heightened credit risk. Lenders allowed risks to be layered one on top of the other during a period of rapid house price appreciation. Loan-to-value ratios (LTVs) at origination increased, the share of loans with low or no documentation of incomes and assets soared, and borrowers were exposed to payment-reset risks. Some loans did not even have property taxes and insurance escrowed.

Access to capital through the ABS market and the view that national house price declines need not get factored into pricing models mostly fueled this risky lending. PLS accounted for 55 percent of MBS issuances in 2005 and 2006. This amount was up from about 20 percent from 1999 through 2003 and 10 percent in 1990. By the end of 2008 PLS accounted for 15 percent of all single-family loans outstanding but fully half of loans with serious delinquencies. As Figure 5.2 shows, the subsequent performance of different loan types and underwriting standards varied considerably during a one-third national home price decline. The worst performers were subprime ARMs followed by subprime FRMs. Prime FRMs held up although these too performed worse than expected. Pricing of the risk was insufficient to cover losses.

Similar loosening of credit standards occurred in the CMBS market—the market for private-label multifamily (five plus unit properties MBS). Although CMBS were not nearly as large a part of the market as PLS were on the single-family MBS side, CMBS performance was similarly dramatically weaker than that of Fannie Mae, Freddie Mac, banks and thrifts, and FHA (Bipartisan Policy Center 2013).

The gargantuan size of Fannie Mae's and Freddie Mac's portfolios (about $1.5 trillion between the two of them by 2007) increased concerns over interest rate risks they were taking, their competitive advantage over other corporations, and the extent to which their potential for oligarchic pricing was leading to less than complete transfer of their benefits to consumers in the form of lower mortgage rates. Accounting scandals rocked both corporations. Their regulator, the Office of Federal Housing Enterprise Oversight, sought much stronger control of them including the authority to impose higher capital standards, but the two powerful corporations resisted. These controls were achieved by transferring its authorities to a new and stronger Federal Housing Finance Agency (FHFA) in 2008.

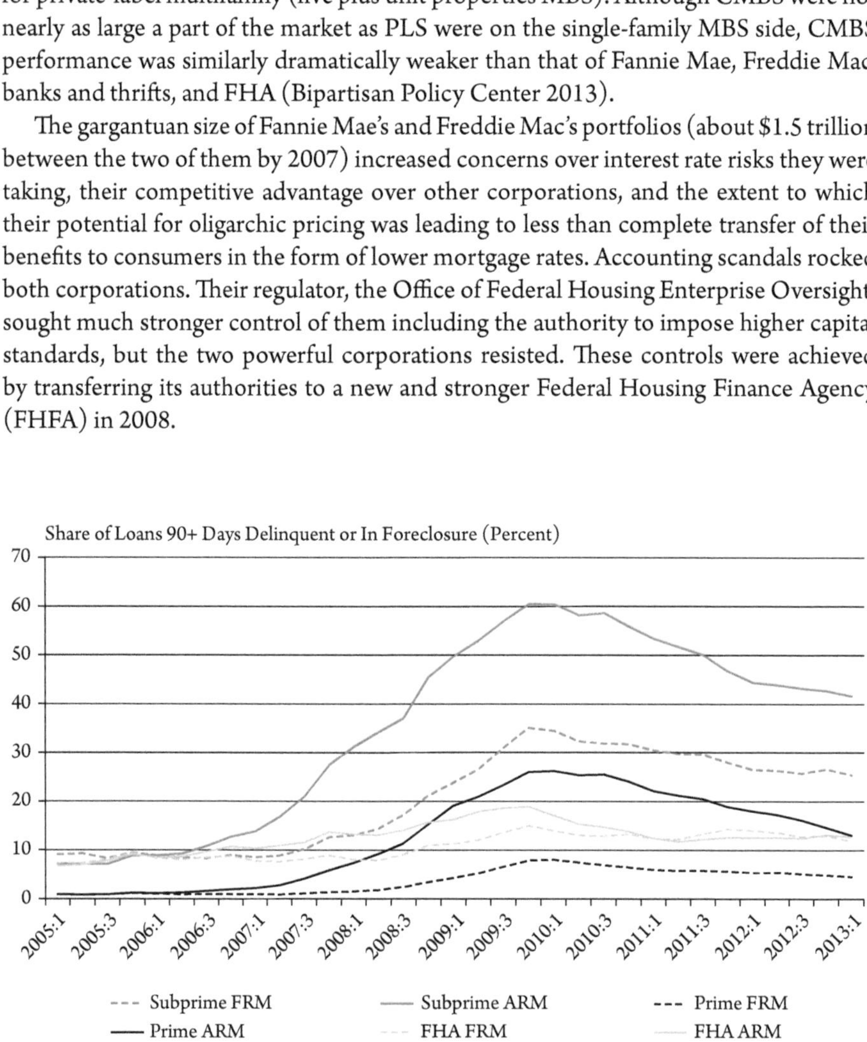

Figure 5.2 Variation of Loan Performance during the Downturn by Loan Type and Underwriting Standards. While delinquency rates increased across loan types, those for subprime and adjustable rate mortgages surged the most. Note: Loan delinquency and in-foreclosure rates are not seasonally adjusted. Source: Mortgage Bankers Association, National Mortgage Delinquency Survey.

Post 2007: Credit Crunch and Mortgage Credit Risk Nationalized

Mortgage loan performance on PLS eroded sharply throughout 2007. By September, investors in these securities lost any appetite for new issuances and the PLS new issuance market shut down. As of 2013, the ABS market for new PLS issuances remained all but closed and accounted for only 1 percent of new MBS issuances.

A year after the PLS new issuance market stalled, the federal government took Fannie Mae and Freddie Mac into conservatorship and the Treasury Department infused them with capital. Concerns that losses would exceed the ability of Fannie Mae and Freddie Mac to cover them led the federal government to step in under authorities created for it under the Housing and Economic Recovery Act of 2008 (HERA). FHA, VA, and Ginnie Mae went from a few percentage points of originations to one-quarter of them and to an even larger share of purchase originations.

As Figure 5.3 shows, credit standards tightened dramatically. The shifting composition of FHA originations and of new issuances and purchases by Fannie Mae and Freddie Mac—altogether now about 90 percent of the market—tell the tale. Average credit scores of each book of business annually continued to increase from 2008 to 2012. Borrowers with low credit scores were mostly locked out of the market. Borrowers with erratic incomes (such as self-employed individuals and business owners) found getting a loan very difficult. Apart from FHA, low down payment loans were scarce. Documentation requirements became onerous and reports surfaced of widespread low appraisal leading to contracts falling through.

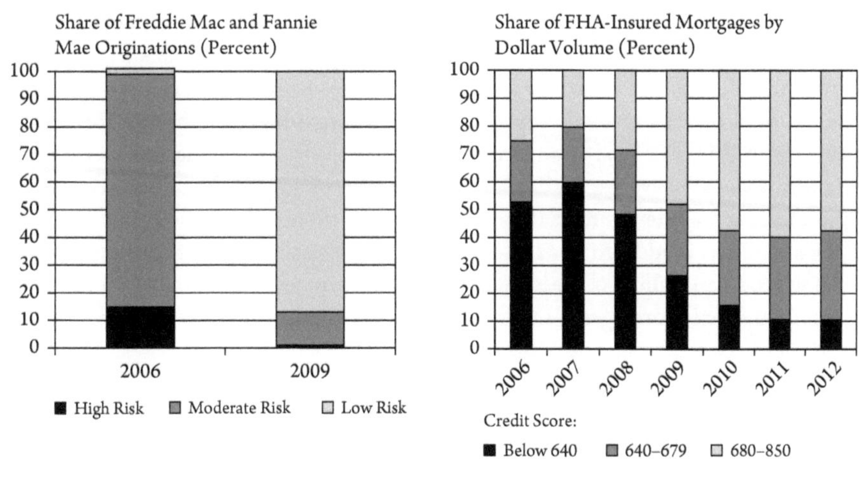

Figure 5.3 Mortgage Credit in the Aftermath of the Financial Crisis. Beginning in 2008, Freddie Mac, Fannie Mae, and FHA reduced lending to higher risk borrowers, which tightened mortgage credit dramatically. Notes: High (low) risk loans are to borrowers with credits scores under 690 (above 750) and have loan-to-value ratios above 85% (below 75%). FHA data exclude records without credit scores. Sources: Barclays Capital, *GSEs: Back to the Future, US Interest Rates Strategy*, 2009; U.S. Department of Housing and Urban Development.

FHA and VA played an outsized role in home purchase loan markets, especially for minorities. Before the mid-2000s, wealth was the most common and binding constraint on would-be homebuyers. Wealth constraints returned with a vengeance in the 2010s. Low-wealth borrowers flocked to FHA because it still permitted down payments of only 3½ percent of the purchase so long as their credit scores exceeded 580.

The initial response to the lax underwriting and NTMs came in regulatory guidance. This guidance failed to prevent the industry from continuing down its dangerous path because it did not cover the shadow banking system and was not required.

The first meaningful round of regulatory actions occurred in 2008 through HERA's creation of the FHFA and the Secure and Fair Enforcement for Mortgage Licensing Act's creation of minimum licensing and registration requirements for state-licensed mortgage brokers. The second meaningful round of regulatory initiatives was launched under existing HOEPA, TILA, and RESPA authorities. The Federal Reserve created a "higher cost" loan category with a safe harbor of 1.5 percentage points above the prevailing mortgage interest rate for first liens and 3.5 percent for second liens.

Dodd-Frank Wall Street Reform and the Consumer Protection Act

The more substantial response came in the form of the Dodd-Frank Wall Street Reform and the Consumer Protection Act of 2010, with its more than 200 separate rules and its establishment of the Consumer Financial Protection Bureau (CFPB). The most important of the mortgage rules to date is the qualified mortgage (QM) definition. This rule prohibits lending without full documentation of income, without regard to ability to repay, or without factoring in a fully indexed rate. It also prohibits the following loans from being QMs: interest-only loans, negative amortization loans, loans with terms of more than 30 years, and balloon payment loans unless from small lenders or for properties in rural or underserved areas. The rule also provides a safe harbor for compliance with an ability-to-repay standard for loans with fully verified income and assets of the borrowers that have a total debt-to-income ratio of 43 percent or less, a 3 percent cap on fees, and a rate no more than 1.5 percentage points above the prime mortgage rate. Fannie Mae, Freddie Mac, FHA, VA, and rural loans are automatically qualified for seven years. Loans falling outside these thresholds can have a rebuttable presumption of being qualified mortgages if the lender documents that the borrower has sufficient income and assets after paying debts to cover living expenses.

Reforming Federal Backstops of Mortgage Markets

One group argues that the federal government should entirely or mostly exit from providing federal backstops of any sort, perhaps limiting them to at most 10 to 15 percent of the market through FHA in its current or a reformed form (Wallison, Pollock, and Pinto 2011). This group sees the federal backstop as encouraging recklessness in lending due to principal-agent problems, fostering financial institutions that become too-big-too-fail, and placing taxpayers at unfair risk while preventing markets from fully sanctioning lender misbehavior through failures.

Another camp sees a federal backstop of a relatively broad part of the market as essential to ensuring liquidity to an $11 trillion plus mortgage market and sees advantages of doing so in terms of credit access, availability of long-term FRMs, cost-effective forward rate locks, and narrower spreads to benchmark interest rates due to very deep and liquid capital market funding of residential mortgages (Center for American Progress 2011; Bipartisan Policy Center 2013).

Consensus among those calling for a broad role appear to be converging around a system in which the federal government would provide catastrophic reinsurance of MBS behind private issuers that would have to hold substantial capital against losses, contract with third-party insurers to hold it, or use capital market executions to fully fund it (Bipartisan Policy Center 2013). Regardless of the form of the private credit enhancement, the federal reinsurance agency would set capital standards and closely monitor its counterparties to ensure that they maintained the required capital levels. In return for this reinsurance, issuers would pay a guarantee fee to the federal reinsurance agency sufficient to cover the agency's operating costs and capitalize a catastrophic risk insurance fund aimed at absorbing losses beyond what is expected from a large price decline.

This consensus view has detractors as described by DeMarco (2013). Some believe that private capital would not come back into the space if the government reinsurance required capital reserves sufficient to withstand expected losses in a 25 percent or more price decline scenario. They remain concerned that private capital, if it did come in, might be quick to exit if expected losses looked like they would exceed actual losses, or would demand such a high price to cover risk at these moments that it would shut down the market and defeat the goal of ensured countercyclical liquidity. Another camp proposes allowing the federal government to set an "attachment point" past which its guarantee would kick in so that in times of stress the government could move the attachment point up so that the private sector would have to take only a small or no portion of the first-loss credit risk (Millstein 2012). Others feel that during such times of stress Congress should have to decide if private insurance requirements need to be temporarily waived or reduced (Bipartisan Policy Center 2013).

Although trade groups and think tanks floated dozens of proposals, FHFA was taking many steps to prepare for a world without Fannie Mae and Freddie Mac, including moving toward a common and single platform for securitization through which both PLS and any agency securities could be issued, involving common pooling and servicing agreements. The FHFA had also begun risk-sharing experiments with the private sector on the multifamily side and in 2013 was on the verge of expanding to the single-family side.

Regulating the Mortgage Market

Another debate also continues to rage around how much and in what ways to regulate mortgage markets and financial intermediaries. To one group, the CFPB and the Dodd-Frank Act are an anathema and overreaching. To another, they are vital and may not yet have gone far enough. Although regulations prohibiting excessively risky lending would likely have prevented that risk from pervading the market, Kling (2010, 31) notes, "The fact is, securitization, house price inflation, and the lack of understanding of risk-taking on the part of executives were little influenced by specific relaxation of financial regulation."

Some view the CRA and GSE goals as culprits in driving risky lending (Pinto 2010). Many others view pinning the causes for the housing market boom and bust or the financial crisis on these two regulations as unsupportable (Kroszner 2008; Avery and Brevoort 2011; Apgar 2012). Indeed, ample evidence exonerates CRA and evidence exonerates the GSE goals. CRA lenders operating in areas in which they were assessed for CRA performance commanded only 6 to 9 percent of the high-cost loan market at its peak, compared to about 30 percent of the prime lending market in these areas, as measured by HMDA data (Kroszner 2008). Fannie Mae and Freddie Mac similarly played disproportionately small roles in high-cost loans when compared with PLS and private conduits (Belsky and Richardson 2010). Indeed, Alt-A loans, which were the principal drivers of credit losses at the GSEs, were not at all goal rich, though they were associated with price bubbles (Berkovec, Chang, and McManus 2011). According to CoreLogic, about 80 percent of these loans did not have full documentation so they could not be counted toward affordable lending goals.

Another regulatory debate centers on the relative importance of ensuring that issuers of MBS have capital at risk tied to the long-run performance of their issuances. These issues have been encapsulated in the debate over the Qualified Residential Mortgage established under the Dodd-Frank Act. This rule will require securitizers to retain 5 percent of the risk on MBS that fall outside this definition. An initial proposal to consider only loans with 20 percent or more down for exemption from the risk retention rules set off a firestorm over the wide swath of the market that would fall outside the standard.

The Fate of Long-Term Fixed-Rate Mortgages

Another hotly debated topic is the role of FRMs in mitigating or exacerbating risks and for whom. On the one hand, long-term FRMs transfer the risk of rising interest rates away from homeowners to lenders and investors. On the other, during periods of house price declines accompanied by interest rate declines, FRMs may prevent homeowners from refinancing to lower rates because the declines place some borrowers in a negative net equity or too-high LTV situation. Borrowers holding ARMs under such circumstances simply ride rates down.

At issue in the debate over whether government should support liquidity for 30-year FRMs is how interest rate risk should be allocated and the consequences of different arrangements. With respect to falling rates, this risk has long been transferred to lenders and investors through the widespread adoption of pre-payable mortgages. With respect to rising rates, this risk has been shared. In the case of ARMs, homeowners bear the risk and in the case of FRMs lenders bear it.

But homeowners are arguably the least able to manage the risk of rising interest rates because the likelihood they will hedge or pick a proper hedge is much lower than it is for lenders and investors. While lenders are in a better position to bear this risk, lenders surely can and have failed to protect themselves adequately from interest risk in rising rate environments. The S&L industry failed to address the mismatch in duration between assets (loans) and liabilities (deposits) in the late 1970s and early 1980s. Hedging strategies and instruments have proliferated since then but they have a cost and can go astray. Still, the prospect of leaving this risk on the shoulders of homeowners is troubling. When rates spiked in Canada in the 1980s where ARM loans dominated, skyrocketing rates led to skyrocketing loan defaults, whereas in the United States homeowners clung to their low FRMs.

Alternatives to FRMs and short-term ARMs are available in the form of hybrid fixed-adjustable mortgages with initial fixed-rates for several years that adjust thereafter on a regular schedule, say annually or every five years. Indeed, hybrid ARMs with 30-year amortization schedules and a prepayment option have been around for decades.

Some suggest that the presence of FHA, Fannie Mae, and Freddie Mac have tilted the playing field toward 30-year FRMs (Woodward 2010; Lea and Sanders 2011). These three agencies certainly have attracted deep pools of capital to funding such mortgages through highly liquid MBS, lowering the costs of such loans. A serious risk exists that if the TBA agency market and agency CMO/REMICs disappeared, the cost of FRMs would increase and consumers would be steered toward ARMs through pricing and underwriting decisions of bank lenders who would prefer to lay interest rate risk on homeowners.

The Scope for Modeling and Compensating Factors in the New System

Faith in the capacity of credit risk models to estimate and price risk was justifiably shaken as a result of the financial crisis (Coval, Jurek, and Stafford 2008). Still, in many cases the problem was less the accuracy of these models in relating various factors to default probabilities and severities, and more in the economic stress scenarios to which these models were subjected in estimating losses and severities. In others, the problem was reliance on methods other than modeling actual loan performance (such as movements in CDS pricing) that created a problem that should and need not be repeated. In still other cases, the problem was the potential for small differences in risk estimates across tranches of MBS when combined into so-called CDO squared that led to large errors in estimating risks.

The last of this long list of reasons for modeling failures has been mitigated by the 2007–2012 period. This afforded a disastrous natural experiment in how extreme stress on national and local home price declines on the order of 30 percent or more—and in the context of low inflation—affected the loan performance of a remarkably diverse range of product features and underwriting standards. With the digital capture of much of this information on literally tens of millions of loans, federal regulators (or any federal reinsurance agency that may emerge from housing finance reform) would have an ample basis upon which to model risk.

The advantage of risk modeling is that it uses actual experience with particular lending products to identify opportunities to discriminate good risks from bad in a more precise fashion than relying on simple rules of thumb and proscriptive limits on a handful of underwriting variables seen as key, notably loan-to-value ratios, debt-to-income ratios, and credit scores. Modeling the many variables that may or may not influence actual probabilities and severities of default allows greater flexibility in underwriting which allows more creditworthy borrowers to qualify. Credit risk analysts in the 1990s discovered that tightening one or more credit standards is often sufficient to offset the risk of loosening one or more.

The question now is whether Congress and the regulators will get comfortable again with the idea of allowing this sort of flexibility in underwriting outside of Fannie Mae, Freddie Mac, and FHA, all of which use them. While these agencies remain intact, a related question is what level of expected risk regulators will accept. Models now set a cutoff based on a decision about the maximum tolerable expected lifetime default of the riskiest marginal borrower. If Congress and regulators get comfortable with this approach instead of proscriptive standards, a key question is what maximum tolerable expected lifetime default gets used and based on what degree of stress to performance. Although new regulations such as the QM definition push in the direction of proscriptive debt-to-income ratios, using compensating factors still dominates the market because Fannie Mae, Freddie Mac, FHA, VA, and the Rural Housing Services are all exempt from the QM rules for seven years, leaving them free to continue using compensating factors to originate qualified mortgages.

Defining Acceptable Risk for Purposes of Underwriting and Pricing

A central policy tension around which much of the policy debate about the future of the mortgage market revolves is between balancing access to mortgage credit with maintaining an acceptable level of risk to individuals, communities, and the financial system. Yet, a striking absence of a public debate exists about what constitutes acceptable risk. Some observers note this, and call for such a debate to begin (Belsky and Richardson 2010; Pinto 2012).

Having such a debate would help to draw out three important issues that could help advance policy in this area. First, what is an acceptable level of risk from a policy perspective? For example, is this level a 1 in 10 chance the marginal loan applicant will ever default, a 2 in 10 chance, a 1 in 20 chance, or a 1 in 100 chance? Policy makers have paid insufficient attention to what different levels of risk for the marginal applicant might mean for individuals, communities, and the financial system. Some contend that no limit should exist on the level so long as the lender prices the risk properly and is required to hold capital sufficient to cover expected losses. However, if the risk is elevated a strong chance exists that the community could be injured due to negative externalities of defaults on property owners and neighborhood safety. This is especially true if the probability of default is high and concentrated enough to produce negative neighborhood-wide price externalities.

Second, how are expectations of default probabilities formed? This is a vitally important subject that policy makers should be concerned about and understand. At least since the mid-1990s, statistical risk models have formed the basis for these expectations. Now that tens of millions of loans with various product features and underwriting standards have been subjected to extreme economic and housing market stresses, an opportunity exists to evaluate the strength of risk models under a wider variety of stress scenarios. This should be a central aim of the FHFA and other financial regulators. Given FHFA's ready access to data, the modeling expertise at the GSEs, and the great level of detail on loan characteristics and performance available in datasets aggregated by commercial vendors, such an initiative would be feasible and illuminating.

Third, should the same stresses be used to decide on an acceptable level of risk as for pricing of the risk? The system could potentially be designed to hold enough capital to withstand a once in an 80-year severe downturn but underwrite to a more typical recession scenario. To underwrite to an infrequently realized set of events could deprive generations of households of the financial benefits from owning their homes during more normal periods.

The Impact of Leverage and Low Down Payment Lending

Low down payment lending is vital to preserving access to homeownership in the United States because so many renter households have limited wealth. Yet, high levels of leverage can pose greater systemic risk and are clearly associated with higher default probabilities. The impact on loss severity is more ambiguous, however. Mortgage insurance is usually required on loans with less than 20 percent down payments. If the mortgage insurer priced the risk properly and retained capital sufficient to cover the additional risk, severities should be no different or perhaps slightly less because coverage often extends below 80 percent of the initial home price.

Evidence exists that sharply reducing the defaults and loss severities associated with low down payment lending is possible simply by ensuring such loans do not have other especially risky features. A study of millions of loans originated from 2000 to 2008 finds that netting out certain dangerous loan types dropped default rates significantly more than the total number of loans outstanding. The default rate as of February 2011 (90 + day delinquent, foreclosed, or in foreclosure) was 11 percent for all loans. However, the default rate was 5.8 percent after netting out loans with less than full documentation, balloon payments, initial adjustment periods of less than five years, maturities over 30 years, or prepayment penalties (Quercia, Ding, and Reid 2012). This was lower than the 7.7 percent rate on prime conventional loans and sharply lower than the 22.3 percent on Alt-A loans and the 32.3 percent on subprime loans. Imposing a 10 percent down payment restriction on top of these product restrictions would remove 31 percent of those who got loans that were still performing in 2011 while imposing a 20 percent down requirement would have eliminated 60 percent. Moving to a 20 percent down requirement would get rid of 10 performing loans for every one prevented default, a 10 percent down requirement would knock out 9 performing loans for every one prevented default, and a 3 percent down requirement would do away with six performing loans for every prevented default.

Summary and Conclusions

The amount of mortgage capital in the United States is 5.7 times greater than the second largest mortgage market in world (the United Kingdom) (Lea 2010). Without the run up in Treasury debt in response to the Great Recession, home mortgage debt outstanding today would be the largest class of credit outstanding on the balance sheets of the United States. The Flow of Funds of the Federal Reserve shows home mortgages at 25 percent (adding multifamily lifts the share to 27 percent) and Treasury securities at 29 percent as of the fourth quarter of 2012, followed distantly by corporate bonds at 14 percent.

That the system continued to function in the midst of a financial crisis, brought on in no small measure by the risks lenders were taking in U.S. real estate, is a testament to the fact that the Depression era supports came through, though not without problems to the system, the broader economy, and the taxpayer in the form of bailouts. The greatest challenge today is finding a way forward that weans the system off of such massive federal credit supports and addresses the future of Fannie Mae, Freddie Mac, and FHA.

The crisis revealed various issues that have yet to be addressed in convincing ways. One is the regulation of ratings agencies. These agencies were and still are compensated for their ratings of MBS by the firms issuing the MBS. This was a possible reason that the ratings agencies doled out so many AAA ratings on bond tranches that subsequently they downgraded to junk bond status. Another issue is how to prevent second mortgage holders from preventing modifications of first mortgages. Still another is how to construct pooling and servicing agreements so that loan modifications that are net present value positive relative to pursuing foreclosure are made, even when they put some tranche holder's interests ahead of others in a structured MBS/CMO. Still another is the regulation of credit default swaps (CDS) so that sellers of them are monitored to ensure they have the capital to honor their commitments. Another issue is the adequacy of disclosures and protections against interest rate risk as markets soak up low-yielding debt obligations.

Doubtless, debate will continue to rage over what should be learned from the recent crisis, how to avert another one, and the possible unintended consequences of regulatory actions that have already been taken or have yet to be taken but are proposed. With the intersection of business and government at the heart of the structure, conduct, and performance of mortgage markets, the government actions taken will have a profound impact on the cost and availability of mortgage credit in the United States moving forward.

Discussion Questions

1. What benefits did the housing finance system of the 1990s bring to housing consumers?
2. What federal laws have had the most impact on the structure, conduct, and performance of the housing system?
3. What factors contributed to excessive mortgage risk-taking in the 2000s?
4. What debates are likely to shape the future of U.S. housing finance system?

References

Apgar, William. 2012. "Getting on the Right Track: Improving Low-Income and Minority Access to Mortgage Credit after the Housing Bust." Working Paper, Joint Center for Housing Studies, Harvard University.

Avery, Robert B., and Kenneth P. Brevoort. 2011. "The Subprime Housing Crisis: Is Government Housing Policy to Blame?" Finance and Economics Discussion Series Staff Working Paper 2011–2036. Division of Research and Statistics, Board of Governors of the Federal Reserve System.

Belsky, Eric S., and Nela Richardson. 2010. "Understanding the Boom and Bust in the Nonprime Mortgage Market." Working Paper, Joint Center for Housing Studies, Harvard University.

Berkovec, James A., Yan Chang, and Douglas A. McManus. 2011. "Alternative Lending Channels and the Crisis in U.S. Housing Markets." Working Paper, Social Science Research Network. http://ssrn.com/abstract=1976274 or http://dx.doi.org/10.2139/ssrn.1976274.

Bipartisan Policy Center. 2013. "Housing America's Future: New Directions for National Policy." BPC. Alexandria, VA: Bremmer and Goris.

Center for American Progress. 2011. "A Responsible Market for Housing Finance: A Progressive Plan to Reform the US Secondary Market for Residential Mortgages." Prepared by the Mortgage Finance Working Group, Washington, DC.

Coval, Joshua D., Jakub W. Jurek, and Erik Stafford. 2008. "The Economics of Structured Finance." Harvard Business School Finance Working Paper No. 09–060. http://ssrn.com/abstract=1287363 or http://dx.doi.org/10.2139/ssrn.1287363.

DeMarco, Edward J. 2013. "Housing Finance, Systemic Risk, and Returning Private Capital to the Mortgage Market." Remarks as Prepared for Delivery. Federal Reserve Bank of Chicago, 49th Annual Conference on Bank Structure and Competition, May 9. Chicago, IL.

Gates, Susan Wharton, Vanessa Gail Perry, and Peter M. Zorn. 2002. "Automated Underwriting in Mortgage Lending: Good News for the Underserved?" *Housing Policy Debate* 13: 2, 369–391.

Hendershott, Patric, Robert Hendershott, and James Shilling. 2010. "The Mortgage Finance Bubble: Causes and Corrections." *Journal of Housing Research* 19:1, 1–16.

Jackson, Kenneth T. 1987. *Crabgrass Frontier: The Suburbanization of the United States.* Oxford: Oxford University Press.

Kane, Edward J. 1989. *The S&L Insurance Mess: How Did It Happen?* Washington, DC: Urban Institute Press.

Kling, Arnold. 2010. "The Root of the Financial Crisis." Hoover Institution–Stanford University, *Policy Review* 158, 21–33.

Kroszner, Randall S. 2008. "The Community Reinvestment Act and the Recent Mortgage Crisis." Confronting Concentrated Poverty Policy Forum, Board of Governors of the Federal Reserve System, Washington, DC.

Lea, Michael. 2010. "Alternative Forms of Mortgage Finance: What Can We Learn from Other Countries?" Paper prepared for the Joint Center for Housing Studies National Symposium; Moving Forward: The Future of Consumer Credit and Mortgage Finance, Harvard Business School, Boston, MA.

Lea, Michael, and Anthony B. Sanders. 2011. "Do We Need the 30-Year Fixed-Rate Mortgage?" Working Paper, Mercatus Center, George Mason University.

Millstein, Jim. 2012. "A Blueprint for Housing Finance Reform in America." Remarks presented at a conference held at the Woodrow Wilson International Center for Scholars. The Program on America and the Global Economy, Washington, DC.

Munnell, Alicia H., Geoffrey M. B. Tootell, Lynn E. Browne, and James McEneaney. 1996. "Mortgage Lending in Boston: Interpreting HMDA Data." *American Economic Review* 86: 1, 25–53.

Pinto, Edward J. 2010. "Triggers of the Financial Crisis." American Enterprise Institute, Memorandum to staff of FCIC. http://www.aei.org/papers/economics/fiscal-policy/triggers-of-the-financial-crisis/.

Pinto, Edward J. 2012. "FHA Watch: Special Update." American Enterprise Institute. http://www.aei.org/article/economics/financial-services/housing-finance/fha-watch-special-update/#mbl.

Pollock. Alex J. 2005. "American 'Housing GSEs': Past Triumphs, Present Tensions, Possible Futures." *Housing Finance International* 19:3, 41–46.

Pozsar, Zoltan. 2008. "The Rise and Fall of the Shadow Banking System." *Regional Financial Review* 44:1, 13–15.

Quercia, Roberto G., Lei Ding, and Carolina Reid. 2012. "Balancing Risk and Reward: Underwriting Standards for Qualified Residential Mortgages." Research Report, Chapel Hill, NC: Center for Community Capital, University of North Carolina.

Sanders, Anthony B. 2002. "Government Sponsored Agencies: Do the Benefits Outweigh the Costs?" *Journal of Real Estate Finance and Economics* 25: 2/3, 121–127.

Seidman Ellen, and Andrew Jakabovics. 2009. "Learning from the Past: The Asset Disposition Experiences of the Home Owners' Loan Corporation, The Resolution Trust Corporation, and the Asset Control Area Program." Federal Reserve Bank of San Francisco, *Community Investment Review* 5:1, 43–52.

Wallison Peter J., Alex J. Pollock, and Edward J. Pinto. 2011. "Taking the Government Out of Housing Finance: Principles for Reforming the Housing Finance Market." An American Enterprise Institute White Paper. http://www.aei.org/paper/100189.

White, Lawrence J. 1991. *The S&L Debacle: Public Policy and Thrift Regulation*. Oxford: Oxford University Press.

White, Lawrence J. 2003. "Focusing on Fannie and Freddie: The Dilemmas of Reforming Housing Finance." *Journal of Financial Services Research* 23:1, 43–58.

Woodward, Susan E. 2010. "The Future of the Capital Markets: Connecting Primary Consumer and Mortgage Credit Markets to Global Capital Markets." Working Paper MF 10–14, Joint Center for Housing Studies, Harvard University.

6

Mortgage Markets: International

KYUNG-HWAN KIM

President, Korea Research Institute for Human Settlements (KRIHS),
Professor of Economics, Sogang University, Korea

MAN CHO

Professor of Public Policy and Management, The KDI School of Public Policy and Management
and Director, The Real Asset Research, Korea Development Institute (KDI), Korea

Introduction

Housing is the most expensive durable consumption good and the most important asset for most households around the world. Mortgage loans enable consumers to purchase homes with long-term financing and to consume a flow of housing services over an extended period of residence as well as providing opportunities to accumulate home equity. Therefore, access to affordable mortgage loans makes homeownership available to more consumers.

For some financial institutions, mortgage lending constitutes a major business line in consumer finance. For other institutions, mortgage loans or securities backed by mortgages can be an important investment asset. At the macroeconomic level, the mortgage market serves as a lynchpin between the housing sector and the wider economy through several channels. Mortgage lending affects demand for new housing and construction. It enables consumers to increase spending through home equity withdrawal, taking a home equity loan using increased home value as collateral (Muellbauer 2012).

The mortgage market can be a source of financial instability. Mortgage lenders relax underwriting criteria during a house price run-up phase and tighten them in the contracting phase of the market cycle. As a result, the volume of mortgage lending increases during a housing boom and decreases during a housing market downturn. Such pro-cyclical mortgage lending behavior exacerbates the housing boom-bust cycle. The unwinding of a housing boom results in a pro-cyclical increase in nonperforming mortgage loans. It impairs the asset position of lending institutions and possibly jeopardizes soundness of the overall financial system.

The housing finance system of a particular country evolves over time, influenced by the level of development, the depth and the width of the financial market, and regulatory frameworks governing mortgage lending and tax subsidy policies. As a result, the size and the structure of mortgage markets exhibit huge differences across countries. This chapter makes international comparisons of mortgage markets in terms of size and key features. Key features include the types and terms of loan products offered, funding, risk management, and government intervention. It also seeks to assess the contributions of mortgage markets to furthering housing policy goals.

Comprehensive international comparative studies of mortgage markets require detailed knowledge of the individual markets and their institutions and policy frameworks. Given the data constraint, this chapter attempts to identify and tap the best available sources of information.

The rest of this chapter is organized as follows. It begins by presenting a brief review of international comparative studies of mortgage markets and their performance. The chapter then provides an overview of mortgage finance systems and the key features of mortgage markets of 21 countries. Next, it provides the results of an empirical analysis of mortgage markets of those countries with reliable data. The chapter then characterizes ideal housing finance systems and provides a taxonomy of countries based on a set of criteria. The final section provides a summary and suggestions for future research.

An Overview of the Literature

The literature on international mortgage markets includes publications of agencies such as the Bank for International Settlements (BIS), the International Monetary Fund (IMF), and the Organization for Economic Co-operation and Development (OECD). The chapter does not provide a comprehensive review of the extended literature but instead focuses on selected studies and key issues.

This literature can be grouped into comparative studies and case studies of specific countries, although some papers offer a combination of the two. Major contributions in the first category include the European Central Bank (ECB 2009), Financial Stability Board (FSB 2011), International Monetary Fund (2004, 2011), Lea (2010a, b), and Warnock and Warnock (2008, 2012). Most of these studies are about developed economies and only Warnock and Warnock cover some emerging economies. Ben-Shahar, Leung, and Ong (2008) examine various countries including China, India, Singapore, Hong Kong, Japan, Ghana, South Africa, Israel, and Poland as well as comparative studies of the Czech Republic, Hungary, Slovakia, Slovenia, and Russia. Smith, Elsinga, O'Mahony, Eng, Wachter, Green, and Kim (2012) discuss mortgage market character and trends in Africa, Brazil, China, France, Germany, India, Italy, Japan, Korea, Mexico, the United Kingdom, and the United States. The European Mortgage Federation (2012a) provides descriptions of housing and mortgage markets in European Union (EU) countries.

Warnock and Warnock (2008, 2012) explain the variations in the size of mortgage markets across countries. Typically, the ratio of mortgage debt outstanding (MDO) to gross domestic product (GDP) is regressed on a set of explanatory variables such as per capita income, population, urbanization rate, indicators of mortgage market infrastructure, and measures of government intervention.

Another research focus relates to the terms of loan products offered, funding of mortgages and risk management (Lea 2010a; European Mortgage Federation 2012a). The proportion of fixed rate mortgages to the total has implications for the stability of housing markets. The International Monetary Fund (2004) reports a negative correlation among 18 developed countries between the standard deviation of annual growth rates in real house prices over 1971 to 2003 and the proportion of fixed rate mortgages. The International Monetary Fund (2011) conducts more comprehensive analyses of the relationships between housing prices, mortgage credit, and housing finance characteristics. The prevalence of variable rate loans lead to a fast growth in mortgage credit during the 2004–2007 housing price boom, which resulted in a steeper housing price downturn and a faster growth in non-performing loans during 2007–2009.

A third subject of research concerns government intervention in mortgage markets. Whether a government guarantee is necessary for a sustainable mortgage securitization market is one such topic. Lea and Sanders (2011) contend that government support of a fixed rate mortgage is unnecessary while Lam (2011) argues that governments are entwined in the mortgage market in other international markets such as Canada and Europe.

An Overview of Mortgage Finance Systems

The essence of the mortgage business is sharing risks among borrowers, lenders, and investors. Countries have different housing finance systems depending on their legal and regulatory frameworks as well as government intervention in the mortgage market, especially on whether the public sector is directly involved in mortgage lending through government funds or government housing banks. The division of the four key mortgage functions—origination, servicing, risk management, and funding—shapes the mortgage business model of a particular country.

The mortgage market system can be classified into deposit-based and capital-market-based funding mechanisms (Lea 2010b; Campbell 2012). In a deposit-based model, banks mobilize funds through short-term deposits, originate loans, service the loans, and manage risks. This model is known as the *originate-to-hold model* because the lenders hold the mortgages until the borrowers are projected to repay the principal and interest in full. Because the lenders keep the mortgage loans on their balance sheets, they have an incentive to apply caution in assessing loan applications, and to modify the terms as required by a fall in house prices. On the other hand, the scope of lending is limited by the ability to raise funds and is subject to interest rate risk from the mismatch between deposits and mortgage loan terms.

The capital-market-based model consists of a primary market for loan origination and a secondary market with securitization or issuance of covered bonds. In the securitization or originate-to-distribute (OTD) model, the originators sell the mortgages to a third party, a conduit or a special purpose vehicle (SPV). The third party packages the mortgages into securities backed by the cash flow from the repayment of the loans, selling the mortgage-backed securities (MBS) to capital market investors. Since the originators do not hold the mortgages, they have weak incentives to conduct careful analysis of the creditworthiness

Table 6.1 **Key Features of Mortgage Markets in Asia-Pacific Countries and Territories and North America**

Asia-Pacific	*Lender*	*Capital Market*	*Covered Bonds*	*MBS*	*ARM*	*Term*	*LTV*	*Prepay Penalty*	*IMF Index*
Australia	Banks Mortgage banks Building and loan associations Mortgage brokers	16.7	NA	16.7	79	25	70(95)	Increase in financing rate of interest	0.31
China	Banks	NA	NA	NA	99	30	70(40) for 1-unit (2-unit) owner	NA	0.38
Hong Kong	Banks	–	NA		99	10~29	50–70(95)	NA	
Japan	Banks Mortgage banks	10	NA	10	36	20–30	70–80	No	0.38
Malaysia	Banks	4 Cagamas	NA	4					0.38
Singapore	Banks	NA	NA	NA	99	35	80(90)	Yes	0.75
Korea	Banks	5	NA	5	95	10~30	Bank: 60 Housing Finance Corporation: 70	Yes	0.44
Taiwan	Banks	5	NA	5	Floating rate Hybrid	20~30	70 or more Second Homes:50(60)	NA	0.31

Table 6.1 **continued**

North America	*Lender*	*Capital Market*	*Covered Bonds*	*MBS*	*ARM*	*Term*	*LTV*	*Prepay Penalty*	*IMF Index*
Canada	Banks Mortgage brokers	32	1	31	31 Hybrid fixed rate for 1–5 years	24 Some 35–40	75–95	Loss of interest rate changes 3 months interest	0.44
United States	Banks Mortgage banks Mortgage brokers	64.1	NA	64.1	4 (Mainly floating rate)	15/30	80(100)	ARM: Up to 5 percent	0.56

Note: This table summarizes key features of mortgage markets in eight Asia-Pacific countries and in both Canada and the United States. Mortgage market percentage point shares are for the capital market, covered bonds and MBS, and the ARM share. NA = not applicable.

Table 6.2 **Key Features of Mortgage Markets in Europe**

	Lender	*Capital Market*	*Covered Bonds*	*MBS*	*ARM*	*Term*	*LTV*	*Prepay Penalty*	*IMF Index*
Austria	Banks Savings banks	17.4	15	2.4	33 (Foreign currency loans)	25–30	80	No	0.19
Denmark	Banks Mortgage banks	142.8	142.8	NA	Minimal	30	80(100)	No for FRM	0.25
France	Banks Mortgage banks	31	28.9	2.1	11.5	15–20	80(100)	Interest up to 6 months 3 percent of balance	0.31
Germany	Banks Savings banks	20.9	19.2	1.7	10	20–30	80 (Local loans) 60 (Pfandbrife funding)	FRM: Loss of interest rate changes	0.19
Ireland	Banks Building and loan associations Mortgage brokers	68.6	23	45.6	91	21–35	90(100)	No	0.25
Italy	Banks	46.9	14	32.9	62.8	20	80	No	0.25
Netherlands	Banks Mortgage banks Mortgage brokers	53.3	8.5	44.8	1	30	112	FRM: Loss of interest	0.5
Russia	Banks Mortgage banks Co-ops	7.7	NA	7.7					0.44

Table 6.2 **continued**

	Lender	*Capital Market*	*Covered Bonds*	*MBS*	*ARM*	*Term*	*LTV*	*Prepay Penalty*	*IMF Index*
Spain	Banks	81	55.4	25.6		30	80(100)	FRM: 2.5 percent	0.31
	Savings banks				99			ARM: 0.5 percent	
	Mortgage brokers								
Sweden	Banks	69.1	69.1	NA	Floating	30–45	70(90)		
	Mortgage banks				rate			No	
United Kingdom	Banks	41.2	13.4	27.8	47	25	Internal decision	FRM: 3 months interest	0.13
	Building and loan associations								
	Mortgage Brokers								

Note: This table summarizes key features of mortgage markets in European countries. Mortgage market percentage point shares are for the capital market, covered bonds and MBS, and the ARM share. NA = not applicable.

of the borrowers because they transfer the credit risk by selling the mortgages. Credit enhancement such as a guarantee on the repayment of principal and interest is required when investors who purchase MBS do not have sufficient information about the quality of the underlying mortgages.

The *covered bond model*, or the *mortgage-backed bond (MBB) model*, is another way to fund mortgages from the capital market. Covered bonds are issued against a collateral pool that is identified and ring-fenced but the cash flow from the mortgages is not dedicated to the bonds. Rather, covered bonds are collateralized obligations of the issuer. Unlike in securitization using MBS, the underlying mortgages are not sold to a third party but remain on the balance sheet of the lenders. The lenders take full responsibility for repaying the principal and interest to the investors. In case some mortgages become insolvent, the issuer of the covered bonds must replace the non-performing loans with other mortgages, which provides a strong incentive to be careful with origination. Covered bonds bear a lower interest rate than MBS issued by the same institution because they provide the investors with recourse to both the collateral and the lenders (Lea 2012).

The composition of mortgage loan products varies widely across countries, depending upon funding sources, consumer preferences, and monetary policy. Mortgage loan products can be classified according to several criteria such as the loan term (short-term or long-term), interest rate fixity—fixed rate mortgages (FRMs), adjustable rate mortgages (ARMs), and mixed mortgages (instruments with elements of both types)—and repayment scheme such as equal installment payments of principal and interest or interest only. Outside of the United States, ARMs are typically called *variable rate mortgages*.

Underwriting criteria are crucial in managing credit and default risks of mortgage borrowers. Key variables include the loan-to-value (LTV) ratio, debt-service-to-income (DTI) ratio, and a prepayment penalty. In recent years, policy makers in various countries have used LTV and DTI as tools of macro-prudential policy aimed at containing systemic risks that can arise from mortgage markets. The existence of a prepayment penalty and its amount vary among countries depending on the mortgage interest regime. The extent and the modality of government intervention in mortgage markets also vary across countries.

Table 6.1 summarizes key features of mortgage markets in eight countries in the Asia/Pacific and two in North America. Table 6.2 provides the same information for 11 European countries. The tables provide information about the key lenders, funding mechanisms, loan products offered, and government intervention. The index of government intervention is from the International Monetary Fund (2011), as a composite based on information about eight categories of intervention in the mortgage markets. Larger numbers mean more intervention.

Empirical Analysis of International Mortgage Markets

This section presents an empirical analysis of the size and the structure of mortgage markets around the world and how they affect the housing market outcomes such as the homeownership rate, the rate of house price growth, and its volatility.

SIZE OF MORTGAGE MARKETS

The single most popular summary metric used in international comparative studies of mortgage markets is MDO-to-GDP. Figure 6.1 provides the MDO-to-GDP ratio of 44 countries and the average for 27 countries in European Union in ascending order. The sample represents the maximum number of countries with verifiable data. Figure 6.1 shows a huge variation in the size of the mortgage market among the countries represented. Switzerland has an MDO of 140 percent of GDP, which stands out as an outlier even among the countries with large market sizes. Switzerland is an unusual case because it has a low homeownership rate, but a high ratio of mortgage debt. Switzerland's tax system encourages debt holding by households but discourages home ownership. As a result, Switzerland has the lowest home ownership rate in the sample. Russia has the smallest sized mortgage market at a meager 2.6 percent of GDP.

High-income countries have the largest mortgage markets. As Figure 6.2 shows, a positive correlation exists between a country's level of development and the size of its mortgage market.

The level of economic development appears to be the most important determinant of the mortgage market size of a country. The simple regression reported in Figure 6.2 suggests that the variation in logarithm of per capita GDP in purchasing power parity terms explains more than 40 percent of the variation in MDO-to-GDP ratio. Such a positive relationship makes sense in that the depth and the width of financial systems are positively correlated with the level of economic development. Although the data are not presented here, the pace of mortgage market expansion appears to be positively correlated with the pace of economic growth. The growth of mortgage debt is higher in countries with faster GDP growth from 2000 to 2010.

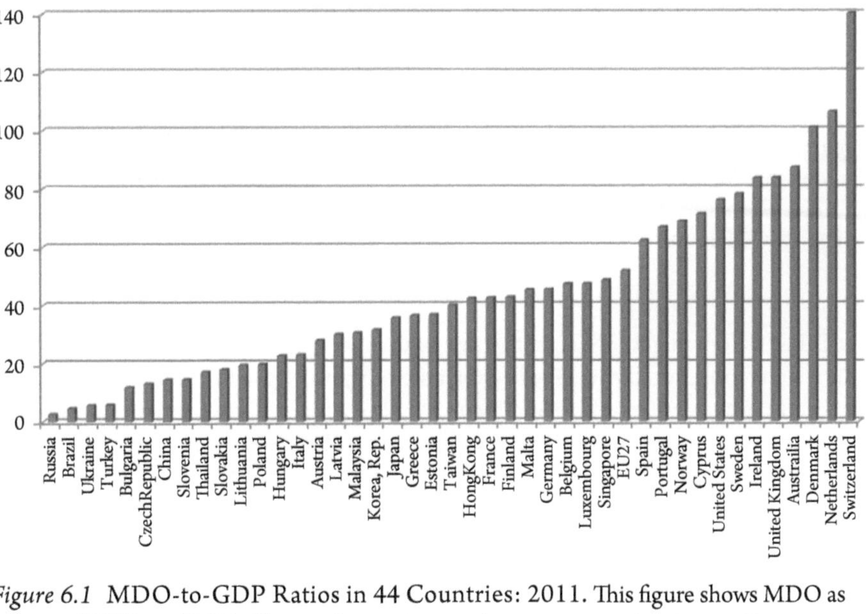

Figure 6.1 MDO-to-GDP Ratios in 44 Countries: 2011. This figure shows MDO as a share of GDP as of 2011. The number varies greatly across countries. Sources: European Mortgage Federation (2012a) and other national sources.

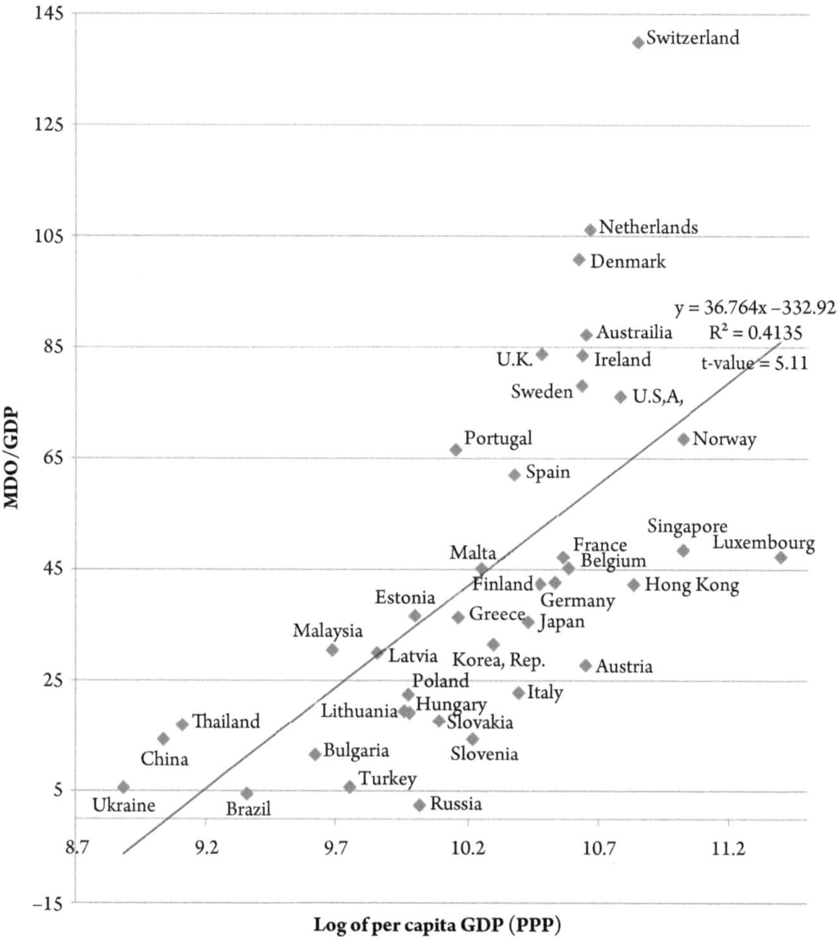

Figure 6.2 The Relationship between a Country's Level of Development and the Size of Its Mortgage Market. This figure shows a strong positive correlation between per capita income, which is based on purchasing power parity (PPP) in logarithmic form, and the MDO-to-GDP ratio.

Other factors might influence the size of the mortgage market. Another section of this chapter examines the linkage between the composition of the mortgage loan products and mortgage market size and focuses on the impact of government intervention in the mortgage market. A positive correlation exists between the magnitude of the tax break to mortgage lending and the MDO-to-GDP ratio in 17 OECD countries (Andrews, Sanchez, and Johansson 2011).

MORTGAGE INTEREST REGIME

The *mortgage interest regime* relates to the length of period during which mortgage interest remains fixed. It can be broken down into fixed to maturity, fixed for an initial period, fully variable, and other mortgage regimes. The breakdown in market share can be based on either total MDO or new lending. Monetary policy that sets a target rate, the spread between the fixed rate and the variable rate, expectation about future interest rates, the slope of the yield curve, borrowers' attitude toward interest risk, as well as funding mechanisms affects the composition of mortgage loan products by interest regime in a country. Therefore, the relative shares of interest types vary across countries and over time within a country.

Several sources of information are available on mortgage interest regimes, with some inconsistencies among different sources regarding the number of categories of interest type and the grouping of some individual countries. Both the European Central Bank (ECB) (2009) and the European Mortgage Federation (EMF) (2012b) group EU countries into fixed rate and variable rate types. The International Monetary Fund (2004) classifies 18 countries into three types: FRMs, ARMs (also called variable rates mortgages), and mixed. Warnock and Warnock (2008) identify the dominant mortgage interest type in 55 countries including both developed countries and emerging market economies in more detailed groupings: fixed, fixed (mixed), fixed/variable, fixed/choice mixed, variable (mixed), and variable. The International Monetary Fund (2011) classifies the dominant mortgage interest type of 16 developed countries and 17 emerging economies as of 2008 into mixed and variable types.

Lea (2010a) provides a detailed breakdown of mortgages offered in 10 developed economies into variable, short-term fixed, medium-term fixed, and long-term fixed. The United States is unique with a very high proportion of long-term FRMs. Andrews et al. (2011) provide information on the prevailing type of mortgage interest rate for 34 member countries as well as the shares of different types for some countries. The Financial Stability Board (2011) also provides information on the shares of different interest types for 23 countries based on the responses to a questionnaire.

Several important points concern the breakdown of mortgage interest type and its implications for housing market stability. First, as Tables 6.1 and 6.2 show, a wide variation exists in the composition of mortgage interest types across countries. Second, the composition of interest types in some EU countries has changed substantially in recent years possibly due to changes in monetary policy (European Mortgage Federation 2012b). In the case of Denmark, the dominant interest type was traditionally a 30-year FRM. But the share of FRM in total outstanding mortgages fell from 43.5 percent in 2008Q4 to 26.9 percent in 2011Q4. Now the dominant product is the medium-term FRM. During the same period, the share of ARMs rose from 49.2 percent to 71.9 percent in the United Kingdom. In Belgium, the share of FRMs in new mortgage lending fell from 85.4 percent in 2007Q3 to 28.8 percent in 2010Q1 but climbed back to 88.0 percent by 2011Q4. On the other hand, the relative shares of different interest types remained very stable during the same period.

Third, ARMs offer more affordable options for financing home purchases because they carry lower interest rates than FRMs. FRMs require wholesale capital market funding, which has a scale advantage over deposit-based funding. Therefore, countries with FRM-dominated mortgage markets are likely to have larger market size and those with ARM-dominated mortgage markets are likely to have higher homeownership rates. Although Table 6.3 suggests this finding, more careful analysis is needed to reach a

Table 6.3 **Mortgage Interest Type, Mortgage Market Size, and Housing Market Outcomes**

	FRM Type	*Mixed Type*	*ARM Type*
Number of countries included	6	6	20
Average MDO-to-GDP	69.7	41.0	47.0
Average owner occupation rate	59.0	65.4	76.3
Standard deviation of real house price increases			
1995–2000	2.69	3.01	7.70
2000–2007	3.25	3.85	6.95
2007–2011	3.23	4.43	4.75
1995–2011	4.76	5.35	8.57

Note: As this table shows, countries in which ARMs are the dominant loan products have smaller mortgage markets, higher homeownership rates, and larger volatility in housing price compared with those in which FRMs are the dominant products. The same analysis was conducted for two groups, i.e., FRMs vs. Mixed and ARMs combined, with similar results.

FRM type: Belgium, Denmark, France, Germany, The Netherlands, and the United States.

Mixed type: Austria, Canada, Italy, Japan, Russia, and Switzerland.

ARM type: Australia, Brazil, China, Finland, Greece, Hong Kong, Hungary, Indonesia, Ireland, Korea, Luxembourg, Malta, Norway, Poland, Portugal, Singapore, Slovenia, South Africa, Spain, Sweden, Thailand, and the United Kingdom.

definitive conclusion because this observation is based on a simple average of a small sample of countries for which data are available.

MORTGAGE MARKETS, GOVERNMENT INTERVENTION, AND HOUSING OUTCOMES

A crucial test of a successful mortgage finance system concerns its contributions to housing outcomes. This section examines the impact of mortgage market size and mortgage interest regime on the homeownership rate, the price of housing and its volatility, and the production of new housing. It also looks into the consequences of government intervention in mortgage markets.

The first topic examined is the impact of the expansion of mortgage lending on housing price and new residential investment. Figure 6.3 illustrates the relationships between MDO growth rate and the housing price appreciation between 2000 and 2011. The growth of mortgage lending was a contributory factor to the housing price boom in the 2000s though MDO growth had no significant impact on residential investment. These findings seem to suggest that the growth of mortgage lending led to a large price response but a small quantity response in the United States and Europe.

The second topic concerns the relationships between the growth of mortgage debt and homeownership. A simple correlation coefficient shows a negative correlation between the MDO-to-GDP ratio and the owner-occupancy rate, which might seem

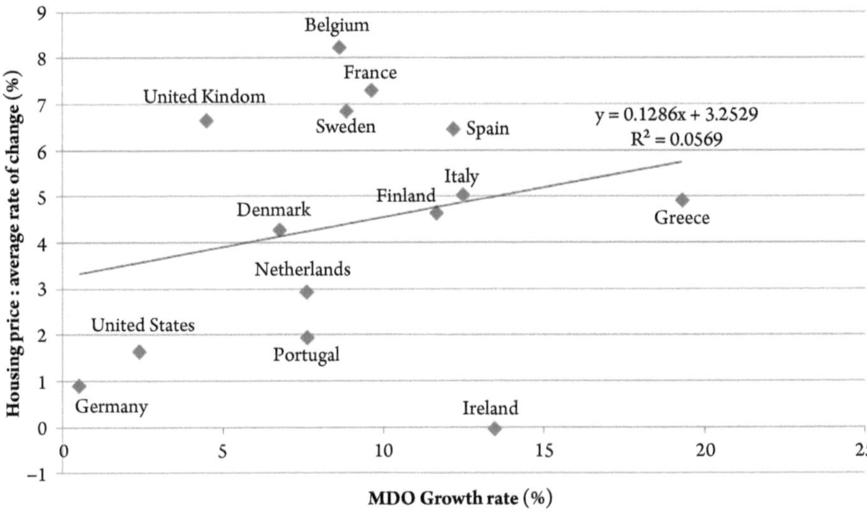

Figure 6.3 MDO Growth and Housing Price Appreciation: 2000–2011. This figure shows a positive correlation between the rate of MDO growth and the rate of increase in housing price during the period 2000–2011 in selected developed economies.

counterintuitive. This is understandable because a negative correlation exists between per capita income and the owner-occupancy rate and a positive correlation exists between per capita income and the MDO-to-GDP ratio among the countries represented in our data set. However, the suggested pair wise relationships are based on the simple correlations without controlling for other factors. For example, homeownership is lower in countries with higher incomes and high MDP-to-GDP ratios because house prices have been rising faster than income or income distribution has become more concentrated.

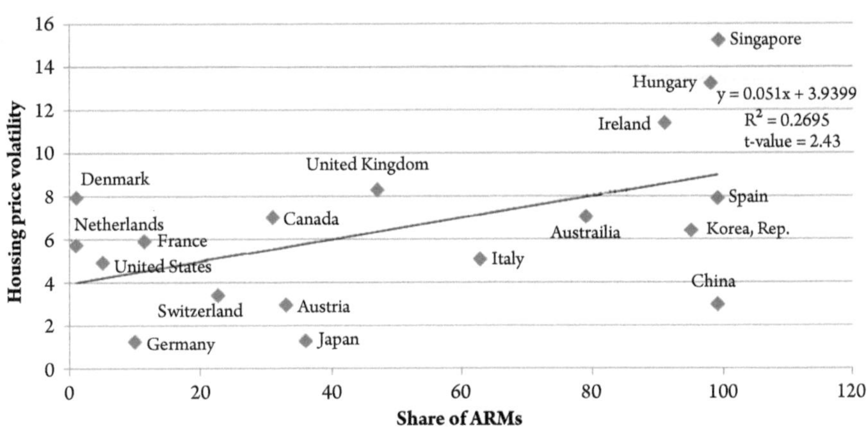

Figure 6.4 Share of ARMs and Housing Price Volatility. This graph shows that countries with larger shares of ARMs tend to have greater volatility in housing price, measured in the standard deviation of the rate of change in real housing prices.

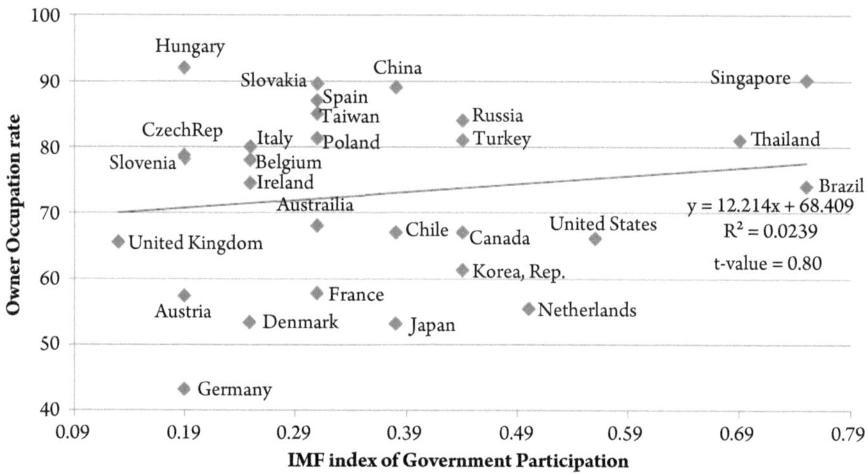

Figure 6.5 Government Intervention in Mortgage Markets and Homeownership. This figure shows that the linkage between government intervention in mortgage markets and owner occupation rate is weak.

The third topic involves the relationship between the mortgage interest regime and housing price volatility. Figure 6.4 shows that housing price volatility measured by the standard deviation of the rate of change in real housing prices tends to increase with the share of ARMs. This is consistent with the finding of International Monetary Fund (2004) based on the price data for the period 1971–2003.

Finally, the impact of government intervention in mortgage markets on homeownership is examined using two measures of government intervention. Andrews et al. (2011) suggest that a tax break in the form of interest deductibility on mortgage has no effect on the owner occupation rate in the 17 OECD countries but it lowers the effective mortgage interest rate to borrowers. Figure 6.5 shows that a similar pattern exists using the IMF index of government participation in mortgage markets constructed from a weighted sum of eight types of measures such as subsidies to first-time or other buyers upfront, mortgage interest deductibility, housing funds or government guarantee, and capital gains tax deductibility.

Characterizing Ideal Housing Finance Systems

What is the best mortgage finance system? Giving a definitive answer is difficult, if not impossible, given the diverse market conditions and institutional characteristics across countries. Nonetheless, the literature on this topic advances several criteria that can help answer the question.

CRITERION 1: INTERMEDIATION AND PRICING EFFICIENCY

The first criterion is the intermediation efficiency (IE). Having lower net intermediation costs for issuing and servicing a mortgage contract of a particular type leads to both a more efficient and social welfare-enhancing mortgage finance system (Diamond and Lea 1992). Cho (2007) translates IE as the excess yield (δ) in mortgage lending:

$$\delta = r_m - r_f - RP \tag{6.1}$$

where r_m and r_f represent the mortgage lending rate and risk-free rate, and the risk premium (RP) for mortgage repayment risk is the additional cost item to control. Diamond and Lea estimate and compare δ for selected OECD countries. As Cho elaborates, a positive δ, as perceived by market participants, will induce the participation of, and the competition among, for-profit business entities in the mortgage lending and funding markets. Furthermore, low transaction costs associated with underwriting and issuing loans, via Automated Underwriting System (AUS) or other information technology solutions, will also reduce δ and result in an efficiency gain.

Nonetheless, using δ as a performance indicator poses measurement issues in consistently estimating and comparing it across countries and time periods. The most fundamental issue has to do with quantification of a forward-looking *RP* for mortgage contracts of diverse sorts. From a conceptual viewpoint a mortgage contract represents a composite bundle of three financial assets, for which one should apply disparate cash flow analytics: a scheduled or contracted payment of principal and interest, and two competing options of (borrower's) default and prepayment (Kau, Keenan, and Muller 1993; Chinloy and Megbolugbe 1994; Deng, Quigley, and Van Order 2000).

The literature advances several conceptual frameworks for measuring the competing risks embedded, for each of these three risk components. Measuring these risk components poses several open-ended measurement issues. For example, in the United States, the 15-year or 30-year FRM with the level paying, fully amortizing, and no prepayment penalty features has been the standard contract since the Great Depression era. The prepay-option-adjusted spread (OAS) has long been the standard measure of the risk premium since the mid-1980s, which controls the prepayment risk involved with originating and funding such mortgage contracts (Fabozzi, Bhattachaya, and Berliner 2011). However, for other mortgage products with more complicated cash flow features such as the subprime option ARM, the same prepay-OAS is not applicable, and one should develop an alternative framework for measuring risk pricing. An important unresolved issue in developing such measurement frameworks is how to properly reflect a forward-looking housing price distribution (i.e., expected mean and volatility of collateral value during loan lives), for which Yang, Lin, and Cho (2011) demonstrate that risk premium can vary widely depending on how one constructs the expression for housing price volatility.

For default risk, researchers advance three main theoretical frameworks: (1) the Mertonian structural or distance-to-default model (Merton 1974; Jarrow and Turnbull 1995; (2) the bond-spread-based reduced form model (Jouini and Kallal 1995; Duffie and Singleton 1999); and (3) the Z-score type scoring model (Altman and Hotchikis 2006). Here again, the real world practice essentially follows a heuristic scoring model fitted with historical loan performance data. In the United States, the credit spread, or the risk premium for covering the mortgage default risk, corresponds to the likelihood of early payment delinquency (EPD) as well as the loss severity, or the loss given default (LGD). EPD represents the probability that a non-repayment event occurs within a few years from loan origination, while LGD measures the amount of expected loss if and when the loan defaults. A close to zero credit spread exists for a premium consumer credit score such as a Fair Isaac Company (FICO) credit score above 740 and a low leverage ratio with a LTV ratio below 60 percent. The credit spread is at least 200 basis points for a less creditworthy borrower with a FICO below 620 and a LTV above 90 percent (Chinloy and Macdonald 2005). In the international context, especially for emerging market countries, where the credit quality tends to be less reliable, loans are priced based on average credit risk so that loans incorporate a fixed credit spread for most of loans issued.

The main implication for emerging market economies and other countries with less well-developed mortgage finance systems is twofold. First, intermediation efficiency is an important criterion for minimizing transaction costs in mortgage lending. Second, proper measurement of the risk premium using a well-established analytical framework and accumulated historical data, and a marginal, rather than an average, pricing of embedded mortgage cash flow risks, is needed to achieve efficient mortgage intermediation. A related issue is the development of a depository of historical mortgage loan performance data, which enables a model- and data-driven measurement of the risk premium.

In the context of international comparison of the housing finance system, a more advanced system generally exhibits a bigger risk appetite, and market participants institute a risk-based or marginal pricing for the risk premium by measuring and pricing using a more model- and data-driven method. Table 6.4 presents two risk-based criteria for housing finance system comparison: the appetite for mortgage credit risk and for interest rate risk. Each criterion encompasses several indicators, both quantitative and qualitative. For interest rate risk, these indicators include: (1) the share of long-term FRMs in total mortgage outstanding mortgages, (2) the share of mortgage loans funded through wholesale funding vehicles such as MBS or covered bonds, and (3) the use, or non-use, of a prepayment penalty and how strictly it is enforced for a standard loan contract. For default risk, the criteria considered are: (1) maximum LTV either regulated by government or set by market participants and (2) the extent of a mortgage insurance (MI) program.

CRITERION 2: ACCESSIBILITY TO MORTGAGE CREDIT AND MARKET COMPLETENESS

The second criterion, which is a mirror image of the risk appetite, represents accessibility of mortgage credit to low-income and less-creditworthy borrowers. Often referred to as *market completeness*, this standard assesses several attributes of the housing finance system related to the accessibility of mortgage credit including: (1) the diversity of mortgage products offered, (2) the extent of market penetration to low-income and less-creditworthy borrowers, (3) the diversity of business channels (in terms of types of mortgage lenders and guarantee providers), and (4) the availability of counseling and consumer education (Mercer Oliver Wyman 2005; Lea 2010b). Based on these attributes, the United Kingdom and Denmark have the most inclusive mortgage finance systems (Mercer Oliver Wyman 2005). This chapter uses three indicators of accessibility that represent both aggregate volume of residential mortgage lending and micro-structure of the housing finance system: (1) the MDO-to-GDP ratio, (2) the extent and the diversity of mortgage lending business channel, and (3) targeted subsidy programs by government for first-time home buyers and other consumer cohorts.

Several issues are worth mentioning about the second criterion. First, extending mortgage credit to broader groups of marginal borrowers is critically linked to risk appetites. These risk appetites should be in a lockstep with the capability of properly measuring and pricing the risk premium in terms of data, analytics, and relevant experience on the part of market participants.

Second, a trade-off exists between raising DTI and LTV limits or other non-price terms in lending and mortgage cash flow risk. This trade-off occurs whether it is caused by the characteristics of borrowers, collateral, or loan products. As a case in point, consider the positive correlation between the maximum LTV allowed in each country and the volatility of house prices, or the magnitude of appreciation during a boom. Hence, public policy should consider both the benefit of increased inclusiveness of the lending system from raising DTI or LTV regulations against the ability of the system to efficiently price the heightened lending risk.

Third, for easing credit constraints for wealth-constrained households, usually young borrowers with limited accumulation of liquid assets, establishing an effective risk-sharing mechanism is an important enabling factor. A case in point is an active and well-functioning mortgage insurance system. Finally, as reflected in the Dodd-Frank Act of 2011 and establishment of the Consumer Financial Protection Bureau (CFPB) in the United States, protecting financial consumers from predatory and fraudulent lending practices is an important public policy issue.

CRITERION 3: SYSTEM STABILITY

The third criterion is the system stability of the banking system and the macro economy from a boom-bust of housing and mortgage markets. Having received heightened attention after the global financial crisis (GFC), this issue concerns imposing a market-wide rather than a financial institution-level restriction on lending practices, often referred to as *macro-prudential regulations*. Such regulations include DTI and LTV limits or capital charges in a counter-cyclical fashion, given the established fact that real estate driven systemic risk inflicts contagion upon the wider economy through various channels. As Muellbauer (2012) notes, a housing and mortgage credit cycle can affect the entire economy through private consumption or the wealth effect, through housing and non-housing investment, and through banking activities from the rise of non-performing loans and their impact on capital cushions and lending.

Ensuring system stability via DTI and LTV limits automatically sets a cap on the risk appetite as well as the extent of mortgage credit apportioned to wealth- or income-constrained households. Hence, in designing the macro-prudential policy, each country should consider all three dimensions in assessing the housing finance system to lay out the specifics of the regulation in question. The effectiveness of different policy instruments from explicit LTV and DTI limits and capital regulations should be compared with other possible regulatory means including fiscal policy mechanisms such as taxation of real estate and mortgages and subsidies for home ownership or utilizing monetary policy tools (Crowe, Dell'Ariccia, Igan, and Rabanal 2011).

Table 6.4 **Taxonomy of Mortgage Finance Systems**

	High	*Medium*	*Low*
Accessibility to mortgage credit	• **Mortgage Debt Outstanding-to-GDP ratio > 70 percent:** Australia Denmark, Ireland, The Netherlands, Sweden, the United Kingdom, and the United States	• **Mortgage Debt Outstanding-to-GDP ratio 40~70 percent:** Finland, France, Germany, Portugal, Spain, Norway	• **Mortgage Debt Outstanding-to-GDP ratio < 40 percent:** China, Hong Kong, Hungary, Greece, Italy, Korea, Poland, and Russia
	• **Highly diversified lending channel:** Australia, Ireland, The Netherlands, the United Kingdom, and the United States (3~4 types of major financial institutions)	• **Moderately diversified lending channel:** Canada, Denmark, France, Germany, Japan, Spain, and Sweden (banks and mortgage banks)	• **Minimally diversified lending channel:** China, Korea, Malaysia, Singapore, and Taiwan (predominantly by commercial banks)
	• **Well-developed targeted subsidy programs:** Australia, Singapore, Taiwan, and the United States	• **Moderately developed targeted subsidy programs:** Canada, China, Korea, Malaysia, and The Netherlands	• **Less-developed targeted subsidy programs:** Denmark, Germany, Ireland, Italy, and the United Kingdom
Risk appetite: Upside and downside interest rate risk	• **Long-term FRM share > 80 percent:** Denmark, The Netherlands, and the United States (strongly correlated with the share of whole-sale funding)	• **Long-term FRM share 20~80 percent:** Japan, Germany, and the United Kingdom	• **Long-term FRM share < 20 percent:** Australia, China, Ireland, Korea, Singapore, and Spain
	• **Whole-sale funding via MBS/CB > 60 percent:** Denmark, Spain, and the United States	• **Whole-sale funding via MBS/CB 30~60 percent:** Canada, Ireland, The Netherlands, and the United Kingdom	• **Whole-sale funding via MBS/CB < 30 percent:** Australia, China, Germany, Japan, Korea, and Singapore
	• **Predominantly no prepayment penalty:** Denmark and the United States	• **Prepayment penalty being flexibly enforced:** The United Kingdom and most European countries (e.g., wavering on relocation, medical emergency)	• **Prepayment penalty being strictly enforced:** Korea and most Asian countries

Table 6.4 **continued**

	High	*Medium*	*Low*
A. Risk appetite (2): Borrower default risk	• **Max LTV non-regulated or above 90 percent:** Australia, The Netherlands, Portugal, Spain, France, Sweden, the United Kingdom, and the United States	• **Max LTV non-regulated or set at 80~90 percent:** Canada, Denmark, Germany, Italy, Japan, and Switzerland	• **Max LTV regulated and set below 80 percent:** China, Korea, Singapore, and Taiwan (the QRM debate in the United States after the GFC); DTI, CB. and other lending criteria being relevant as well
	• **Highly active MI programs:** Australia, Canada, France, The Netherlands, and the United States	• **Moderately active MI programs:** Hong Kong, Israel, Italy, Spain, Sweden, and the United Kingdom	• **Minimal or inactive MI programs:** China, Korea, India, and Thailand

Note: This table provides a taxonomy of mortgage finance systems in various countries according to the three broad criteria each of which is subdivided into two or three sub-indicators.

The housing finance systems of various countries can be assessed based on each of the following three criteria: (1) access to mortgage lending service, (2) the appetite for credit risk, and (3) the appetite for interest rate risk. Table 6.4 summarizes the criteria and the groupings of countries into each category. Each cell has two or three indicators and consequently a particular country can fall into different categories depending on the indicators.

Three indicators of access to mortgage credit (market penetration) should be considered. The first is the familiar MDO-to-GDP ratio. High MDO-to-GDP countries include The Netherlands, Denmark, the United Kingdom, Ireland, Sweden, and the United States. The medium MDO-to-GDP countries are Norway, Spain, and Portugal. The low MDO-to-GDP countries are Germany, France, Greece, Italy, Austria, Japan, and Korea. The second indicator concerns the diversity of available lending channels. In China, Korea, and Singapore, commercial banks are the dominant lending channel. The United States and the United Kingdom have three to four lending channels. The third indicator is about the existence of targeted subsidies. Australia, Singapore, and the United States have well developed subsidy programs while such programs are less well developed in Germany and United Kingdom.

The appetite for interest rate risk is the second criterion to be considered. The first indicator for this criterion is the share of long-term FRMs. The groupings are consistent with those of mortgage interest regime discussed in the earlier section. The second indicator concerns the share of the wholesale capital market funding through MBS or covered bonds. Denmark, Spain, and the United States score high on this index, whereas Australia, Japan, and Singapore fall behind. The third indicator is the existence of a prepayment penalty. The United States represents one extreme where long-term FRMs dominate the market but no prepayment penalty is enforced. Korea and other Asian countries are at the other extreme with ARMs and a prepayment penalty.

The third criterion is the appetite for borrower default risk. Some countries have LTV ceilings exceeding 90 percent such as Australia, The Netherlands, and the United States. Other countries such as China, Korea, and Taiwan enforce ceilings on LTV at 80 percent or below. Mortgage insurance is widely used in Canada, The Netherlands, and the United States, while it is in minimal usage or inactive in China and Korea (Financial Stability Board 2011).

Summary and Conclusions

This chapter focuses on an international comparative analysis of mortgage markets. Key findings of the analysis reveal the following.

- The size of mortgage market, measured by the share of MDO as a percentage of GDP, varies across countries.
- Mortgage market size is positively correlated with the level of economic development, measured in per capita income. On the other hand, government intervention appears to have a negligible impact on the size of the mortgage market except the interest deductibility from taxable income in some OECD countries.

- Variations exist in the make-up of lending institutions, funding mechanisms, terms of loan products offered, and the extent and modality of government interventions in mortgage markets around the world. Although these characteristics change slowly over time, a shift in interest rate type can occur over a reasonably short period in some countries.
- Funding sources and the dominant interest type of mortgage loans are interrelated because long-term funding through capital markets is the most suitable for fixed rate mortgages.
- The growth of mortgage lending and the interest type of mortgage loans have affected house price appreciation and its volatility. The rapid expansion of mortgage credit was a key driver of the latest global house price boom. The countries with ARMs as the dominant loan product tend to have more volatile changes in house prices.
- Although a major goal of a well-functioning mortgage market is to promote homeownership, the correlation between the size of the mortgage market and the owner-occupation rate is negative. This is because a well-functioning mortgage market is strongly positively correlated with per capita income, whereas owner occupancy has a negative correlation with per capita income. However, other factors such as high house price-to-income ratios or skewed income distribution may be at work.

An ideal housing finance system should assess the positive and negative aspects of mortgage markets of various countries based on specific criteria related to the desirable features. Although difficulties exist in reaching a consensus on an ideal housing finance system, the evidence suggests desirable features of mortgage markets intermediation and pricing efficiency, accessibility to mortgage credit and market completeness, and system stability. Table 6.4 presents a taxonomy of countries based on an assessment of the mortgage markets for specific indicators pertaining to access to mortgage lending services, appetite for credit risk, and appetite for interest rate risk.

The availability of attractive mortgages is a necessary but not a sufficient condition for affordable housing. The increased demand fueled by mortgage lending constrained by inelastic housing supply will lead to large price responses and a small quantity response (Kim 1995; Malpezzi and Wachter 2005). The analysis of a small sample suggests that growth of the mortgage market did not significantly affect new residential investment. In this context, finding no clear positive correlation between the size of the mortgage market and the homeownership rate in some countries is not surprising. In fact, a country with a very large mortgage market and a highly inelastic housing supply system can have a low homeownership rate, despite large tax relief for borrowing costs. The Netherlands is an example.

Another policy issue concerns the diversity of loan products offered. Some housing finance products appear in the market to disappear later due to changes in demand or government policy. More financing options enhance consumer welfare only when consumers receive accurate information about loan products and they have sufficient financial literacy to process the information in order to make rational choices. Therefore, consumers could be worse off with too much product diversity and hence it might be best if a small number of standardized loan products be made available (Scanlon, Lunde, and Whitehead 2008).

Going forward, an important question is how mortgage markets will play out once the housing market recovers from the hangover of the global financial crisis. Lenders reduced the volume of new lending and imposed tight loan underwriting criteria. Some product innovation introduced in Europe during the 1990s and early 2000s reversed in the wake of the crisis (Scanlon, Lunde, and Whitehead 2011). Governments have heightened regulatory interventions through macro-prudential instruments. The question is how best to enhance financial inclusion by extending access to credit to more households while maintaining financial stability.

Discussion Questions

1. Identify a popular indicator to measure the size of a country's mortgage market and its key determinants.
2. Identify two main funding methods for mortgage lending and discuss the pros and cons of each.
3. Discuss the general characteristics of ARMs and FRMs in terms of their impact on housing market outcomes.
4. List the criteria that can be used to gauge how well a country's mortgage finance system is functioning.

Acknowledgments

The authors acknowledge valuable comments by Michael Lea and research assistance by In Sik Koo.

References

Altman, Edward I., and Edith Hotchikis. 2006. "Corporate Credit Scoring—Insolvency Risk Models." In Edward I. Altman and Edith Hotchkiss, eds., *Corporate Financial Distress and Bankruptcy*, 3rd edn., 233–264. Hoboken, NJ: John Wiley & Sons.

Andrews, Dan, Aida Caldera Sanchez, and Asa Johansson. 2011. "Housing Markets and Structural Policies in OECD Countries." OECD Economics Department Working Papers No. 836.

Ben-Shahar, Danny, Charles Leung, and Seow-Eng Ong. 2008. *Mortgage Markets Worldwide*. New York: Blackwell.

Campbell, John. 2012. "Mortgage Market Design." *Review of Finance* 17:3, 1–33.

Chinloy, Peter, and Nancy Macdonald. 2005. "Subprime Lenders and Mortgage Market Completion." *Journal of Real Estate Finance and Economics* 30:2, 153–165.

Chinloy, Peter, and Isaac Megboluge. 1994. "Hedonic Mortgages." *Journal of Housing Research* 5:1, 1–21.

Cho, Man. 2007. "180 Years' Evolution of the US Mortgage Banking System: Lessons for Emerging Mortgage Markets." *International Real Estate Review* 10:1, 171–212.

Crowe, Christopher, Giovanni Dell'Ariccia, Deniz Igan, and Pau Rabanal. 2011. "Policies for Macrofinancial Stability: Options to Deal with Real Estate Booms." IMF Staff Discussion Note SDN/11/02.

Deng, Yongheng, John Quigley, and Robert Van Order. 2000. "Mortgage Termination, Heterogeneity and the Exercise of Mortgage Options." *Econometrica* 68:2, 275–307.

Diamond, Douglas, and Michael Lea, 1992. "Housing Finance in Developed Countries: An International Comparison of Efficiency." *Journal of Housing Research* 3:1, 1–271.

Duffie, Darrell, and Kenneth J. Singleton. 1999. "Modeling Term Structure of Defaultable Bonds." *Review of Financial Studies* 12:4, 687–720.

European Central Bank (ECB). 2009. "Housing Finance in the EURO Arena." Occasional Discussion Paper, European Central Bank.

European Mortgage Federation. 2012a. *HYPOSTAT 2011: A Review of Europe's Mortgage and Housing Markets*. Brussels: European Mortgage Federation.

European Mortgage Federation. 2012b. *Study on Mortgage Interest Rates in the EU*. Brussels: European Mortgage Federation.

Fabozzi, Frank, Anand Bhattacharya, and William Berliner. 2011. *Mortgage Backed Securities: Products, Structuring, and Analytical Techniques*. 2nd edn. Hoboken, NJ: John Wiley & Sons.

Financial Stability Board. 2011. *FSB Principles for Sound Mortgage Underwriting Practices*. Washington, DC: Financial Stability Board. http://www.fsb.gov.

International Monetary Fund. 2004. Chapter 2, "Three Current Issues." In *World Economic Outlook*. Washington, DC: International Monetary Fund.

International Monetary Fund (IMF). 2011. "Housing Finance and Financial Stability—Back to the Basics." *Global Financial Stability Report*. Washington, DC: International Monetary Fund.

Jarrow, Robert M., and Stuart M. Turnbull. 1995. "Pricing Derivatives on Financial Securities Subject to Credit Risk." *Journal of Finance* 50:1, 53–85.

Jouini, Elyès, and Hédi Kallal. 1995. "Martingales and Arbitrage in Multiperiod Securities Markets." *Journal of Economic Theory* 66:1, 179–197.

Kau, James, Donald Keenan, and William Muller III. 1993. "An Option-Based Pricing Model of Private Mortgage Insurance." *Journal of Risk and Insurance* 60:2, 288–299.

Kim, Kyung-Hwan. 1995. "Access to Credit, Terms of Housing Finance and Affordability of Housing." *Housing Finance International* 9:4, 22–27.

Lam, Alan. 2011. "Government Interventions in Housing Finance Markets: An International Overview." Working Paper, Housing and Urban Development Department, Washington, DC.

Lea, Michael. 2010a. "International Comparison of Mortgage Product Offerings." Research Institute for Housing America. http://www.housingamerican.com.

Lea, Michael. 2010b. "Alternative Forms of Mortgage Finance: What Can We Learn from Other Countries." Paper prepared for Harvard Joint Center for Housing Studies National Symposium.

Lea, Michael. 2012. "Covered Bonds." In Susan J. Smith, Marja Elsinga, Lorna Fox O'Mahony, Ong Seow Eng, Susan Wachter, and Anthony B. Sanders, eds., *International Encyclopedia of Housing and Home*, Volume 1, 255–261. Oxford: Elsevier.

Lea, Michael, and Anthony B. Sanders. 2011. "Government Policy and the Fixed Rate Mortgage." *Annual Review of Financial Economics* 3: 223–234.

Malpezzi, Stephen, and Susan M. Wachter. 2005. "The Role of Speculation in Real Estate Cycles." *Journal of Real Estate Literature* 13:2, 143–164.

Mercer Oliver Wyman. 2005. *Risk and Funding in European Residential Mortgages: Responding to Changes in Mortgage Demand*. London: Mortgage Insurance Trade Association.

Merton, Robert C. 1974. "On the Pricing of Corporate Debt: The Risk Structure of Interest Rates." *Journal of Finance* 29:2, 449–470.

Muellbauer, John. 2012. "When Is a Housing Market Overheated Enough to Threaten Stability?" Paper presented at the BIS-Bank of Australia Conference, Sydney, Australia.

Scanlon, Kathleen, Jens Lunde, and Christine Whitehead. 2008. "Product Development in European Mortgage Markets: More Choice, More Risk." *European Journal of Housing Policy* 8:2, 109–131.

Scanlon, Kathleen, Jens Lunde, and Christine Whitehead. 2011. "Responding to the Housing and Financial Crises: Mortgage Lending, Mortgage Products and Government Policies." *International Journal of Housing Policy* 11:1, 23–49.

Smith, Susan J., Marja Elsinga, Lorna Fox O'Mahony, Ong Seow Eng, Susan Wachter, Richard K. Green, and Kyung-Hwan Kim, eds. 2012. *International Encyclopedia of Housing and Home,* Volume 4. Oxford: Elsevier.

Warnock, Francis E., and Veronica C. Warnock. 2012 "Developing Housing Finance Systems." In *Reserve Bank of Australia-Bank for International Settlements Conference Volume,* 49–67.

Warnock, Veronica C., and Francis E. Warnock. 2008 "Markets and Housing Finance: 2008." *Journal of Housing Economics* 17:3, 239–251.

Yang, Tyler, Che-Chun Lin, and Man Cho. 2011. "Collateral Risk in Residential Mortgage Defaults." *Journal of Real Estate Finance and Economics* 42:2, 115–142.

7

Development of the Market for Mortgage-Backed Securities

STEPHEN A. BUSER
Emeritus Professor of Finance, The Ohio State University

JOHN J. MCCONNELL
Emanuel T. Weiler Distinguished Professor of Management, Purdue University

Introduction

This chapter has four main objectives. The first is to provide a historical context for the development and evolution of mortgage-backed securities (MBS). Factors arising from continuing government support for homeownership are considered along with the economic interests of providers and consumers of mortgage finance. The second objective is to provide a summary of the evolving nature of the MBS market. The trend in the volume of aggregate MBS offerings is considered in addition to innovations in MBS products. The third is to summarize studies that evaluate the economic effects that the market for MBS has had on the cost and availability of mortgage finance. The final objective is to consider lessons that can be learned from the development of the MBS market.

Historical Foundation

The ability to pledge real estate as collateral for a loan has been traced to English common law as early as 1190 A.D. (Jones 1882). Mason (2001) and others have observed that nominal maturities for early mortgage loans were short by current standards, often three to five years. Periodic payments were typically limited to interest only. The full principal amount would be due as a balloon payment at maturity. Although such provisions might have been reasonable for wealthy borrowers in need of temporary liquidity, they were more challenging for potential borrowers of modest means. New structures arose for mortgage lending in response to subsequent industrial development and corresponding growth in the middle class.

The building and loan society (B&L), which has been traced to England in the eighteenth century, provided an alternative structure (Bodfish 1931). A defining feature of early B&Ls was that their members owned them. Each member of a B&L was required to make periodic investments until attaining a minimum level of investment. The member was then eligible for a mortgage loan. The required initial investment effectively served as the down payment, and continuing payments to the B&L represented interest and principal payments on the mortgage. Although nominal maturities remained relatively short, as an equity investor of a B&L, even a member of the middle class had an enhanced expectation for timely renewal of a mortgage.

Based on the success of English B&Ls, similar institutions emerged in other developing economies, including the United States, where the first B&L was created in Philadelphia in 1831 (Mason 2001). As the middle class continued to grow, households seeking mortgages grew faster than the established members of B&Ls who had repaid their loans and were able to contribute funds for new mortgages. As a result, B&Ls began to adopt the commercial bank practice of accepting temporary deposits of short-term funds to supplement scheduled contributions from members. The shift from equity to deposit financing led to a corresponding relabeling from "building and loan" to "savings and loan," or simply "thrift."

The thrift industry grew rapidly. By 1930 the National Association for U.S. Building and Loan Societies included 11,777 member institutions (Ewalt 1964). As a reflection of the underlying change in financial structure for member associations in 1930 the National Association became the U.S. Savings and Loan League.

Frederiksen (1894) documents efforts to meet the growing demand for mortgage funding with closer ties to the modern MBS market. As early as the 1850s, some lenders in the United States adopted the practice of originating mortgage loans and selling rights to third party investors to receive principal and interest payments. Mortgages were typically adjustable rate loans secured by farm property. Nominal loan maturities remained in the customary range of three to five years.

Early mortgage banks were referred to as a mortgage guarantee houses. Each mortgage bank guaranteed the payment of interest and principal of the loans it originated and sold. The ultimate investors were wealthy individuals who expected to retain their investments until the maturity of the loans because no secondary market existed for trading either whole loans or interests in them. According to Klaman (1959), this general model of early mortgage banking remained intact until the early 1930s. Following the collapse of real estate prices that accompanied the onset of the Great Depression of the 1930s, many mortgage guarantee houses could not redeem their outstanding mortgage bonds. Mortgage guarantee houses disappeared as a major source of funding for real estate markets, at least temporarily.

The Great Depression was difficult for financial institutions and especially for thrifts. Many workers with mortgages lost their jobs and defaulted. Workers who either lost their jobs or had their working hours reduced began to draw down their savings rather than add to them. Both trends, mortgage defaults and deposit withdrawals, presented major challenges for thrifts. The threat that a given institution would be unable to meet the withdrawal demands of its deposit customers led to runs on deposits. Such runs, and even the mere concern about potential runs, reduced the ability and willingness of institutions to refinance mortgages as they came due.

During the Great Depression, the federal government created new agencies. The Federal Housing Administration (FHA) was created in 1933 and offered federal government guarantees to mortgage lenders offering long-term, fixed rate, and fully amortizing mortgages (Green and Wachter 2005). In 1944, the Veterans Administration (VA) established a similar guarantee program. In 1946, the Farmers Home Administration (FmHA) was established to insure farm and rural loans.

The federal government established the Federal National Mortgage Association in 1938, commonly referred to as Fannie Mae. The ostensible objective of Fannie Mae was to provide liquidity to lenders by offering to purchase mortgages that met certain standards, including the requirement that loans have fixed rates of interest and be fully amortizing loans with 30-year maturities. Although the charter for Fannie Mae allowed for the issuance of MBS products, the early approach was to purchase whole loans and hold them in portfolio as a long-term investor. To fund these purchases, Fannie Mae issued bonds of its own, much like mortgage guarantee houses did as early as the late 1800s (Fannie Mae, 1966). In contrast to private guarantee houses, and despite the public-private nature of the entity, investors generally viewed Fannie Mae bonds as having an implicit federal guarantee (Frame and White 2007).

In 1968, which was the same year Fannie Mae was fully privatized, the federal government created the Government National Mortgage Association, or GNMA, commonly referred to as Ginnie Mae. In 1970 the federal government created the Federal Home Loan Mortgage Corporation, or FHLMC, commonly referred to as Freddie Mac. As in the case of Fannie Mae, Freddie Mac was a shareholder-owned corporation with no explicit federal government guarantee. However, Ginnie Mae had a slightly different charter. At its inception, Ginnie Mae was authorized to issue MBS products where the underlying mortgages were FHA, FmHA, and VA loans. Ginnie Mae was also authorized to guarantee the timely payment of interest and principal on loans used in support of Ginnie Mae MBS.

Efforts to promote homeownership by stabilizing the funding and operation of banks and thrifts were generally successful. However, the practice of relying on short-term funding for long-term investments gave rise to a new problem referred to as a *maturity mismatch*. The early development of the MBS market provided an opportunity for mortgage lenders to mitigate the maturity mismatch by selling a portion of their portfolios. By virtue of the restrictions on loans eligible for early MBS pools, there was a corresponding limit on the ability of financial institutions to reduce the maturity mismatch problem by selling mortgages they had underwritten.

The effects of these structural problems became increasingly severe in the 1970s when the U.S. Treasury had to sharply increase its rate of borrowing to finance growing costs of the Vietnam War. In response to increasing Treasury rates, banks and thrifts had to increase the rates of interest they offered on deposits. Higher rates on deposits led to higher interest rates for new mortgages. The higher interest rates on new mortgages caused a decline in the value of mortgages with lower fixed rates already in thrift portfolios. Ultimately, the reduction in the value of existing mortgages caused a corresponding reduction in equity value for thrifts.

In response to the severity of the maturity mismatch problem, the federal government relaxed certain regulatory standards for banks and thrifts that had been in place since the Great Depression. The government relaxed restrictions for the types of deposits banks and thrifts were permitted to accept and the interest rates banks and thrifts were permitted to offer on deposits. Collectively, the restrictions on forms of deposits and interest rates offered had been referred to as Regulation Q, or simply "Reg Q," by virtue of the specific section of a bill that had been passed in response to the Great Depression. The government also relaxed restrictions on the types of investments that federally insured banks and thrifts could make. These restrictions were initially introduced in yet another bill, termed the Glass-Steagall Act, which had been passed in the aftermath of the Great Depression.

The elimination of Reg Q was intended to provide greater access to funds for banks and thrifts. However, the repeal led to increased competition and a corresponding reduction in profit margins. With respect to the repeal of the Glass-Steagall Act, banks and thrifts could use the new freedom to take positions in financial products such as interest rate derivatives, to hedge against maturity mismatch risks. Unfortunately, the new freedom also permitted financial institutions to engage in risk enhancing rather than risk mitigating investments.

Despite the arguably good intentions of regulatory authorities and perhaps as a result of these efforts, nearly one half of all thrifts either failed or were sold before failure between 1986 and 1995 (Federal Deposit Insurance Corporation, 2014). As a result of the failures, the Federal Savings and Loan Insurance Corporation (FSLIC) was itself declared insolvent in 1989. A new government entity, the Resolution Trust Corporation, was created to manage thrift liquidations with the FDIC taking over deposit insurance. As discussed in the next section, the virtual collapse of the former savings and loan industry set the stage for a rapid expansion of the MBS market.

Formal Development of the Modern MBS Market

Ginnie Mae issued the first MBS in 1970. The initial offering had a face value of $70 million, and all of the underlying loans were fully amortizing with 30-year maturities. Guarantees by the VA or insurance by the FHA or FmHA covered all loans. The initial Ginnie Mae MBS was structured as a simple pass through. Each investor who bought a given fraction of the MBS received a corresponding share of any monthly payments of interest and principal from the underlying mortgage loans.

As had been the case for even earlier private offerings by mortgage guarantee houses, mortgage bankers originated the underlying loans for Ginnie Mae MBS. They retained the right and the obligation to service the underlying loans. Such service included collecting monthly mortgage payments of principal and interest along with payments for taxes and insurance. The mortgage bankers remitted these payments to appropriate parties, net of an agreed upon servicing fee. Each originator as servicer accepted the additional obligations of pursuing delinquent mortgagors, foreclosing on loans in default, securing and selling any properties recovered from foreclosures, and remitting recoveries on foreclosed properties to the ultimate investors. Except for relatively modest variations, this general model for the originator and servicer has remained largely intact through the present time.

Freddie Mac and Fannie Mae made their initial MBS offerings in 1971 and 1981, respectively. As with Ginnie Mae, the initial offerings by Freddie Mac and Fannie Mae were simple pass-through securities. The pool of underlying mortgages was limited to fully amortizing 30-year mortgages that were insured either by the FHA or FmHA or guaranteed by the VA.

Innovations in MBS have generally taken one of two forms. One class of innovations relates to the payment structure of the MBS. The second has to do with the underlying collateral. With respect to payment structure, cash flows for certain MBS, referred to as *collateralized mortgage obligations* (CMOs), are reorganized into tranches that enable investors to choose among a wide array of payoff patterns. With respect to collateral, the MBS market currently consists of two sectors.

One sector, the agency market, offers a guarantee of timely payment of interest and principal to investors. The agency market includes MBS sponsored by Ginnie Mae, Fannie Mae, or Freddie Mac. The last two agencies are known as *government sponsored mortgage enterprises* (GSEs). Only loans that meet certain criteria are acceptable for securitization under the auspices of one of the GSEs. Such loans are referred to as "conforming."

The other sector has no explicit or implicit federal guarantee. The collateral risk of default is covered within the MBS or by private insurance. The private sector has developed the *private label MBS market*. Loans backing private label MBS include non-agency loans and so-called "subprime" and "Alt-A" loans, which are collectively referred to as *nonprime loans*.

Freddie Mac issued the first CMO in 1983 (Roll 1987a, b). Early CMOs were structured such that holders of the first tranche initially received all principal payments, plus appropriate interest, until the first tranche was fully repaid and thus retired. Principal and interest payments were then paid to the second tranche until that tranche was fully retired, and so on until all of the underlying loans were fully repaid. During the period in which the tranches were being retired in order of priority, each of the tranches received its pro rata share of the monthly interest payments. The payment was based on the remaining amount of principal outstanding in the tranche and the tranche's stated coupon interest rate. Such structures were named *sequential pay bonds* in recognition of the fact that principal payments were made according to the sequential ordering of the tranches.

Early CMOs were backed by GSE insured or guaranteed mortgages. As a consequence, investors in these MBS had little concern about default of the underlying loans. In the mid-1990s, private entities began offering MBS of their own. Certain features were similar for the private label and GSE MBS, such as the design of tranches and the scheduled payment structures. For private label MBS, investors bear the risk that mortgagors will default on underlying loans. Arguably, this risk is compounded because mortgage loans that do not meet the GSE criteria of conforming loans support most private label CMOs. Indeed, private label issuers could even include nonprime loans in their respective mortgage pools.

CMOs with default risk are structured so as to provide credit protection for more senior tranches in the event of defaults on underlying mortgages. For many MBS structures, loan originators retain the most credit sensitive tranche, which is sometimes referred to as the *residual* or *equity tranche*. However, as events between 2007 and 2009 demonstrated, even for a senior tranche, an investor bears credit risk when enough of the underlying loans default.

The continuing evolution of the market for MBS products has given rise to a corresponding restructuring of risks for investors. Investments in the underlying collateral generally have two forms of risk: interest rate risk and credit or default risk. Given that either the federal government or the GSEs guaranteed the earliest MBS, investors recognized credit risk but it played a relatively limited role. Hence, as in the case of early pass through securities, for early CMO products offered by GSEs, the more consequential risk was interest rate risk. By virtue of the restructuring of cash flows interest rate risk can have a complex effect on the pricing of CMOs tranches.

Given their long maturities, fixed rate 30-year mortgages are susceptible to the customary risk of any fixed rate bond. If rates rise dramatically, the price of the bond can decline dramatically and the investor can suffer substantial losses in value. Fixed rate mortgages, especially FHA, VA, and most GSE conforming loans, can be fully paid off at any time without penalty. If interest rates decline, mortgagors have an incentive to pay off their loans early and to refinance into a lower rate loan. This ability to pay off the loan before maturity is the borrower's *prepayment option*.

Thus, investors in MBS products bear two types of interest rate risk. If rates rise, the value of their investment declines. If rates fall, such that the value of a fixed rate bond increases, the mortgagor has the option to prepay the underlying loans. The former risk is *interest rate risk* and the latter risk is so-called *prepayment risk*.

Even with sequential pay tranches, considerable uncertainty remains as to when the early pay tranches will be paid off. To reduce this uncertainty further, tranches were created that specified a range in which early payoffs would be directed to the first pay tranche with excess payoffs being directed to later tranches. Such tranches were labeled *planned amortization class* (PAC) or *targeted amortization class* (TAC) bonds.

Even these bonds bear interest rate risk as the underlying mortgages are fixed rate loans. An increase in rates is likely to slow prepayments and depress the value of even shorter term PAC and TAC tranches. To reduce interest rate risk further, issuers introduced floating rate bonds. Since the underlying loans are fixed rate, a floating rate bond meant that another tranche with a rate that moved opposite of the floating rate was required. This gave rise to the *inverse floating rate tranche*. In concert with the creation of other types of tranches, issuers created securities in which one tranche received only the interest (IOs) from the mortgages, which meant the creation of a security that received only principal (POs).

Creating one tranche that bears less risk does not mean that the risk disappears. It just means that the risk is shifted to another tranche. Less risky tranches are subject to less prepay and interest rate risk than are MBS pass-throughs, which means that other tranches are more subject to prepay and interest rate risk. At their peak, some CMOs were issued with as many as 50 different tranches with some tranches bearing extreme interest rate and prepayment risk.

The Rise, Fall, and Partial Recovery of the MBS Market

The MBS market grew slowly at first. According to the Securities Industry and Financial Markets Association (SIFMA), by 1996 the total face value for all MBS offerings was still less than $500 million. Private label MBS offerings accounted for only 10 percent of this modest total. By 1998, the volume of MBS offerings had more than doubled to exceed $1 trillion. Private label offerings had increased by a factor of four. In 2003, the annual levels for GSE and private label MBS offerings were $2.8 trillion and $400 million, respectively. In concert with a subsequent decline in GSE offerings, the market for private label offerings continued to grow, reaching an all-time high of more than $900 million in 2006.

As fate would have it, 2006 was also the initial year of what has since been called the "Great Recession." During 2008 the face value for new private label MBS offerings was only $45 million or 5 percent of the peak of $900 million in 2006. The effects of the Great Recession were not as severe for the GSEs. According to SIFMA, GSE offerings of MBS reached a low of $1.2 trillion in 2006. During 2009 GSE offerings of MBS had recovered to $2.0 trillion. In contrast, the level of private label MBS offerings was $30 million in 2009.

Both the pattern and timing of changes in issuing volume for MBS were similar to those in real estate prices. According to the Case-Shiller House Price Index, home prices increased nationwide by more than 80 percent from the beginning of 1996 through July 2006, and then declined by more than 30 percent from July 2006 through the end of 2009. Between 2006 and 2009, the rate of prime home mortgage defaults increased by more than a factor of six. The average prices for AA-rated and AAA-rated nonprime CMO tranches originated in 2006 declined by 70 percent and 20 percent, respectively. This interval witnessed the demise of the major investment banks Bear Stearns, Lehman Brothers, and Merrill Lynch along with major mortgage originator/servicers including Countrywide, Downey, and IndyMac. In each case, linkages were made to investments in MBS.

Economic Effects of the MBS Market

One rationale for establishing the GSEs was the belief that a national secondary market for mortgages would reduce the cost of homeownership by providing greater liquidity for lenders. The creation of government sponsored MBS was a step toward this goal. The argument customarily advanced is that tradable MBS would attract a wider set of investors to the mortgage market that, in turn, would lower the cost of housing finance.

The creation of CMOs was another step along this path. Specifically, the idea was that some investors were reluctant to become active in the MBS market. Long-term maturities coupled with the mortgagor's prepayment option meant that the actual maturity of the security was unknown. This exposed a potential investor to interest rate risk and uncertainty as to the actual maturity date of the security. Issuers viewed sequential pay CMOs as a way to overcome the disadvantages of simple pass through MBS. The notion was that an investor who prefers a shorter-term security buys an early pay tranche. Someone who is willing to bear more risk, presumably for a higher expected yield, purchases a later pay tranche.

One rationale for the creation of MBS is the idea that such securities, especially those with a government guarantee, can be traded in an anonymous market in which investors need not search for information about ultimate borrowers. This reduction in search cost on the part of investors can reduce the cost of mortgage financing which provides greater access to funding at lower cost to homeowners.

An offsetting argument is that shareholders owned Fannie Mae and Freddie Mac. If the management of the GSEs acts in the interests of shareholders, any value created by the GSEs' securitization activities will be passed on to shareholders in the form of higher dividends and stock prices. That is, if securitization creates value, why would management of the GSEs pass on those benefits to mortgagors? Whether the GSEs' MBS programs actually reduce the cost of mortgage credit and increased homeownership are empirical questions.

Hendershott and Shilling (1989) examine the impact of the GSEs' MBS programs on the cost of mortgage credit. Over the period 1977 through 1987, the interval during which Fannie Mae and Freddie Mac became active in the MBS market, the percentage of loans that conformed to agency standards that were securitized increased from less than 5 percent to more than 50 percent. One factor that determines whether a loan is eligible for securitization by the GSEs is the size of the loan. Hendershott and Shilling examine loans originated in California in 1978 and 1986 that were conforming on all dimensions except loan size. After controlling for other factors, they find that rates on conforming loans were 15 to 30 basis points less than those of "non-conforming jumbo" loans. The authors conclude that the potential for securitization reduces the cost of mortgage financing to homebuyers.

Kolari, Fraser, and Anari (1998) conduct a cointegration analysis using data for 1985 through 1995. Their dependent variable is the yield spread between residential mortgage loans and Treasury securities. Their key independent variable is the fraction of all mortgage loans securitized during a quarter. They find that a 10 percent increase in the fraction of loans securitized leads to a 20 basis point decline in mortgage rates.

Ambrose, Buttimer, and Thibodeau (2001) provide a slightly different perspective on the interest rate differential of jumbo versus conforming loans. Mortgage rates are a function of the volatility of the underlying asset. Using data from the Dallas, Texas area, they estimate the volatility of property prices underlying jumbo and non-jumbo loans. They find that properties underlying jumbo loans have a higher volatility than those underlying conforming loans. After controlling for the difference in volatilities, and using simulation analysis, they attribute a maximum yield differential of 16 basis points to GSE activities.

Naranjo and Toevs (2002) distinguish between the two different forms of GSE activities, mortgage purchases and securitizations. They use a cointegration analysis along with data on conforming and non-conforming originations from 1986 through 1998 to separate the two effects. They find that GSE purchases and securitizations result in a jumbo/non-jumbo rate differential of 21 basis points. They conclude that the effect of purchases is much stronger than that of securitizations.

Ambrose, LaCour-Little, and Sanders (2005) adopt an even broader perspective on the conforming/non-conforming rate differential. Non-conforming loans can differ from conforming loans on dimensions other than loan size. They use 26,179 loans originated from 1995 through 1997 and initially replicate the results of earlier studies by documenting a yield spread for conforming versus non-conforming loans of 25 basis points. When they control for additional loan and borrower characteristics, such as credit scores, they find an implied spread of only 9 basis points.

Todd (2001) examines the average coupon rate for new Freddie Mac mortgages and aggregate securitization volume and CMO issuances during 1984 through 1995.

He finds no significant relationship between mortgage rates and securitization activity, whether measured as aggregate MBS or CMO activity. He further finds no significant relationship between origination fees and securitization activity.

Lehnert, Passmore, and Sherlund (2008) use a vector autoregressive approach with data on mortgage rates, GSE purchases, and MBS offerings during 1993 through 2005. They ask whether GSE activity leads to reductions in mortgage rates in time series data. In contrast to prior studies, they find that GSE securitizations do not have any effect on mortgage rates.

In 1969, the year before the first GSE offering of an MBS, the rate of homeownership in the United States was 64.3 percent. As of 1993, the rate was 64.0 percent. On that basis, mortgage securitizations appear to have no effect on the rate of homeownership. However, beginning in 1994 the rate of U.S. homeownership increased steadily and reached a peak of 69 percent in 2006 before declining to 67.4 percent in 2009. Over this same time frame, nonprime mortgage securitizations flourished (1994–2006) and then virtually disappeared (2007–2009). Thus, growth in the nonprime (private label) securitizations appears to have been associated with a significant increase in homeownership. Several studies examine this connection in greater detail.

Gabriel and Rosenthal (2006) use Home Mortgage Disclosure Act (HMDA) and census tract data to study the relationship between loan denial rates and secondary mortgage market purchases during 1992 through 2002. Their results do not strictly apply to securitizations alone because they include all secondary loan purchases as their independent variable. Over that period the rate of homeownership increased from 64.1 percent to 67.5 percent. The fraction of loans in low-income and minority neighborhoods sold into the secondary market increased from 33 percent to 81 percent. After controlling for other factors, they find that increases in secondary market activity are associated with a significant decline in loan denial rates. They conclude that secondary market activity significantly expanded the supply of mortgage credit.

Nadauld and Sherlund (2009) and Mian and Sufi (2009) are concerned directly with whether securitization led to the increase in nonprime lending. Both employ HMDA data and compare credit standards and securitizations at the zip code level. Zip codes are classified as prime and nonprime. Nadauld and Sherlund consider 1997 through 2007, whereas Mian and Sufi study 1992 through 2006. Nadauld and Sherlund find that investment banks that securitized loans were more likely to purchase loans in nonprime than in prime zip codes. Mian and Sufi find that the rate of loans securitized from nonprime zip codes was significantly greater than from prime zip codes. This relationship was especially strong during 2002 through 2005, primarily due to private label securitizations. Both studies find that during 2006 and 2007 default rates were significantly higher for zip codes with higher fractions of nonprime securitizations. Both studies conclude that private label MBS offerings expanded the supply of credit during the early 2000s and were associated with higher defaults rates during 2006 and 2007.

Keys, Mukherjee, Seru, and Vig (2010) address the policy question of whether the additional regulation of financial institutions muted or exacerbated the inclination of mortgage lenders to originate and securitize nonprime loans. They find that highly regulated banks were more likely to originate and securitize nonprime loans than were lightly regulated mortgage bankers.

Is the MBS Market a "Market for Lemons"?

Various explanations have been proposed to account for the nature and extent of difficulties experienced by markets for MBS during the period from 2007 through 2010. Some assert that the ability of lenders to separate the economic functions of loan origination and loan underwriting contributed to a general decline in lending standards. Others observe that additional political objectives resulted in the explicit relaxation of lending standards for products sold by GSEs. Still others contend that credit rating agencies (CRAs) not only permitted such effects but also contributed to such problems by relaxing standards of their own.

In addition to such issues, many interpret the dramatic increase in mortgage defaults and corresponding economic losses suffered by investors in MBS as evidence that investors were in fact duped as a result of relaxed standards. Accordingly, some assert that the MBS market is effectively a market for lemons. However, even if some or all of the underlying assertions are valid, the ultimate conclusion need not be true. On the contrary, as with the evaluation of any risky investment, returns during any single period of limited duration and limited representation do not establish that, ex ante, prices and yields were naïve or inappropriate. The alternative, and customary economic null hypothesis, is that investors were in fact generally aware of the appropriate risks, including the risks of declining standards, and reasonable expectations of such effects were incorporated in the prices and yields for MBS products. Accordingly, the following summary of economic investigations seeks to incorporate issues of risk pricing as well as risk assessment per se.

Downing, Jaffee, and Wallace (2009) address the question of whether the MBS market is a market for lemons by examining individual pools of Freddie Mac MBS created during 1991 through 2002. They focus on prepayment risk. They find that MBS used to create CMOs tend to perform worse from the investor's perspective. Mortgagors exercise their prepayment option more aggressively in MBS used to create CMOs than borrowers in the original MBS. They compare actual MBS yields with estimated appropriate yields for MBS used to create CMOs. These appropriate yields are consistent with market participants recognizing the lemons problem and pricing MBS accordingly.

Purnanandam (2011) notes that some banks specialize in originating mortgage loans with the intent of securitizing them. This mode of operation is labeled the *originate-to-distribute* (OTD) *model*. Purnanandam studies banks according to their degree of involvement in the OTD market during 2006 through 2008. Banks heavily involved in the OTD market tend to originate lower quality loans. He interprets this finding as evidence that the OTD model embeds weaker incentives for lenders to screen loans, directly contributing to the increase in nonprime defaults. A separate question is whether market participants recognized the lower quality of the loans and priced MBS products appropriately.

Dell'Ariccia, Igan, and Laeven (2012) study nonprime loans originated during 2000 through 2006. They report that lending standards declined among nonprime lenders and that this decline was greater for loans originated in geographic areas where mortgage securitizations were greater. However, as with Purnanandam (2011), they do not address the question of whether investors appropriately priced the higher risks presented by lower credit standards.

Keys et al. (2010) exploit an oft cited rule-of-thumb to address the question of whether securitization affects lending standards. They propose viewing a credit score of 620 as a proxy for whether a nonprime loan is likely to be used to support an MBS. Loans with scores just above that level are more likely to be securitized than loans with scores just below that level. Holding constant all other observable factors, they find that securitized loans with scores just above 620 are significantly more likely to default than non-securitized loans with scores just below this level. The authors argue that the potential for securitization reduces lenders' incentives to screen borrowers. As with Purnanandam (2011) and Dell'Ariccia et al. (2012), Keys et al. do not address the question of whether investors appropriately price the potential adverse selection in MBS.

Krainer and Laderman (2014) study mortgage loans originated in California during 2000 through 2007. They find that loans securitized in private label MBS default at a higher rate than those either held in the originator's portfolio or loans securitized by the GSEs. The authors also report that such loans provide a premium yield. This result is consistent with investors recognizing that such loans present the investor with greater risk. Investors recognize the potential lemons problem in MBS and adjust prices. The authors note that in the absence of a well-established pricing model, they cannot determine whether the price adjustment was appropriate.

Demyanyk and Van Hemert (2011) focus on nonprime mortgages originated during 2001 through 2007. Although they do not consider the role of securitization, the authors report that the quality of nonprime loans deteriorated dramatically. They also observe that loan securitizers appear to have been aware of this phenomenon. The yield spread on high-risk loans widened relative to the yield spread of low-risk loans.

Demiroglu and James (2012) directly examine whether investors price the adverse selection potential in MBS. They focus on Alt-A loans because these are the types of loans in which unobservable information may play a larger role in determining credit risk. The authors classify investors in MBS in terms of the degree of affiliation with the originator. Loan performance is worse (i.e., defaults and losses are greater) for investors with less direct ties to the originator. They find that the degree of affiliation matters for pricing. After controlling for other factors, yields are higher and overcollateralization is greater for MBS bought by investors with weaker ties to originators.

Based on these findings, and as might be expected in a market populated by sophisticated participants, investors appear to recognize the potential for adverse selection. They adjusted prices and yields in response to increased risk of adverse selection. Investors demanded and received higher yields as the risk of adverse selection increased. This conclusion is consistent with all sides recognizing the potential for a market for lemons in the nonprime MBS market. The unanswered question is whether the magnitude of the increase in yields was sufficiently high, ex ante; the increase was certainly not high enough ex post.

Credit Rating Agencies in the MBS Market

Three CRAs dominate the U.S. market for credit ratings of publicly traded securities: Moody's Investor Service (Moody's), Standard & Poor's Financial Services (S&P), and Fitch Ratings (Fitch). These agencies rate debt securities according to the likelihood of default and recovery in the case of default. CRAs do not rate CMOs backed by GSE sponsored MBS because an explicit or implicit federal government guarantee supports the securities. Thus, for many years, CRAs played no role in the issuance of MBS or CMOs. However, during the late 1990s and especially during the early 2000s, the volume of private label CMOs expanded the demand for CRAs to rate the credit quality of CMO tranches.

Mathis, McAndrews, and Rochet (2009) study nonprime CMOs issued during 2000 through 2008. During 2000 through 2006, the authors report that, after controlling for characteristics of the underlying loans, the fraction of nonprime CMO tranches rated AAA increased significantly. Ashcraft, Goldsmith-Pinkham, and Vickery (2010) also study nonprime securitizations during 2001 through 2007. Ignoring other factors, the fraction of securitizations rated AAA declined from 2001 through the end of 2004 and then remained flat through mid-2007. Even after adjusting for other factors, the fraction of tranches rated AAA declined between 2001 and 2004. However, the fraction of tranches rated AAA increased significantly between 2005 and mid-2007. The authors find that nonprime MBS tranches issued during 2006 and 2007 experience higher levels of delinquencies and defaults. These findings are consistent with ratings drift by the CRAs.

The related question is the extent to which investors relied on ratings when buying MBS tranches. Did investors recognize the potential drift in ratings and price tranches accordingly? To address that question, Adelino (2009) investigates whether yield spreads of CMO tranches predict future performance after taking into account credit rating. The sample is yield spreads for tranches of 87,017 securities issued during 2003 through 2007. After controlling for credit ratings, he finds that CMO yield spreads have predictive power for future tranche performance where performance includes future rating downgrades and defaults. Adelino does note an exception to his finding: investors did not rely exclusively on ratings when buying and selling CMOs. Investors' discriminatory power appears to have been at work for lower rated tranches only. Within AAA rated tranches, yield spreads appear to have had no predictive power for future performance.

He, Qian, and Strahan (2012) address a key question about the role of rating agencies. Some cite the pay-for-rating method in which issuers pay the rating agencies to rate their issuances as leading to an incentive problem. The CRAs are potentially rewarded for inflating ratings by the issuer that brings more business to the CRA. Using CMOs issued during 2000 through 2006, CMOs issued by frequent issuers received higher ratings than those from less frequent issuers. Further, yields were lower for more frequent than for less frequent issuers during 2001 through 2003. This pattern reverses between 2004 and 2006. The authors interpret their findings to mean that investors had come to recognize the potential for drift in CRA ratings.

Lessons Learned from the History of the MBS Market

Debate continues over the roles played by the federal government and the GSEs in the mortgage market. A common presumption about such intervention in the MBS market is that enhanced securitization reduces the cost and increases the availability of mortgage credit. Whether that presumption is justified is the subject of a set of empirical articles. Indeed, with the extreme difficulties confronted by GSEs and the MBS markets during 2007 through 2009, the common presumption that securitization has a beneficial impact on housing markets is even more fiercely debated.

Models for the valuation of MBS offerings have come under attack. Some contend that model inadequacies allowed banks and other investors to take on investment risk they did not understand and could not manage. Formal mathematical models have lost some of their luster because they appear to have failed during the recession of 2007–2009. Nevertheless, models of some sort are necessary for investors to evaluate risks and possible returns. The development of better models is undoubtedly an area for continuing research. The specific form of the earliest MBS offerings by Ginnie Mae enabled Dunn and McConnell (1981a, b) to focus on the emerging analytic tools on issues of special significance for practitioners. Subsequent extensions paved the way for practical expansions of the MBS markets to areas such as private labels. Growth in the complexity of MBS offerings presented new challenges for pricing models. Addressing these challenges led to expanded efforts to capture the essential features of specific forms of MBS products. Researchers developed new sets of tools, such as reduced form models, as essential supplements to more traditional structural models. Moreover, both forms of models presented demands for relevant data to provide accurate estimates of value for specific MBS offerings.

Some commentators raised questions as to whether the development of the MBS market has lowered the effective borrowing cost for homeowners. At an even more fundamental level, some questioned whether the development of the MBS market has enhanced the general availability of homeownership. Policy makers even questioned the extent to which growth in the extent and complexity of the MBS market might have played a role in the rise and decline in housing values that occurred during early 2000s.

Sorting out the factors that led to the decline of the MBS market between 2007 and 2009 is likely to require further investigation with an emphasis on policy implications. Perhaps the greatest policy question is what to do with the behemoth GSEs that have been taken into government conservatorship. The question is what role, if any, should the federal government play in the market for securitized mortgage loans?

In light of the general importance of homeownership to individual families and to the economy, financial innovation was required to fill an essential void following the collapse of the savings and loan industry in the 1980s. Even the most vocal critics of the MBS market will likely concede that creating the foundation for a new financial structure was no small undertaking. Within a relatively few years, MBS markets were providing financing for homeownership in excess of $1 trillion per year. Such success does not imply that mistakes were not made or that the MBS market necessarily operates at an ideal level. On the contrary, the MBS securities markets will continue to evolve to service home buyers seeking funding.

Summary and Conclusions

The MBS market has its origins in the earliest mortgage bankers who originated loans and sold the cash flows to third party investors. The MBS market had its official start with the introduction of the simple pass-through MBS issued by Ginnie Mae in 1970.

Innovations included the creation of CMOs in which the cash flows from the underlying MBS were allocated to tranches. In tandem with the creation of private label MBS, homeownership in the United States reached its highest ever level. MBS had a positive role in increasing homeownership. That increase appears to be attributable to private sector MBS rather than government-sponsored MBS. The downside of this increase in homeownership has been an increase in loan defaults and delinquencies. Many questions remain about the effect of MBS on the cost and level of homeownership. Among those is what role, if any, should be assigned to GSEs?

Discussion Questions

1. Define a mortgage and discuss what a typical home buyer expects in a mortgage. How does the standard mortgage of today meet those needs in comparison to the standard mortgage of several hundred years ago?
2. What is a MBS?
3. Describe both the political and economic factors that have contributed to the development of the MBS market.
4. To what extent, and in what specific ways, has the MBS market allowed for greater separation of the traditional functions of originating mortgages and investing in mortgages?
5. Identify some economic advantages for home buyers that have resulted from the development of the MBS market.
6. Discuss whether the empirical evidence indicates that securitization has been beneficial for home buyers.

Acknowledgments

In addition to references identified in the chapter, the authors draw from their earlier article McConnell and Buser (2011).

References

Adelino, Manuel. 2009. "Do Investors Rely Only on Ratings? The Case of Mortgage-Backed Securities." Working Paper, Sloan School of Management, Massachusetts Institute of Technology. http://ssrn.com/abstract=1425216/.

Ambrose, Brent W., Richard Buttimer, and Thomas Thibodeau. 2001. "A New Spin on the Jumbo/conforming Loan Rate Differential." *Journal of Real Estate Finance and Economics* 23:3, 309–335.

Ambrose, Brent W., Michael LaCour-Little, and Anthony B. Sanders. 2005. "Does Regulatory Capital Arbitrage, Reputation, or Asymmetric Information Drive Securitization?" *Journal of Financial Services Research* 28: 1–3, 113–133.

Ashcraft, Adam, Paul Goldsmith-Pinkham, and James Vickery. 2010. "MBS Ratings and the Mortgage Credit Boom." Working Paper, Staff Report No. 449, Federal Reserve Bank of New York.

Bodfish, Morton, ed. 1931. *History of Buildings & Loans in the United States.* Chicago: United States Building and Loan League.

Dell'Ariccia, Giovanni, Deniz Igan, and Luc Laeven. 2012. "Credit Booms and Lending Standards: Evidence from the Subprime Mortgage Market." *Journal of Money Credit and Banking* 44: 2–3, 367–384.

Demiroglu, Cem, and Christopher James. 2012. "How Important Is Having 'Skin in the Game'? Originator-Sponsor Affiliation and Losses on Mortgage-Backed Securities." *Review of Financial Studies* 25:11, 3217–3258.

Demyanyk, Yuliya, and Otto Van Hemert. 2011. "Understanding the Subprime Mortgage Crisis." *Review of Financial Studies* 24:6, 1848–1880.

Downing, Chris, Dwight Jaffee, and Nancy A. Wallace. 2009. "Is the Market for Mortgage-Backed Securities a Market for Lemons?" *Review of Financial Studies* 22: 7, 2457–2494.

Dunn, Kenneth B., and John J. McConnell. 1981a. "A Comparison of Alternative Models for Pricing GNMA Mortgage-Backed Securities." *Journal of Finance* 36:2, 471–484.

Dunn, Kenneth B., and John J. McConnell. 1981b. "Valuation of GNMA Mortgage-Backed Securities." *Journal of Finance* 36:3, 599–616.

Ewalt, Josephine Hedges. 1964. *A Business Reborn: The Savings and Loan Story, 1930–1960*. Chicago: American Savings and Loan Institute Press.

Fannie Mae. 1966. *Background and History 1938–1966*. Washington, DC: Fannie Mae.

Federal Deposit Insurance Corporation. 2014. "Historical Statistics on Banking." http://www2.fdic.gov/hsob/HSOBRpt.asp.

Frame, W. Scott, and Lawrence J. White. 2007. "Charter Value, Risk-Taking Incentives and Emerging Competition for Fannie Mae and Freddie Mac." *Journal of Money, Credit and Banking* 39:1, 83–103.

Frederiksen, Ditlew Morad. 1894. "Mortgage Banking in America." *Journal of Political Economy* 2:2, 203–234.

Gabriel, Stuart A., and Stuart S. Rosenthal. 2006. "Secondary Mortgage Markets and Access to Credit: 1992–2002." Working Paper, Lusk Center for Real Estate, University of Southern California.

Green, Richard K., and Susan M. Wachter. 2005. "The American Mortgage in Historical and International Context." *Journal of Economic Perspectives* 19:4, 93–114.

He, Jie, Jun Qian, and Philip Strahan. 2012. "Are All Ratings Created Equal? The Impact of Issuer Size on the Pricing of Mortgage-Backed Securities." *Journal of Finance* 67:6, 2097–2137.

Hendershott, Patric H., and James D. Shilling. 1989. "The Impact of the Agencies on Conventional Fixed-rate Mortgage Yields." *Journal of Real Estate Finance and Economics* 2:2, 101–115.

Jones, Leonard A. 1882. *A Treatise on the Law of Mortgages of Real Property*. Volume 1. Boston: Houghton, Mifflin.

Keys, Benjamin J., Tanmoy Mukherjee, Amit Seru, and Vikrant Vig. 2010. "Did Securitization Lead to Lax Screening? Evidence from Subprime Loans." *Quarterly Journal of Economics* 125:1, 307–362.

Klaman, Saul B. 1959. *The Postwar Rise of Mortgage Companies*. New York: Columbia University Press.

Kolari, James W., Donald R. Fraser, and Ali Anari. 1998. "The Effects of Securitization on Mortgage Market Yields: A Cointegration Analysis." *Real Estate Economics* 26:4, 677–693.

Krainer, John, and Elizabeth Laderman. 2014. "Mortgage Loan Securitization and Relative Loan Performance." *Journal of Financial Services Research* 45:1, 39–66.

Lehnert, Andreas, S. Wayne Passmore, and Shane M. Sherlund. 2008. "GSEs, Mortgage Rates, and Secondary Market Activities." *Journal of Real Estate Finance and Economics* 36: 3, 343–363.

Mason, David L. 2001. "From Building and Loans to Bail-Outs: A History of the American Savings and Loan Industry, 1831–1989." PhD dissertation, Ohio State University.

Mathis, Jérôme, James McAndrews, and Jean-Charles Rochet. 2009. "Rating the Raters: Are Reputation Concerns Powerful Enough to Discipline Rating Agencies?" *Journal of Monetary Economics* 56: 5, 657–674.

McConnell, John J., and Stephen A. Buser. 2011. "The Origins and Evolution of the Market for Mortgage-Backed Securities." *Annual Review of Financial Economics* 3: 173–192.

Mian, Atif R., and Amir Sufi. 2009. "The Consequences of Mortgage Credit Expansion: Evidence from the U.S. Mortgage Default Crisis." *Quarterly Journal of Economics* 124:4, 1449–1496.

Nadauld, Taylor D., and Shane M. Sherlund. 2009. "The Role of the Securitization Process in the Expansion of Subprime Credit." Working Paper 2009–28, Federal Reserve Board.

Naranjo, Andy, and Alden Toevs. 2002. "The Effects of Purchases of Mortgages and Securitization by Government Sponsored Enterprises on Mortgage Yield Spreads and Volatility." *Journal of Real Estate Finance and Economics* 25: 2/3, 173–195.

Purnanandam, Amiyatosh. 2011. "Originate-to-distribute Model and the Subprime Mortgage Crisis." *Review of Financial Studies* 24:6, 1881–1915.

Roll, Richard. 1987a. "Collateralized Mortgage Obligations: Characteristics, History, Analysis." In Frank J. Fabozzi, ed., *Mortgage-Backed Securities*, 7–43. Chicago: Probus Publishing.

Roll, Richard. 1987b. "Recent Innovations in Collateralized Mortgage Obligations." *Housing Finance Review* 6:Winter, 193–234.

Todd, Steven. 2001. "The Effects of Securitization on Consumer Mortgage Costs." *Real Estate Economics* 29:1, 29–54.

8

Prepayment and Default Risk

STEPHEN L. BUSCHBOM

Graduate Assistant, Department of Insurance, Legal Studies and Real Estate, Terry College of Business, University of Georgia

JAMES B. KAU

Professor Emeritus of Real Estate, Department of Insurance, Legal Studies and Real Estate, Terry College of Business, University of Georgia

DONALD C. KEENAN

Professor, UFR d'Économie et Gestion, THEMA Université de Cergy-Pontoise

Introduction

In the endogenous approach to prepayment and default, a borrower rationally decides to terminate a mortgage contract though either default or prepayment when circumstances dictate that this is the best course of action. A basic assumption in the contingent claims framework valuing these two options is that the borrower seeks to minimize the market cost of the mortgage they owe.

Termination, either through default or prepayment, is a decision that is possible at any moment of time. Interest rates and property values are the two major considerations influencing a borrower's actions. Borrowers must consider both the current and expected future levels of interest rates and home values in reaching their decision to terminate a loan at a particular time. A borrower is highly unlikely to immediately default given the realization of *negative equity* where the value of the home is less than the outstanding mortgage balance. Instead, a borrower considers future possible home values and the borrower's decision becomes an expected net present value. Other considerations than just the future value of the house enter into the rational valuation of the default decision such as the alternative of prepayment. Such factors are discussed as the chapter proceeds.

The borrower may also default or prepay a mortgage due to an exogenous shock such as unemployment, divorce, or change of employment, though these events are not easily anticipated. Given that such shocks are non-trivial, the recent literature attempts to incorporate the effects of such event shocks in various mortgage-modeling scenarios.

This chapter discusses the two most common frameworks used to predict termination of either the endogenous or the exogenous kinds: the structural and reduced form approaches. These approaches are presented primarily in the context of valuing a standard fixed rate mortgage (FRM). The next section provides a discussion of a borrower's motivation to terminate a mortgage followed by an overview of both structural and reduced form modeling of mortgage termination.

Residential Mortgage Termination

Mortgages contracts are complex in structure and the value is sensitive to many factors: interest rates, home prices, loan-to-value (LTV), points or fees paid at origination, mortgage insurance, and borrower characteristics. Because mortgages are long-term instruments, interest rates and home prices should not be assumed constant when valuing a contract. Given that future economic conditions are uncertain, mortgage valuation requires incorporating a stochastic economic environment into the valuation process. Modeling the borrower's future decisions (continuation, default, or prepayment) based on a stochastic economic environment involving interest rates and home prices is the foundation of mortgage valuation.

Before discussing modeling techniques and assumptions, a basic framework is set forth to conceptualize when and why a borrower terminates a mortgage contract assuming that execution is always done optimally. *Optimal execution* in the present context is the assumption that the borrower terminates due to only those financial considerations involving minimizing the market cost of the mortgage contract. This primarily involves anticipating house prices and interest rates.

One well-known theoretical paper on mortgage termination is Kau, Keenan, Muller, and Epperson (1992). The value of the mortgage contract to the borrower, $V(H,r,t)$, is

$$V(H,r,t) = A(r,t) - D(H,r,t) - C(H,r,t), \tag{8.1}$$

where $A(r, t)$ is present value of the remaining mortgage payments at time t discounted by the current interest rate r. To account for termination options, the borrower deducts the option value of default $(D(H, r, t))$ and prepayment $(C(H, r, t))$, with both options dependent on home price H and the current interest rate r at time t, from this present value of discounted monthly mortgage payments. Figure 8.1 graphically shows the borrower's position immediately before a mortgage payment date where $\mathrm{F}\left(\tau_t^-\right)$ is the loan's face value plus accrued interest.

Although prepayment can occur at any point in time, a borrower would only default when a payment is due, given they can freely enjoy usage of the house until that payment date. In Figure 8.1, the interaction between interest rates and home prices is apparent. Assuming a decrease in the spot interest rate (r), a simultaneous increase in home prices moves the borrower toward the prepayment region (V = F) while a decrease in home prices moves the borrower toward the default region (V = H). At r* in Figure 8.1, the borrower will always terminate the loan, defaulting when $H < \mathrm{F}\left(\tau_i^-\right)$ and prepaying when $H > \mathrm{F}\left(\tau_i^-\right)$. As interest rates approach infinity, the present value of remaining mortgage payments approaches zero and the borrower will always default when the home value is less than the mortgage payment.

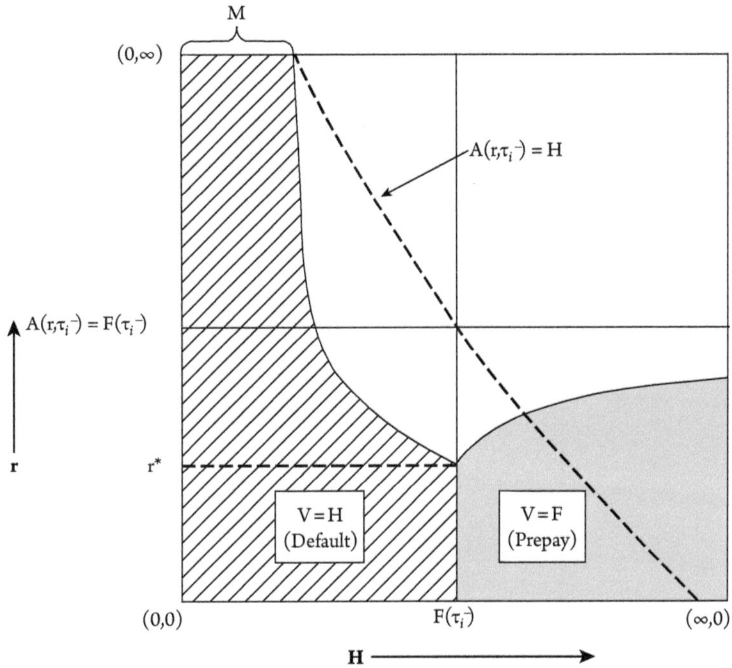

Figure 8.1 Mortgage Termination State Space Immediately before a Payment. The prepayment/default decision at time $t = \tau_i^-$ is just before the ith payment of size *M*. $F(\tau_i^-)$ is the unpaid mortgage balance plus accrued interest. A borrower is indifferent between default and prepayment below r*. The area of negative equity is below the line $A(r, \tau_i^-) = H$. Source: Adapted from Kau et al. (1995).

As mentioned, prepayment is a continuous option, whereas default only becomes a reasonable event on a payment date. Figure 8.2 shows the borrower's decision immediately after a payment is made. At sufficiently low interest rates, the borrower will prepay the mortgage after a payment is made, at $t = \tau_i^+$, whereas they would have anticipated defaulting in this same region immediately before making a payment, at $t = \tau_i^-$.

The previous framework is an example of structural modeling of the option to terminate and is one of the two dominating methods for mortgage valuation. The other method is reduced-form modeling which is similar to a hazard model but includes a second layer of uncertainty so that it can be described as doubly stochastic (termination is an uncertain event as well as the hazard of termination itself). While structural models are an excellent choice when examining the impact of prepayment and default on mortgage valuation under specific assumptions about the economic environment, reduced-form models are better suited for empirical work because they use historical observations of behavior to estimate termination rather than endogenous ideal calculations. The following section provides a discussion of both models with consideration of the theoretical model and the empirical estimations each model yields, along with other possible approaches to mortgage termination found in the recent literature.

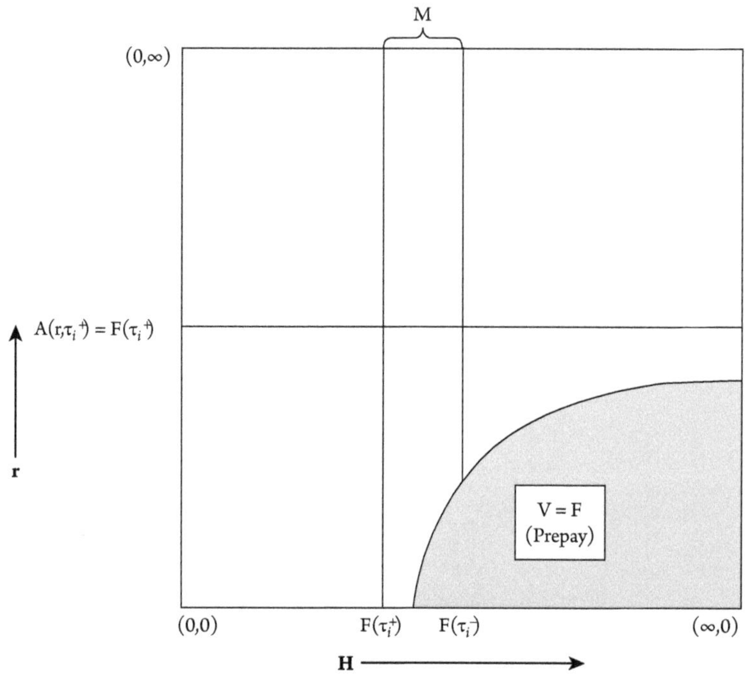

Figure 8.2 Mortgage Termination State Space Immediately after a Payment.
The prepayment/default decision at time $t = \tau_i^+$ is just after the ith payment of size M. $F\left(\tau_i^{+/-}\right)$ is the unpaid mortgage balance plus accrued interest after (+) and before (–) payment M. Source: Adapted from Kau et al. (1995).

STRUCTURAL MODELS

Structural models describe home price and interest rate movements as stochastic processes (via mean value, volatility, and drift) with default or prepayment only occurring once reaching a critical boundary during the evolution of these processes. A borrower's financial position is based on future expectations and, assuming perfect execution, will immediately default or prepay once attaining such a boundary point. Valuing a mortgage requires knowing the boundaries where a borrower defaults or prepays their mortgage and knowing the boundaries at a particular time one must have similarly found the mortgage values and boundary over possible interest rates and house prices in the future. The framework above from Kau et al. (1992) achieves all this by proceeding backwards in time from the end of the contract. The value of a mortgage contract on the last payment date is the minimum of the last mortgage payment or the home value. With this knowledge one can solve the choice problem at the next moment in backward time and so forth. In this manner, a numerical solution technique is possible allowing explicit valuation of default prepayment options.

The stochastic process for nominal home prices in Kau et al. (1992) is

$$\frac{dH}{H} = (\alpha - s)dt + \sigma_H dz_H, \tag{8.2}$$

where z_H represents a standard Wiener process, s is the homeowner's service flow, a is the instantaneous total expected return and σ_H is the proportional variance. The instantaneous default-free nominal interest rate process is the Cox, Ingersoll, and Ross (1985) mean-reverting process

$$dr = \gamma(\theta - r)dt + \sigma_r \sqrt{r}\, dz_r, \tag{8.3}$$

where interest rates r revert to the long-term rate of θ at a speed of γ. The terms σ_r and dz_r are interpreted in the same manner as σ_H and dz_H from Equation 8.2. With the stochastic economic environment defined in Equations 8.2 and 8.3, valuation of the borrower's assets can be determined by the backward partial differential equation (PDE)

$$\begin{aligned}&\frac{1}{2}H^2\sigma_H\frac{\partial^2 X}{\partial H^2} + \rho H\sqrt{r}\,\sigma_H\sigma_r\frac{\partial^2 X}{\partial H \partial r} + \frac{1}{2}r\sigma_r^2\frac{\partial^2 X}{\partial r^2} + \gamma(\theta - r)\frac{\partial X}{\partial r}\\ &+ (r-s)H\frac{\partial X}{\partial H} + \frac{\partial X}{\partial t} - rX = 0,\end{aligned} \tag{8.4}$$

where $dz_r = dz_H = \rho dt$, X denotes the value of the relevant asset and ρ is the correlation between the stochastic terms for home prices and interest rates.

Using the notation introduced earlier, the terminal condition for the value of a mortgage is

$$V\left(\bar{_i}\right) = Min\left[V\left(\tau_i^+\right) + M, H\right] \quad i < n \tag{8.5}$$

so that a monthly payment is made only when continuation is financially logical. If a payment is not made, the lender receives the house, H. The borrower's optimal default occurs when first $H(t) = V(r,t)$ and in earlier time optimal prepayment occurs when first $F(t) = V(r,t)$, where these boundaries' locations are endogenously determined in the course of minimizing V.

The intuition is that a borrower will always choose to default when the home is no longer worth more than the mortgage contract, including the options to terminate in the future, and will always prepay when the face value of the loan (unpaid principal balance plus accrued interest) is no longer less than the value of the mortgage contract, again including future termination options. The aforementioned equalities are referred to as *free boundary conditions*, whereas ordinary boundary conditions restrict asset values given extreme values of H and r. Both sets of boundary conditions, as well as the terminal condition, are necessary for valuation using the backward PDE in Equation 8.4.

Until this point, termination is assumed to be endogenously determined so that the borrower only terminates the mortgage when it minimizes the market cost of the mortgage. Exogenous prepayment, however, also occurs at "suboptimal" points in time where the borrower is not actually minimizing the value of the mortgage. This is not to say that the borrower is acting irrationally. A borrower may be forced to relocate for a job, sell the property during a divorce, or move for a variety of other reasons. While structural models are inappropriate to predict exogenous prepayment, the impact of exogenous prepayment on mortgage values is quantifiable. A simple means of introducing exogenous prepayment is by appending a Poisson process to the terminal condition in Equation 8.5 as described in Kau et al. (1992) and Kau and Keenan (1995).

Mortgage insurance can also be evaluated using the existing structural model framework. While the borrower's actions determine the value of mortgage insurance, insurance does not enter into the valuation of borrower's position. The terminal condition for insurance is

$$I(\tau_i^-)=\begin{cases} I(\tau_i^+) \text{ if } V(\tau_i^-)=V(\tau_i^+)+M \quad (\text{no default}) \ i<n \\ \max\left[0,\min\left[F(\tau_i^-)-H,\ \Phi F(\tau_i^-)\right]\right] \text{if } V(\tau_i^-)=H \ (\text{default}). \end{cases} \tag{8.6}$$

The value of insurance becomes the future value of insurance upon continuation. In the event of default, the insurer must pay the difference between the home value and the loan's face value up to a specified percentage, Φ, of the face value. Kau et al. (1992) show that given a range of home price volatility rates between 10 and 20 percent and an initial LTV of up to 95 percent, insurance provides little, if any, value with coverage greater than 25 percent of the loan's face value. The result is not surprising because a structural model predicts that without explicit transaction costs a borrower will choose to default well before negative equity becomes substantial. While 25 percent coverage may seem insufficient protection against mortgage losses in view of the 2008 financial crisis, it is important to realize the impact of home price volatility in the structural model. If home price volatility is increased beyond 20 percent, the value of insurance rapidly increases.

Mortgage valuation is based on the absence of arbitrage. Thus, the value of a mortgage contract must be equal to the loan amount at origination less any upfront points charged. The arbitrage free contract condition at origination is then

$$V(H(0),r(0);c)+I(H(0),r(0);c)=(1-\delta)F(0), \tag{8.7}$$

where δ is the number of upfront points charged and c is the annual contract rate of the mortgage. The arbitrage free principle is best understood in a hypothetical setting where a borrower receives a 100 percent LTV mortgage and housing values are stochastic. Given a sufficient decline in home prices, the borrower can enjoy the services of the house for one month and then default. Given such a scenario, the contract must contain either insurance or points to balance and be free from arbitrage.

Table 8.1 shows a comprehensive summary of the total effects for all variables discussed up to this point (Kau, Keenan, Muller, and Epperson 1995). A mortgage contract is priced at multiple LTV points intersecting with four different economic environments. A noteworthy result of this simulation is that the prepayment option is the dominant factor influencing mortgage value until LTV reaches 90 percent. Consistent with option pricing theory, the options to prepay and to default increase in value with increased volatility in interest rates and home prices, respectively. As LTV increases to 95 percent and above in these scenarios, the value of default gains significance relative to prepayment. The increasing significance of default as LTV increases is certainly intuitive, but less intuitive is the corresponding decrease in contract rate. Figure 8.3 helps to clarify this result.

Curve A in Figure 8.3 assumes the scenario where $\sigma_H = \sigma_r = 10$ percent from Table 8.1. The corresponding contract rate is 11.85 percent. The dotted curve represents a scenario where σ_H increases to 15 percent but σ_r remains at 10 percent. The increase in home price volatility increases the value of the default option, indicating a higher likelihood

Table 8.1 **Changes in Interest Rate and House Price Variables**

Loan-to-Value		***Contract Rates (c)***		***Value of Payments (A)***		***Default (D)***		***Insurance (I)***		***Prepayment (P)***	
	σ_H / σ_r	***5%***	***10%***	***5%***	***10%***	***5%***	***10%***	***5%***	***10%***	***5%***	***10%***
80%	5%	10.68%	10.60%	84,355	83,796	9	732	3	460	5,531	4,724
	10%	12.10%	12.06%	95,345	95,038	3	525	1	151	16,544	15,864
85%	5%	10.68%	10.54%	89,590	88,592	42	1,525	16	970	5,841	4,311
	10%	12.10%	11.99%	101,301	100,437	31	1,498	4	424	17,549	15,640
90%	5%	10.67%	10.47%	94,790	96,257	254	2,782	92	1,827	5,974	3,652
	10	12.09%	11.85%	107,213	105,264	261	3,772	35	1,093	18,337	13,936
95%	5%	10.62%	10.40%	99,680	97,914	1,294	4,518	480	3,097	5,292	2,918
	10%	12.05%	11.70%	112,793	109,878	2,277	7,542	284	2,318	17,219	11,078
100%	5%	10.53%	10.34%	104,145	102,528	4,182	6,735	1,788	4,886	3,251	2,181
	10%	11.92%	11.61%	117,543	114,843	10,504	12,401	1,572	4,113	10,110	8,055

A level term structure (10% spot interest rate, r(0). 10% steady rate, θ), the service flow, s, is 8.5%, points, δ, are 1.5%, the correlation coefficient, ρ, is 0, and the insurance coverage, Φ, is 25%. A "level term structure" refers to the initial spot rate, r(0), versus the steady state rate, θ, and not to the slope of the zero coupon yield curve.

Note: Contract rate and value for a fixed rate mortgage is found for increasing LTV ratios (by row) for two levels of interest rate volatility (by row) and home price volatility (by column).

Source: Kau et al. (1995).

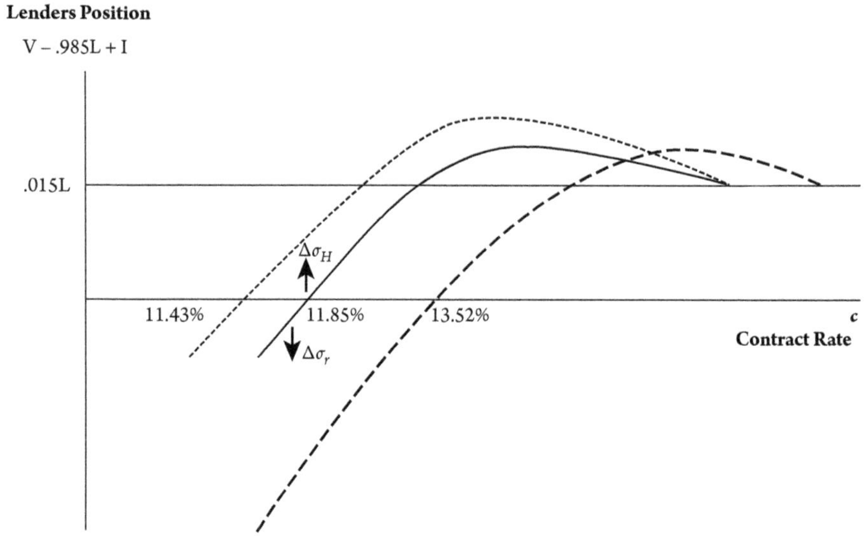

Figure 8.3 Changes in Mortgage Contract Value with an increase in Home Price and Interest Rate Volatility. The solid line represents the case where $\sigma_H = \sigma_r = 10$. The dotted curve represents a scenario where σ_H increases to 15 percent but σ_r remains at 10 percent. The contract rate adjusts down to 11.43 percent to restore equilibrium. The dashed curve represents a scenario where σ_r increases to 15 percent while σ_H remains at 10 percent. The contract rate adjusts up to 13.52 percent to restore equilibrium. Source: Adapted from Kau et al. (1995).

of future default. The increased likelihood of default eliminates future paths that previously resulted in prepayment. The presence of insurance in this mortgage contract paid upfront is then the key element explaining why the contract rate decreases from 11.85 percent to 11.43 percent given an increase in home price volatility. Insurance protects the lender from a loss in principal upon default while at the same time the lender is less exposed to prepayment termination. With the shift in termination patterns a lower contract rate suffices for the no-arbitrage condition to be satisfied and equilibrium to be restored. In the other scenario where σ_r increases to 15 percent while σ_H remains at 10 percent (the dashed curve), the prepayment option becomes more valuable to the borrower which results in a higher contract rate needed to the lender. The contract rate in this scenario increases to 13.52 percent to restore equilibrium.

The aforementioned framework of Kau et al. (1992) is very common in the academic literature but is difficult to implement and so is of limited usefulness to the finance industry. The trouble with executing a structural options model in backward time lies in the computational complexity involved in the numerical solution. A finite difference method is used in the numerical solution of the PDE thereby requiring the repeated approximation of derivatives. The idealized model uses continuous time, so space and time steps must be finely specified in order for the numerical solution to converge to an accurate value. This particular model required approximately 30,000 time steps (at least 50 steps per month), which introduces a substantial computational burden.

An alternative to the finite difference model described above is the bivariate binomial options technique of Hilliard, Kau, Keenan, and Muller (1995). The assumptions about home prices and interest rates remain unchanged from the finite difference model. The two differences come in the form of the process to calculate solution values and the number of time steps required to achieve convergence. The bivariate binomial options approach uses a jump process where two states are determined along with their respective probabilities. The values of the home and interest rates in each of the independent states then allow for the calculation of the mortgage value which in turn allows for the valuation of default and prepayment in the course of determining similar boundary conditions. The bivariate binomial option requires only 1,800 time steps (five per month) to converge.

The results of the Kau et al. (1992) and Hilliard et al. (1995) stress the importance of valuing both default and prepayment options simultaneously. An increase in interest rate volatility paired with a decrease in home price volatility shifts option value from default to prepayment. Following intuition, as LTV increases along with home price volatility, the value of the default option approaches or exceeds the value of prepayment. The last point is particularly relevant given changes in the mortgage market, subsequent to the development of the model, which allowed an increasing number of borrowers to obtain low down payment loans. Even if home prices are increasing, Deng, Quigley, and Van Order (1996) show that the cost of default is non-negligible assuming a 90 percent LTV. Most academic literature regarding mortgages before the 1990s focused heavily on the value of prepayment because default rates were much lower than the rates experienced in the 1990s and 2000s when underwriting standards and cash down payments declined. Mian and Sufi (2009) evaluate 18 years of mortgage origination and find that 2002–2005 is the only period with negative correlation between the growth of income and of mortgage credit. The precipitous decline in underwriting standards leading up to the subprime crisis clearly increased the value of the default option so that any model focusing only on prepayment would have been inappropriate to assess termination risk.

A common complaint leveled against structural modeling of mortgage terminations is the large gap between when terminations should apparently occur and what is empirically observed. A common conjecture is that transactions costs for both default and prepayment would substantially help by constraining the borrowers' ability to terminate a mortgage. Although transaction costs do account for some termination delay, Dunn and Spatt (2005) find that reasonable assumptions for refinance costs fail to explain much of the gap between expected and observed prepayment rates. This result in consistent with earlier work by Kau, Keenan, and Kim (1994) and Kau and Kim (1994) where they also show transaction costs account for only a small portion of the option execution gap. A theoretically more satisfying explanation is achieved by considering the future value of default and prepayment which rationally lead one to delaying termination. If the default option is in the money so that there is negative equity, the possibility exists that the house's value will increase so that the default option is no longer in the money. Even if the house does not increase in value, the borrower can always default in the future. Adding another variable increases the complexity of estimating a structural model (Brunson, Kau, and Keenan 2001) and so there is limited ability to adapt the model to be more realistic. The need for additional explanatory power and flexibility is satisfied by reduced form modeling.

REDUCED FORM MODELS

While structural models require precise assumptions about the behavior of the borrower to endogenously explain mortgage termination, reduced form models estimate termination using historical terminations. Kau, Keenan, and Smurov (2006) provide an overview of reduced form models and a comparison to the structural model alternative. The modeler identifies the explanatory variables describing the loan or borrower characteristics and then examines how these covariates shift a baseline hazard. The *baseline hazard* is defined as the shared, underlying pattern of mortgage terminations over time. The supposition within reduced form modeling is that in addition to the termination risk of an individual loan given its hazard rate, the hazard rate itself is also random. These models are therefore commonly deemed doubly stochastic.

A reduced form model, such as a proportional hazard model, seems already doubly stochastic because some of its covariates are random but the model would then only rely upon the uncertainty of the term structure and house price, which is empirically inadequate to explain termination. The gap unexplained by such covariate uncertainty suggests the presence of an additional source of innate risk. Therefore, the assumption adopted is that the baseline hazard be uncertain in addition to the randomly varying covariates. Unlike structural modeling, a reduced form model assumes default and prepayment events arrive randomly and so termination is not restricted to optimal or even "in-the-money" points in time. Relaxing the assumption of optimal termination is convenient given that prepayment is often observed to occur at suboptimal points in time. Reduced form modeling accounts for these historical instances of suboptimality to the extent they are present in the data and can therefore project some level of noisy terminations provided the explanatory variables contain sufficient predictive power.

Kau, Keenan, Lyubimov, and Slawson (2011) present a reduced form model for mortgage valuation where the baseline hazard rate is randomized for each discrete cohort of mortgage originations. The randomization produces a dynamic baseline hazard that serves as the prime second layer of uncertainty. The model uses two baseline hazard rate processes for default (d) and prepayment (p), $\lambda_0^d(t)$ and $\lambda_0^p(t)$, which follow the CIR processes for time varying trends to propagate through time. The hazards are represented as

$$d\ \ln\lambda_0^l(t) = k_l(\theta_l - \ln\lambda_0^l(t))dt + \sigma_l dw_l(t) \quad l = d, p, \tag{8.8}$$

where $W_d^{\mathbb{P}}$ and $W_p^{\mathbb{P}}$ are white noise processes assumed to be independent with a multiplicative impact on the hazard variance σ_l. The hazards are linear in the logarithm and mean revert to a rate of θ_l at a speed of k_l. The white noise process rules out negative values. This is important given that hazard rate values are typically rather small, particularly for default, and there can easily be zero observed defaults at a particular point in time. These latent processes materialize at each payment date to yield the realized discrete hazard rate process

$$\lambda_i^l = e^{\beta_l' \mathbf{X}(t(i))} \lambda_0^l(t(i)) \quad l = d, p, \tag{8.9}$$

where $X(t(i))$ is the vector of covariates and β is the vector of estimated coefficients. The covariates are run against both forms of termination with prepayment and default acting as substitutes in the manner emphasized in the structural approach of Kau et al. (1992).

In addition to the stochastic baseline hazard process, two other sources of uncertainty must be addressed: interest rates and home prices. The authors use a two-state form for the interest rate process where the spot interest rate $r(t)$ is expressed as the sum of two independent latent CIR processes $x_i(t)$ (Chen and Scott 2003), so that

$$r(t)=x_1(t)+x_2(t), \tag{8.10}$$

where

$$dx_i(t)=k_i(\theta_i-x_i(t))dt+\sigma_i\sqrt{x_i(t)}dw_i(t) \quad i=1,2. \tag{8.11}$$

As is standard, a downward drift adjustment for each factor $x_i(t)$ must take place to obtain the risk-neutral term structure. The parameters k_i, θ_i, σ_i, an $W_i^{\mathbb{P}}$ are interpreted in the same manner as in Equation 8.8. The drift adjustment is an additive term taking the form $\Phi^i\sqrt{x_i}$. The interest rate process is estimated using a Kalman filter with results similar to previous literature.

Incorporating a home price process is a unique contribution of Kau et al. (2011). Accounting for the uncertainty regarding future home prices allows termination in a manner similar to the approach taken by loan originators. The forecasts can then be used to reveal lenders' risk perception as indicated by comparisons to actual loan valuation. The home price process is influenced by the term structure

$$q(t)=\frac{H(t)\exp\left(\int_0^t\left[s-\varphi^q(u)\right]du\right)}{B(t,T+t)}. \tag{8.12}$$

Here the numerator represents the risk-adjusted accumulative returns to the house and the denominator is the similar returns of rolling over into a T-period discount bond. The service flow of the house is s and φ^q is the price of risk associated with the home price process. According to Kau et al., the price of risk should be trendless because no expectation exists of a consistent deviation between home price returns and bond returns. The price of risk takes the form of $\varphi^q = \varphi^0 + \varphi^1 q$ and is estimated for each of the 20 metropolitan statistical areas (MSAs) in the Case-Shiller Home Price Appreciation index using empirical data and satisfying the trendless requirement previously mentioned. The home price process can then be predicted for each of the 20 MSA's separately, using the form

$$dq(t)=q(t)\left[k_q\left(\theta_q-q(t)\right)dt+\sigma_q\sqrt{q(t)}dW_q(t)\right]. \tag{8.13}$$

According to the estimated term structure and home price process for San Diego, California, there is only an 8 percent chance of a 30 percent home price decline within four years after September 2004. There was little possibility the lending community could have foreseen the impending house price declines assuming they employed a similar model.

Estimation of the Real Hazard Process

The difficulty with estimating the prepayment and default hazard intensity processes is the gap between the *state model* and the *observation equations.* Stochastic differential equations, which assume the latent variables propagate through continuous time, drive the *state model*. The *observation equations* simply identify instances where the latent variables materialize and a termination decision takes place, which occurs once a month. As the termination intensity processes are known to be nonlinear in their path and non-Gaussian in their density, Kalman filter estimation will yield inconsistent results and is therefore inappropriate. Instead, a simulation-based approach for estimating dynamic random models is more appropriate.

Two of the most common estimation techniques are particle filters (analogous to sequential Monte Carlo or SMC) and Monte Carlo Markov chains (MCMC methods). In the spirit of these other techniques, particle filters use the initial prior distribution of a state variable to draw a large number of samples (particles), propagate the state variable through time, and then weight the state variable by the likelihood of an observed historical outcome at a given payment date. In contrast, MCMC make use of all state variables simultaneously in unweighted samples. Each estimation technique must be evaluated for its appropriateness of application. For example, particle filters may fail to produce meaningful estimates if the data sample is not sufficiently large while MCMC convergence is dependent on how well the state space is connected as well as by the time step specification (pseudo-convergence and multimodality; Geyer 2010). Doucet, De Freitas, and Gordon (2001) and Doucet and Johansen (2009) provide further discussion of particle filter technique estimation and Harrison and West (1997), Gamerman and Lopes (2006), and Geyer (2010) offer more discussion of MCMC estimation.

Calibration of the Risk Neutral Process

In order to obtain risk-neutral results for the hazard processes above, a calibration process must take place. Empirical data contain both information about termination probabilities and market-adjusted hazards. The arbitrage free assumption mentioned earlier requires that the value of the mortgage calculated using market-adjusted probabilities be equal to the loan amount adjusted for points at origination, so that the mortgage contract is balanced, avoiding instantaneous default or prepayment.

Kau et al. (2011) avoid consideration of upfront points in their calibration process specification since they lack that information, but note that subprime borrowers are typically reluctant to pay a substantial number of points. The calibration process uses a random sampling of the data to estimate the parameters of the hazard processes necessary to satisfy the arbitrage-free contract requirement at origination. The difference between the predicted and actual loan values are then incorporated into a standard approximation procedure where the sum-of-squared errors for the calibration process are minimized over the sample of chosen loans.

In the case of calibrating prepayment parameters, Kau, Keenan, and Smurov (2004) note care should be exercised. Any arbitrary increase in the multiplicative or additive prepayment hazard can trigger immediate prepayment. With a data set of sufficient size and diversification, conducting a two-stage calibration process can isolate the effect of prepayment. By selecting a sample of loans with low LTVs, the default component for these mortgages is numerically trivial, allowing the prepayment parameter estimates to be free from interference by default in the first-stage. The second-stage for the default adjustments then involves estimating the remaining parameters from a sample of loans above the chosen LTV cutoff. Kau et al. (2004) provide further discussion about the calibration process.

An important result of Kau et al. (2011) is identifying when lenders adjusted market pricing due to changed perceptions of risk. In February 2005, the expected loss parameter in the calibration process reached an upper bound of plausibility under the old calibration, signaling a bifurcation of risk pricing between older and more newly originated loans.

Discussion of Results from a Reduced Form Example

Kau et al. (2004) employ a model similar to the aforementioned work of Kau et al. (2011) with the exception of a home price process. The data include a diverse sample of mortgages and borrower profiles outside the subprime dataset used by Kau et al. (2011). The results of the estimated risk-adjusted baseline hazard processes produce a default rate which conforms to the smoothed standard SDA default schedule published by the Public Securities Administration (PSA) while the prepayment rate deviates from the standard PSA prepayment schedule in later years. The prepayment rate increases at the end of the loan term and is consistent with the notion that a mortgage payment eventually becomes a "nuisance" once the outstanding balance is at a low enough level. Jegadeesh and Ju (2000), using nonparametric estimation, find a similar pattern for prepayment consistent with the "nuisance" explanation.

In order to isolate the impact of the free parameters most commonly associated with termination (LTV, contract rate, and the 10-year Treasury rate), Kau et al. (2006) vary each free parameter of interest using a base loan evaluated by the estimated model. The base loan is originated in January 2001 with a 90 percent LTV, a 7 percent contract rate, no origination points, and an original principal balance of $150,000. An interesting result is the impact of LTV at origination on mortgage value. The relationship shown in Figure 8.4 seems somewhat surprising at first glance but is completely logical.

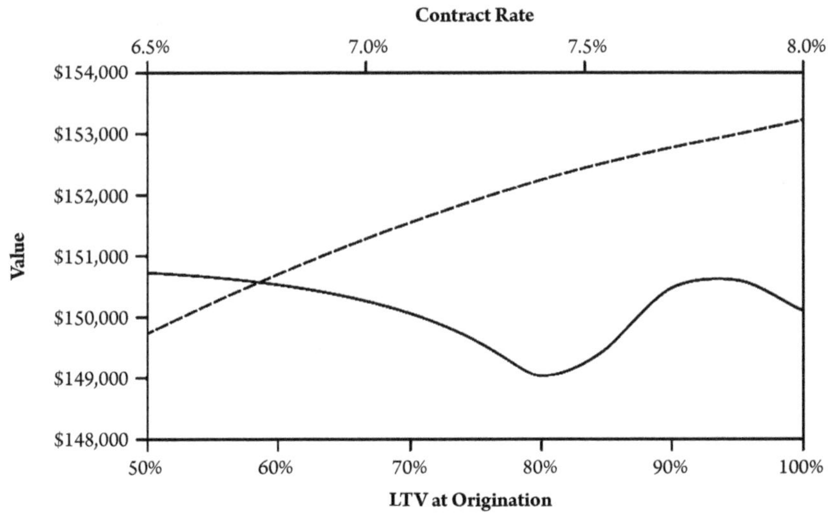

Figure 8.4 Loan Value by LTV at Origination and Contract Rate. Loan value decreases with LTV until 80 percent where mortgage insurance is introduced. The decline continues once LTV is high enough so that the value of default dominates the value of insurance. Loan value monotonically increases with contract rate. Source: Adapted from Kau, Keenan, and Smurov (2006).

The declining trend, which reverses at 80 percent, occurs due to the introduction of mortgage insurance protecting the lender from a loss upon default. The probability of default increases with LTV and the contract rate increases to compensate for the increased risk. The value of the mortgage continues to increase until LTV is sufficiently high that the risk of default dominates the value of insurance.

The contract and 10-year Treasury rates affect the value of a mortgage in a predictable manner for the base loan. The dashed line in Figure 8.4 shows that as contract rate increases, the value of a mortgage increases monotonically. The 10-year Treasury rate affects value in the opposite manner so that the value of a mortgage decreases monotonically as the Treasury rate increases.

Figure 8.5 graphs two of the three free parameters with mortgage value decomposed into two components: the value of mortgage payments and the value of prepayment. The value of default is not shown but monotonically increases with increases in all three free parameters (contract rate, LTV, and the 10-year Treasury rate). The value of prepayment is generally the dominant contributor to a mortgage's value. Substitution is also apparent so that as contract rate increases, both prepayments and defaults increase in place of regular payments. Increases in the 10-year Treasury rate cause prepayments to decline while both regular payments and default increase. Finally, increasing LTV at origination increases default at the expense of future payments and prepayment. However, the interaction of default and prepayment for high Treasury rates in this example should be read with caution. The value of default overtakes prepayment at roughly an 8.5 percent 10-year Treasury rate, but this rate is in the upper range typically observed for loan originations in the data sample.

Deng, Quigley, and Van Order (2000) address a topic not treated by Kau et al. (2004) due to data limitations: the impact of borrower characteristics on termination

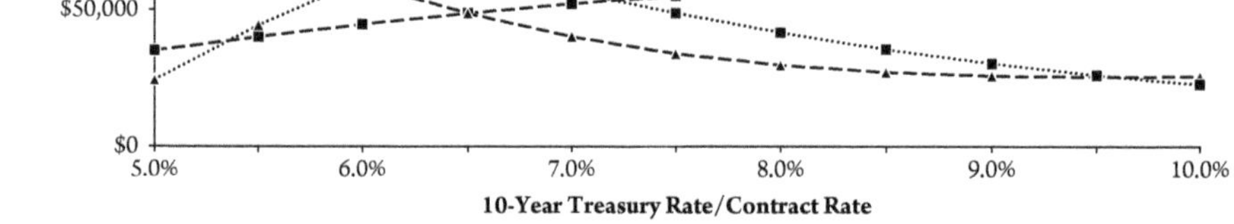

Figure 8.5 Elements of Loan Value by the 10-Year Treasury Rate and Contract Rate. The value of payments increases (decreases) as the 10-year Treasury rate (contract rate) increases. The opposite trend is generally true for the value of prepayment in this example. The value of prepayment decreases (increases) as the 10-year Treasury rate (contract rate) increases. The value of prepayment begins to reverse direction at sufficiently high contract rates. The value of default is not shown but is of lower value than prepayment and monotonically increases with increases in both 10-year Treasury rates and contract rates.
Source: Adapted from Kau, Keenan, and Smurov (2006).

hazard. The authors find significant heterogeneity among borrowers in the execution of the termination option, with prepayment affected the most. Of particular interest, the results show that borrowers with the higher LTV at origination are more likely to terminate not only through default but also through prepayment.

Topics in Residential Mortgage Termination

Terminations are sensitive to various factors affecting the timing and intensity of prepayment and default. Recent literature is leveraging richer data better describing borrower and associated risk factors in order to probe the effect on terminations. Some of the most common topics in this area include second mortgages, borrower mobility, and borrower heterogeneity.

SECOND MORTGAGES

Over the past decade, second mortgages became more common as underwriting standards and risk tolerance changes resulted in greater mortgage liquidity. Borrowers seeking a mortgage with an LTV above 80 percent often want to avoid making monthly mortgage insurance payments. As an alternative, the borrower could take out two mortgages: one for 80 percent of the home value and a second loan carrying a higher coupon rate for the remaining amount of debt. Second mortgages are often called "piggyback" loans, as they accompany a first mortgage in the encumbrance of a property. Avery, Brevoort, and Canner (2007) evaluate Home Mortgage Disclosure Act (HMDA) data and 22 percent of first-lien home-purchase loans for one- to four-family residences involve a piggyback loan. Goodman, Ashworth, Landy, and Yin (2010) estimate that 50 percent of first-lien mortgages in private securitizations carry a second lien. The presence of a second mortgage alters the borrower's termination behavior, especially default, given the borrower has a second set of options to evaluate.

Eriksen, Kau, and Keenan (2013) use a unique data set obtained from one of the nation's largest lenders to evaluate the impact of second mortgages. Typically, performance data are available for either the first mortgage or second mortgage but rarely both simultaneously. Agarwal, Ambrose, Chomsisengphet, and Liu (2006) find significant differences in termination rates for first and second mortgages but cannot distinguish single loan borrowers from those with a first and second mortgage. Research from Sherlund (2008), Demyanyk and Van Hemert (2009), and Pennington-Cross and Ho (2010) identify first mortgages with known second mortgages at origination but lack subsequent performance data on the second mortgages.

Eriksen et al. (2013) find that over the period 2002–2010, borrowers with a second mortgage were 62.7 percent more likely to default on their primary loan each period. In order to evaluate equivalent risk profiles, the first and second mortgages are combined and then compared to a single loan with equivalent attributes. Interestingly, combined loan borrowers are 58.3 percent less likely to default on their first mortgage than single loan borrowers. Borrowers treat the first and second mortgages as sequential put options. As the second mortgage lender is paid off last in the event of a foreclosure, that lender is unlikely to initiate foreclosure when negative equity is sufficiently high because the net recovery yields little, if any, payoff. As a result, the borrower may intentionally stop making payments on the second mortgage while keeping the first mortgage current. The second mortgage lender and the borrower now have partially aligned interests regarding future housing values. The second mortgage lender retains the option to foreclose in the event home prices increase or amortization reduces principal on the first mortgage to a sufficient level.

The defaulted borrower of the second mortgage, aware of the second mortgage lender's position, will then only continue making payments on the first mortgage if the value of consumption placed on their continued occupancy of the property exceeds the payment on the first mortgage. However, the borrower can always bring the second mortgage current in the event of sufficient price appreciation.

Kau, Keenan, and Lyubimov (2013) investigate strategic default with simultaneous consideration of first and second mortgage pairs. Strategic default is not defined in the traditional sense of a borrower acting in a goal-seeking manner, but rather in a context consistent with game theory. In this context, *strategic default* means that the borrower is aware of the lender's position, including transaction costs, and reacts accordingly. An important contribution of the paper is the analysis of the loan pairs beyond the period they first default, which allows for instances where a borrower brings one or both loans current. The results are mixed in support of strategic default where a borrower defaults on the second loan but not the first. While the authors find second loan default propensity increase as the second loan recovery rate approaches zero, they also find an increase in the propensity to default on the first loan.

An interesting result from Kau et al. (2013) is the opposite scenario where a borrower defaults on the first loan but not the second. Here 88 percent of the first-only defaults have collateral values in excess of the first loan. The second loan lender could possibly realize a positive recovery in the event the second lender chooses to foreclose. In addition, first loan modifications are somewhat common for first-only defaults with 15.7 percent of borrowers receiving a modification within six months. These results suggest the possibility some borrowers may default on the first loan in hopes of a modification while avoiding foreclosure from the second loan.

BORROWER MOBILITY

The prepayment of a mortgage occurs for one of three reasons: refinancing, sale of the house (move), or full payment of the outstanding loan in cash. A cash payoff with no new debt is a rare event worth mentioning but will be ignored hereafter. The other two reasons, refinance and sale, are often grouped together without differentiation in many discussions of prepayment. The primary reason differentiation does not occur is the lack of historical data. In a perfect setting, a researcher could observe all mortgage originations and match borrowers as well as property addresses so full information would be available about refinance and sale transactions. Because researchers work with highly incomplete information, prepayments require significantly more effort if one wishes to explain borrower mobility.

Clapp, Goldberg, Harding, and LaCour-Little (2001) separate refinance and sale transactions by using loan data from a national lender in conjunction with transaction data from the California Market Data Corporative, Inc. (CMDC). Prepayment terminations from a move (where property is sold) can be identified by matching the property address contained in the two data sources as well as by matching the property sale date to the loan origination date. With prepayments categorized, the three competing risks of termination—default, refinance, and moves—are analyzed. The results indicate that the market price of the loan, the original loan balance, and current LTV influence refinance, while a borrower's characteristics (age, minority status, and income) and the probability of negative equity influence a move. Accounting for the two sources of prepayment risk separately increases termination prediction ability compared to a model where the source of prepayment is undifferentiated.

Deng, Pavlov, and Yang (2005) find similar results looking at California data and highlight the significantly different prepayment termination patterns, both from refinance and move, for borrowers in an affluent area of Los Angeles County. An, Clapp, and Deng (2010) perform more recent work about borrower mobility by using a nested multinomial logit model to correct for the correlation of sale and default due to omitted borrower mobility characteristics.

BORROWER HETEROGENEITY

The assumption that borrowers are homogeneous (beyond FICO scores) implies that borrower characteristics have no differential effect on termination decisions. Relaxing the assumption of homogeneity introduces the problem of how to classify borrowers if different groups of borrowers present significantly different risk profiles and thus termination patterns. Archer, Ling, and McGill (1996) show collateral or income constraints significantly reduce the impact of option value on prepayment. The problem of heterogeneity is particularly problematic in reduced form modeling given the role of baseline hazard rates in predicting termination.

Deng et al. (2000) address borrower heterogeneity. They use a Cox proportional hazard model (Cox and Oakes 1984) where prepayment and default are estimated jointly as dependent competing risks. There are three mass points in the distribution of unobserved borrower heterogeneity, which permits risk differentiation among high and low risk borrower types. This process, known as *mass point mixed hazard* (MMH), uses probability mass points to capture unobserved heterogeneity. Unobserved borrower heterogeneity plays an important role in the propensity to terminate a loan. Heterogeneity particularly affects prepayment. High-risk borrowers are 4.58 times riskier than low-risk borrowers in prepayment. A particularly interesting finding is the increased propensity to terminate, both by default and prepayment, for high LTV borrowers.

The difficulty with MMH estimation is that the model may fail to converge to a solution, which then requires strong parametric assumptions about the shape of the baseline hazard function (Clapp, Deng, and An 2006). An et al. (2010) use a nested multinomial logit model to account for unobserved heterogeneity. The authors note that the termination risk for sale and default are likely to be correlated with the unobserved borrower characteristics. As a result, a standard multinomial logit model, which prohibits correlation among termination risks, is inappropriate for modeling unobserved heterogeneity as it relates to mortgage termination.

Summary and Conclusions

Accurate estimation of mortgage termination is critical for the valuation of a mortgage asset. While structural models are prominent choices for predicting borrower default and prepayment, reduced form models have gained traction as they lend themselves to estimation based on observed behavior rather than generating termination endogenously. Additionally, reduced form models allow for a greater number of explanatory variables than structural models, which typically only use home price and interest rate as explanatory variables. The ability to incorporate borrower characteristics, macroeconomic variables, and mortgage contract features provides flexibility that helps researchers evaluate the evolving mortgage market. The 2008 mortgage crisis highlighted the unreasonable assumptions in mortgage underwriting and valuation. The reduced form framework should serve as a foundation for understanding how such modeling assumptions affect mortgage valuation through the estimation of prepayment and default.

Discussion Questions

1. Identify which modeling technique assumes only optimal termination execution and explain why this is the case.
2. Explain why a borrower would not immediately default upon the realization of negative equity.
3. Discuss why the absence of arbitrage is important for mortgage pricing.
4. Explain why a reduced form model is appealing for estimating mortgage termination.

References

Agarwal, Sumit, Brent W. Ambrose, Souphala Chomsisengphet, and Chunlin Liu. 2006. "An Empirical Analysis of Home Equity Loan and Line Performance." *Journal of Financial Intermediation* 15:4, 444–469.

An, Xudong, John M. Clapp, and Yongheng Deng. 2010. "Omitted Mobility Characteristics and Property Market Dynamics: Application to Mortgage Termination." *Journal of Real Estate Finance and Economics* 41:3, 245–271.

Archer, Wayne R., David C. Ling, and Gary A. McGill. 1996. "The Effect of Income and Collateral Constraints on Residential Mortgage Terminations." *Regional Science and Urban Economics* 26:3, 235–261.

Avery, Robert B., Kenneth P. Brevoort, and Glenn B. Canner. 2007. "2006 HMDA Data." *Federal Reserve Bulletin* 93:December, A73–A109.

Brunson, Andrew L., James B. Kau, and Donald C. Keenan. 2001. "A Fixed-rate Mortgage Valuation Model in Three State Variables." *Journal of Fixed Income* 11:1, 17–27.

Chen, Ren-Raw, and Louis Scott. 2003. "Multi-factor Cox–Ingersoll–Ross Models of the Term Structure: Estimates and Tests from a Kalman Filter Model." *Journal of Real Estate Finance and Economics* 27:2, 143–172.

Clapp, John M., Yongheng Deng, and Xudong An. 2006. "Unobserved Heterogeneity in Models of Competing Mortgage Termination Risks." *Real Estate Economics* 34:2, 243–273.

Clapp, John M., Gerson M. Goldberg, John P. Harding, and Michael LaCour-Little. 2001. "Movers and Shuckers: Interdependent Prepayment Decisions." *Real Estate Economics* 29:3, 411–450.

Cox, John C., Jonathan E. Ingersoll Jr., and Stephen A. Ross. 1985. "A Theory of the Term Structure of Interest Rates." *Econometrica* 53:2, 385–407.

Cox, David R., and David Oakes. 1984. *Analysis of Survival Data*. Volume 21. Boca Raton, FL: Chapman & Hall/CRC.

Demyanyk, Yuliya, and Otto Van Hemert. 2009. "Understanding the Subprime Mortgage Crisis." *Review of Financial Studies* 24:6, 1848–1880.

Deng, Yongheng, Andrey D. Pavlov, and Lihong Yang. 2005. "Spatial Heterogeneity in Mortgage Terminations by Refinance, Sale and Default." *Real Estate Economics* 33:4, 739–764.

Deng, Yongheng, John M. Quigley, and Robert Van Order. 1996. "Mortgage Default and Low Downpayment Loans: The Costs of Public Subsidy." *Regional Science and Urban Economics* 26:3, 263–285.

Deng, Yongheng, John M. Quigley, and Robert Van Order. 2000. "Mortgage Terminations, Heterogeneity and the Exercise of Mortgage Options." *Econometrica* 68:2, 275–307.

Doucet, Arnaud, and Adam M. Johansen. 2009. "A Tutorial on Particle Filtering and Smoothing: Fifteen Years Later." In Dan Crisan and Boris Rozovskii, eds., *Oxford Handbook of Nonlinear Filtering*, 656–704. Oxford and New York: Oxford University Press.

Doucet, Arnaud, Nando De Freitas, and Neil Gordon. 2001. *Sequential Monte Carlo Methods in Practice*. New York: Springer.

Dunn, Kenneth B., and Chester S. Spatt. 2005. "The Effect of Refinancing Costs and Market Imperfections on the Optimal Call Strategy and the Pricing of Debt Contracts." *Real Estate Economics* 33:4, 595–617.

Eriksen, Michael, James Kau, and Donald Keenan. 2013. "The Impact of Second Loans on Subprime Mortgage Defaults." *Real Estate Economics* 41:4, 858–886.

Gamerman, Dani, and Hedibert F. Lopes. 2006. *Markov Chain Monte Carlo: Stochastic Simulation for Bayesian Inference*. Volume 68. Boca Raton, FL: Chapman & Hall/CRC.

Geyer, Charles. 2010. "Introduction to Markov Chain Monte Carlo." In Steve Brooks, Andrew Gelman, Galin Jones, and Xiao-Li Meng, eds., *Handbook of Markov Chain Monte Carlo: Methods and Applications*, 3–48. Boca Raton, FL: Chapman & Hall/CRC.

Goodman, Laurie S., Roger Ashworth, Brian Landy, and Ke Yin. 2010. "Second Liens: How Important?" *Journal of Fixed Income* 20:2, 19–30.

Harrison, Jeff, and Mike West. 1997. *Bayesian Forecasting and Dynamic Models*. 2nd edn. New York: Springer.

Hilliard, Jimmy E., James B. Kau, Donald C. Keenan, and Walter J. Muller. 1995. "Pricing a Class of American and European Path Dependent Securities." *Management Science* 41:12, 1892–1899.

Jegadeesh, Narasimhan, and Xiongwei Ju. 2000. "A Non-parametric Prepayment Model and Valuation of Mortgage-backed Securities." *Journal of Fixed Income* 10:1, 50–67.

Kau, James B., and Donald C. Keenan. 1995. "An Overview of the Option-theoretic Pricing of Mortgages." *Journal of Housing Research* 6:2, 217–244.

Kau, James B., and Taewon Kim. 1994. "Waiting to Default: The Value of Delay." *Real Estate Economics* 22:3, 539–551.

Kau, James B., Donald C. Keenan, and Taewon Kim. 1994. "Default Probabilities for Mortgages." *Journal of Urban Economics* 35:3, 278–296.

Kau, James B., Donald C. Keenan, and Constantine Lyubimov. 2013. "First Mortgages, Second Mortgages, and Their Default." Working Paper, University of Georgia.

Kau, James B., Donald C. Keenan, and Alexey A. Smurov. 2004. "Reduced-form Mortgage Valuation." Working Paper, University of Georgia.

Kau, James B., Donald C. Keenan, and Alexey A. Smurov. 2006. "Reduced Form Mortgage Pricing as an Alternative to Option-pricing Models." *Journal of Real Estate Finance and Economics* 33:3, 183–196.

Kau, James B., Donald C. Keenan, Constantine Lyubimov, and V. Carlos Slawson. 2011. "Subprime Mortgage Default." *Journal of Urban Economics* 70:2, 75–87.

Kau, James B., Donald C. Keenan, Walter J. Muller III, and James F. Epperson. 1992. "A Generalized Valuation Model for Fixed-rate Residential Mortgages." *Journal of Money, Credit and Banking* 24:3, 279–299.

Kau, James B., Donald C. Keenan, Walter J. Muller III, and James F. Epperson. 1995. "The Valuation at Origination of Fixed-rate Mortgages with Default and Prepayment." *Journal of Real Estate Finance and Economics* 11:1, 5–36.

Mian, Atif, and Amir Sufi. 2009. "The Consequences of Mortgage Credit Expansion: Evidence from the US Mortgage Default Crisis." *Quarterly Journal of Economics* 124:4, 1449–1496.

Pennington-Cross, Anthony, and Giang Ho. 2010. "The Termination of Subprime Hybrid and Fixed Rate Mortgages." *Real Estate Economics* 38:3, 399–426.

Sherlund, Shane M. 2008. "The Past, Present, and Future of Subprime Mortgages." Finance and Economics Discussion Series 2008–2063. Washington, DC: Federal Reserve Board.

9

Commercial Mortgages and Commercial Mortgage-Backed Securities

XUDONG AN

Associate Professor of Finance, College of Business Administration, San Diego State University

KERRY D. VANDELL

Dean's Professor of Finance and Director of the Center for Real Estate, The Paul Merage School of Business, University of California–Irvine

Introduction

Commercial mortgages are loans secured by income-producing property. Commercial properties include any real property interest providing a cash flow through lease payments. In addition to conventional investable assets such as office buildings, they include nontraditional assets such as infrastructure, single-family rental housing, and even billboards (Deloitte Center for Financial Services 2013). Commercial mortgages have a priority claim on cash flows, are senior to equity interests, but do not share in property returns. They are considered debt, but there are also hybrid structures that offer equity participation.

Before the Industrial Revolution, the primary class of investment property was agricultural land. Tenant farmers were typically obligated to the landed gentry for rents, paid as a percentage of the crop production. The option to pay down the indebtedness and take fee ownership of the land was limited (Linklater 2013).

In the United States the federal government retained ownership of newly acquired land, permitting fee ownership by small landholders. Supported by the Homestead Act of 1862, the price initially was low. But as re-trading of land rights occurred, prices rose relative to incomes making land not affordable. The response was the initiation of the mortgage banking industry. Mortgage banks provided loans to farmers, acting as correspondents for large banks and insurance companies (Lederman 1993).

Industrialization and urbanization were raising land and property prices in urbanizing areas. The East Coast financial institutions provided debt capital for acquisition and development of commercial sites. Terms were short at five years or less, with little amortization and a loan-to-value ratio (LTV) of 50 percent or less. As stringent as the terms may seem, this capital was indispensable for permitting rental housing and commercial development (Keehn and Smiley 1977).

Because land speculation was unregulated, many booms and busts occurred in the commercial property market in the nineteenth and early twentieth century. The largest bust was the Great Depression, which formally began with the stock market crash of October 1929, but was fueled earlier by real estate speculation. The predecessors of the later CMBS market were first tested with the issuance of mortgage bonds on commercial properties. These mortgage bonds perished during the 1930s, together with much of the rest of the commercial mortgage market (Pedrelli 1999).

The commercial mortgage market did not recover until after World War II, with the help of reforms during Roosevelt's New Deal. Commercial banks were assigned primacy in providing short-term commercial mortgage debt and lending for acquisition and construction. Insurance companies, often through mortgage banking correspondents, handled longer term financing (Dennis 1981).

Pension funds were growing during the postwar years, but were not active in commercial mortgage lending until the Employee Retirement Income Security Act of 1974 (ERISA) mandated diversification in pension fund investment portfolios. The result was increased allocations to debt and equity interests in commercial real estate. The Garn-St. Germain Depository Institutions Act of 1982 freed savings and loans to compete with banks for lending in the commercial mortgage market. The repeal of the Glass-Steagall Act in 1999 removed the distinction between the commercial and investment banks, further increasing the options for commercial mortgage lending. Additional capital came from cross-border investing by oil economies, emerging markets, and sovereign wealth funds (Hendrickson 2011).

The tax laws encouraged real estate investors to make heavier use of debt. The Economic Recovery Tax Act of 1981 (ERTA) provided incentives to invest in commercial development, with high permitted rates of tax depreciation without recapture, high initial-period write-offs, low capital gains tax rates, and the ability to offset taxable losses against taxable gains from other sources.

The 1980s marked the first tentative steps toward the development the modern commercial mortgage-backed securities (CMBS) market. CMBS products were based on pricing models and a diversified pool of loans rather than individual bonds on single properties. CMBS securities were created by the pooling of commercial mortgage loans through a conduit process that placed them into a trust or special purpose vehicle (SPV). The SPV qualified to be treated as a real estate mortgage investment conduit (REMIC) in the Tax Reform Act of 1986 (TRA 86), rendering the trust a passive vehicle avoiding federal income taxes at the entity level.

The CMBS market was patterned after earlier Ginnie Mae securities using Federal Housing Administration (FHA) and Veterans Administration (VA) residential loans and pass-through residential mortgage-backed securities (RMBS) issued by Freddie Mac and Fannie Mae. S&P and other agencies began developing ratings for these security instruments in the mid-1980s, but were hindered until more definitive evidence on the default risk inherent in these pools was available.

After the REMIC legislation of 1986, other innovations in the CMBS market appeared. Following innovations in the CMO market, cash flows from the mortgage pools began to be carved up into "tranches" and placed into securities. Because various protections mitigated prepayment risk for most commercial mortgages, most attention in the shaping of tranches focused on default risk (CRE Finance Council 2010).

Senior-subordinate structures became common, in which the senior A rated bonds retained first claim on principal and interest and the junior B-piece bonds were assigned the first-loss position from delinquencies or defaults. However, there still was little appetite for the development of the CMBS market because of the fallout from TRA 86. Until the late 1980s, the commercial mortgage market was growing, while the CMBS market remained in its infancy.

Figures 9.1 and 9.2 portray commercial mortgage debt issuance over 1980Q1 to 2013Q1. By year-end 1989, commercial mortgages reached $1.088 trillion outstanding, surpassing the Treasury market ($430.6 billion) and of comparable magnitude to

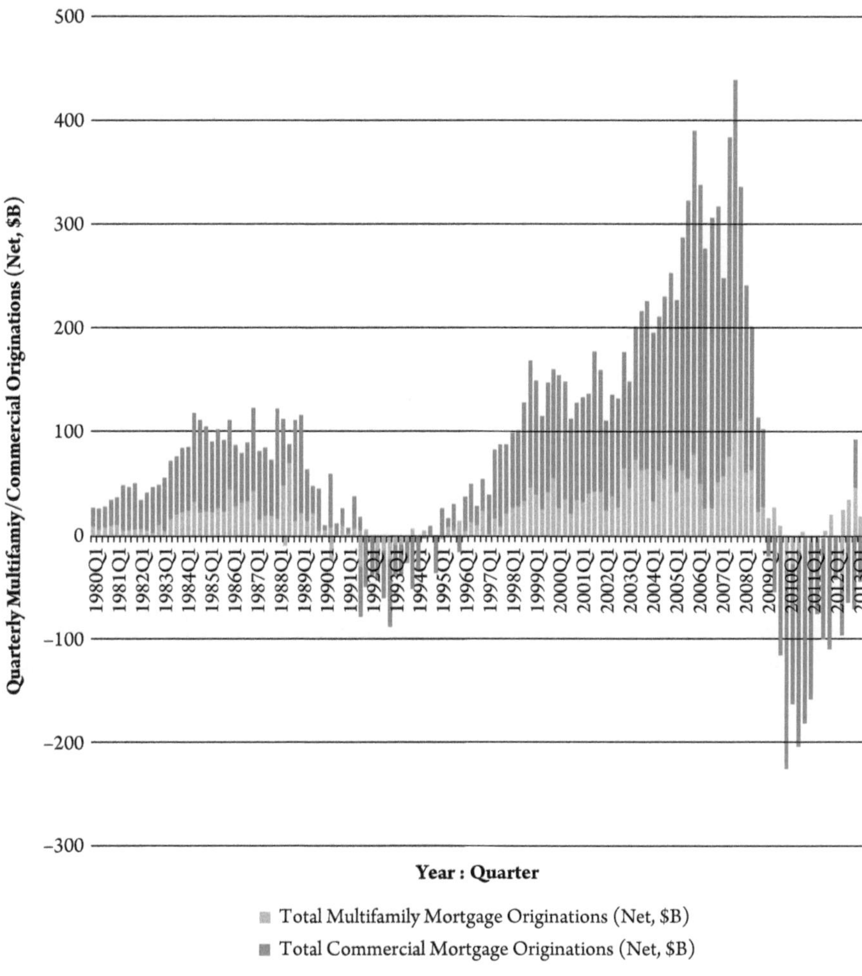

Figure 9.1 Quarterly Multifamily and Commercial Mortgage Originations: 1980Q1 to 2013Q1. This figure illustrates the cycles of activity in the multifamily and commercial mortgages markets. Dramatic retrenchment occurred in 2008, followed by the recent recovery, and the stability of the multifamily sector relative to the nonresidential commercial sector. Source: U.S. Board of Governors of the Federal Reserve System (2013).

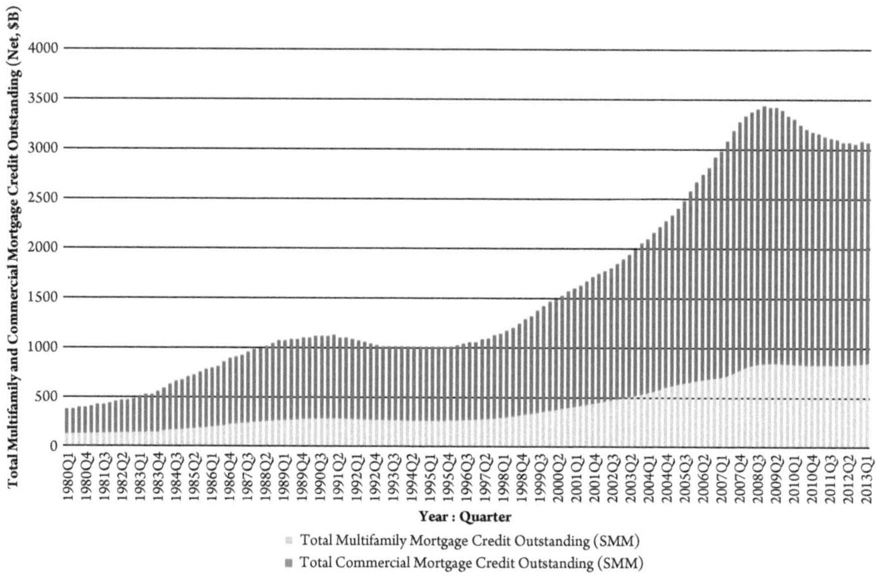

Figure 9.2 Total Multifamily and Commercial Mortgage Credit Outstanding (Net, $B): 1980Q1 to 2013Q1. This figure illustrates the trend in outstanding balances in the commercial and multifamily mortgage markets over at 33-year period. A decline started in 2008 followed by the beginning of recovery in 2012. Source: U.S. Board of Governors of the Federal Reserve System (2013).

the tax-exempt state and local securities market ($1.130 trillion). However, only 3.2 percent of commercial mortgage credit outstanding was securitized, primarily through FHA and government-sponsored enterprise (GSE) multifamily securities, not private-issue CMBS.

The savings and loan (S&L) crisis of the late 1980s and early 1990s provided the first major challenge to delivering debt capital to the commercial real estate market through portfolio lenders or as whole loans. The crisis on the whole-loan side was a major impetus for the development of the CMBS market. The federal government created the Resolution Trust Corporation (RTC) in 1989 to resolve defaulted mortgages and other assets that had resulted from the crisis, totaling close to $153 billion in 1999 dollars (Curry and Shibut 2000). In 1992 the RTC began issuing CMBS securities made up of pools of performing and non-performing loans. Federal guarantees on these securities were necessary at first but gradually eliminated, and spreads began to decline. Structures emerged that no longer were confined to a single-property class, but were diversified. By 1995 the securitization activities of the RTC ended, and private entities took advantage of the jump-start provided. The international risk-based capital standards imposed by the Basel Accords (Basel I) in 1988 gave a higher capital rating to senior CMBS tranches than to whole loans. Although CMBS products could create value through diversification, liquidity, and risk allocation, they did not reduce credit risk in the underlying commercial mortgages.

The second major crisis to beset the commercial mortgage and CMBS markets was the global financial crisis that began in 2007. Some assign primary blame to the expansion of the non-agency private-issue RMBS sector. However, commercial mortgage and CMBS markets were also subjected to speculative pressures, spurred by rapid capital formation and inflows from newly emerging economies and institutional investors. Interest rates remained low, and federal regulators exercised lax oversight (Coleman, Lacour-Little, and Vandell 2008). As the economy expanded, growth in demand arose for commercial property, especially office. Commercial property values across all sectors and regions rose steadily through mid-2007 (Taylor 2009).

By 2007 lenders and CMBS market makers had begun to tighten credit standards. This and the weakening economy resulted in a reduction in both the demand for and supply of mortgage credit. By the end of 2007 through 2009 the economy, employment, and commercial property prices were in free-fall. The downturn caused a disruption in lending, downgrading and price reductions in CMBS securities, and illiquidity in the whole loan and securitized market. Unlike the crisis of the early 1990s when overbuilding dominated, the dominant factor was on the demand side. The previous high levels of employment in office and other sectors driving real estate demand were ultimately unsustainable, resulting in high vacancy rates.

Commercial mortgages did not include a subprime sector as did the residential market, but had other characteristics that rendered them vulnerable to the downturn. Beyond cash flow insolvency by tenants resulting in high vacancy and delinquency rates and declines in effective rents, there was balloon or rollover risk. Most commercial mortgage products had interest only (IO) or amortization longer than the terms to maturity, which left a balloon payment due at maturity (Jacob and Fastovsky 1999). Under ordinary circumstances, the note would refinance at a new rate and term. If the lender faced liquidity and capital adequacy problems, it called the note. If market values had dropped, the lender also required additional cash before refinancing to maintain required minimum LTVs. These actions increasingly precipitated defaults.

A third factor that increased default risk was structured finance instruments, especially mezzanine debt (Berman 2007). Mezzanine debt was inserted between equity interests in the property and the first lien. Sometimes considered priority equity and other times subordinate debt, these instruments had hybrid characteristics. The intent was to reduce traditional equity and debt capital, raise equity yields, and provide opportunities for mezzanine investors to achieve high-yield returns. In exchange, these investors took a first loss position on the debt, but the byproduct was to increase leverage. As with traditional second liens, mezzanines leave the traditional first-lien lender in the same priority of claim, but increase the likelihood of default during a market downturn owing to the reduced equity position.

A fourth factor in CMBS pools creating risk was the special servicer (Ambrose, Sanders, and Yavas 2009). Unlike the primary and master servicers who handled the processing and allocation of ordinary payments into the pool, the special servicer handled unique payment events, including delinquencies. Delinquencies required careful decision-making not to violate the pooling and servicing agreement to obtain maximization of the recovery of principal and interest on a net present value basis in the event of default. Investors in different tranches had different interests in default resolution. Special servicers were often B-piece investors at risk of first losses, while being the initial controlling class on the securities and ultimately the property. This situation normally aligned interests. In major market declines, however, special servicers had incentives not to foreclose but to "extend and pretend." The special servicer extended the maturity term of a troubled loan to avoid an immediate realization of default loss from a distressed sale. This preserved their status, fees, and potential future cash flows in the event of market recovery. A foreclosure would wipe out their investment and lose fee income as special servicers to a new controlling class. However, the "extend and pretend" may not be at the best interest of other investors.

By early 2010 the commercial property and mortgage crisis began slowly to abate. Capitalization (cap) rates and vacancies on commercial property declined, while effective rents stabilized. "Extend and pretend" became less of an issue as market fundamentals improved. CMBS default rates peaked in 2011 and began to drop. Defaults on bank portfolio loans were declining by early 2010. GSE multifamily loans and pools continued to perform because of cherry picking of the highest-quality loans.

Commercial mortgage issuance dropped from $352.3 billion in 2007 to a net redemption of $174.7 billion in 2010. By 2012, the net redemption was only $19.7 billion. In fact, 2012Q4 showed net positive issuance of commercial mortgage debt (Figure 9.1), and the first balance increase since 2008 (Figure 9.2).

The lenders that fared best during the crisis were those most adversely affected by defaults in earlier credit crises: insurance company-originated commercial mortgages and FHA and GSE multifamily loans. The GSEs had experienced high defaults during the fallout from the S&L crisis, but strengthened their underwriting standards and took advantage of their implicit federal government guarantee of their debt, allowing them to increase market share from 1.0 percent to 8.6 percent in 2012. Insurance companies reduced market share from 22.7 percent in 1990 to 9.3 percent by 2009 but began to cherry pick loans carefully after the financial crisis and resumed an important presence.

Commercial banks and CMBS conduits fared the worst, with the highest default rates during the financial crisis. Banks and other depositories suffered high losses after the S&L crisis. They had a 59.0 percent market share in 1987, dropping to 48.6 percent by 2012, losing out primarily to the GSEs and CMBS. The CMBS market began its rise in the early 1990s, to a 25.9 percent market share in 2007, then falling to 21.6 percent by 2010 with defaults and redemptions, before showing signs of recovery by 2012.

From 1990 to 2007, CMBS issues would come to dominate the form in which commercial debt was held. From 0.7 percent of commercial mortgage debt outstanding in 1981Q4, CMBS rose to a peak of 25.5 percent by 2007Q2. The multifamily sector was even more securitized than nonresidential. The securitized share of multifamily debt rose from 1.5 percent in 1981Q3 to 32.6 percent by 2003Q3. Nonresidential CMBS grew from 0.1 percent in 1985Q1 to 25.8 percent by 2007Q3. These markets evaporated after 2007Q2, when CMBS issuance dropped from $75.9 billion to zero by 2008Q3.

Policy makers gave consideration to a covered bond in which the issuer retained risk in the event of default. The Dodd-Frank Wall Street Reform and Consumer Protection Act of 2010 ultimately resulted in a less severe credit risk retention reserve. The industry responded with CMBS 2.0 requiring more stringent loan underwriting, disclosure, and pool structuring than before the financial crisis without the risk retention. While CMBS 2.0 has been accepted from a credit risk standpoint, the political outcome is still uncertain (Sargent 2011). Although the CMBS market has recovered from essentially no issuance during the period 2008Q3 to 2010Q1, to $44.4 billion in 2012, this amount is far less than the $230.2 billion in 2007.

Commercial Mortgage Terms and Underwriting

Differences exist between commercial and residential mortgages. First, commercial mortgages are usually balloon loans. As Table 9.1 shows, such mortgages amortize over a 20 to 30 year period but mature in a shorter timeframe, with a remaining balance payoff. Short maturity reduces interest rate risk borne by lenders while the long amortization lowers borrowers' monthly payment. To further reduce monthly payment, many commercial mortgages are interest-only (IO) or have IO periods.

To control the elevated default risk caused by balloon payment, IO features and property value volatility, lenders limit loan-to-value ratio (LTV). Table 9.1 shows LTV generally below 70 percent. Lenders require the debt-service coverage ratio (DSCR), defined as net operating income (NOI) divided by the mortgage payment, to be higher than a certain level. The average DSCRs of loans made in 2012Q4 are all above 1.4, with some hotel loans as high as 3.0. To mitigate default risk, reserve requirements are common. From Table 9.1, apartment loans can have reserves of $275 per unit per year. Office and retail loans can have reserves of $0.20 per square foot annually.

Commercial mortgages are more likely to be recourse, with debt payable in full even if foreclosure does not satisfy the outstanding balance. A general obligation of the borrower or a personal guarantee from the owner is common.

Controlling LTV and DSCR, capital reserves, and recourse are measures to reduce default risk. Commercial mortgage lenders charge spreads to compensate for remaining default risk. The average spread of 30-year conforming residential mortgages over the 10-year Treasury is 170 basis points (bps) over 1971–2013 based on Federal Reserve data, while the spreads of commercial mortgages are typically over 250 bps. Table 9.1 shows that in 2012Q4 office, retail, and hotel loans had average spreads of 345, 305, and 369 bps, respectively. Even the safest apartment loans had an average spread of 284 bps.

Unlike residential mortgages, commercial mortgages are usually restricted from prepayment. Lockouts prohibit the borrower from prepaying, usually in the first few years of the term. According to An, Deng, Nichols, and Sanders (2013a), 85 percent of CMBS loans originated after 1998 have a lockout. Prepayment penalty or yield maintenance is usually used after the lockout period. In the former, borrowers pay percentage of the remaining balance, to pay off the loan early. In the latter, the borrower pays the present value of the difference between the scheduled interest payment and a lower market rate.

Since 2000, defeasance is the preferred alternative to handling prepayment for CMBS loans. In a defeasance, real estate collateral is substituted with a portfolio of Treasury or agency securities that matches the cash flow of scheduled mortgage payments, including the balloon. Defeasance strengthens the predictability of commercial mortgage payment streams for investors while providing borrowers with flexibility in selling or refinancing. From Moody's (2006), defeasance covered more than 2,000 CMBS loans in 2005 with a balance of $29.7 billion, more than 12 percent of outstanding issuance.

Commercial mortgages have other covenants on the property and borrowing entity. Maintaining and insuring the property, paying property taxes, and prohibiting sale without lender approval are minimum requirements. Other covenants include lender approval of leases, including modification; generally accepted accounting principles (GAAP); property operating statements submission; and notification of major capital expenditure, regulatory violations, condemnation, insurance claims, or lawsuits.

Table 9.1 **Commercial Mortgage Terms: 2012Q4**

	Apartment	*Office*	*Retail*	*Industrial*	*Hotel*	*Golf*	*Senior Housing*	*Mfg Housing*	*Res-taurant*	*Self Storage*	*Special Purpose*
Maturity											
Avg	20.50	8.00	6.20	11.46	7.80	9.00	13.65	9.15	7.45	6.10	7.85
Min	3	3	3	3	5	5	3	5	3	3	3
Max	40	30	10	30	30	30	25	30	15	10	20
Amortization											
Avg	27	25	24	24	22	20	24	25	20	27	20
Min	15	15	15	15	15	15	15	15	15	15	15
LTV											
Avg	73	68	70	69	65	63	70	70	62	68	62
Min	50	50	50	50	50	50	50	50	50	50	50
Max	90	80	80	85	80	80	90	80	75	80	80
DSCR											
Avg	1.43	1.70	1.43	1.50	1.64	1.66	1.56	1.42	1.71	1.67	1.70
Min	1.10	1.15	1.05	1.15	1.00	1.20	1.12	1.15	1.15	1.15	1.15
Max	1.96	2.25	2.25	2.15	3.00	2.40	2.30	2.05	2.40	2.75	2.10
Spread over 10-year Treasury											
Avg	2.84	3.45	3.05	2.93	3.69	5.80	3.33	3.99	4.71	5.11	4.83
Min	0.70	1.05	0.75	1.05	1.20	1.20	1.45	0.99	2.10	1.05	2.00
Max	6.85	6.85	7.16	6.85	11.26	11.50	8.22	8.22	11.52	6.85	12.00

Table 9.1 **continued**

	Apartment	*Office*	*Retail*	*Industrial*	*Hotel*	*Golf*	*Senior Housing*	*Mfg Housing*	*Res-taurant*	*Self Storage*	*Special Purpose*
Interest rate											
Avg	4.49	5.10	4.70	4.58	5.34	7.45	4.98	5.64	6.36	4.70	6.48
Min	2.35	2.70	2.40	2.70	2.85	2.85	3.10	2.64	3.75	2.40	3.65
Max	8.50	8.50	8.81	8.50	12.91	13.15	9.87	9.87	13.17	8.81	13.65
Reserve requirement											
Typical	275 $/unit	0.20 $/sf	0.18 $/sf	0.18 $/sf	5.0 of EGI	2500 $/unit	300 $/unit	75 $/unit	3.0 of EGI	65 $/unit	0.18 $/sf
Min	150	0.15	0.15	0.10	4.0	1000	250	25	2.0	25	0.10
Max	300	0.25	0.20	0.25	5.0	5000	400	150	5.0	80	0.20

Note: The table shows terms including maturity in years, DSCR, LTV, interest rate, and spread over Treasuries are in percentage points. Avg = average, Min = minimum, and Max = maximum.

Source: RealtyRates.com (2013).

LTV and DSCR are the main focuses of commercial mortgage underwriting. The LTV ratio is the classical underwriting criterion that focuses on collateral. Commercial mortgage underwriting has required the LTV to be 75 percent or lower with value based on an independent appraisal (Brueggeman and Fisher 2011). Loans with higher risk are often limited to lower LTV (Archer, Elmer, Harrison, and Ling 2002; Grovenstein, Harding, Sirmans, Thebpanya, and Turnbull 2005). Guarantees and credit enhancements, competition, and expectations of a rising market may push lenders to relax the LTV limit. A constraint on LTV at loan maturity is often examined and assures that the borrower can refinance or sell the property to repay.

The DSCR requirement focuses on repayment capacity. The typical minimum DSCR requirement is 1.3, meaning that the NOI is 30 percent above the level required to cover the periodic mortgage payment. The DSCR can vary across cycles and properties. Some variations in calculating NOI include subtracting capital expenditures from cash flow, which is an above the line treatment, and applying more conservative assumptions about rent, vacancy, and operating expenses.

Commercial mortgage lenders do not examine credit scores as closely as residential lenders. They use credit status of the borrower, from past experience in investment, operations, mortgage repayment, and business relationships. Lenders also look at the borrower's social network, capability to manage the property, and reputation and integrity of the key principals making financial and asset decisions.

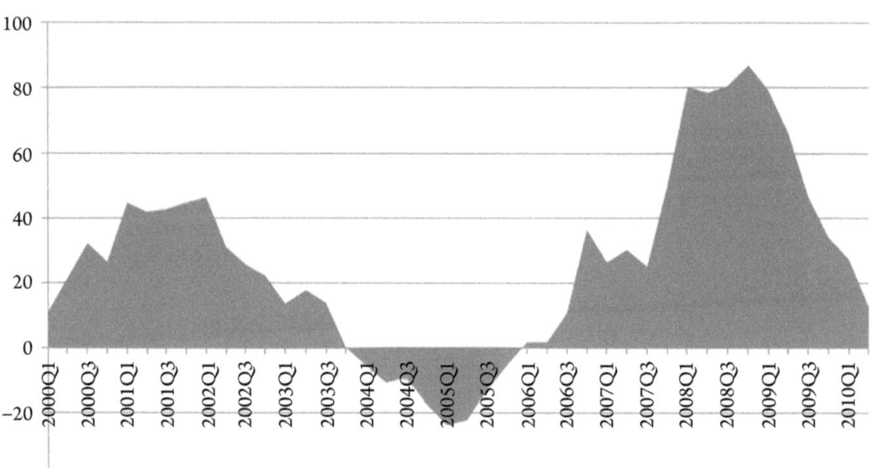

Figure 9.3 Net Percentage of Lenders Tightening Commercial Real Estate Credit. This figure shows the net percentage of lenders reported to have tightened credit on commercial real estate loans. This quarterly survey by the Federal Reserve Board includes about 60 large domestic banks and 24 U.S. branches and agencies of foreign banks. Source: Federal Reserve Senior Loan Officer Survey (April 2010).

Figure 9.3 plots the net percentage of domestic banks tightening standards for commercial real estate loans (including construction loans) from the Federal Reserve Senior Loan Officer Survey. It shows that commercial real estate lenders loosened credit during 2004Q1 to 2005Q4 but then tightened credit during 2006 through 2009.

This cyclicality is not reflected in the underwriting ratios (LTV and DSCR) of commercial mortgage loans. Based on survey data from RealtyRates.com, commercial mortgage loans maintained relatively stable LTVs and DSCRs during 2002–2010 (An and Sanders 2010). Consistent with the RealtyRates.com survey data, underwriting information from CMBS loans shows no signs of substantial underwriting changes before, during, or after the financial crisis. This is apparently paradoxical compared with the Federal Reserve data suggesting cyclical underwriting. What explains this paradox?

First, commercial mortgage loans originated may have been based on inflated property values. According to Cohen and Manuszak (2013), Moody's adjusted DSCRs based on stabilized cap rates declined during 2002–2007 while LTVs increased to over 100 percent in 2007. Second, lenders may have changed underwriting in other dimensions, such as allowing more IO loans and relaxing loan covenants. Third, lenders may have changed underwriting standards in unperceivable ways such as decreasing the collection of "soft" information as Rajan, Seru, and Vig (2014) suggest for subprime mortgages.

Default Risk of Commercial Mortgages

Default is the signature risk of commercial mortgages. Compared to residential mortgages, commercial mortgages have higher default rates, due to volatility of commercial property values, risky loan features such as balloons and IO, and borrowers being more ruthless in exercising default options (Vandell 1995; Geltner, Miller, Clayton, and Eichholtz 2007; Ciochetti, Deng, Gao, and Yao 2002; Ciochetti, Deng, Lee, Shilling, and Yao 2003).

During normal times, the annual default rate (90 + day delinquency rate) of commercial mortgages is between 0.6 and 2.4 percent (Esaki 2002), in contrast to the 0.1 to 0.6 percent in the Standard Default Assumption (SDA) for residential mortgages. Within a 10-year period, 16 percent of commercial mortgages default compared with less than 2 percent for residential mortgages.

This pattern changes with recent data. Figure 9.4 shows that starting from late 2006 a surge in the prime ARM default rate occurred, surpassing the conduit CMBS default rate. From 2007 through 2009, the default rate of conduit CMBS loans was even lower than that of prime conventional fixed rate mortgages (FRMs). Over the entire period, the conduit CMBS default rate remained lower than subprime FRMs and adjustable rate mortgages (ARMs).

Figure 9.5 has 30 + day, 60 + day, and 90 + day delinquency rates of conduit CMBS loans during 2000Q1 through 2010Q2. The 30 + day delinquency rate had been below 1 percent before a wave of defaults hit the CMBS market during 2002–2004. Delinquency rates trended down during 2005–2006 and became historically low in the first half of 2007, 0.3 percent. They rose to over 8 percent in 2010. Serious delinquency rates were lower at the start of the recent recession compared with 1990–1991, but they accelerated much more rapidly.

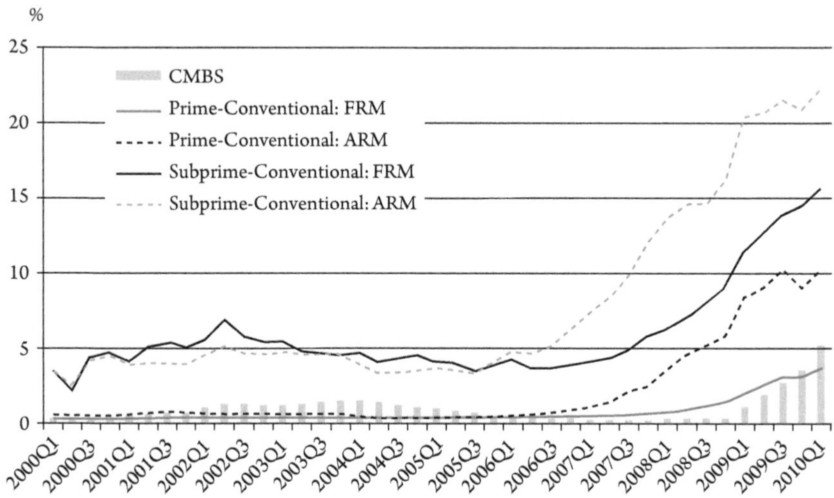

Figure 9.4 Serious (90 + Day) Deliquency Rates: Conduit CMBS Residential Mortgages. This figure shows the serious delinquency rate of conduit CMBS loans compared with those of different types of residential mortgage loans including prime FRMs, prime ARMs, and subprime FRMs ARMs. Source: CRE Finance Council (2010) and Mortgage Bankers Association (2010).

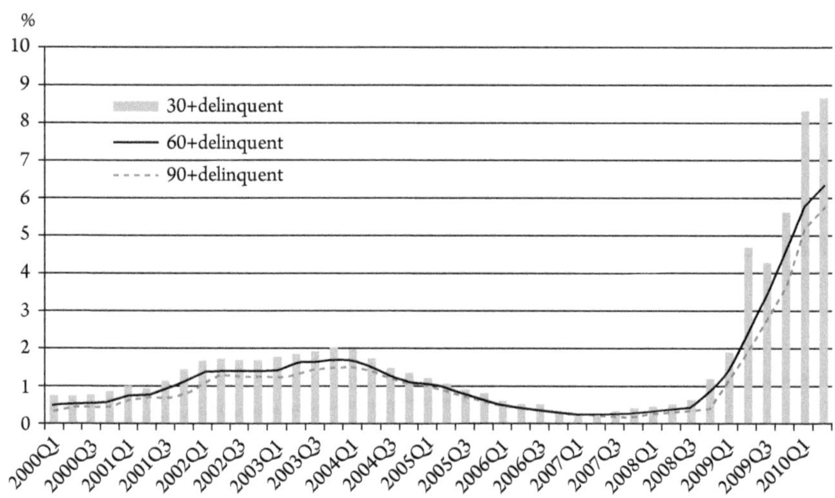

Figure 9.5 Conduit CMBS Loan Default Rate: 2000Q1 to 2010Q2. This figure shows the 30-day, 60-day, and 90-day delinquency rates of conduit CMBS loans. Source: CRE Finance Council (2010).

The CMBS market contained troubled commercial mortgages in the early 1990s because the RTC securitizations liquidated nonperforming portfolios of failed thrifts. The CMBS developments since 2000 have brought uniform underwriting standards, transparency, and efficiency gains (An, Deng, and Gabriel 2009). Therefore, comparing default rates of CMBS loans with those of other lending channels is relevant. An and Sanders (2010) show that default rates of conduit CMBS loans and commercial mortgages held by banks and thrifts have been comparable. They were low during 2000–2007 and both reached unprecedented levels in the subsequent three years. The default rate for conduit CMBS loans is more cyclical. It had higher peaks and lower troughs, consistent with their funding fluctuations in the capital market.

There are different types of default. *Term default* is the failure to make monthly payments during the term of the loan. *Balloon default* is when at loan maturity the borrower cannot sell the property at a price to cover the remaining balloon payment or cannot refinance into a large enough loan. *Technical default* is a failure to pay taxes or insurance premiums, to keep the property in repair, or to violate other loan covenants.

An obvious reason for the borrower's term default is property NOI shortage. When the property value falls below the loan value, an optimal option action is to put the property to the lender (Kau, Keenan, Muller, and Epperson 1987; Titman and Torous 1989). Goldberg and Capone (2002) contend that neither negative cash flow nor negative equity is a sufficient condition of default. The borrower can delay the option to default if positive cash flow occurs after servicing the debt (Vandell 1995). A double trigger exists of both negative equity and negative cash flow.

Property value and NOI are factors for balloon default as well. If income has dropped, the DSCR may be insufficient to permit refinancing. Similarly, if value has dropped, the LTV will be too high to permit refinancing, or the sales price will not pay off the loan. If interest rates rise substantially, the borrower may be unable to refinance due to insufficient DSCR. Additionally, tightening of underwriting standards can cause refinance difficulty and balloon default.

Idiosyncratic default risk factors exist. The borrower may not be a special purpose entity, so problems from other assets may cause a bankruptcy or default of the current loan. Inadequate escrows for capital expenditures, tenant improvements, and leasing commissions are also risks.

Kau et al. (1987), Titman and Torous (1989), and Childs, Ott, and Riddiough (1996) have developed structural models for commercial mortgage default, in which mortgages are contingent claims on interest rates and property value. Standard option pricing techniques are used to value mortgages and default risk.

Reduced-form models such as linear regression, logit, and hazard models are used to analyze default probabilities. Studies have identified negative equity (Vandell 1992; Vandell, Barnes, Hartzell, Kraft, and Wendt 1993; Seslen and Wheaton 2012; An, Deng, Nichols, and Sanders 2013a) and negative cash flow (Goldberg and Capone 2002; Seslen and Wheaton 2012) as critical drivers of default risk. Underwriting LTV, loan size, prepayment incentives and constraints, and property type also matter (Goldberg and Capone 2002; Ciochetti et al. 2002, 2003). Other factors include macroeconomic variables such as yield curve slope and interest rate volatility, property location, legal environment, originator type, and special servicers (Yildirim 2008; Archer et al. 2002; Titman and Tsyplakov 2010; Black, Chu, Cohen, and Nichols 2012; Chen and Deng 2013). An et al. (2013a) show that local economic conditions such as commercial real estate vacancy, absorption, unemployment, and house price appreciation affect CMBS default. Lenders, investors, credit rating agencies (CRAs), and regulators use default probability and loss recovery models in underwriting, pricing, credit rating, and stress testing of commercial mortgages and CMBS (Chen and Zhang 2011; Bernanke 2013).

Default is not a one-stage process but a multiple-stage dynamic game between the borrower and lender. The borrower first decides whether to miss a scheduled monthly payment. If a payment is missed and the loan becomes 30-days delinquent, late fees apply. When a commercial mortgage is 60-days overdue, a notice of default (NOD) is sent to the borrower. The servicing is transferred from the primary (sub) servicer to a special servicer, who first seeks a workout or restructuring. If a workout is unsuccessful, the lender through the special servicer starts the foreclosure process after the loan is over 90-days delinquent.

Foreclosure results in a sale (trustee sale in non-judicial foreclosure states), which usually falls short of the remaining balance plus fees and legal costs. An unsuccessful foreclosure sale leads to real estate owned (REO). During any of the stages, the borrower can bring the loan current by paying the late fees, penalties, legal charges, and overdue payments. The borrower's strategy depends on the gains or losses from acceptance, rejection, or a counter-offer from the lender and the likelihood of each response. The borrower can also file a bankruptcy to stop foreclosure, if not preempted by the mortgage contract. Figure 9.6 depicts the default process.

Lenders and borrowers are incentivized for a workout given the deadweight loss caused by foreclosure. Loan modification workouts include a reduced interest rate or payment, reduction in principal, and extension of term, or extend and pretend.

The primary or sub-servicer conducts regular services, collecting monthly payments, keeping records, and maintaining escrows. The special servicer is involved only when a loan becomes more than 60 days delinquent. The special servicer, controlled by or the first-loss bondholder is empowered to extend, restructure, and foreclose. Chen and Deng (2013) find that special servicers are successful in default resolution. They foreclose if the property has cash flow and if market conditions improve. Liu and

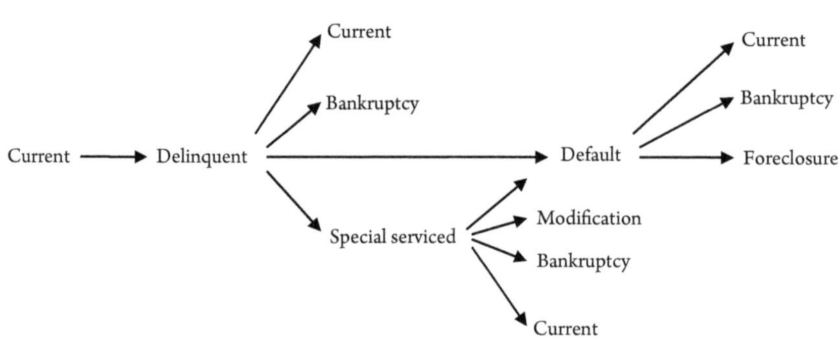

Figure 9.6 The Process of Commercial Mortgage Default Resolution. This figure depicts the multiple stages of the default resolution process of commercial mortgages and shows possible outcomes in each stage.

Quan (2013) demonstrate that a special servicer holding first-loss bonds of the CMBS deal postpones foreclosure at the expense of senior-bond holders.

Commercial Mortgage-Backed Securities (CMBS)

In CMBS, default risk is handled through a senior-subordinated structure. Underwriters pool commercial mortgages and carve out tranches with different seniority. A simplified senior-subordinated structure includes credit qualities from AAA, AA (senior tranche), to BB, B (subordinated) and unrated (first loss).

The cash flow distribution rule is a *waterfall*. Any return of principal generated by amortization, prepayment, and default is allocated first to the highest-rated tranche and then to lower-rated tranches. Subordinated tranches will not receive any principal until the senior tranches are retired. Losses from default are charged against the principal balance of the lowest-rated tranche outstanding or first-loss piece. This is a *reverse waterfall structure*. Interest received from outstanding principal is paid to all tranches. The most subordinate bond class outstanding is the controlling class, with priority in approving special servicer action.

CMBS structures can have an IO tranche that absorbs excess interest payments. Tranches could have the same credit rating but different duration, and other tranches include principal only (PO) bonds (companion class), floaters, and inverse floaters.

Given the different risks borne by senior and subordinated tranches, investors are compensated with different rates of return. Investors in subordinated tranches can receive a spread of 500 bps or more over comparable Treasuries. Those in AAA tranches have lower spreads because they are protected by the subordinated tranches.

In theory, securitization enhances liquidity, capitalizing on specialization and diversification. In CMBS, the senior-subordinated structure meets the demand of different investors with various risk-return combinations and creates value through risk separation and allocation, a central activity of modern financial intermediaries (Allen and Santomero 1996). It also creates custom tailored bonds to meet the asset-liability needs against interest rate risk matching duration and convexity. Securitization reduces commercial mortgage spreads (An, Deng and Gabriel 2009) and mitigates information asymmetry (An, Deng, and Gabriel 2011).

However, the securitization process creates distance between the lender, investor, and borrower, and causes information destruction or under-utilization (Rajan et al. 2014). When interests of investors, investment bankers, originators, and servicers are not aligned, there is moral hazard in underwriting (Bernanke 2008; Keys, Mukherjee, Seru, and Vig 2010; Purnanandam 2011). It creates challenge for borrowers and servicers in workouts, given information barriers and incentive and control problems. The institutional complexity creates difficulty to negotiate flexibility and concessions into loan contract.

For each CMBS tranche, the *subordination level* is the proportion of principal outstanding of other tranches with a lower rating. It reflects the credit support for that tranche. In a CMBS deal, if the subordination level for the AAA tranche is 15 percent, then the AAA tranche is unaffected until more than 15 percent of the pool is eroded. As the outstanding lowest-rating tranches realize losses, the subordination level of the senior tranches declines.

Figure 9.7 shows the average initial subordination levels for non-agency AAA and BBB CMBS bonds issued during 1999 and 2012. Over the period 1999–2012, the average initial subordination levels dropped from 31 to 14 percent for the AAA tranches and from 10 to 3 percent for BBB tranches, extending decline in CMBS subordination levels in the 1990s (Sanders 1999; Geltner, Miller, Clayton, and Eichholtz 2007).

Moody's, Standard and Poor's (S&P), and Fitch are the three major CMBS rating agencies. The CMBS underwriter assembles a pool of loans and passes the information to the CRAs. The CRAs work independently to examine the subordination for the tranches to reach ratings such as AAA, AA, A, and BBB for a prospective deal structure (An, Deng, and Sanders 2008). An underwriter may choose to remove or add loans to the pool and ask the CRAs to re-design the structure. Usually two or more rating agencies rate a CMBS issue and the proposal-revision process for subordination progresses iteratively. The rating agencies provide their final credit risk assessment: bond ratings for each CMBS tranche.

The subordination level should reflect the underlying credit risk of the CMBS pool. However, An, Deng, Nichols, and Sanders (2013b) find that besides credit risk, market forces affect subordination levels as do clientele effects usually seen in financial product design (Van Horne 1985).

CMBS bonds can be upgraded or downgraded. In the last quarter of 2006, Moody's upgraded 110 CMBS bond classes from 44 CMBS transactions. Moody's downgraded eight CMBS classes of the WBCMT 2006-C26 deal in November 2012. During the financial crisis, the CRAs downgraded many CMBS and collateralized debt obligation (CDO) bonds.

The large wave of CMBS downgrade during the crisis has triggered heated debates about the subjectivity and efficacy of the CRAs' credit ratings. The CRAs are alleged to have conflicts of interest, being paid by security issuers and not investors, which have possibly led to biased assumptions and inflated credit ratings for CMBS and related

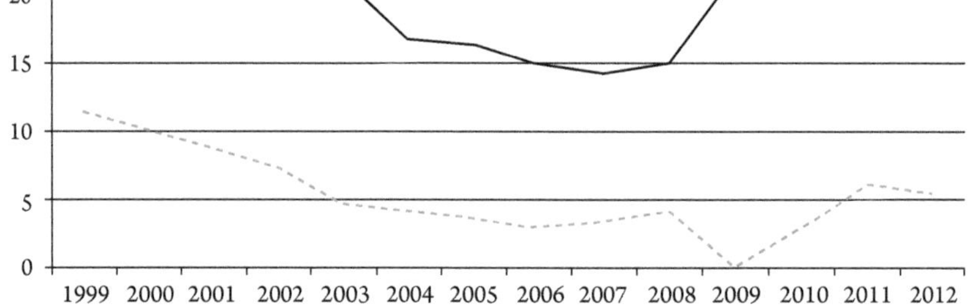

Figure 9.7 Average Initial Subordinations Levels of AAA and BBB CMBS Bonds. This figure shows the average initial subordination levels of AAA and BBB CMBS bonds issued in each year from 1999 to 2012. Source: CMAlert (2012).

structured finance vehicles (Griffin and Tang 2011; Bolton, Freixas, and Shapiro 2012; Griffin and Tang 2012; Stanton and Wallace 2012). *Rating shopping* suggests that issuers choose the CRA that provides favorable ratings (Riddiough and Zhu 2009; Bongaerts, Cremers, and Goetzmann 2012).

The CRAs responded that they never claimed to predict with perfect accuracy. They issued ratings based upon stress tests undertaken for a disclosed set of assumptions about expected future market dynamics. CRAs have also undertaken actions to restore credibility. Moody's tightened rating standards on CMBS in 2007 and proposed adding volatility scores and loss sensitivities to existing ratings in 2008. In recent years, investor-paid credit ratings have gained increased attention (Bruno, Cornaggia, and Cornaggia 2011).

The Commercial Real Estate Finance Council (CREFC) and others have proposed reforms to commercial mortgage securitization. As a result, we see changes in the CMBS market. Sargent (2011) compares the WFRBS C4 and DBUBS C3 issues of 2011 (CMBS 2.0) with the average CMBS deal issued in 2007 (CMBS 1.0). CMBS 2.0 deals are smaller, have fewer loans, and have a higher average DSCR and a lower average LTV. The percentage of IO and partial IO loans are lower in CMBS 2.0 deals. Subordination levels of the AAA bonds of CMBS 2.0 deals are higher.

Other changes have occurred in CMBS 2.0 at the deal, bond, and loan level that involve cash management procedures, loan terms, and representations and warranties. Waterfall changes are made in interest payment allocations when property appraisals are reduced. Recourse carve-out or "bad boy" guarantees are more strictly enforced. The special servicer replacement process has been changed to address perceived abuses by the first loss piece in CMBS 1.0. To deal with extend and pretend, the lender must approve replacement of independent directors with prior written notice. Cash management of loans is more stringent. A hard lockbox requires tenants to send rental payments to a lender-controlled account. Information provided to hired CRAs is to be made available to non-hired CRAs.

CMBS AAA and BBB bond spreads are generally smaller than corporate AAA and BBB spreads. However, CMBS spreads were more volatile during the recent financial crisis. The CMBS BBB spread jumped to over 1300 bps in 2008Q1. No CMBS BBB bonds were issued during 2009Q3 through 2010Q1. After 2011, the issuance of CMBS BBB bonds returned, but their spreads are higher than those of corporate BBB.

An, Deng and Gabriel (2011) analyze the determinants of the overall spread of a CMBS deal. Results show the CMBS spread is positively related to the corporate credit spread, and negatively related to the yield slope and the CMBS market cap, a proxy for liquidity in the CMBS market. Deal characteristics such as the property type distribution and geographic diversification of the underlying collateral affect CMBS spreads. In addition, CMBS investors are willing to pay more for conduit than portfolio deals, attributable to less information asymmetry in conduit CMBS deals.

Summary and Conclusions

Commercial real estate finance has evolved since its role in the nineteenth century of providing the yeoman farmer the opportunity to acquire land as a fee estate. It has benefited from innovations, including securitization and structured finance, which have integrated it with capital markets and created opportunities to make available credit at more favorable terms to a broader set of investors in commercial property.

The commercial mortgage and CMBS markets are suffering from adverse reputational effects stemming from the recent financial crisis. Over time, innovations in technology and capital market instruments and institutional structures for the delivery of capital will provide further opportunities to render the market for commercial property more efficient and complete.

Since the deregulation of the S&Ls in the 1980s and of the banks in the 1990s, an unfortunate legislative and regulatory attitude implicitly assumed markets would behave. Evidence shows they did not always do so, resulting in economic dislocation, which has invariably been followed by a period of enhanced regulatory scrutiny and increased command and control regulation. A more productive approach, in our opinion, would be a joint effort by the government and the commercial mortgage and CMBS sectors to render these markets competitive, transparent, and free from the market imperfections that may have played a role in precipitating periodic high levels of systemic risk, bubbles, and other threats to the economy.

Discussion Questions

1. Explain how the sources of financing for commercial real estate evolved over time.
2. Indicate how commercial mortgages differ from residential mortgages.
3. Identify the major factors influencing commercial mortgage default.
4. Describe how the senior-subordinate structure works in CMBS.
5. Give four examples of changes in the CMBS market after the recent financial crisis.

References

Allen, Franklin, and Anthony M. Santomero. 1996. "The Theory of Financial Intermediation." Working Paper, Wharton Financial Institutions Center.

Ambrose, Brent W., and Anthony B. Sanders. 2003. "Commercial Mortgage-Backed Securities: Prepayment and Default." *Journal of Real Estate Finance and Economics* 26:2/3, 179–196.

Ambrose, Brent W., Anthony B. Sanders, and Abdullah Yavas. 2009. "CMBS Special Servicers and Adverse Selection in Informed Intermediation: Theory and Evidence." Working Paper, Pennsylvania State University.

An, Xudong, and Anthony B. Sanders. 2010. "Default of Commercial Mortgage Loans during the Financial Crisis." Working Paper, San Diego State University.

An, Xudong, Yongheng Deng, and Stuart A. Gabriel. 2009. "Value Creation through Securitization: Evidence from the CMBS Market." *Journal of Real Estate Finance and Economics* 38:3, 302–326.

An, Xudong, Yongheng Deng, and Stuart A. Gabriel. 2011. "Asymmetric Information, Adverse Selection and the Pricing of CMBS." *Journal of Financial Economics* 100:2, 304–325.

An, Xudong, Yongheng Deng, and Anthony B. Sanders. 2008. "Subordination Levels in Structured Financing." In Arnoud Boot and Anjan Thakor, eds., *Corporate Finance*, Volume 3: *Financial Intermediation and Banking*, 41–60. Amsterdam: Elsevier.

An, Xudong, Yongheng Deng, Joseph B. Nichols, and Anthony B. Sanders. 2013a. "Local Traits and Securitized Commercial Mortgage Default." *Journal of Real Estate Finance and Economics*, forthcoming.

An, Xudong, Yongheng Deng, Joseph B. Nichols, and Anthony B. Sanders. 2013b. "Credit Risk and Subordination Levels in Commercial Mortgage-backed Securities (CMBS)." Working Paper, San Diego State University.

Archer, Wayne R., Peter J. Elmer, David M. Harrison, and David C. Ling. 2002. "Determinants of Multifamily Mortgage Default." *Real Estate Economics* 30:3, 445–473.

Berman, Andrew. 2007. "Risks and Realities of Mezzanine Loans." *Missouri Law Review* 72:4, 993–1030.

Bernanke, Ben S. 2008. "Remarks on Mortgage Crisis." Speech delivered to the National Community Reinvestment Coalition, March 14.

Bernanke, Ben S. 2013. "Stress Testing Banks: What Have We Learned?" Presented at Federal Reserve Bank of Atlanta, April.

Black, Lamont K., Chenghuan Sean Chu, Andrew Milman Cohen, and Joseph Nichols. 2012. "Differences across Originators in CMBS Loan Underwriting." *Journal of Financial Services Research* 42:1, 15–134.

Bolton, Patrick, Xavier Freixas, and Joel Shapiro. 2012. "The Credit Rating Game." *Journal of Finance* 67:1, 85–111.

Bongaerts, Dion, K. J. Martijn Cremers, and William N. Goetzmann. 2012. "Tiebreaker: Certification and Multiple Credit Ratings." *Journal of Finance* 67:1, 113–152.

Brueggeman, William B., and Jeffrey D. Fisher. 2011. *Real Estate Finance and Investments*. New York: McGraw-Hill.

Bruno, Valentina, Jess Cornaggia, and Kimberly J. Cornaggia. 2011. "The Information Content of Credit Ratings: Compensation Structure Does Matter." Working Paper, American University.

Chen, Jun, and Yongheng Deng. 2013. "Commercial Mortgage Workout Strategy and Conditional Default Probability: Evidence from Special Serviced CMBS Loans." *Journal of Real Estate Finance and Economics*, forthcoming.

Chen, Jun, and Jing Zhang. 2011. *Modeling Commercial Real Estate Loan Credit Risk: An Overview*. Moody's Analytics Quantitative Research Report.

Childs, Paul D., Steven H. Ott, and Timothy J. Riddiough. 1996. "The Pricing of Multiclass Commercial Mortgage–Backed Securities." *Journal of Financial and Quantitative Analysis* 31:4, 581–603.

Ciochetti, Brian A., Yongheng Deng, Bin Gao, and Rui Yao. 2002. "The Termination of Lending Relationships through Prepayment and Default in Commercial Mortgage Markets: A Proportional Hazard Approach with Competing Risks." *Real Estate Economics* 30:4, 595–633.

Ciochetti, Brian A., Rui Yao, Yongheng Deng, Gail Lee, and James Shilling. 2003. "A Proportional Hazard Model of Commercial Mortgage Default with Originator Bias." *Journal of Real Estate Finance and Economics* 27:1, 5–23.

CMAlert. 2012. CMBS. http://www.cmalert.com/about_cmbs.php.

Cohen, Andrew, and Mark Manuszak. 2013. "Ratings Competition in the CMBS Market." *Journal of Money, Credit and Banking* 45:1, 93–119.

Coleman, Major, Michael LaCour-Little, and Kerry D. Vandell. 2008. "Subprime Lending and the Housing Bubble: Tail Wags Dog?" *Journal of Housing Economics* 17:3, 272–290.

CRE Finance Council. 2010. *CMBS E-Primer*. Washington, DC: CRE Finance Council.

Curry, Timothy, and Lynn Shibut. 2000. "The Cost of the Savings and Loan Crisis: Truth and Consequences." *FDIC Bank Review* 13:2, 26–35. http://www.fdic.gov/bank/analytical/banking/2000dec/brv13n2_2.pdf.

Deloitte Center for Financial Services. 2013. *Non-Traditional Commercial Real Estate: Capitalizing on the REIT Opportunity*. http://deloitte.wsj.com/cfo/files/2013/06/Non-traditionalCommercialRealEstate.pdf.

Dennis, Marshall. 1981. *Mortgage Lending Fundamentals and Practices*. New York: Reston.

Esaki, Howard. 2002. "Commercial Mortgage Defaults: 1972-2000." *Real Estate Finance* 18:4, 43–51.

Federal Reserve Senior Loan Officer Survey. 2010. April. http://www.federalreserve.gov/boarddocs/snloansurvey/201005/default.htm.

Geltner, David M., Norm G. Miller, Jim Clayton, and Piet Eichholtz. 2007. *Commercial Real Estate Analysis and Investments*. Mason, OH: Thomson.

Goldberg, Lawrence, and Charles A. Capone, Jr. 2002. "A Dynamic Double-Trigger Model of Multifamily Mortgage Default." *Real Estate Economics* 30:1, 85–113.

Griffin, John M., and Dragon Yongjun Tang. 2011. "Did Credit Rating Agencies Make Unbiased Assumptions on CDOs?" *American Economic Review Papers and Proceedings* 101:3, 125–130.

Griffin, John M., and Dragon Yongjun Tang. 2012. "Did Subjectivity Play a Role in CDO CreditRatings?" *Journal of Finance* 67:4, 1293–1328.

Grovenstein, Robert A., John P. Harding, C. F. Sirmans, Sansanee Thebpanya, and Geoffrey K. Turnbull. 2005. "Commercial Mortgage Underwriting: How Well Do Lenders Manage the Risks?" *Journal of Housing Economics* 14:4, 355–383.

Hendrickson, Jill M. 2011. *Regulation and Instability in U.S. Commercial Banking: A History of Crises*. Palgrave MacMillan Studies in Banking and Financial Institutions. New York: Palgrave Macmillan.

Jacob, David P., and Peter Fastovsky. 1999. "Understanding and Managing the Balloon Risk in Commercial Mortgages." In Frank Fabozzi and David Jacob, eds., *The Handbook of Commercial Mortgage Backed Securities*, 2nd edn., 275–285. New Hope, PA: Frank J. Fabozzi Associates.

Kau, James B., Donald C. Keenan, William J. Muller III, and James F. Epperson. 1987. "The Valuation and Securitization of Commercial and Multifamily Mortgages." *Journal of Banking and Finance* 11:3, 525–546.

Keehn, Richard H., and Gene Smiley. 1977. "Mortgage Lending by National Banks." *Business History Review* 51:4, 474–491.

Keys, Benjamin, Tanmoy Mukherjee, Amit Seru, and Vikrant Vig. 2010. "Did Securitization Lead to Lax Screening? Evidence from Subprime Loans." *Quarterly Journal of Economics* 125:1, 307–362.

Lederman, Jess, ed. 1993. *The Handbook of Mortgage-Banking: Trends, Opportunities and Strategies*. New York: McGraw-Hill.

Linklater, Andro. 2013. *Owning the Earth: The Transforming History of Land Ownership*. New York: Bloomsbury USA.

Liu, Peng, and Daniel Quan. 2013. "Foreclosure of Securitized Commercial Mortgages—A Model of the Special Servicer." *Journal of Real Estate Finance and Economics* 46:3, 321–338.

Moody's. 2006. *U.S. CMBS: Strong Real Estate Appreciation Drives Defeasance to Record Levels. Moody's Investors Service Structured Finance Special Report*. New York: Moody's.

Mortgage Bankers Association. 2010. *U.S. Residential Mortgage Delinquency Rates*. Washington, DC: Mortgage Bankers Association.

Pedrelli, Nino D. 1999. "Volatility and Performance Analysis of Two Past Real Estate Markets: Mortgage Bonds of the 1920's and Land Warrants of the 1850's." PhD dissertation, University of Wisconsin.

Purnanandam, Amiyatosh. 2011. "Originate-to-Distribute Model and the Sub-Prime Mortgage Crisis." *Review of Financial Studies* 24:6, 1881–1915.

Rajan, Uday, Amit Seru, and Vikrant Vig. 2014. "The Failure of Models That Predict Failure: Distance, Incentives and Defaults." *Journal of Financial Economics*, forthcoming.

RealtyRates.com. 2013. *Investor Survey*. http://www.realtyrates.com/matrixg.html.

Riddiough, Timothy J., and Jun Zhu. 2009. "Shopping, Relationships, and Influence in the Market for Credit Ratings." Working Paper, University of Wisconsin, Madison.

Sanders, Anthony B. 1999. "Commercial Mortgage-Backed Securities." In Frank J. Fabozzi, ed., *The Handbook of Fixed-Income Securities*, 615–628. New York: McGraw-Hill.

Sargent, Patrick C. 2011. "CMBS 2.0: An Overview of Changes and Challenges." New York: Andrews Kurth LLP.

Seslen, Tracey, and William C. Wheaton. 2012. "Contemporaneous Loan Stress and Termination Risk in the CMBS Pool: How 'Ruthless' Is Default?" *Real Estate Economics* 38:2, 225–255.

Stanton, Richard, and Nancy Wallace. 2012. "CMBS Subordination, Ratings Inflation, and Regulatory Capital Arbitrage." Working Paper, University of California, Berkeley.

Taylor, John B. 2009. *Getting Off Track: How Government Actions and Interventions Caused, Prolonged, and Worsened the Financial Crisis*. Stanford, CA: Hoover Institution Press.

Titman, Sheridan, and Walter N. Torous. 1989. "Valuing Commercial Mortgages: An Empirical Investigation of the Contingent-Claims Approach to Pricing Risky Debt." *Journal of Finance* 44:2, 345–373.

Titman, Sheridan, and Sergey Tsyplakov. 2010. "Originator Performance, CMBS Structures and Yield Spreads of Commercial Mortgages." *Review of Financial Studies* 23:9, 3558–3594.

U.S. Board of Governors of the Federal Reserve System. 2013. *Flow of Funds Accounts: Historical Data*. Tables L 219, L 220, F 219, and F 220. Washington, DC: Federal Reserve.

Vandell, Kerry D. 1992. "Predicting Commercial Mortgage Foreclosure Experience." *Journal of the American Real Estate and Urban Economics Association* 20:1, 55–88.

Vandell, Kerry D. 1995. "How Ruthless Is Mortgage Default? A Review and Synthesis of the Evidence." *Journal of Housing Research* 6:2, 245–264.

Vandell, Kerry, W. Barnes, David Hartzell, Dennis Kraft, and William Wendt. 1993. "Commercial Mortgage Defaults: Proportional Hazards Estimations Using Individual Loan Histories." *Journal of the American Real Estate and Urban Economics Association* 21:4, 451–480.

Van Horne, James C. 1985. "Of Financial Innovations and Excesses." *Journal of Finance* 40:3, 621–631.

Yildirim, Yildiray. 2008. "Estimating Default Probabilities of CMBS with Clustering and Heavy Censoring." *Journal of Real Estate Finance and Economics* 37:2, 93–111.

10

The Subprime Mortgage Crisis

ANTHONY B. SANDERS
Professor of Finance, School of Management, George Mason University

Introduction

National average house prices in the United States rose 94 percent between 1997 and their peak in 2007 based on the FHFA Purchase Only house price index. Some markets such as Los Angeles, Phoenix, and Las Vegas experienced even stronger house price growth than the national average. The large price increases were sustainable from a user cost perspective due to falling mortgage interest rates. Such rates fell from 8.52 percent in May 2000 to 3.54 percent in May 2013. Due partly to rising house prices, serious single-family mortgage delinquencies remained below 3 percent until the fourth quarter (Q4) 2007. From 2007Q4 onward, serious delinquencies rose to more than 10 percent in 2012. The unemployment rate was stable at 4.7 percent as of October 2007. So, at the beginning of 2007Q4, unemployment and serious delinquencies were low.

The purpose of this chapter is to define a subprime mortgage and discuss how subprime mortgages became so toxic to mortgage-backed securities (MBS) investors as well as to consumers. Furthermore, legislation aimed at diminishing subprime mortgages in the United States is discussed.

The remainder of the chapter has the following organization. The next section defines and discusses subprime mortgages. This is followed by sections on underwriting standards and mortgage products, the government's role in the subprime crisis, and subprime mortgages and collateralized mortgage obligations. The chapter then discusses securitization after the recession and legislative responses such as Dodd–Frank and the Consumer Financial Protection Bureau. The final section offers a summary and conclusions.

Subprime Mortgages

The term *subprime mortgage* is a misnomer because there is no such thing as a subprime mortgage, only a subprime borrower. Further, the definition of a subprime borrower varies according to which company is measuring subprime. Hancock, Lehnert, Passmore, and Sherlund (2006) discuss this issue as summarized in Table 10.1. The context is regulatory approaches that banks face on capital requirements and the impact

Table 10.1 **Summary of Conventional Mortgage Market Segment Decisions**

Credit Score	***Loan-to-Value Ratio***		
	< 80 percent	*80–90 percent*	*> 90 percent*
660 or higher	Prime	Near-prime	Subprime
581 to 659	Near-prime	Near-prime	Subprime
580 or lower	Subprime	Subprime	Subprime

Note: This table classifies prime, near-prime, and subprime borrowers based on a combination of credit score and LTV ratio.

Source: Hancock et al. (2006).

on mortgage rates. Table 10.1 shows criteria for classifying prime, near-prime, and subprime borrowers. For example, all borrowers with a 10 percent or less down payment are defined as subprime. If the borrower has a credit score below 660, the borrower is classified as "near prime" or "subprime." If the borrower has a credit score of 660 and above as well a down payment in excess of 20 percent, the borrower is classified as "prime." Sengupta and Emmons (2007) offer the following alternative definition of a subprime borrower as being previously delinquent, foreclosed or previously bankrupt, having a low credit score, or having a debt service-to-income (DTI) ratio in excess of 50 percent.

Figure 10.1 provides information of subprime borrower volume, total mortgage volume, and the Case-Shiller 20 city house price index. Mortgage volume and house prices moved together until 2004 (Sanders 2008). At that point, total mortgage volume declined while subprime volume increased although far lower than total mortgage volume.

Another factor driving subprime mortgage origination during the 2000s is the Federal Housing Administration (FHA), which originated a large share of high loan-to-value (LTV) ratio loans. The FHA high LTV share hovered around 80 percent during the early to mid-2000s. The high share is not surprising given that the FHA's clientele is typically low down payment and first-time home buyers. On the credit side, the FHA had around an 80 percent share of borrowers with Fair Isaac Corporation (FICO) credit scores of less than 680. Using the previous definition of subprime borrowers, the FHA was clearly a lending participant in the subprime market.

Fannie Mae and Freddie Mac, the government sponsored enterprises (GSEs), also contributed to the subprime crisis. To observe the dangers to households and taxpayers of low down payment loans coupled with low credit (FICO) scores, the Federal Housing Finance Agency (FHFA 2010) characterizes the loan performance of the government mortgage enterprises. For example, for the 2007 vintage of enterprise-purchased mortgages, the serious delinquency rate for credit (FICO) scores < 620 and LTVs ≥ 97.5 and ≤ 104.9 was 51.6 percent.

The study examines the characteristics and performance of single-family mortgages originated between 2001 and 2008 and sold into the secondary market. According

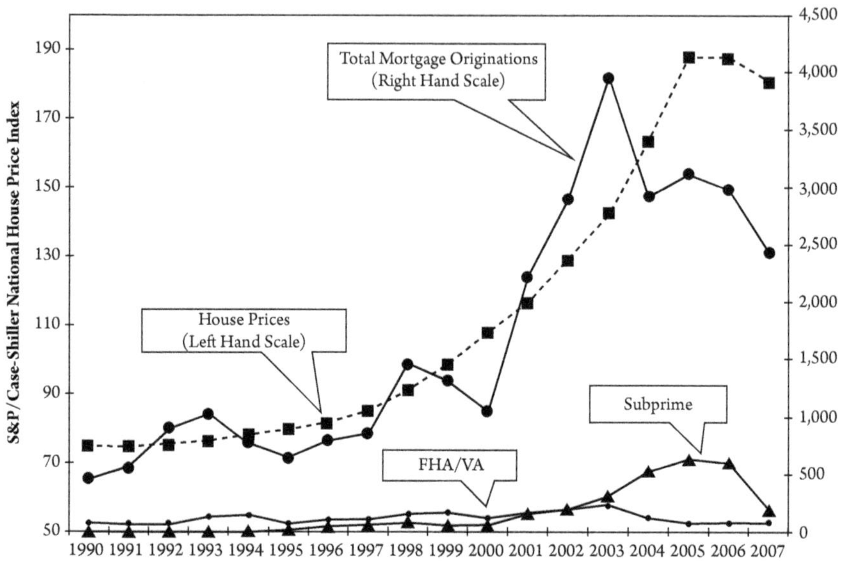

Figure 10.1 Mortgage Volume and House prices. This graph shows house prices and mortgage origination volume from 1990 to 2007. House prices rose with mortgage originations through 2003. After 2003, house prices continue to rise with the rise in subprime mortgage volume. Sources: S&P Case-Shiller, Inside Mortgage Finance.

to the FHFA, the private label securities (PLS) market had an even broader credit bucket than Fannie Mae and Freddie Mac and worse performance. The differences lie in each of the following categories: credit scores, LTV ratios, and increased adjustable rate origination. Mortgage origination has developed statistical models that include borrower characteristics, but notably on payment performance. That performance is in the credit score, with the FICO score tabulated from 300 to 950 being used as a benchmark. Higher scores indicate better-quality borrowers, and a minimum of 620 is conventionally used to indicate a prime mortgage candidate. Higher scores have lower probabilities of delinquency and ultimate default. Of Fannie Mae and Freddie Mac borrowers, 84 percent had FICO scores above 660 during the 2001 to 2008 origination period. Only 5 percent of mortgages purchased had FICO scores below 620. For private-label MBS, only 47 percent of loans were to borrowers with FICO scores above 660. Borrowers with FICO scores below 620 were 32 percent of private-label mortgages securitized.

The data set excludes second and other liens, which increase the debt obligations and the risk of default. Using first mortgages alone, Fannie Mae and Freddie Mac acquisitions had 82 percent of loans below an 80 percent LTV. Only 9 percent of Fannie Mae and Freddie Mac acquisitions had LTVs above 90 percent. By comparison, only two-thirds of private-label MBS had an LTV ratio at or below 80 percent. For loans above a 90 percent LTV, the proportion was 11 percent. The proportion of high LTV primary loans decreased over time as borrowers increased their usage of second loans, resulting in rising cumulative LTV.

Private-label mortgages had higher proportions of adjustable rate loans. These adjustable rates often had the additional feature of having even lower teaser rates on which the borrower qualified for a loan. Fannie Mae and Freddie Mac had 88 percent of their originations between 2001 and 2008 as fixed rate mortgages (FRMs). Private-label MBS had 70 percent as adjustable rate mortgages (ARMs).

Fannie Mae and Freddie Mac had 5 percent of their FRMs and 10 percent of their ARMs become more than 90 days delinquent of the 2001 to 2008 origination dates by the end of 2009. Among private-label loans, 20 percent of FRMs and 30 percent of FRMs had become more than 90 days delinquent by the end of 2009.

Clearly, low down payment and low credit score loans are subprime. However, another contributing factor to the subprime crisis was subprime borrowers using mortgage products that accentuated the risk for the borrower, such as exotic ARM products including option ARMs and limited or no-documentation loans. *Limited or no documentation loans* are loans that require only a credit score or minimal information and are not fully underwritten loans.

Underwriting Standards and Mortgage Products

The worst performing mortgage product was the ARM with substantially higher defaults than FRMs. One of the primary causes of subprime ARM defaults was weaker underwriting, which was encouraged by Housing and Urban Development (HUD) policies. Non-bank lenders largely originated these subprime ARMs (Gwinner and Sanders 2008). Independent non-bank lenders made between 40 and 50 percent of the subprime loans from 2004 to 2006 (Avery, Brevoort, and Canner 2007). Non-bank lenders such as New Century Financial aggressively pursued the originate-to-distribute business model, where it originated loans for sale to the capital markets.

Founded in 1995, New Century was the third largest subprime lender in the country by the end of 2006, with loan production that year of $51.6 billion. New Century filed for bankruptcy protection in April 2007, primarily as a result of insufficient capital to satisfy demands from investors to repurchase defaulted and deficient mortgages. According to the bankruptcy court examiner, New Century had a "brazen obsession with increasing loan originations without due regard to the risks associated with that business strategy" (Missal 2008, 8).

The primary consideration for loan quality was the ability to sell into the secondary market (Sanders 2008). More than 70 percent of loans originated by New Century had low initial teaser rates, and 40 percent were underwritten on a stated income basis. A *stated income loan* is a mortgage where the lender does not verify the borrower's income by looking at pay stubs, W-2 (employee income) forms, income tax returns, or other records. Instead, the lender simply asked borrowers to state their income without verification. Stated income loans were also known as "liar loans." New Century made frequent exceptions to its underwriting guidelines for borrowers who might not otherwise qualify for a loan. Early payment defaults, a sure sign of weak underwriting, rose from 4.38 percent of its loans made in 2003 to 13.1 percent of loans in early 2007 (Missal 2008). An *early payment default* is defined as a default on a loan in the first three months of its life. In essence, the borrower never made a mortgage payment.

New Century was one of several specialized mortgage finance firms using quantitative techniques to underwrite loans not meeting the agencies' underwriting standards. This firm sold the securitized pools of the loans to institutional investors specializing in structured finance securitizations. New Century's originations were $6.2 billion of mortgages in 2001, $14.2 billion in 2002, $27.4 billion in 2003, $42.2 billion in 2004, and $56.1 billion in 2005.

Lenders evaluated subprime mortgage credit with the same techniques as prime mortgage credit. The rating agencies were complicit in rating securities based on subprime credits. Because of the rating agencies' concern with reputational risk, they desired credit enhancement of subprime pools. These pools had credit support to reduce security losses in the event of default risk of the underlying mortgage collateral. This support included mortgage insurance comparable to that on prime loans. Overcollateralization entailed selling securities with a face value exceeding that of the underlying mortgage pool. These subordinated securities for the excess were to take losses from default, protecting securities with higher ratings, including AAA. Security purchasers could also purchase *credit default swaps,* which are insurance policies paying off in the event of default to reduce their risk and reduce regulatory capital against the security.

Subprime borrowers, those with poor credit records, a history of bankruptcy, or who are overextended on their credit, often selected mortgage products that are atypical of prime borrowers that have stronger credit records. Prime borrowers typically choose standard, long-term FRMs and make a down payment of 20 percent or more. Historically, 80 percent of prime originations have been fixed rate in any given year, and 20 percent have been ARMs. Subprime borrowers often made low down payments between zero and 10 percent and chose riskier loan products, including the following.

- Option mortgages allow borrowers to defer some of their payments, resulting in increasing loan balances, also known as *negative amortization mortgages.*
- Convertible mortgages start with fixed rates and then convert to adjustable rates at a pre-specified reset date. Reversing, they start with an adjustable rate including a low teaser, and convert to a fixed rate.
- Low documentation no documentation mortgages occur when the borrower provides no or minimal documentation on such matters as employment and income.

One of the more risky products during the subprime boom was the *hybrid ARM* featuring an initial fixed teaser rate for two or three years that then adjusted to a variable rate linked to a capital market benchmark such as the 1-year Treasury bill plus a spread. As these loans feature 30-year amortization schedules, they are known as 2/28 or 3/27 loans. Foote, Gerardi, Goette, and Willen (2008) show that the initial teaser rate on 2/28 ARMs averaged from 7.3 percent in 2004 to 8.6 percent in 2007, with an average spread of about 300 basis points over the 1-year prime ARM rate. The fully indexed rate fell from 11.5 percent in 2004 to 9.1 percent in 2007. The bulk of subprime ARMs were expected to reset in 2007 and 2008 (Center for Responsible Lending 2008). Interest rate cuts by the Federal Reserve in 2008 somewhat muted the effects of this wave of adjustments.

Demyanyk and Van Hemert (2011) show that most subprime ARM defaults occur before the loans reach their first adjustment date, highlighting the prevalence of weak underwriting rather than the impact of rate adjustments. A borrower defaulting before the first adjustment date is likely to have made few payments on the loan, which is consistent with poor credit quality. Lenders use at least 90 days or three months delinquent before taking actions that lead to default. Subprime lending including ARMs instruments started early in the housing boom. They did not cause earlier problems because house prices were rising. Only when house prices began to decline after 2006 did subprime mortgages lead to defaults.

Changing market conditions and the prevalence of prepayment penalties curtailed the ability of borrowers to refinance before teaser interest rates expired. Many borrowers took out subprime ARMs with the intention of exploiting house price increases and refinancing before the end of the teaser period. Subprime ARMS typically had high prepayment rates. As Foote et al. (2008) show, lenders extended up to 60 percent of the Alt-A loans to borrowers whose credit scores fell short of prime but are believed to be above levels associated with subprime lending.

The design of subprime mortgages was to help borrowers build equity and credit to become prime borrowers. As Bhardwaj and Sengupta (2011) note, subprime ARM cohorts originated between 2000 and 2004 prepaid at 31 to 49 percent in the first two years and 57 to 77 percent in the first three years. Prepayments for the 2005 and 2006 cohorts slowed dramatically to about a 36 percent cumulative rate before 24 months for the 2005 cohort, and slower still at 21 percent for the 2006 cohort. Declining house prices inhibited the ability of highly leveraged 2005 and 2006 borrowers to refinance. Also, an estimated 70 percent of subprime loans carried prepayment penalties as opposed to 2 percent of prime loans (Berson 2006; Center for Responsible Lending 2008).

Geographic concentration of subprime lending also increased loss severity. Agarwal, Ambrose, Chomsisengphet, and Sanders (2012) find that subprime loans tend to be concentrated geographically. In studying the Phoenix, Arizona, area, they report that subprime loans are primarily in older neighborhoods in the inner city. As foreclosures surged in these older neighborhoods, house prices declined more than in neighborhoods or zip codes with higher concentrations of prime loans. High-risk lending in geographically concentrated areas can result in default cascades where the decline in property value can contribute to the decline in neighboring property values and increasing loss severities in these neighborhoods.

As house prices fell and interest rates rose, subprime defaults and foreclosures rose more than expected. As highly leveraged borrowers found themselves with mortgage debt greater than the value of their homes, many tended to ruthlessly default, leaving the lender with the cost of disposing the property, and accepted the damage to their credit records. A *ruthless default* is when a borrower ceases payment even when there is sufficient income to remain current. As Foote et al. (2008) show, the issue with falling house prices stems from the resulting vulnerability to personal financial shocks rather than to the tendency to ruthlessly default. Households with positive equity can sell or refinance, but those with negative equity and a personal financial shock such as a job loss are more likely to be forced into foreclosure.

Lenders made 60 percent of vintage 2006 subprime loans on a stated income basis, without any documentation or verification of the income of the borrower (Fitch 2007). In considering the debt-to-income (DTI) ratio, a standard practice is to verify the loan applicant's income with evidence such as pay stubs, direct verification by employer, or tax returns. In emerging markets, informal borrowers may submit rent receipts, utility bills, payoffs of appliance loans, or contracted savings accounts. Industry terms for stated income loans included "no doc," "low doc," or "liar loans." Although convenient for the borrower, such loans carried spreads of up to 500 basis points above prime lending rates. Stated income loans rely on the lender to verify assets and employment. Lenders should have taken more care to ensure borrowers had more substantial cash equity in the transaction.

Historically, lenders make stated income loans in limited numbers to self-employed professionals or to refinance existing loans held by the lender. The lender could save time when it was familiar with the property, comfortable with the LTV of the new loan, and with its knowledge of the borrower's willingness and ability to pay. However, stated income lending became more widespread in the industry and it became riskier as lenders offered such loans on the expectation of rising house prices and without verifying income or assets.

Studies cited by the Office of the Comptroller of the Currency (OCC) show that borrowers exaggerated their income on 90 percent of surveyed stated income loans and by more than 50 percent. Also, many lenders and mortgage brokers were aware that the borrower lacked the income to pay the loan (Dugan 2007). Stated income loans performed worse than other subprime loans. According to rating agency analysis, 67 percent of early payment defaults for the 2007 vintage were low or no documentation loans (Fitch 2007).

Lenders accepted higher LTV and DTI ratios for both prime and subprime loans during the early 2000s. LTVs rose in two respects: (1) higher LTVs accepted at purchase, and (2) equity extracted by refinancing an appreciated house. Mian and Sufi (2009 find that LTVs and DTI ratios rose substantially in the early 2000s. Foote et al. (2008) document that in New England, for borrowers with FICO scores less than 620, LTV ratios on purchase and refinance loans rose from 82 percent in 1999 and 2000 to 92 percent in 2005 and 2006. DTIs for similar borrowers rose from 36 percent in 1999 through 2000 to 43 percent in between 2005 and 2006. For borrowers with high FICO scores, average LTVs rose to almost 95 percent, and DTIs rose from 36 percent in 2000 to 42 percent in 2005.

At the time of purchase, lenders accepted increasingly higher LTVs, including the possibility of financing 100 percent or more of the house price with a straight first lien, or with simultaneous first and second lien mortgages, known as *piggyback loans*. More traditionally, lenders made mortgages with LTVs greater than 80 percent only when the borrower purchased mortgage default insurance.

Piggyback loans packaged a first lien with a LTV up to 80 percent with a second lien or home equity line of credit. When the second lien was for 10 percent of the appraised value and a home equity loan was for 10 percent of the purchase price, the piggyback package becomes an 80–10–10 capital structure. The 80 percent first lien is eligible for sale to the government-sponsored market at Fannie Mae or Freddie Mac without the payment of mortgage insurance. Because mortgage insurance is payable on the entire loan amount, the borrower saves if the premium is less than the incremental rate on the second. Until 2006, piggybacks provided a tax advantage because interest on the second lien was tax deductible, but the mortgage insurance (MI) premium was not. Piggybacks made up more than 35 percent of subprime originations in 2006 (Fitch 2007).

Calhoun (2005) documents reporting and risk issues with piggyback lending. In 2001 piggyback loans accounted for 20 percent of mortgage originations in dollar volume. By 2004 piggybacks accounted for nearly 40 percent of mortgage volume. These include regional concentrations of piggyback lending to improve affordability. Overall, higher LTV levels and debt burdens coupled with subsequently falling house prices and employment losses created a greater probability of negative equity and default.

Many foreclosed borrowers put little money down and had lived for a short time in their homes. As Foote et al. (2008) report, 40 percent of foreclosures in New England were of mortgages with zero down payments, and that 40 percent had owned their homes for less than three years in 2007. Because foreclosures usually take six months or more in Massachusetts, most recent foreclosed borrowers spent little time in their homes before financial problems occurred. In New England, house prices fell 12 percent between the first quarter of 2006 and the first quarter of 2008. During this period, unemployment fell 0.4 percent, so financial pressure on owners remained muted.

Many foreclosures have been for subprime loans to formerly prime borrowers. According to Foote et al. (2008), 70 percent of homes lost to foreclosure in 2006 and 2007 in Massachusetts were initially purchased with prime loans, but 45.2 percent of defaulted mortgages were subprime. The 45.2 percent subprime share of foreclosures occurred because many borrowers who purchased homes with prime loans later refinanced into subprime and then defaulted.

Mayer and Pence (2008) find that subprime originations were heavily concentrated in fast-growing parts of the country with considerable new construction, such as Florida, California, Nevada, and the Washington, DC, area. These areas also experienced rapid price appreciation. They also find a heavy concentration of subprime loans in zip codes with more residents in the moderate credit score category and more black and Hispanic residents. Areas with lower income and higher unemployment had more subprime lending, but these associations are smaller in magnitude.

Credit rating agencies were at the core of the meltdown in the private-label mortgage market. An ongoing debate exists as to whether the failure of these securities was due to conflicts of interest at the rating agencies, rating agency incompetence, or unpredicted market forces. The widespread reliance on ratings produced a system whereby there was little countervailing force to the rating agency opinions. Many called for increased regulation of rating agencies and increased competition and transparency. Others called for a change to buyer compensation of rating agencies. Whether implementing any of these remedies will address reliance of investors on ratings is unclear. A shift to reserves based on financial risk of the underlying securities might reduce the reliance on ratings.

The senior-subordinated structure is dominant in the private-label MBS market. The risk in the underlying asset pool is portioned among different investors with senior or A-rated bonds or tranches receiving priority on principal payments. The junior- or B-rated bonds or tranches receive the losses on default first. This partitioning of risk allows investors to select their risk exposure in credit-sensitive products such as subprime asset-backed securities (ABS).

Although the senior-subordinated structure seems fairly straightforward, it suffers from two fundamental problems in practice. First, the tranches in the senior-subordinated deals can have amany tranches, resulting in the B-rated tranches being thin. The subordination level between tranches is small enough that losses quickly eat through the tranche. During a spike in defaults, a thin tranche can go from par value to zero very quickly.

Second, the rules governing cash flows in a senior-subordinated structure can be complex. While complexity per se is not a problem, the difficulty arises in whether investors understand their exposure to collateral risk from both defaults and prepayments and the apportionment of cash flows. For example, complex triggers may cause the priority of cash flows to change within a structure. These triggers differ from deal to deal and may lead investors to underestimate risk.

CREDIT DEFAULT SWAPS

A *credit default swap* (CDS) is a financial product related to subprime mortgages and a relatively recent innovation. Substantial trading in CDSs in the mortgage market did not begin until mid-2005 when several dealers created a standard form of contract known as the *pay as you go* (PAUG) contract. It differs from CDS used in other markets in that the design of the mortgage contract was to reflect the underlying cash flows of MBS bonds rather than to be triggered by a corporate default. A CDS in the mortgage market operates much like a leveraged long or short position in the underlying bond.

In 2006, Markit launched ABX.HE, a subprime mortgage-backed credit derivative index on home equity loans as assets. The introduction of the ABX contract dramatically increased the volume of trading in synthetic MBS positions. Subprime MBS traditionally were classified as *asset-backed securities* (ABS). With the collapse of the subprime mortgage market, ABX remained one of the few liquid trading vehicles. ABX prices are widely used to benchmark the pricing of other mortgage instruments. CDS and ABX have had a mixed impact on the market. The introduction of CDS and ABX may have allowed for rational pricing to reenter the mortgage market by more accurately pricing risk. However, these tools created additional risk in the market because they multiply the amount of credit risk in the market. Furthermore, some contend that the ABX does not represent a true market basket of ABS. Thus, if the collateral is not representative, hedging based on ABX can be problematic. As with over-the-counter (OTC) markets, regulators have difficulty assessing the amount of contracts outstanding. An exchange or other mechanism could likely reduce some of the risks created by these instruments.

Government's Role in the Subprime Crisis

Subprime lending actually provided only limited access to mortgage finance. More than half of the subprime loans were for refinancing existing mortgages rather than purchasing a house. In the United States, individuals frequently replace existing FRMs with new ones to take advantage of declining market rates or to extract equity from the house by refinancing at a higher LTV. Many subprime borrowers refinanced to pay off riskier ARMs before they reached the end of their low teaser interest rate period. As such, refinancing did not allow borrowers to procure more real estate. Further, not all subprime lending has been for low-income households. Lenders made many subprime loans to higher income earners who had blemished credit records.

Despite the dramatic improvement in housing quality and a homeownership rate of 66.3 percent in 1998, the U.S. Department of Housing and Urban Development (HUD) (1995) created the "National Homeownership Strategy: Partners in the American Dream," which partnered with lenders (banks) and the GSEs (Fannie Mae and Freddie Mac) to cut transaction costs, reduce down payment and mortgage costs, and increase availability of financing. Furthermore, the Act aimed to promote fair housing by removing barriers to purchasing, removing barriers to capital and credit for buying, owning, and maintaining a home and removing employment and career barriers in business and professional environments that can open markets for underserved groups.

The policy of President Clinton and HUD was to encourage removing barriers to credit and lower down payments. This pro-ownership strategy continued under Presidents Bush and Obama. Alternative tenure choice support by the government goes to renters. In the rental market, the underserved through the rental market have vouchers or certificates for housing under section 8 of the Housing Act of 1937. Such rental subsidies cover fewer than 3 percent of households.

Subprime Mortgages and Collateralized Mortgage Obligations

The global market for *collateralized debt obligations* (CDOs) witnessed explosive growth over the 1997–2006 period, as the stock of global issuance expanded from $300 billion to almost $2 trillion. CDO issuance importantly supported the market for subprime MBS, via the re-packaging of relatively illiquid assets into derivative CDO securities.

In a stunning market about-face, new issuance of CDOs ceased in 2007, in the wake of implosion and wholesale re-pricing of credit risk in the capital markets. The surge in issuance of subprime-backed CDOs coincided with a marked tightening in subprime MBS-Treasury spreads, suggesting some measurable effect of this market-completing vehicle on the supply/demand balance and pricing of MBS. In 2007 and in the wake of the implosion in the CDO market, spreads on MBS widened markedly.

CDOs are financial structures where a set of assets is held in a trust formed as a *special purpose vehicle* (SPV). The trust issues a series of tranches with different exposures to the risks of the underlying assets. A CDO cash-flow structure allocates the interest and principal payments of the underlying collateral pool of debt instruments to the CDO tranches. Although many variations are available, a *cash CDO* is a senior-subordinated structure where the senior CDO debt tranches are paid first followed by the mezzanine and lower-subordinated notes. Any remaining cash flow is available to equity. In the CDO structure, a set of assets, such as corporate bonds, collateralized MBS, or residential MBS, can be packaged into claims and sold to investors.

The rules for distributing the cash flows of the CDO bonds' underlying collateral are relatively straightforward, but the valuation of the debt and equity tranches can be complicated. The reason for this complexity is that CDOs often contain a large portfolio of assets and credit exposures with diverse risk profiles in default, loss, and recovery as collateral. Many possible capital structures for debt and equity can be issued. Unlike mortgage obligations where prepayment risk is the dominant focus, the primary focus in CDO valuation is typically on the credit risk.

What went wrong with CDOs that were backed by subprime mortgages? For example, assume a mortgage pool rated as BBB when the pool's cash flows are allocated into various tranches including AAA to unrated. While investors in the AAA tranches may have thought that this was a safe investment, the decline of housing prices coupled with rising unemployment rates led to mortgage defaults. Default costs exhausted the lower-rated tranches. That event led to a drop in value of these AAA-rated tranches and ratings downgrades to B or worse (Wall Street Journal 2007).

Securitization after the Fall

The high delinquency and default rates on subprime mortgages signaled the need for a reexamination of methods of securitization. When a loan is originated, three kinds of credit risk are created: systematic, idiosyncratic, and operational. *Systematic risks* relate to future events such as changes in home prices. *Idiosyncratic risks* involve changes such as those in the income of the borrower. *Operational risks* are related to the quality of the underwriting and servicing. An example of an underwriting risk is to determine whether lenders appropriately verified the borrower's income and current home value. Investors are often well positioned to bear systematic risks and diversify idiosyncratic risks, but cannot assess the risks of poor underwriting and servicing. The securitization process should ensure sufficient motivation and capital for originators to manage and bear the risks of underwriting and servicers to fulfill their obligations to the investors.

The securitization market has relied on representation and warranties to protect investors against poor underwriting and loan practices. Although several remedies are available to protect investors, the general solution to a violation of representations and warranties is for the original lender to repurchase the poorly underwritten loans or provide equivalent collateral. Under normal market conditions, the representation and warranties approach to providing comfort to investors works well. Yet, it is vulnerable in the presence of numerous requests or court cases for loan repurchases or if a lender has systematically let underwriting standards deteriorate. The original lender may have insufficient capital to repurchase the loans in question. If the lender declares bankruptcy, it will be able to avoid honoring the representations and warranties causing investors in securities to bear this risk from systematically poor quality originators.

One proposal is to require assignee liability so that investors are responsible for the fraudulent actions of originators against borrowers. Additional proposals want originators to keep "skin in the game", which mean to have incurred monetary risk by being invested in achieving a goal. These remedies to protect borrowers or security investors also contribute to angst in the global capital market. Some view government intervention into private market contracts with skepticism. The U.S. government has intervened in the past in the mortgage market to prevent predatory lending and redlining, namely refusing to lend in low income or high crime areas.

Dodd–Frank and the Consumer Financial Protection Bureau

One solution to the subprime crisis was the Dodd–Frank Wall Street Reform and Consumer Protection Act, which President Barack Obama signed into federal law on July 21, 2010. This legislation created the Consumer Financial Protection Bureau (CFPB) with the primary responsibility for regulating consumer protection regarding financial products and services in the United States. Specifically, Congress gave the CFPB the authority to adopt mortgage rules for fair lending such as ability to repay and qualified mortgage standards under Regulation Z of the Truth in Lending Act of 1968.

The qualified mortgage requirement makes subprime mortgage origination considerably more challenging. The final rule describes certain minimum requirements for creditors making ability-to-repay determinations, but does not dictate that they follow particular underwriting models. At a minimum, creditors generally must consider eight underwriting factors: (1) current or reasonably expected income or assets; (2) current employment status; (3) the monthly payment on the covered transaction; (4) the monthly payment on any simultaneous loan; (5) the monthly payment for mortgage-related obligations; (6) current debt obligations, alimony, and child support; (7) the monthly DTI ratio and residual income after debt service; and (8) credit history. Creditors must generally use reasonably reliable third party records to verify the information they use to evaluate the factors.

The rule provides guidance for applying these factors under the statute. For example, monthly payments must generally be calculated by assuming that the loan is repaid in substantially equal monthly payments during its term. For ARMs, the monthly payment must be calculated using the fully indexed rate as well as the introductory rate.

The line the CFPB is drawing is one that has long been recognized as a rule of thumb to separate prime loans from subprime loans. Indeed, under the existing regulations that the Board adopted in 2008, only higher-priced mortgage loans are subject to an ability to repay requirement and a rebuttable presumption of compliance if creditors follow certain requirements. The new rule strengthens the requirements needed to qualify for a rebuttable presumption for subprime loans and defines with more particularity the grounds for rebutting the presumption. Specifically, the final rule provides that consumers may show a violation with regard to a subprime qualified mortgage if at the time the loan was originated the consumer's income and debt obligations left insufficient residual income or assets to meet living expenses.

The Dodd–Frank Act sets certain product-feature prerequisites and affordability underwriting requirements for qualified mortgages and vests discretion in the CFPB to decide whether additional underwriting or other requirements should apply. The final rule implements the statutory criteria, which generally prohibit loans with negative amortization, interest-only payments, balloon payments, or terms exceeding 30 years from being qualified mortgages. So-called "no-doc" loans where the creditor does not verify income or assets also cannot be qualified mortgages. Finally, a loan generally cannot be a qualified mortgage if the points and fees paid by the consumer exceed 3 percent of the total loan amount, although certain bona fide discount points are excluded for prime loans.

Dodd–Frank and the CFPB effectively put an end to subprime mortgages if that definition includes no-documentation, negative amortization, or interest-only mortgages. Lenders can still originate interest-only loans if they are willing to post additional capital.

Summary and Conclusions

The subprime mortgage crisis resulted from the confluence of a bursting housing bubble, rising unemployment, and granting loans to borrowers with minimal down payments and low credit scores. Subprime mortgages that had no specific definition during the last decade included low down payment mortgages, no or low documentation loans, and loans to low credit score borrowers. Loans that featured low down payments and low credit scores performed particularly poorly.

Government housing policies such as the National Homeownership Act of 1994 contributed to the aggressive encouragement of low down payments and streamlined credit analysis. The result was a near collapse of the banking system and Fannie Mae and Freddie Mac being placed under government conservatorship.

Subprime mortgages were particularly devastating in transferring risk to other sectors of the economy through ABS and CDOs. The reaction to the subprime crisis has been legislation such as the Wall Street Reform and Consumer Protection Act of 2010, or Dodd–Frank and the formation of the CPFB. This legislation has diminished lenders' willingness to originate mortgages that are either non-prime or not qualified. Lenders can still post higher capital for certain non-prime mortgage products, but credit overlays are daunting. America experimented with a massive expansion of mortgage credit, but suffered greatly because of it.

Discussion Questions

1. Explain whether the pursuit of higher homeownership rates contributed to the housing bubble and burst.
2. Discuss how the federal government contributed to the subprime mortgage crisis.
3. Discuss whether the government should encourage mortgages with LTVs greater than 90 percent or credit scores below 660.
4. Explain the involvement of non-bank lenders and HUD in the subprime crisis.
5. Discuss the contribution of CDOs in the subprime crisis.

Acknowledgments

The author thanks Stuart Sanders for his excellent research support.

References

Agarwal, Sumit, Brent W. Ambrose, Souphala Chomsisengphet, and Anthony B. Sanders. 2012. "Thy Neighbor's Mortgage: Does Living in a Subprime Neighborhood Affect One's Probability of Default?" *Real Estate Economics* 40:1, 1–22.

Avery, Robert B., Kenneth P. Brevoort, and Glenn B. Canner. 2007. "The 2006 HMDA Data." *Federal Reserve Bulletin* 93:September, 73–109.

Berson, David W. 2006. "Challenges and Emerging Risks in the Home Mortgage Business." Presentation to the National Housing Forum, Office of Thrift Supervision, Washington, DC.

Bhardwaj, Geetesh, and Rajdeep Sengupta. 2011. "Subprime Mortgage Design." Working Paper, Federal Reserve Bank of St Louis.

Calhoun. Charles A. 2005. "The Hidden Risks of Piggyback Lending." Working Paper, Calhoun Consulting.

Center for Responsible Lending. 2008. "A Snapshot of the Subprime Crisis." http://www.responsiblelending.org/mortgage-lending/tools-resources/snapshot-of-the-subprime-market.pdf.

Demyanyk, Yulia, and Otto Van Hemert. 2011. "Understanding the Subprime Mortgage Crisis." *Review of Financial Studies* 24:6, 1848–1880.

Dugan, John C. 2007. "Remarks by John C. Dugan Comptroller of the Currency before the Neighborhood Housing Services of New York." http://www.occ.gov/news-issuances/speeches/2007/pub-speech-2007-2048.pdf.

Federal Housing Finance Agency. 2010. "Data on the Risk Characteristics and Performance of Single-Family Mortgages Originated in 2001–2008 and Financed in the Secondary Market." http://www.fhfa.gov/webfiles/16711/RiskChars9132010.pdf.

Fitch. 2007. "Fitch Says Confident in 'AAA' Subprime Ratings." Fitch U.S. Subprime Rating Surveillance Update, July 2007. http://www.reuters.com/article/2007/07/18/usa-subprime-fitch-idUSN1831999120070718.

Foote, Christopher L., Krisopher Gerardi, Lorenz Goette, and Paul S. Willen. 2008. "Subprime Facts: What (We Think) We Know about the Subprime Crisis and What We Don't." Federal Reserve Bank of Boston Public Policy Discussion Papers No. 08–2.

Gwinner, William B., and Anthony B. Sanders. 2008. "The Sub Prime Crisis: Implications for Emerging Markets." World Bank Policy Research Working Paper 4726.

Hancock, Diana, Andreas Lehnert, Wayne Passmore, and Shane Sherlund. 2006. "The Competitive Effects of Risk-Based Capital Regulation: An Example from U.S. Mortgage Markets." Finance and Economics Discussion Series 2006–46, Board of Governors of the Federal Reserve System.

Mayer, Chris, and Karen Pence. 2008. "Subprime Mortgages: What, Where, and to Whom?" Finance and Economics Discussion Series. Washington, DC: Federal Reserve Board.

Mian, Atif R., and Amir Sufi. 2009. "The Consequences of Mortgage Credit Expansion: Evidence from the U.S. Mortgage Default Crisis." *Quarterly Journal of Economics* 124:4, 1449–1496.

Missal, Michael. 2008. *Final Report of Michael Missal, Bankruptcy Court Examiner, in re: New Century Holdings, Inc. Chapter 11, Case No. 07–10416 (KJC)*, U.S. Bankruptcy Court of the District of Delaware, February.

Sanders, Anthony B. 2008. "The Subprime Crisis and Its Role in the Financial Crisis." *Journal of Housing Economics* 17:4, 254–261.

Sengupta, Rajdeep, and William R. Emmons. 2007. "What Is Subprime Lending?" *Federal Reserve of St Louis Economic Synopses*, No. 13, 1. http://research.stlouisfed.org/publications/es/07/ES0713.pdf.

Stevens, David. 2013. "AEI–FHA Panel Discussion." Washington, DC: Mortgage Bankers Association, January 25. http://www.aei.org/files/2013/01/24/-david-stevens-fha-presentation_110822825627.pdf.

U.S. Department of Housing and Urban Development. 1995. "The National Homeownership Strategy: Partners in the American Dream." http://confoundedinterest.files.wordpress.com/2013/01/nhsdream2.pdf.

Wall Street Journal. 2007. "Wizardry Amplified Credit Crisis." December 27, Online edition, http://online.wsj.com/article/SB119871820846351717.html.

Part Three

PUBLIC EQUITY MARKETS AND INVESTMENTS

11

REITs: Structure and Performance

WALTER I. BOUDRY
Assistant Professor of Real Estate,
School of Hotel Administration, Cornell University

JARL G. KALLBERG
Alvin C. Wolff Distinguished Professor of Real Estate,
Washington State University

Introduction

REITs are attractive to investors, particularly institutional investors, due to their high dividend payouts and ability to provide more liquidity to the underlying market for direct real estate investment. This chapter analyzes the performance of real estate investment trusts (REITs). It compares the returns on REITs with those on more traditional asset classes, specifically bonds and mid-cap equities, and surveys the academic literature dealing with the diverse issues related to valuation. The chapter also examines the linkages between REIT performance and the behavior of the underlying real estate market. Because the chapter takes the perspective of a U.S.-based investor, it does not directly address the broader issues of global REITs.

REIT Performance

The original design of REITs was to provide individual investors with more liquid access to commercial real estate markets. Their structure as an essentially tax-free conduit with severe restrictions on possible investments and dividend payout made REITs a very transparent and liquid asset class that has undergone many structural changes. This section documents the explosive growth and inconsistent performance of REITs.

MARKET SIZE

REITs have undergone a remarkable spurt of growth since their introduction in 1965 with the listing of Continental Mortgage in the United States. Figure 11.1 shows the

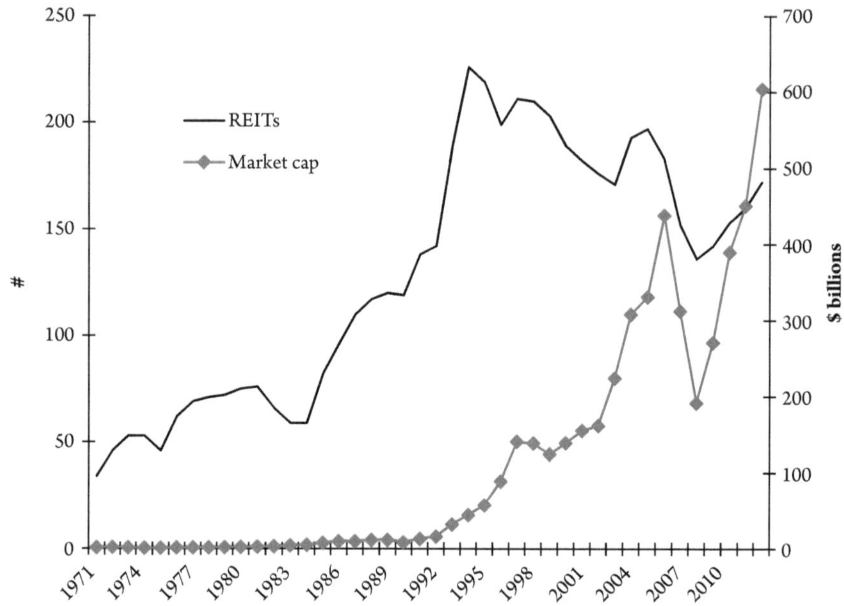

Figure 11.1 REIT Market Capitalization. This figure shows the number of REITs and the total market cap in billions of U.S. dollars from 1971 to 2012. The data include equity, mortgage, and hybrid REITs.

number of REITs and market capitalization (cap) in billions of U.S. dollars from 1971 until the end of 2012. In 1971 there were 34 public REITs with a total market cap of $1.5 billion. By the end of 2012 this figure grew to 172 REITs, which was down from its highest level of 226 reached in 1994, with a total market cap of $603.4 billion. This figure also underscores the immense shocks that this sector was exposed to during the financial crisis. From the 2006 level of $438.1 billion, REIT capitalization plummeted to $191.7 billion by 2008, which was followed by a remarkable recovery to its current level.

Figure 11.1 data (taken from http://www.REIT.com) include equity REITs (those that own property), mortgage REITs (those that make loans or own MBS), and hybrid REITs (those that do both). In the earlier periods, mortgage REITs were the majority of the total REIT population, but by 1976 equity REITs eclipsed mortgage REITs as measured by market cap. The hybrid REIT market was comparable in size to the mortgage REIT sector until 2001 when the latter market enjoyed substantial growth. Mortgage REITs from a 2000 level of $1.6 billion have become a $59 billion market (almost 10 percent of the total REIT capitalization) while the hybrid REIT has essentially disappeared. This chapter focuses only on equity REITs.

REAL ESTATE RETURNS

Endowment funds, pension funds, mutual funds, and other types of institutional investors view real estate as an important investment category. This investment is done through securitized or direct form. Securitized real estate is through holding REITs or real estate mutual funds. Direct investment is via ownership of real estate assets. Thus, a subject of considerable importance is the different performance of direct as opposed to securitized real estate investment.

A great advantage of publicly traded REITs is their transparency. By trading on major exchanges, like any public equity, determining historical return characteristics is straightforward and offers comparability. The National Association of Real Estate Investment Trusts (NAREIT) maintains an extensive website at http://www.reit.com. NAREIT offers detailed information on REIT performance by type and geographic region. The NAREIT index, which is used in this chapter, provides an accurate benchmark for the performance of U.S. commercial real estate.

For direct investment in real estate, performance measurement is more complex, largely due to the infrequency of trades. This lack of transaction prices requires inferring market values through appraisals. For many years the most important index was the *NCREIF Property Index*, which is an appraisal-based measure of the unlevered return on investment grade properties. Appraisal-based measures have several flaws, notably their tendency to smooth returns, which understates the true volatility. Chinloy, Cho, and Megbolugbe (1997) discuss this and other possible appraisal biases. The research surrounding this topic is extensive, as in Gatzlaff and Geltner (1998) and Geltner and Goetzmann (2000). Fisher, Geltner, and Pollakowski (2007) develop a quarterly transaction-based index (TBI) of property-level investment performance for major property types included in NCREIF. Their methodology extends earlier work by Geltner (1991) on commercial real estate indexes. The following empirical work primarily focuses on the TBI index.

COMPARATIVE RETURNS

To help frame the remainder of the analysis, presenting an overview of the returns on REITs and other major investment classes is instructive. Figure 11.2 shows the growth of $1 invested in five broad asset classes: (1) 10-year government bonds, (2) 90-day Treasury bills, (3) REITs as measured by the FTSE NAREIT index, available from http://www.reit.com, (4) capital appreciation on direct real estate investment as measured by the MIT TBI transaction-based index, available from http://web.mit.edu/cre/research/credl/tbi.html, and (5) returns on mid-cap stocks. The last is a value-weighted index constructed from U.S. equities in the third to seventh deciles of market cap, based on data from Wharton Research Data Services (WRDS). The data begin in the first quarter of 1984 to coincide with the initiation of the TBI index and end in the last quarter of 2012.

Over this 29-year period, a dollar invested in government bonds grew to 10.6 (a geometric annual return of 8.48 percent); a dollar invested in Treasury bills grew to 3.24 (a geometric return of 4.14 percent); and a dollar invested in mid-cap equities returned 18.26 (a geometric return of 10.54 percent). The REIT index geometric return was 9.11 percent. This return is in sharp contrast to the very modest gains shown by the TBI index, which had a geometric return of only 2.35 percent. The real estate slump of the 1990s depressed this index; it returned to its 1984 value only in 1997 and its current level of 196 is similar to values attained in 2006. These observations indicate that REIT

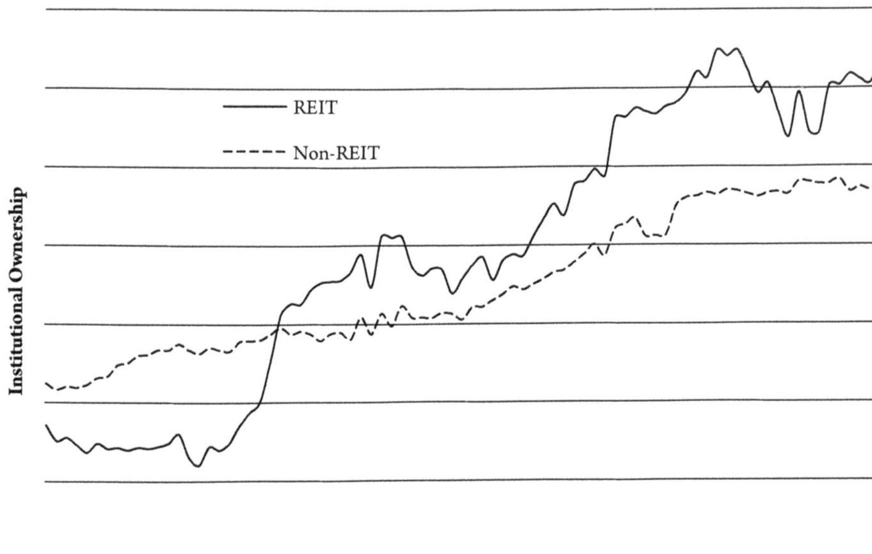

Figure 11.2 Institutional Ownership: REITs and Non-REITS. This figure reports the level of institutional ownership for equity REITs and non-REIT firms from 1990 to 2010. Thomson Reuters 13(f) data served as the basis for calculating institutional ownership.

returns come primarily from income rather than capital appreciation. Decomposing the total REIT return into these two components over the entire period for which data are available from 1978 to 2012 results in an average annual return from capital appreciation of 3.48 percent. The average annual return from income is 8.83 percent.

Figure 11.2 suggests that REIT returns are most closely correlated to the returns on mid-cap equities. The correlation with direct real estate and with bond returns is of lower magnitude. Figure 11.3, which computes the rolling five-year correlations between the REIT returns and other three indexes, makes these observations more precise. Over the entire sample period the correlation between REIT and mid-cap returns is 0.66. However, using a GARCH approach, Jirasakuldech, Campbell, and Emekter (2009) show significant differences in the volatility structure of REITs versus small-cap equities. The REIT correlation with the TBI returns is only 0.058 and with bond returns it is –0.065. NCREIF returns are only weakly correlated (0.175) with REIT returns. The correlation with bond returns is positive until about 2000 and then is generally significantly negative. These results are consistent with earlier REIT empirical analysis. For example, Liu and Mei (1992) use a Generalized Method of Moments (GMM) approach to uncover the time varying risk premiums.

The lack of correlation of REIT returns with appreciation of the underlying properties is an important characteristic of REITs and will be explored further. These results are generally consistent with those obtained in Feldman (2003) during the 1987–2001 period. Similarly, using a vector autoregression approach, Glascock, Lu, and So (2000) show that REITs are more correlated with small stocks and less correlated with bonds after 1992.

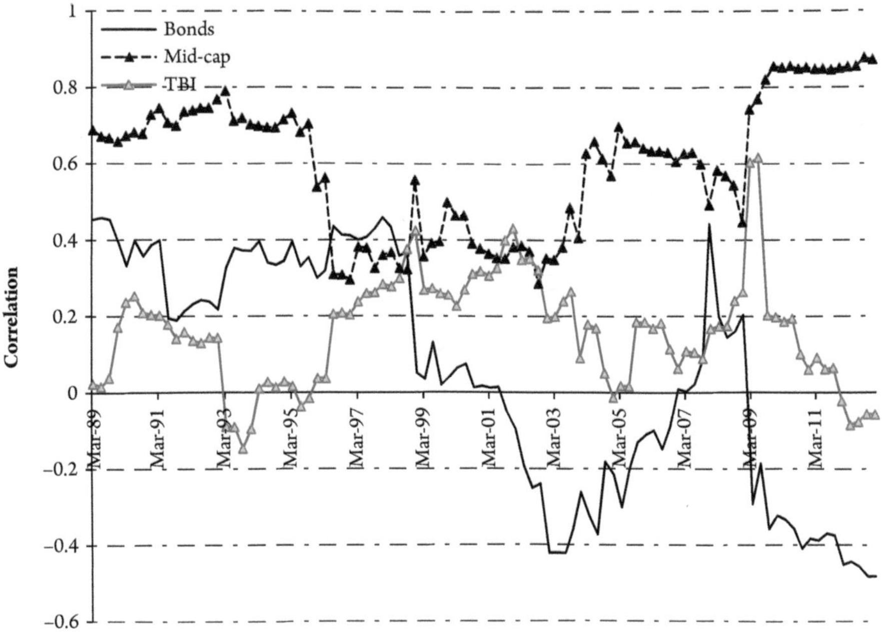

Figure 11.3 Rolling Correlations. This graph shows the rolling five-year correlations between the REIT index returns on the returns on 10-year government bonds, mid-cap equities, and the MIT/TBI index of real estate capital appreciation.

Table 11.1 summarizes the key statistics for the return series studied in this chapter. Again the table shows that REIT returns more closely resemble the returns from mid-cap equities than the returns on the underlying real estate or bonds. REIT total returns lie between the returns on riskless bonds and the returns on mid-cap equities. These results are typical of those obtained in much earlier studies such as Goetzmann and Siegel (1984). With the exception of the REIT income returns, the series show moderate skewness, with the typical slightly negative skewness for the REIT and equity returns. Each series shows excess kurtosis or peakedness.

SHARPE RATIOS

An important way to measure the efficiency of investment in REITs versus more traditional instruments is via the *Sharpe ratio,* which is a standard measure of the (retrospective) risk-return trade-off as the excess return over the riskless rate divided by the return's standard deviation. However, the data from Table 11.1 show significant departures from the assumption of normally distributed returns, suggesting some caution in interpreting the Sharpe ratio in this context (Leland 1999). Figure 11.3 graphs the rolling six-year Sharpe ratio for the four return series. Specifically, the average realized quarterly returns net of the 90-day Treasury bill rate is computed for that quarter. This average excess return is divided by the standard deviation over the corresponding rolling six-year period. This estimation is rolled forward by one quarter until the data end.

Table 11.1 **Summary Statistics for Asset Returns from 1984 to 2012**

Variable	*Mean*	*Median*	*Standard Deviation*	*Skewness*	*Kurtosis*
90-day Treasury bill	5.16	5.01	3.54	0.62	3.32
10-year government bond returns	8.86	5.65	9.16	0.73	3.49
REIT capital returns	3.48	4.51	17.81	−0.69	6.40
REIT income returns	8.83	8.30	1.55	3.28	22.59
MIT TBI index	0.78	0.99	8.16	−0.55	1.23
Mid-cap index total returns	12.93	15.62	16.16	−0.63	3.85
S&P 500	9.45	12.67	16.21	−0.54	3.61

Note: This table presents the basic statistics for the return sample. The basic data are quarterly returns annualized beginning in the first quarter of 1978 and ending in the last quarter of 2012, except the TBI index, which begins in the first quarter of 1984. The data sources are NCREIF (http://web.mit.edu/cre/research/credl/) and WRDS. The means, medians, and standard deviations are in percentages.

Over the entire sample bonds have the highest ratio (0.537), followed by mid-cap equities (0.456) and REITs (0.354). The TBI has a negative ratio (−0.080). The Sharpe ratio for REITs is negative for the first few years of the 1990s but then remains positive for the remainder of the sample period. The REIT index has a lower standard deviation than the mid-cap equity series. Nevertheless, its average Sharpe ratio is still lower than that for mid-cap. These series show considerable nonstationarity, notably in the two real estate ones for REITs and TBI. Recent evidence suggests that REIT returns exhibit very significant and abrupt regime shifts (Peng and Schulz 2012; Bianchi and Guidolin 2013).

FACTOR MODELS

The final analysis of REIT returns is through estimation of a simple return-generating model. These models establish a linkage between the REIT index returns and return indexes of related investments. Such models usually relate REIT returns to a bond index since their high dividend payout makes REITs a reasonable substitute for bonds. The models also include an equity index because REITs are a type of mid-cap equity. The third factor relates to the returns on the underlying real estate market. The estimated model is the following:

$$\mathrm{R}_t = \alpha + \beta_1 \mathrm{Bond}_t + \beta_2 \mathrm{Mid\text{-}cap}_t + \beta_3 \mathrm{TBI}_t + \beta_4\ \mathrm{NCREIF}_t + \varepsilon_t \tag{11.1}$$

where R_t is the REIT index return in quarter t; α is a constant; Bond_t is the 10-year government bond return in quarter t; $\mathrm{Mid\text{-}cap}_t$ is the return on the mid-cap index in quarter t; TBI_t is the appreciation in the TBI index in quarter t; and NCREIF_t is the return on the

Table 11.2 **Factor Model Regressions**

Estimation Interval	*Bond*	*Mid-cap*	*TBI*	*NCREIF*	*Adjusted R^2*	*F statistic*
1984 to 1993	6.128 (1.93)	0.496 (4.33)	0.036 (0.12)	−0.291 (−0.62)	0.405	7.64
1994 to 2003	0.936 (0.23)	3.84 (3.10)	0.139 (0.72)	−1.787 (−1.62)	0.197	3.39
2004 to 2012	15.548 (2.64)	1.487 (8.19)	0.145 (0.59)	−0.058 (−0.12)	0.745	22.61

Note: This table reports the estimation of the four-factor model:

$$R_t = \alpha + \beta_1 Bond_t + \beta_2 Mid\text{-}cap_t + \beta_3 TBI_t + \beta_4 NCREIF_t + \varepsilon_t$$

where R_t is the REIT index return in quarter t; α is a constant; $Bond_t$ is the 10-year government bond return in quarter t; $Mid\text{-}cap_t$ is the return on a mid-cap index in quarter t; TBI_t is the appreciation in the TBI index in quarter t; and $NCREIF_t$ is the return on the NCREIF index in quarter t. The estimation is done separately over the periods 1984 to 1993, 1994 to 2003, and 2004 to 2012. The t-values are given in parentheses.

NCREIF index in quarter *t*. Using both real estate return indexes can hopefully capture the income and the capital appreciation components of the returns on direct investment in real estate.

Table 11.2 shows the estimates from this regression over the periods 1984 to 1993, 1994 to 2003, and 2004 to 2012. The table shows that the only consistently significant factor is the mid-cap return, which is significant at the 0.01 level in each of the three regressions. The bond factor is significant in the first and last period only. What is interesting is the varying ability of the model to match REIT returns. The R^2 in the first period is 0.405 and then falls to 0.197 in the second period before taking on its highest value of 0.745 over the most recent period. Clayton and MacKinnon (2003) document the rise in REIT idiosyncratic risk in the middle period. They attribute the decline in systematic risk to increased information flows and the greater presence of institutional investors. However, the results in Table 11.2 for the most recent decade make this explanation less plausible. This factor model estimation has some noteworthy implications: (1) it is highly nonstationary (i.e., the weights on the factors and the overall fit are quite different in the three estimation periods); (2) the bond factor is much less important than the mid-cap equity factor; and (3) the two return series for the underlying real estate returns are insignificant.

A subsequent section discusses further some reasons for and implications of the apparent lack of a linkage between the returns on direct and securitized real estate. Some of the main hypotheses for why securitized returns in the form of REITs may differ from returns on the underlying real estate as measured by the TBI are the following. First, REITs are a levered investment, while the TBI is unlevered. Because the market value of REIT debt or the REIT's cost of debt is not observed, accurately de-levering the REIT returns or levering the TBI returns to make them perfectly comparable to the REIT index is difficult.

Second, because REITs are traded equity, their value should impound expectations of future economic conditions in an efficient market. The TBI may embed future economic conditions through the most recent transactions underlying the index. However, it is unlikely to be as forward looking as the publicly traded equity markets. Several studies analyzing the lead-lag relationship between real and securitized real estate markets generally find that the securitized market leads the underlying market. Yavas and Yildirim (2011) provide recent example using a dynamic conditional correlation GARCH model.

Third, the TBI may not actually measure underlying real estate returns very well. All underlying real estate returns are subject to estimation error or appraisal smoothing, depending on the index construction technique. Most properties do not sell during a given year. For those not selling, the valuation is estimated by an appraisal. That appraisal is smoothed when a previous valuation is adjusted by a preset percentage. Although such errors could be small, no guarantee exists that this is the case. The potential also exists that the assets in the TBI are not a perfect match for those owned by REITs. In hedging terminology, Boudry, Coulson, Kallberg, and Liu (2013) examine this basis risk for the TBI. They show that the tracking of the TBI to individual real estate properties is roughly comparable to the tracking of the S&P 500 (SPX) to its individual components.

Fourth, REIT returns can be distorted due to noise trading (Black 1986). A *noise trader* makes investment decisions based on perceived market movements rather than a security's fundamentals. Thus, a noise trader buys when others are buying and sells when others are selling. Because REITs are traded equities, noise traders in the public equities markets potentially drive prices away from fundamental values. In such a situation, the correlation between REITs and the underlying real estate could be quite low, especially when the costs to exploit such mispricing are high. The references cited in the following section dealing with momentum in the return generating process develop these ideas further.

RELATED LITERATURE ON REIT RETURN PROCESSES

Although the previously discussed REIT return-generating results are similar to those presented in Clayton and MacKinnon (2003), they are not strictly comparable. The authors study REITs over a much earlier sample period: 1979 to 1998. Their return-generating process includes a large-cap and small-cap equity index, bond returns, and the NCREIF returns. Furthermore, they orthogonalize their factors and use a variance decomposition approach.

This subject remains an active area of research interest. Chui, Titman, and Wei (2003) and Derwall, Huij, Brounen, and Marquering (2009) provide considerable support for the presence of a momentum factor in REIT pricing. More recently, Goebel, Harrison, Mercer, and Whitby (2013) study momentum together with a "characteristic-based" approach in the spirit of Daniel and Titman (1998). This technique uses the underlying characteristics of a security such as the book-to-market ratio to explain differences in returns. Goebel et al. find that larger returns are associated with higher book-to-market ratios, less liquidity, and lower levels of institutional ownership. They further find that the premium associated with high book-to-market ratios is present only during periods of monetary expansion.

REITS AS PART OF AN INVESTMENT PORTFOLIO

Given the above discussion, one issue is how REITs fit within a typical pension or endowment fund portfolio. The early literature suggests that a 10 to 20 percent allocation to real estate is plausible (Fogler 1984; Firstenberg, Ross, and Zisler 1988). Kallberg, Liu, and Grieg (1996) use actual cash flow data from a portfolio of direct investment in real estate to re-examine this issue. Using integer programming to capture inherent "lumpiness" of real estate investment, they show that an allocation of about 9 percent is optimal. This latter figure seems to match the figures quoted by practitioners. For example, in a survey of more than 700 U.S. pension and endowment funds, Clayton (2007) finds that equity real estate represented 6.1 percent of total assets in 2006. Fugazza, Guidolin, and Nicodano (2009) show that adding REITs to the investment opportunity set can (out-of-sample) improve the investor's Sharpe ratio.

Factors Driving REIT Performance

The remainder of this chapter addresses the determinants of differences in REIT performance. Although the following analysis is not exhaustive, it examines several possible factors.

- *Corporate governance.* Does the degree to which the REIT's governance structure binds shareholders and managers influence value?
- *Insider ownership.* How does the increasing presence of institutional investors affect REIT returns?
- *Dividends.* Given the severe constraints on dividend payouts, can REIT dividend policy sway valuations?
- *Underlying real asset market.* How closely are REIT returns linked to the underlying asset market?

REIT VALUATION AND CORPORATE GOVERNANCE

The separation of ownership and control of the firm provides much of the impetus for corporate governance. Shleifer and Vishny (1997) provide a review of the corporate governance literature. Researchers have devised various control mechanisms including performance-based compensation contracts, board structures, anti-takeover provisions, ownership structure, and takeovers in an attempt to mitigate the potential shareholder-manager conflicts. A relevant issue is whether a REIT's governance structure influences its valuation. On the surface, corporate governance should not appear to have a major influence on REIT valuation. The restrictions on the payout of net income greatly reduce the possibility for diverting free cash flows as originally established by Jensen (1986). This restriction also necessitates REITs maintaining their access to capital markets. Additionally, REITs are more transparent than regular corporations because they are constrained to engage only in passive real estate activities and are essentially a collection of tangible assets. Buttimer, Hyland, and Sanders (2005), who find no evidence of long-term REIT post-initial public offering (IPO) outperformance, corroborate this observation.

Conversely, the lack of large blocks of shareholders suggests the need for corporate governance in REITs (Ling and Ryngaert 1997). McConnell and Servaes (1990) cite a substantial holding by insiders as a powerful governance mechanism. Friday, Sirmans, and Conover (1999) document a non-linear relationship between insider ownership and market-to-book ratios. For equity REITs, levels of insider ownership below 5 percent lead to higher levels of market-to-book; higher levels have a negative impact. Analyzing Tobin's Q and insider ownership, Han (2006) finds a similar result when accounting for the UPREIT structure. Edelstein, Sureda-Gomila, and Urošević (2010), who offer a more recent theoretical and empirical approach, show that the aggregate insider stake in a REIT declines over time.

Because many diverse governance mechanisms can be considered as substitutes, several studies use aggregated governance measures. Bianco, Ghosh, and Sirmans (2007) use the Gompers-Ishii-Metrick G-measure (Gompers, Ishii, and Metrick 2003), which uses 24 governance characteristics usually coded in binary form and then added to measure the strength of shareholder rights. They conclude that the impact of governance and valuation is unresolved. This result may be partially due to the relative scarcity of hostile takeovers.

Using Tobin's Q, Hartzell, Kallberg, and Liu (2008) show that corporate governance plays an important role in the IPO valuation of a REIT. Q is defined as the (offer price × shares outstanding + total assets – book equity) divided by total assets. It is measured at the IPO stage to mitigate possible endogeneity problems. After including various control variables to explain the IPO Q, the authors find that higher valuations are associated with lower management fees or compensation, more variable or incentive-based compensation, and greater insider ownership. More than half of publicly traded REITs are incorporated in Maryland, usually as trusts. Maryland offers greater liability protection, easier bylaw amendments and protection against hostile takeovers. A strong negative valuation effect also occurs for incorporation in Maryland, which is a state known to be management friendly. They find similar results regarding post-IPO performance and governance.

More recently, Bauer, Eichholtz, and Kok (2010) use the Corporate Governance Quotient index of Institutional Shareholder Services to examine the linkage between the level of corporate governance and REIT performance. They find that governance is significantly related to firm value only for REITs with low payout ratios. These low payout ratios can result from multiple sources, including managerial compensation, non-property expenses or high levels of capital expenditures.

INSTITUTIONAL OWNERSHIP AND FIRM PERFORMANCE

In many ways REITs act like regular corporations and in other ways they do not. Institutional ownership is one place where REITs as an industry are likely to behave differently from non-REITs. The reason for this is that ownership tests form part of the requirements to maintain REIT status. So unlike regular firms that do not face these restrictions, regulation imposes a friction on the ownership structure of REITs.

REIT OWNERSHIP REQUIREMENTS

Internal Revenue Code section 856 provides the ownership requirements that REITs face in order to maintain REIT status. REIT ownership essentially has two requirements. First, as stated in section 856(a)(5), the firm must have at least 100 beneficial owners. For most publicly traded companies, this is unlikely to be a major restriction. However, it is potentially an issue for private investors wanting to use the REIT structure. Second, the firm cannot be closely held, which is covered in section 856(h). This second restriction is what is commonly referred to as the "five or fewer" rule, and essentially states that no five or fewer persons can own 50 percent or more of the REIT. Although the rule itself is somewhat more complicated than it is commonly phrased, the end result is that serious limits exist on concentrated ownership.

The Omnibus Reconciliation Act of 1993 included a *look-through provision* related to pension fund ownership in REITs. This provision allowed a fund to be considered as the set of its beneficiaries, rather than as a single entity. The impact of this provision was to make all the beneficiaries of the pension fund individual owners from the perspective of the five or fewer rule. As Downs (1998) shows, this made institutional investment in REITs by pension funds a much more attractive proposition and led to an increase in institutional ownership in REITs.

REIT INSTITUTIONAL OWNERSHIP

Figure 11.4 reports the level of institutional ownership for equity REITs (solid) and non-REIT (dotted) firms from 1990 to 2010. Thomson Reuters 13(f) data serve as the basis for calculating the level of institutional ownership. Before 1994, fairly low levels of institutional ownership in REITs occurred. This is consistent with the finding of Chan, Leung, and Wang (1998) who show that before 1994 on a size-matched basis REITs had lower levels of institutional ownership than non-REITs. After 1994 and the enactment of the look-through provision, a sharp increase took place in the level of institutional ownership in REITs. By 1996 the average level of institutional ownership was higher in the REIT market than for non-REITs.

Institutional ownership remained steady during the late 1990s and started to increase again around 2001. Although a similar upward trend in ownership occurred for non-REITs during the post 2001 period, it is more dramatic in the REIT sample. The likely explanation for this is that the first REITs entered the S&P 500 in 2001. Ambrose, Lee, and Peek (2007) show that index inclusion caused a change in the price dynamics of REITs. Included REITs became more highly correlated with the index, but spillover effects arose for the rest of the REIT industry, making non-index REITs more highly correlated with the general stock market. Along these same lines, Chiang (2010) shows that higher levels of institutional ownership are related to higher levels of synchronicity with REITs of the same asset type.

Finally, the impact of the global financial crisis can be seen on the level of REIT institutional ownership in the latter part of the sample. Although ownership levels remained

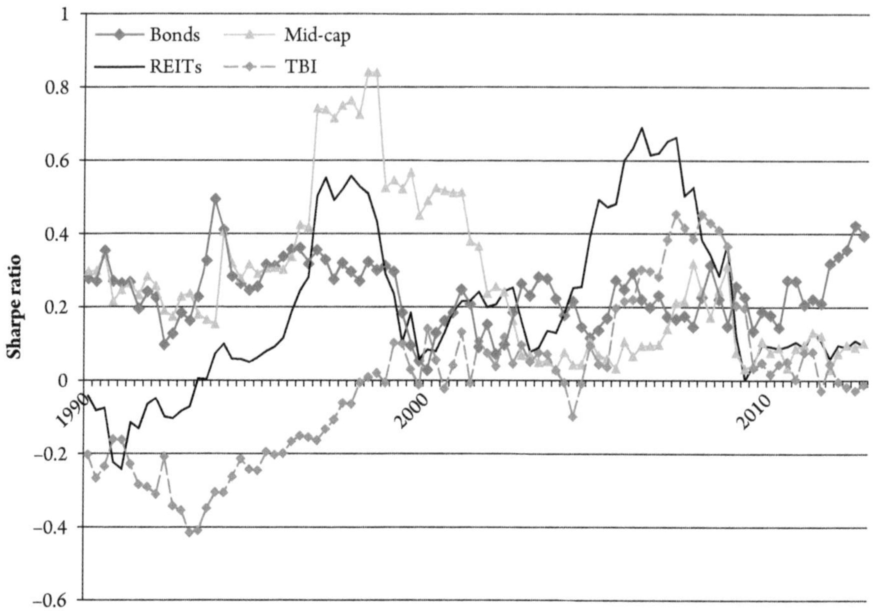

Figure 11.4 Sharpe Ratios. This figure shows the rolling six-year Sharpe ratios for the four return series emphasized in the analysis.

fairly stable for non-REITs, REIT institutional ownership fell dramatically at the start of the financial crisis but has since rebounded to near pre-crisis levels. Devos, Ong, Spieler, and Tsang (2013) show that during this period, institutional investors displayed a flight to quality by investing in REITs that were larger and had lower betas.

Table 11.3 reports ownership data by market cap decile for 138 firms in the FTSE/NAREIT equity REIT index in the first quarter of 2013. The source of the FTSE/NAREIT index constituent list is the NAREIT web page (http://www.reit.com) and SNL is the source for all other data. Three results are apparent from the table. First, only small REITs appear to have low levels of institutional ownership on average. Apart from the first decile of REITs, all other size deciles have institutional ownership greater than 70 percent. The REITs in the bottom decile are true micro-cap stocks. They have an average market cap in the bottom 5 percent of all Center for Research in Securities Prices (CRSP) listed stocks. Second, a nearly monotonic relationship exists between size and institutional ownership. Institutional owners almost exclusively hold large firms. Finally, an inverse relationship exists between inside and institutional ownership. Inside ownership tends to decline as firms become larger, while institutional ownership increases.

THE IMPACT OF INSTITUTIONAL OWNERSHIP ON PRICING

The prevailing assumption in corporate finance is that higher levels of institutional ownership have a positive influence on equity returns (McConnell and Servaes 1990). Institutional ownership could affect firm performance through several potential mechanisms. Gompers and Metrick (2001) describe one channel where institutional ownership is associated with higher returns. They contend that if the demand and supply

Table 11.3 **REIT Ownership**

Decile	*Number of Firms*	*Average Institutional Ownership*	*Average Inside Ownership*	*Average Market Capitalization (in millions)*
1	13	37.4	13.6	147
2	14	72.5	7.5	488
3	14	72.2	9.5	755
4	14	73.4	10.0	1,121
5	14	80.7	8.6	1,573
6	14	88.9	4.0	1,996
7	14	83.3	5.3	2,845
8	14	90.9	3.2	3,925
9	14	92.2	2.7	6,813
10	13	93.1	4.6	21,166
Sample	138	78.7	6.9	1,757

Note: This table reports ownership data by market cap decile for 138 equity REITs in the FTSE/NAREIT equity REIT index in the first quarter of 2013. Average institutional ownership is the average level of institutional ownership for firms in a given decile. Firms with ownership greater than 100 percent were winsorized to 100 percent. Average inside ownership is the average level of ownership of firm insiders for a given decile. Average market cap is the average market cap of firms in a given decile. The FTSE/NAREIT index constituent list is from NAREIT's web page (http://www.reit.com). SNL is the source for all other data.

curves for stocks are not perfectly elastic, then demand shocks could cause changes in stock prices and thus returns. This is often called the *price pressure effect*. In this sense, institutional ownership may predict stock returns. Furthermore, if institutional investors have preferences for certain firm characteristics, then a shock to institutional ownership will have a disproportionately large effect on firms with those characteristics. Gompers and Metrick show that this appears to be the case for a large sample of firms. Institutions tend to favor larger, more liquid stocks that generally have low past returns. Higher levels of institutional investment predict higher future returns.

Conversely, institutional investors may exhibit herding or return chasing behavior by channeling capital flows to REITs with recent superior performance. Using quarterly Federal Reserve Flow of Funds data, Ling and Naranjo (2003) find no empirical support for return chasing behavior in the modern post-1992 REIT era. However, their results indicate that capital flows can influence REIT returns. Ling and Naranjo (2005) use a vector autoregression approach on monthly and weekly mutual fund flows. They show some evidence of return chasing behavior and that inflows can positively influence REIT returns.

According to Ling and Ryngaert (1997), institutional ownership may lead to a change in price dynamics around REIT IPOs. They find that in the 1970s and 1980s, REIT IPOs tend to be overpriced and subsequently exhibit underperformance compared to other REITs during the 100 days after an IPO. This relationship reverses itself in the IPOs of the early 1990s. In this market, characterized by higher institutional ownership, IPOs tend to be underpriced by 3.6 percent on average. They modestly outperform other REITs during the 100 days after an IPO.

Rather than being due to demand shocks, Yan and Zhang (2009) contend that returns and institutional ownership are positively correlated because of information. Institutions may be better informed than other investors and exploit their informational advantage. In particular, they argue that short-term active investors are more likely to trade on information. Their evidence indicates that the total level of institutional ownership does not predict returns, but rather the ownership levels of short-term investors.

Institutional owners can also affect firm performance through a corporate governance mechanism. If one believes that institutional investors are better monitors than retail investors, then ownership may affect performance through better oversight of management. Chung, Fung, and Hung (2012) show institutional ownership has a positive effect on REIT efficiency.

REIT VALUATION AND DIVIDENDS

Because the majority of REIT returns come from the dividend cash flow, various studies investigate how REIT dividend policy influences REIT valuation. Kallberg, Liu, and Srinivasan (2003) show a tie between REIT values and their dividend payout. They find that, unlike for equity indexes, present value and dividend pricing models cannot be rejected for REITs, reinforcing the link between REIT values and dividend payouts. This result is in contrast to the rejection of these models for equity indexes (Campbell and Shiller 1988).

The market reaction to dividend cuts by REITs is similar to the results obtained for regular corporations: dividend cuts (increases) receive a negative (positive) announcement effect (Wang, Erickson, and Gau 1993). Although this finding suggests that REIT managers have some discretion of dividend payouts, the issue of REIT dividends and performance remains an open question. As Boudry (2011) discusses, REIT dividends can be decomposed into discretionary and non-discretionary components. Because of the dividend distribution requirements imposed on REITs in order to maintain status, REITs in practice typically distribute at least 100 percent of their taxable income and capital gains in dividends each year. REITs are required to distribute 90 percent of funds from operations after reserves.

REITs apparently use discretionary dividends that do not have an obvious tax motivation to smooth the overall level of dividends. So the meaning of a high dividend payout for a REIT is unclear. The firm could have high taxable income or could be paying large discretionary dividends. Because the discretionary and non-discretionary make up of dividends is only known during the subsequent period, examining the market's reactions to discretionary and non-discretionary dividends is difficult.

REITS AND THE UNDERLYING REAL ESTATE MARKET

A central debate in the REIT literature is the issue of how linked are REITs and the underlying asset markets. The issue is important from a practical standpoint because pension fund and other investment portfolios often view REITs as a more liquid mechanism for participating in the real estate market. Their alternative is direct real estate investment with all of its problems with illiquidity, high transactions costs, and lack of transparency. Many practitioners believe that REITs and direct real estate have different risk and return properties. Feldman (2003) confirms this intuition using a mean-variance analysis. MacKinnon and Al Zaman (2009) present an opposing viewpoint.

However, the results in Tables 11.1 and 11.2, as well as Figure 11.2 suggest that REIT returns more closely resemble those on mid-cap stocks as opposed to the underlying real properties. A problem with much of the extant literature is its focus on short-term structural relations between the two markets. Boudry et al. (2012) use a cointegration framework to link the TBI index with REIT returns. Although they find that securitized returns lead the underlying real market, the two markets share a long-run equilibrium. Both REITs and direct property returns adjust toward this equilibrium.

Hartzell, Kallberg, and Liu (2005) examine a final aspect of the linkage between REITs and the underlying market. They find that the demand for investment capital drives the volume of REIT IPOs rather than adverse selection. This fact again suggests a complex temporal interaction between the two markets.

Summary and Conclusions

This chapter has analyzed the historical performance of U.S. equity REITs and some factors underlying the differences in this performance. Measured in diverse ways including means and standard deviations of quarterly returns, Sharpe ratios, and factor models contemporaneously, the data show that REIT returns are more similar to mid-cap equities than to bonds or to the returns on the underlying real estate. These data also show how dynamic these relationships are. The Sharpe ratios vary widely over the sample timeframe. The R^2s and the factor loadings in the return-generating model are very different in the three sample periods studied.

The second part of this chapter studied the possible factors that influence the risk and return of REITs. In general, strong corporate governance and higher levels of institutional ownership positively influence REIT returns. REITs are an important class of investments for institutional investors. The data show that in the largest size decile, institutional ownership is 93.1 percent of the total.

A REIT is often considered an equity that is relatively easy to value because of the constraints on its investment activities and its transparency. Yet, the literature surveyed in this chapter suggests a complex relationship between REIT returns and their possible determinants. In particular, the link between REIT returns and dividend policy is hard to characterize. Despite the recent refinements in measures of the returns on direct real estate investment, many issues remain unresolved concerning the linkages between the real and securitized real estate markets.

Discussion Questions

1. Discuss the reasons for the apparent lack of a contemporaneous link between the performance of REITs and the performance of the underlying real asset market.

2. Explain why REITs may not require as strong a corporate governance structure as typical corporations.
3. Discuss why institutional investors hold an increasing percentage of REIT shares.
4. Compare the historical performance of REITs with mid-cap equities and riskless bonds.

Acknowledgments

The authors thank Sujith Puram, a finance doctoral candidate at Arizona State University, for assistance in preparing this manuscript.

References

Ambrose, Brent W., Dong Wook Lee, and Joe Peek. 2007. "Industry Comovement after Joining an Index: Spillovers of Nonfundamental Effects." *Real Estate Economics* 35:1, 57–90.
Bauer, Rob, Piet Eichholtz, and Nils Kok. 2010. "Corporate Governance and Performance: The REIT Effect." *Real Estate Economics* 38:1, 1–29.
Bianchi, Daniele, and Massimo Guidolin. 2013. "Can Linear Predictability Models Time Bull and Bear Real Estate Markets? Out-of-Sample Evidence from REIT Portfolios." *Journal of Real Estate Finance and Economics* 43:2, 1–49.
Bianco, Candy, Chinmoy Ghosh, and C. F. Sirmans. 2007. "The Impact of Corporate Governance on the Performance of REITs." *Journal of Portfolio Management* 33:1, 175–191.
Black, Fischer. 1986. "Noise." *Journal of Finance* 41:3, 529–543.
Boudry, Walter. 2011. "An Examination of REIT Dividend Policy." *Real Estate Economics* 39:4, 601–634.
Boudry, Walter, Edward Coulson, Jarl Kallberg, and Crocker Liu. 2012. "On the Hybrid Nature of REITs." *Journal of Real Estate Finance and Economics* 44:1, 230–249.
Boudry, Walter, Edward Coulson, Jarl Kallberg, and Crocker Liu. 2013. "What Do Commercial Real Estate Price Indexes Really Measure?" *Journal of Real Estate Finance and Economics* 45:4, 617–639.
Buttimer, Richard, David Hyland, and Anthony Sanders. 2005. "REITs, IPO Waves, and Long Run Performance." *Real Estate Economics* 33:1, 51–87.
Campbell, John, and Robert Shiller. 1988. "Stock Prices, Earnings and Expected Dividends." *Journal of Finance* 43:3, 661–676.
Chan, Su Han, Wai-Kin Leung, and Ko Wang. 1998. "Institutional Investment in REITs: Evidence and Implications." *Journal of Real Estate Research* 16:3, 357–374.
Chiang, Kevin C. H. 2010. "On the Comovement of REIT Prices." *Journal of Real Estate Research* 32: 2, 187–200.
Chinloy, Peter, Man Cho, and Isaac F. Megbolugbe. 1997. "Appraisals, Transaction Incentives, and Smoothing." *Journal of Real Estate Finance and Economics* 14:1, 89–111.
Chui, Andy, Sheridan Titman, and K. C. John Wei. 2003. "Intra-Industry Momentum: The Case of REITs." *Journal of Financial Markets* 6:3, 363–387.
Chung, Richard, Scott Fung, and Szu-Yin Kathy Hung. 2012. "Institutional Investors and Firm Efficiency of Real Estate Investment Trusts." *Journal of Real Estate Finance and Economics* 45:1, 171–211.
Clayton, James. 2007. *PREA Plan Research Report.* Hartford, CT: Pension Real Estate Association.
Clayton, James, and Gregory MacKinnon. 2003. "The Relative Importance of Stock, Bond and Real Estate Factors in Explaining REIT Returns." *Journal of Real Estate Finance and Economics* 27:1, 39–60.

Daniel, Kent, and Sheridan Titman. 1998. "Evidence on the Characteristics of Cross-Sectional Variation in Common Stock Returns." *Journal of Finance* 52:1, 1–33.

Derwall, Joroen, Joop Huij, Dirk Brounen, and Wessel Marquering. 2009. "REIT Momentum and the Performance of REIT Mutual Funds." *Financial Analysts Journal* 65:5, 24–34.

Devos, Erik, Seow-Eng Ong, Andrew C. Spieler, and Desmond Tsang. 2013. "REIT Institutional Ownership Dynamics and the Financial Crisis." *Journal of Real Estate Finance and Economics* 47:2, 266–288.

Downs, David H. 1998. "The Value in Targeting Institutional Investors: Evidence from the Five-or-Fewer Rule Change." *Real Estate Economics* 26:4, 613–649.

Edelstein, Robert, Antoni Sureda-Gomila, and Branko Urošević. 2010. "Ownership Dynamics with Multiple Insiders: The Case of REITs." *Real Estate Economics* 38:1, 57–90.

Feldman, Barry. 2003. *Investment Policy for Securitized and Direct Real Estate*. Chicago: Ibbotson Associates.

Firstenberg, Paul M., Stephen A. Ross, and Randall Zisler. 1988. "Real Estate: The Whole Story." *Journal of Portfolio Management* 23:1, 22–34.

Fisher, Jeff, David Geltner, and Henry Pollakowski. 2007. "A Quarterly Transactions-Based Index of Institutional Real Estate Investment Performance and Movements in Supply and Demand." *Journal of Real Estate Finance and Economics* 34:1, 5–33.

Fogler, H. Russell. 1984. "20 percent in Real Estate: Can Theory Justify It?" *Journal of Portfolio Management* 10:2, 6–13.

Friday, Swint, Stacy Sirmans, and Mitchell Conover. 1999. "Ownership Structure and the Value of the Firm: The Case of REITs." *Journal of Real Estate Research* 17:1, 71–90.

Fugazza, Carolina, Massimo Guidolin, and Giovanna Nicodano. 2009. "Time and Risk Diversification in Real Estate Investments: Assessing the Ex Post Economic Value." *Real Estate Economics* 37:3, 341–381.

Gatzlaff, Dean, and David Geltner. 1998. "A Transaction-based Index of Commercial Property and Its Comparison to the NCREIF Index." *Real Estate Finance* 15:1, 7–22.

Geltner, David. 1991. "Smoothing in Appraisal-Based Returns." *Journal of Real Estate Finance and Economics* 4:3, 327–345.

Geltner, David, and Will Goetzmann. 2000. "Two Decades of Commercial Property Returns: A Repeated-Measures Regression-Based Version of the NCREIF Index." *Journal of Real Estate Finance and Economics* 21:1, 5–21.

Glascock, John, Chiuling Lu, and Raymond So. 2000. "Further Evidence on the Integration of REIT, Bond, and Stock Returns." *Journal of Real Estate Finance and Economics* 20:2, 177–194.

Goebel, Paul, David Harrison, Jeffrey Mercer, and Ryan Whitby. 2013. "REIT Momentum and Characteristic-Related REIT Returns." *Journal of Real Estate Finance and Economics* 47:3, 564–581.

Goetzmann, Will, and Laurence Siegel. 1984. "Real Estate Returns: A Comparison with Other Investments." *Real Estate Economics* 12:3, 219–242.

Gompers, Paul A., Jay Ishii, and Andrew Metrick. 2003. "Corporate Governance and Equity Prices." *Quarterly Journal of Economics* 118:1, 107–155.

Han, Bing. 2006. "Insider Ownership and Firm Value: Evidence from Real Estate Investment Trusts." *Journal of Real Estate Finance and Economics* 32:4, 471–493.

Hartzell, Jay, Jarl Kallberg, and Crocker Liu. 2005. "The Role of the Underlying Real Asset Market in REIT IPOs." *Real Estate Economics* 33:1, 27–50.

Hartzell, Jay, Jarl Kallberg, and Crocker Liu. 2008. "The Role of Corporate Governance in IPOs: Evidence from REITs." *Journal of Law and Economics* 51:3, 539–562.

Jensen, Michael C. 1986. "Agency Costs of Free Cash Flow, Corporate Finance, and Takeovers." *American Economic Review* 76:2, 323–329.

Jirasakuldech, Benjamas, Robert Campbell, and Riza Emekter. 2009. "Conditional Volatility of Equity Real Estate Investment Trust Returns: A Pre- and Post-1993 Comparison." *Journal of Real Estate Finance and Economics* 38:2, 137–154.

Kallberg, Jarl, Crocker Liu, and Wylie Grieg. 1996. "The Role of Real Estate in the Portfolio Allocation Process." *Real Estate Economics* 24:3, 359–377.

Kallberg, Jarl, Crocker Liu, and Anand Srinivasan. 2003. "Dividend Pricing Models and REITs." *Journal of Real Estate Economics* 31:3, 435–450.

Leland, Hayne. 1999. "Beyond Mean-Variance: Performance Measurement in a Nonsymmetric World." *Financial Analysts Journal* 55:1, 27–36.

Ling, David, and Andy Naranjo. 2003. "The Dynamics of REIT Capital Flows and Returns." *Real Estate Economics* 31:3, 403–436.

Ling, David, and Andy Naranjo. 2005. "Dedicated REIT Mutual Fund Flows and REIT Performance." *Journal of Real Estate Finance and Economics* 32:4, 409–433.

Ling, David, and Michael Ryngaert. 1997. "Valuation Uncertainty, Institutional Involvement, and the Underpricing of IPOs: The Case of REITs." *Journal of Financial Economics* 43:3, 433–456.

Liu, Crocker, and Jianping Mei. 1992. "The Predictability of Returns on Equity REITs and Their Co-Movement with Other Assets." *Journal of Real Estate Finance and Economics* 5:4, 401–418.

MacKinnon, Greg, and Ashraf Al Zaman. 2009. "Real Estate for the Long Term: The Effect of Return Predictability on Long-Horizon Allocations." *Real Estate Economics* 37:1, 117–153.

McConnell, John, and Henri Servaes. 1990. "Additional Evidence on Equity Ownership and Corporate Value." *Journal of Financial Economics* 27:3, 595–612.

Peng, Liang, and Rainer Schulz. 2012. "Does the Diversification Potential of Securitized Real Estate Vary Over Time and Should Investors Care?" *Journal of Real Estate Finance and Economics* 41:4, 409–433.

Shleifer, Andrei, and Robert Vishny. 1997. "A Survey of Corporate Governance." *Journal of Finance* 52:2, 737–783.

Wang, Ko, John Erickson, and George Gau. 1993. "Dividend Policy and Dividend Announcement Effects for Real Estate Investment Trusts." *Journal of the American Real Estate and Urban Economics Association* 21:2, 185–201.

Yan, Xuemin, and Zhe Zhang. 2009. "Institutional Investors and Equity Returns: Are Short-Term Institutions Better Informed?" *Review of Financial Studies* 22: 2, 893–924.

Yavas, Abdullah, and Yildiray Yildirim. 2011. "Price Discovery in Real Estate Markets: A Dynamic Analysis." *Journal of Real Estate Finance and Economics* 42:1, 1–29.

12

REITs: International Dimensions

EHSAN NIKBAKHT
Professor of Finance, Frank G. Zarb School of Business, Hofstra University

GARRETT SMITH
Doctoral Student, Florida Atlantic University

ANDREW SPIELER
Professor of Finance, Frank G. Zarb School of Business, Hofstra University

Introduction

The United States imposes strict criteria for a company to obtain REIT status. However, these strict guidelines provide benefits to the corporation and investors. By effectively having no corporate taxation, a REIT removes the double taxation an investor faces with other entities. The success of the REIT structure in early adopters in the United States and Australia has opened the door for other countries. As of 2013, REIT-type structures operate in 40 countries with 25 having REITs listed on local stock exchanges. Other countries are considering legislation to introduce REITs into their domestic markets. Table 12.1 lists the major REIT countries and the market capitalization of their REITs listed domestically and the year of first listing. The countries with largest market capitalization (cap) of I-REITs as a percentage of country contribution as of December 2012 are the United States (44.8 percent), Hong Kong (11.7 percent), Japan (10.9 percent), Australia (8.1 percent), Singapore (5.1 percent), and United Kingdom (5.1 percent). No other country has at least 5 percent (EPRA 2012).

In 1960, the U.S. Congress passed the REIT Act (contained in the Cigar Excise Tax Act of 1960). The first REIT, Continental Mortgage Investors, was publicly listed in 1965. Just four years later, The Netherlands passed legislation conducive for REIT formation. In 1971, Australia became the third country to accommodate the REIT structure. Surprisingly, only these three markets listed REITs until Malaysia introduced REIT legislation in 1989. In the decade that followed, four countries introduced REIT legislation—Canada, Belgium, Turkey, and Greece. In the early 1990s, the United States and Australia started to allow internally managed trusts. This laid the foundation for the so-called

Table 12.1 **Listing of Major International REIT Markets: Year-end 2011**

Country	*Number of REITs*	*Market Cap (Millions $)*	*Year of First REIT*
United States	187	559,521	1965
Australia	44	82,467	1971
France	41	56,250	2003
Japan	34	46,181	2001
Canada	33	44,192	1993
United Kingdom	20	38,200	2007
Singapore	24	35,299	2002
Hong Kong	8	16,500	2005
The Netherlands	5	8,534	1972
Belgium	14	7,133	1996
Turkey	17	5,756	1997
Malaysia	15	5,361	1989
New Zealand	5	2,149	1997
Germany	5	1,645	2007
South Africa	1	789	2002
South Korea	7	188	2002

Note: This table shows the 16 countries with the largest number of REITs and their market capitalization as of year-end 2011 as well as the year of the first REIT listing in each country.

modern REIT era. A glut of commercial property at depressed prices was a direct result of the savings and loan crisis. This allowed for certain internally managed REITs to be highly successful, signifying the start of the modern REIT era (Whiting 2007). The success of this model aided in the recovery of property prices and provided motivation for Asian countries to consider establishing REITs to help their own recovery from the Asian financial crisis (AFC).

Although the United States is the largest component of the global REIT landscape as measured by percentage of firms, as well as market capitalization, REITs are likely to become increasingly more popular across different markets. This chapter examines why the outlook for international real estate investment trusts is bright.

The first REITs in the United Kingdom and Germany were launched at the beginning of the global financial crisis (GFC) in 2007, when both countries' financial markets were performing poorly. However, the U.K. market has grown considerably since then and ranks as the sixth largest REIT market by capitalization. Although growth of German REITs (G-REITs) has been slow due in part to the legal structure and restrictions, a new rule changing the securitized property landscape has positively affected capital flows. Because of the success of REITs in the United Kingdom and elsewhere, Ireland approved a REIT structure in an effort to stimulate its stagnant real estate market resulting from the GFC in April 2013. The first two REITs listed on the Irish stock market have been well received, with both raising more capital during their respective IPOs than expected (Pirolo, 2014).

Another reason the outlook is bright for I-REITs is the size of the global real estate market itself. Estimates of the total investable global commercial real estate market exceed $12 trillion (Deloitte Touche Tohmatsu 2012; UBS Global Asset Management 2011). The private commercial real estate market is sizable at about $8 trillion (Rehring 2012). Table 12.1 demonstrates that the total REIT 2012 current market capitalization (and by extension, the approximate value of the real estate holdings) is $1 trillion, well short of the total investable market. This figure is double the 2006 estimate (Cauchie and Hoesli 2006). This increase in six years while spanning the GFC illustrates how quickly the I-REIT sector is growing.

On a percentage basis, public real estate markets consequently represent one-twelfth or about 8 percent of total investable property worldwide. This estimate is in line with alternative estimates that the total securitized portion of investable real estate is between 5 and 10 percent. Expanding holdings of the investable property market will partly fuel the growth of the REIT sector. Additionally, the breakdown in securitized real estate is skewed toward Europe and North America, with about 70 percent of the investable property contained in these two locations. Australasia (Australia and Asia) comprises the remaining 30 percent. According to Whiting (2007), REITs in this region owned about 60 percent of the investable property in Australia as of 2004. This is not the case for Asia. The anticipated growth of Asian cities, particularly in China, India, and Southeast Asia, will lead to an increase in both supply and demand for investable property. Conservatively, even if the current level remains constant at 5 to 10 percent of Asian investable property, the aggregate size of the REIT markets is expected to grow considerably. This may be a substantial underestimate if REIT formation in Asia expands rapidly.

As large institutional investors such as pension funds, endowments, and sovereign wealth funds continue to amass assets, they will reduce risk through diversification. REITs and particularly I-REITs will be a constituent in these investors' portfolios. For example, the California Public Employees' Retirement System (CalPERS) was the first U.S. pension fund to allocate capital to I-REITs in 2006 (Jacobius 2006). CalPERS invested over $1 billion in these investments, which represented less than 1 percent of its portfolio. CalPERS is the largest pension fund in the United States with more than $250 billion in assets as of January 2013. Other states such as Ohio, Oregon, Massachusetts, and Pennsylvania have followed suit. As a further illustration of the growth of real estate as an asset class, the Yale endowment's second largest asset class is now real estate with 20.2 percent in 2011 (Yale 2012).

The research concerning I-REITs is heavily skewed toward the Asian markets because of their anticipated importance and relative maturity compared with Europe. The most developed lines of research involve the integration of I-REITs between two or more countries and other asset classes. Market segmentation effects can be tested directly between equities, fixed income, real property and REITs, or between REIT markets in different countries. Investigating diversification benefits received from I-REITs is a third topic. Other areas include factors influencing I-REIT returns and capital structure, as well as how regulation and other country-specific factors affect REIT development.

Legal and Regulatory Framework

Because of the heterogeneity in the legal, political, and economic climate, no unified structure dictates how I-REITs operate on a global scale. The country of incorporation solely determines the laws defining REIT operation. Even within the European Union (EU), no unified REIT legal framework exists to aid in cross-border operations. EU REITs tend to be structured similarly to U.S. REITs. However, important differences exist that affect how financial markets treat REITs in different countries.

To illustrate this point, consider the development of the REIT market in Spain. The Spanish government passed a law in 2009 allowing for the formation of a REIT-type investment vehicle. Under Spanish law, however, the corporation would be subject to taxation. Not surprisingly, after four years no Spanish REITs have listed. Advocates of REITs are lobbying the government to alter the law seeking a framework more similar to the United States or the United Kingdom. Some contend this could help relieve part of the continued stress on the property market (Hutchings 2012).

South Korea is another example of unintentional legal obstruction to REIT development. Pham (2011) outlines the complicated nature of the Korean REIT (K-REIT) statutes. Additionally, the structure of the law imposes constraints resulting in poor performance relative to other Korean assets. While the Korean government has recently loosened some of its initial restrictions, the K-REIT market has not gained the traction seen in other Asian economies.

Ong, Ooi, and Kawaguchi (2011) discuss how the REIT structure operates in Japan and Singapore. Both countries have structures that are close to their U.S. counterparts but with subtle differences. These two nations have the largest market depth in Asia. Newell and Yue (2010) analyze Hong Kong REITs as well as their return and diversification characteristics. Quek and Ong (2008) give an overview of China's securitized property market and report the performance of the two publicly listed REITs with investments in Chinese property. However, neither of these REITs is listed in mainland China. Instead, one is listed in Hong Kong and the other in Singapore. No Chinese exchange lists publicly traded REITs but some private REIT-type companies trade internally between the major banks. Deloitte Touche Tohmatsu (2012) provides a summary of Chinese property investment and regulation.

I-REIT Research

In some countries, historical REIT data are available for research and analysis. In others, the paucity of REITs obliges a reliance on non-REIT data that are deemed a suitable proxy for REIT behavior. Bond, Karolyi, and Sanders (2003) and Bond and Glascock (2006) demonstrate that these proxies are suitable and are statistically and economically indistinguishable from actual I-REIT behavior. Early studies of I-REITs needed these proxies regardless of the markets investigated. Now, these proxies are used in emerging or developed markets with substantial investable real estate. They are also used in firms earning a majority of revenue from property investment but having underdeveloped domestic REIT markets such as South Korea or Sweden.

I-REITs: A Suitable Substitute for Physical International Property

REITs can serve as a proxy for real property investment. However, most studies focus on the U.S. market, based on data availability. Equity and real estate markets may be structured differently enough abroad to prevent REITs from substituting as direct real estate investments. As long as REITs function similar to real property across different countries, retail and professional investors can incorporate this asset class into their portfolios.

Hoesli and Oikarinen (2012) use U.S., U.K. and Australian data to model the relationship between the two asset classes. U.S. and U.K. markets behave in a similar fashion. In the long run, REITs behave more closely to real estate than equities, despite trading on major exchanges and as components of indexes. Interestingly, REITs react before the underlying real estate to external shocks. Based on a three-year holding period, U.S. and U.K. investors receive the same diversification benefits as from holding the less liquid underlying real estate assets. On the other hand, the results from the Australian data are mixed and ultimately inconclusive.

Using a different methodology, Hudgins (2010) obtains similar results. In both the United States and the United Kingdom, REIT returns are weakly correlated with broad equity returns, while strongly correlated to real estate. However, this is not the case for Australia where the opposite finding occurs. Nonetheless, skeptics still abound. According to Whiting (2007, 18), Ben Sanderson, property investment manager at Prudential, PLC, believes that REITs do not replicate physical property.

Market Integration Between REITs and Other Assets

The fact that I-REITs may behave like property does not necessarily imply substantial market segmentation between REITs and other asset classes. This issue warrants an international investigation. Studies investigate the connection among REITs, fixed-income, equity, commodities, and real property for the U.S. market. Nikbakht (2011) tests for volatility spillover from bonds and equity into real property and the I-REIT market over 2000–2009. This period covers both the recovery from the dot-com bubble and the GFC. The results indicate volatility spillover effects from both equities and high-yield bonds to REITs. Little connection exists between REITs and commodities over this period.

Liow (2010) investigates the integration of the four largest securitized real estate markets (the United States, United Kingdom, Japan, and Australia) with the broader global equity market for 1990–2007 using monthly returns. Correlations are weaker between REIT returns and the global market than between the individual equity markets and the global market proxy. While the integration effects are still relatively weak, its effect has been strengthening over time.

Xu and Yang (2011) investigate the impact of U.S. monetary policy on the returns of 18 securitized real estate markets. The primary variables of interest are the target factor and the path factor of interest rates. The *target factor* is the change in the periodic interest rate. The *path factor* is a matrix consisting of various shorter-term rates designed to capture the anticipated movement of future interest rates, as well as the future policy direction of the Federal Reserve (Fed). International markets typically respond differently to Fed shocks than U.S. markets. Although the U.S. markets primarily react to the target rate, international markets respond to the path of future rates. The difference in response of securitized property within a country is correlated with the exchange rate and the level of real economic integration with the United States.

Market Integration Among I-REITs

This section examines the issue of market interdependence and the level of integration between the REIT markets. Forbes and Rigobon (2002) investigate the integration of equities and conclude that during three major international crises, no contagion occurs except an increase in the level of general market volatility. Brière, Chapelle, and Szafarz (2012) expand both the time frame and number of assets under investigation. They conclude that correlations in financial markets are broadly unstable. Structurally, globalization and crisis contagion are very different. Crisis contagion implies that the decline of one market or asset directly causes the decline in another market or asset class. Globalization allows for freer movement of funds. Thus, investors may move funds in anticipation of crisis. In this case, there is no contagion effect, but rather globalization and a flight to safety during times of crisis. These results in the non-REIT environment provide support from the previous section that I-REITs provide diversification benefits.

Deqing and Yung (2007) provide the first study of volatility transmission between I-REITs. They use daily return data between six countries (Australia, Hong Kong, Japan, Singapore, the United States, and the United Kingdom) for January 1, 1999, through December 31, 2003. The authors investigate: (1) if volatility is transmitted within the Asian region and (2) if volatility can be transmitted trans-regionally. Results indicate that the transmission of volatility and the transmission response is asymmetric. The transmission effect is especially strong within Asia. The United States acts like a volatility transmitter to Asia while the United Kingdom acts primarily as a volatility receiver.

Continuing with this theme, Liow (2008) investigates the linkages between the United States, United Kingdom, and eight countries within the Asian region. The author uses a longer time frame than previously employed in the extant volatility transmission literature in securitized real estate prices. In particular, the sample period includes the AFC, which allows a study of long-term and short-term co-movements. The long-term trend and short-term interconnectedness increases after the AFC. Further, the trend strengthens in the years following the AFC, illustrating interdependence within the Asian region exists.

Liow and Chen (2013) continue the theme of examining the Asian REIT sector for integration. They examine eight countries within the region (Australia, Japan, Hong Kong, Singapore, Taiwan, China, Malaysia, and the Philippines) covering 15 years (1995–2009) to test for long-term, time-varying volatility. They market for securitized real estate in Asia is not correlated in the long term. However, during the time period of the GFC, a tendency to exhibit price convergence between the markets occurs.

Yunus (2009) investigates the interconnectedness of seven large securitized property markets and to identify the source of any integration between markets. The study uses weekly data covering the period from January 1990 to August 2007. Although Yunus computes the results in both U.S. dollars and local returns, no material difference exists between the methods. The evidence also shows co-integration among all the country pairs except France and the Netherlands.

Ryan (2011) investigates the market integration of listed property companies including REITs between 12 emerging and developed economies. The periods include pre-crisis, crisis, and recovery for the AFC and for the pre-GFC and GFC. Further, the author considers this question under three different currency regimes: unhedged, fully hedged, and partially hedged. During either crisis period, the correlations change. The implication is that a shift in diversification benefits occurs after the crisis. Those countries providing benefits before the crisis no longer do so after the crisis. Underdeveloped markets before the crisis tend to provide diversification benefits post-crisis. The benefits differ for the hedged and unhedged positions. Short-term investors tend to hedge their positions, while long-term investors tend to use unhedged positions.

Liu, Loudon, and Milunovich (2012) investigate the relationship between the U.S., Australia, Hong Kong, Japan, and Singapore REIT markets. The authors explore the linkages of these five economies using macroeconomic and financial variables, in both U.S. dollar and local currency returns. The credit spread, volatility of global equity markets, volume traded on global equity markets, and inflation rates play a factor in determining the correlation between the markets. Currency plays a limited role based on local or dollar returns. These findings corroborate Yunus (2009), but are at odds with Ryan (2011).

Pham (2012) investigates the correlation of returns with the transmission of volatility between the emerging and developed REIT markets in Asia. Japan, Hong Kong, and Singapore are denoted as developed nations and the other four as emerging. Daily data are from June 2006 to May 2011 for seven countries (Japan, Singapore, Hong Kong, Malaysia, Taiwan, Thailand, and South Korea). Pham constructs three indexes for Malaysia, Thailand, and South Korea but uses the S&P REIT indexes for the remaining four countries. The correlation in REIT markets across Asia is relatively low (0.14 to 0.42) with the highest pair between Hong Kong and Singapore. Further, the average correlation between emerging markets (0.25) is lower than the average correlation between developed nations (0.35). After risk-adjusting returns, the emerging economies outperform the developed economies, a result strengthened when factoring in the relatively poorer performance of the Korean REIT market. For completeness, the author subdivides the periods into pre-GFC, GFC, and post-GFC. During the time period of the GFC, all markets begin to integrate with each other and that decoupling of markets in the post-period has been slow. The transmission analysis finds that Japan and Singapore tend to transmit prices.

Zhou (2012) continues the investigation of I-REIT integration by considering the seven largest REIT markets and examining if, and to what extent, their integration characteristics are time-scale dependent. At the time of the analysis, these seven markets (Australia, France, Hong Kong, Japan, Singapore, the United States, and the United Kingdom) comprise nearly 90 percent of the entire global REIT market. The sample is daily return data from the EPRA/REIT indexes for January 1990–December 2009. The degree of connectedness increases over time.

Zhou (2013) uses a 20-year period (1991–2010) to investigate risk transfer between I-REITs. Instead of using traditional variance transmission effects to test for volatility transmission, the author uses a value at risk (VaR) approach. The goal is to assess if the occurrence of past large risks can be transmitted to another market for the United States, the United Kingdom, and the four major markets in Australasia (Australia, Japan, Hong Kong, and Singapore). The six countries generate a total of 15 market pairs. Zhou also investigates each pair for the direction of transmission. There are 45 directional and country correlation pairs. Only a fraction of the sample is fully integrated (both positive and negative transmission): the United States and the United Kingdom, the United States and Australia, Japan and Singapore, and Hong Kong and Singapore for the full sample investigated. Within sub-periods the integration of markets increases over time. The results also show the transmission of negative (downside) risk more often than positive return spillovers.

Diversification Benefits of I-REITs

I-REITs provide tangible diversification benefits. Worzala and Sirmans (2003) provide a comprehensive review of the securitized real estate investing literature including the benefits of diversification.

Bond et al. (2003) explore the diversification abilities of I-REITs by using the EPRA country-level REIT indexes. The authors explore the return characteristics of 14 countries over the period 1990–2001. The data support the existence of both a global market risk factor and country-specific risk factors in explaining REIT returns. The country-specific risk factor is especially strong in the Asia-Pacific region. Factors providing additional explanatory power for U.S. equity markets, such as value and size, also hold for I-REITs at the country level, but the U.S. factors are not transmitted. Strong regional dependence in returns points to the ability to obtain diversification benefits. More importantly, investors must consider that broad international risk cannot be the only consideration when building a portfolio.

Yunus and Swanson (2007) investigate the diversification benefits provided to a U.S. domiciled investor by investing in the Asian-REIT region. The sample period is January 2000 to March 2006 using daily EPRA/NAREIT indexes for Australia, Hong Kong, Japan, Singapore, and the United States. The authors divide the sample into two different periods based on a common structural break in the data. They find no long-term trends between Asian REITs and U.S. REITs over the whole sample or the early sample period. For the second part of the sample after the structural break, the data begin to show signs of co-movement. This trending appears to only occur because of the U.S.-Australia and U.S.-Singapore relationships. There is no evidence of short-term relationships in the markets.

Niskanen and Falkenbach (2010) use European REIT data combined with a mixed asset portfolio consisting of six equity, three bond, and a commodity benchmark indexes. The authors consider daily returns for a year (March 2006–March 2007). They report significant positive correlation between REITs and equities. This is particularly true between REITs and small cap stocks, and as volatility in the market increases. The correlation between REITs and fixed income securities is negative and increasing (became more negative) as fixed income volatility increases. The correlation with commodities is generally positive. The practical implication is that the short-term hedging benefits of European REITs depend on the volatility of the other financial markets in question.

Serrano and Hoesli (2010) compare the predictability of I-REIT returns with those of common equity. The authors investigate the role of country effects and its potential impact on the predictability of returns. The study uses daily data on the 10 largest REIT markets (the United States, Hong Kong, Japan, Australia, the United Kingdom, France, Singapore, Holland, Germany, and Sweden) comprising roughly 95 percent of the total global market for the period 1990–2007. Return data are for equity, fixed-income, and REIT markets. An active trading strategy based upon an ARMA-EGARCH framework outperforms a buy-and-hold strategy in only three markets for equities, but in over half for REITs. In general, the REIT markets for the United States, Holland, and Australia have the most predictability. These are also the most mature markets, and the only markets with listed REITs for the entire sample. The maturity of the market representing a country effect plays a large role in predicting the returns for securitized property.

Schindler (2011) investigates the efficiency of I-REITs for 16 markets. The sample contains 4 developed and 12 emerging markets over the period 1992–2009. The testing of market efficiency is for autocorrelation on the time series data. With the exception of 2 of the 16 markets, the equity markets do not appear to be a significant factor in explaining efficiency and return predictability for REITs.

Kroencke and Schindler (2012) concentrate on the four largest markets that still exceed 75 percent of global market capitalization. In contrast to previous studies, they also consider the effect of currency risk on I-REIT returns. The asset classes are international bonds and equity from the perspective of a U.S. investor. Substantial diversification benefits occur when adding securitized property to an equity and fixed-income portfolio, beyond those from holding international assets. In the sub-period analysis, they consistently observe diversification benefits except during the GFC, a finding that mirrors other research. Furthermore, the benefit gained from I-REITs is superior to the diversification benefits of adding international equity, confirming previously reported results. Currency risk can affect the interpretation of diversification benefits. Kroencke and Schindler examine the fully hedged portfolio relative to the unhedged one. The currency-hedged portfolio performs significantly better. Currency risk may play a large role in determining benefits of I-REITs used in a mixed-asset portfolio.

Lu, Tse, and Williams (2013) use daily data to compare the returns from U.S. REITs vis-à-vis I-REITs. The authors also use the VaR framework to determine the largest concentration of risk in the given timeframe. They consider the returns from 12 international markets and spanned six-and-a-half years (July 2002–December 2008). The authors construct their own REIT indexes from Datastream data and explore the diversification benefits and integration of the I-REITs with the U.S. REIT market during normal, boom, and recession periods. The U.S. REIT market is a transmitter of price information in all three periods. The correlations between different I-REIT markets and the U.S. REITs increase during the crisis periods. Finally, during normal time periods, emerging markets have the highest contribution to the VaR, showing increased downside risk. However, during the crisis period, the roles are reversed with the developed markets exhibiting increased downside risk.

Regional and Country-Specific Factors Influencing Returns and Operations

The previous discussion focused on how markets may become integrated and the impact on the diversification benefits. A natural extension is to characterize how REIT markets differ or how country factors influence their returns.. A voluminous literature examines the role of analyst coverage for traditional equity markets. However, a new strand has emerged to examine the role of REIT analyst coverage. Furthermore, researchers have used the market reaction to earnings forecast accuracy as a test of market efficiency.

Devos, Ong, and Spieler (2007) investigate the effect on firm value from U.S. REIT analyst coverage. Analyst coverage plays an important role in the development of the REIT asset class. As coverage increases, forecast accuracy improves, which increases transparency within the asset class. Analyst coverage has a positive and significant effect on REIT valuation as measured by Tobin's Q. Gyamfi-Yeboah, Ling, and Naranjo (2012) use I-REIT data to further explore this relationship. The intent of the research is to be international in scope, but a lack of I-REIT data would not allow meaningful international analysis.

Hamelink and Hoesli (2004) investigate the factors that drive I-REIT returns. They collect monthly returns from Global Property Research (GPR) and state returns in dollars to be uniform and unhedged. The authors decompose the return characteristics and investigate the extent to which each of several factors influences the observed returns. The country-specific factor accounts for between 55 and 65 percent of the observed dollar return. The importance of this factor declines over the sample period. As the significance of the country factor declines, the importance of property type increases. One factor not previously investigated but found to be important is a value versus growth factor. The factor is positive and accounts for about 10 percent of the holding period return (HPR) based on a 12-month moving average for the period February 1990–April 2003. Because this factor has a high level of variance, ignoring value can be damaging to the performance of a portfolio containing I-REITs.

Bardhan, Edelstein, and Tsang (2008) investigate the effect of integration on the annual returns of 946 firms from 16 countries from 1995 to 2002. The authors control for market and macroeconomic conditions to determine if the openness of a country, as a proxy for its integration into the global economy, explains the risk-adjusted return differential for the country's securitized real estate market. The level of openness has a significant and negative impact on the risk-adjusted returns of that country. Another implication is that global financial market integration improves the efficiency of both financial and real asset markets.

Schulte, Dechant, and Schaefers (2011) examine the characteristics affecting the pricing of European REITs. This research helps to fill a large gap because most previous studies focus on U.S., U.K., or Asian markets, but largely ignore Continental Europe. Integration of Europe through the introduction of the Euro in 2002 may influence the pricing of European REITs. Integration affects the diversification benefits provided from either the European or international investor's perspective. The study follows the Fama and French (1992) asset pricing methodology, examining whether the size and value factors—small minus big (SMB) and high minus low (HML)—aid in explaining

European REIT returns. The data set used for the paper consists of all traded and delisted real estate and general equity companies from 16 European countries from 1988 to 2009. The sampling procedure yields 15,501 firms after data screening. The real estate (REIT) companies comprise 335 of the observations. Value effects are observed, while size effects are not priced into European REIT returns. These findings show differences in pricing between the U.S. and European securitized real estate markets.

Ooi, Ong, and Neo (2011) use an event study methodology to investigate the abnormal return performance effects from the announcement of property acquisitions by Japanese and Singaporean REITs. The second area of focus is to determine if operational performance improves after acquiring new property. The reported results identify positive cumulative abnormal returns (CARs) for three different event windows. The five-day window (–2, + 2) has a CAR of 0.38 percent. This result is consistent, yet smaller, than the gains reported in similar studies of the U.S. market. Interestingly, all 228 acquisitions are cash transactions. The benefits of property acquisitions appear to arise from economies of scale and better management by the acquiring firm. Conversely, the markets appear to react negatively to REITs acquiring mixed-use properties or when REITs acquire an existing portfolio of properties. The market rewards REITs for corporate focus and operational transparency.

Brounen, Kok, and Ling (2012) investigate the differences in REIT shareholder composition between five different countries (Australia, France, Japan, the United Kingdom, and the United States). They explore the effects of shareholder composition on abnormal returns during extreme market movement days in 2008 and 2009. They find a very large and diverse framework of ownership for REITs in all the subject countries. Large shareholders affect stock returns and share turnover, a finding highlighted during times of stress. In periods of extreme equity price decline, the market shareholder composition influences the response of REITs at the firm level. If the largest shareholder controls more than 25 percent of the REIT, then the returns are significantly greater. Additionally, abnormal turnover is significantly reduced if the largest shareholder controls more than 25 percent of the REIT.

Chikolwa (2011) examines the capital structure of Australian REITs. Studying A-REITs fills a void because most studies analyze U.S. REIT capital structure. The sample includes 208 firm-years covering the period 2003–2008 for a total of 34 firms with panel data methods on this unbalanced sample. The paper investigates the effects on capital structure under the specific framework provided by A-REITs with the traditional equity variables, as described in Rajan and Zingales (1995), but adds additional factors to better explore variables unique to A-REITs. These additional factors include current real estate market conditions, term structure of real estate including leasing conditions and rates, REIT sector, indicator variable for international operations, and stapled management structure. The impact of profitability and growth prospects is small based on the amount of firm leverage. Operational risk is a significant predictor of financial leverage for A-REITs. These two variables exhibit a negative relationship, all else equal. Size and leverage have a positive relationship, supporting both pecking order and static trade-off theories of capital structure. The evidence fails to support the possibility of market timing of either debt or equity. When an A-REIT has either international operations or a stapled management structure, the effects on leverage are negative, as well as economically and statistically significant.

Ong et al. (2011) examine how seasoned equity offerings (SEOs) for Japanese and Singaporean REITs are affected under a variety of market conditions or asset acquisitions. The primary focus is to investigate if REITs use equity issuance to maintain legally required leverage ratios that may be out of line after the issuance of debt for acquisitions. Similar to Chikolwa (2011), they test the market timing theory of issuance. The data used consist of 82 hand-collected observations from press announcements of SEOs made by REITs in Japan and Singapore from 2002 to 2007. The evidence shows a 1.2 percent price decline for the (0, + 1) announcement window, a result in line with previous studies using U.S. data. Additionally, the observed price decline supports the pecking order theory of capital structure. The authors find market conditions to be significant when investigating REIT SEOs. First, a favorable yield spread helps to mitigate the negative announcement returns for the SEO, but not the probability of the event occurring. Second, the increasing value of the equity markets increases the probability that a firm will conduct an SEO. The data provide evidence of clustering effects in Japanese and Singaporean REITs.

Are I-REIT Returns Affected by National Legal Framework and Governance?

La Porta, Lopez-de-Silanes, Shleifer, and Vishny (LLSV) (1997, 1998, 2002) greatly influenced international financial research. The legal framework of a country influences the local financial markets. By extension, seeing how this environment affects the many characteristics of asset classes across borders is possible.

Edelstein, Qian, and Tsang (2011) investigate the LLSV factors' impact on REITs. They report both legal system quality and accounting standards quality affect excess returns for I-REITs. Broadly speaking, these two factors are a byproduct of the country-specific legal system. These results are in line with those found for equities. As Eichholtz, Gugler, and Kok (2011) point out, real estate is by its very existence non-mobile but it may be more susceptible to the financial market environment of its host nation.

Home bias, which is the propensity for investors to focus on domestic assets, exists for all asset classes. However, real estate investment has been subject to this bias even more than equity markets. Eichholtz et al. (2011) propose that this may be a result of the effects of institutional differences across countries. They use a mix of listed property companies, as well as time series data over the period 1996–2007, to investigate the effects of companies operating purely in their domestic market versus companies international in scope. Companies with an international scope underperform those that are pure local players in the early years of the sample. However, this disadvantage dissipates during the sample period and disappears by the end. They attribute the performance difference to institutional environment, the level of economic integration, and the transparency of the real estate market. No difference in performance exists at the end of the sample period. These results suggest that investors seeking diversification can either build a diversified international property portfolio themselves or invest in the limited number of large internationally diversified REITs.

Jones Lang LaSalle (2012), which publishes bi-annual reports on the condition and transparency of real estate markets, notes that 90 percent of the 97 countries it follows had improved scores from 2010. This is good news following the severe drop that occurred due to the GFC. Many improvements in these scores are tied to better corporate governance of REITs, as well as an increase in reliable market data. The question is whether the increase in transparency leads to the increased capital flows already discussed, or whether the increased capital flows force better transparency.

Lecomte and Ooi (2013) use a data set for corporate governance calculated by the Asia Pacific Real Estate Association (APREA) to investigate to what extent corporate governance affects REIT performance on firm-level Singaporean REITs. Although most large REITs in the United States or Australia are internally managed, all of the REITs in Singapore as of 2011 have opted for external management. Several fees are due to the different parties including manager, property manager and trustee. The largest fees are attributed to the manager. While the fee structure is not uniform, the trust manager has a base fee and possibly performance, acquisition/divestment and assets under management-type fees. The trust manager is most directly responsible to the trust sponsor whom has a substantial holding within the REIT. The authors report a weak but positively significant relationship between corporate governance and stock price. However, they fail to find a connection between operating performance and governance. The same governance scoring mechanism can be used to test for the entire Asian REIT universe to broaden their sample and strengthen conclusions. Pica (2011) provides a comprehensive review of governmental regulation, as well as corporate governance issues with REITs as they relate specifically to Asia.

Summary and Conclusions

While I-REITs do not provide financial shelter in time of market upheavals, this statement is true for nearly all asset classes. When investors need diversification benefits the most is when none is available. However, outside of these events, I-REIT diversification benefits exist. This class is a strong proxy for physical property within a country. This is primarily due to the fact that I-REITs derive the vast percentage of their profits from the country in which they are domiciled, and this holds for even the largest REITs globally. REITs allow for a more pure play in gaining country-level diversification benefits.

I-REITs are likely to continue to grow as an asset class. With the growth of this asset class, I-REITs will become an important tool for portfolio diversification for the professional and retail investor alike. The growth of the asset class is assured. The regulatory environment may be one of the few factors that can hold back the growth of the I-REITs.

The empirical literature shows that a volatility transmission effect between different markets. This may have implications for investors and portfolio managers of international REITs. Namely, naïve diversification can jeopardize the risk/return ratio of a portfolio. Portfolio managers should avoid unjustified diversification if the correlation benefit is breaking down among markets. Only through carefully selected portfolios, when a relatively lower inter-market correlation exists, would investors benefit. Table 12.2 shows the result of a simulation where the risk/return ratio of a portfolio, 50 percent in stocks and 50 percent in bonds, is significantly higher than 50 percent in stock, 30 percent in bonds, and 20 percent in global REITs. If volatility continues to spill over from one region to the other, then the risk reduction benefit may not hold true in

Table 12.2 **Asset Allocations Based on Average Annual Return: A Simulation**

Period	*Allocation Scenario 1 (50% U.S. Stocks, 30% U.S. Bonds, and 20% International REITs)*	*Allocation Scenario 2 (50% U.S. Stocks and 50% U.S. Bonds)*
Full period: 2000–2013	Risk: 10.88%	Risk: 12.72%
	Return: 4.79%	Return: 4.66%
	Risk/Return: 2.27	Risk/Return: 2.73
Pre-crisis: 2000–2007	Risk: 8.30%	Risk: 9.44%
	Return: 5.97%	Return: 5.07%
	Risk/Return: 1.40	Risk/Return: 1.86
Post-crisis: 2008–2012	Risk: 13.52%	Risk: 16.23%
	Return: 3.17%	Return: 4.10%
	Risk/Return: 4.27	Risk/Return: 3.96

Note: This table shows the results of a simulation based on two allocations scenarios: (1) 50 percent U.S. stock, 30 percent U.S. bonds, and 20 percent international REITs and (2) 50 percent U.S. stocks and 50 percent U.S. bonds. The risk/return ratio of a portfolio in scenario 2 is much higher than in scenario 1.

every case. The degree of correlation, not merely risk and return, influences the performance of a global portfolio regardless of how measured. The trade-off can use the coefficient of variation as the ratio of standard deviation to mean of returns. Alternatively, the Sharpe ratio measures the excess return per unit of standard deviation.

Discussion Questions

1. Which international REIT markets are as developed as the U.S. market?
2. Why are I-REITs attractive to both domestic and global investors?
3. What are the primary growth factors for I-REITs?
4. How large is the public real estate market as compared to the total investable property worldwide?
5. What are the empirical research findings on the correlation of I-REITs with other major asset classes?

References

Bardhan, Ashok, Robert Edelstein, and Desmond Tsang. 2008. "Global Financial Integration and Real Estate Security Returns." *Real Estate Economics* 36:2, 285–311.

Bond, Shaun, and John Glascock. 2006. "The Performance and Diversification Benefits of European Public Real Estate Securities." Working Paper, Social Sciences Research Network. http://ssrn.com/abstract=896524 or http://dx.doi.org/10.2139/ssrn.896524.

Bond, Shaun, Andrew Karolyi, and Anthony Sanders. 2003. "International Real Estate Returns: A Multifactor, Multicountry Approach." *Real Estate Economics* 31:3, 481–500.

Brière, Marie, Ariane Chapelle, and Ariane Szafarz. 2012. "No Contagion, Only Globalization and Flight to Quality." *Journal of International Money and Finance* 31:6, 1729–1744.

Brounen, Dirk, Nils Kok, and David Ling. 2012. "Shareholder Composition, Share Turnover, and Returns in Volatile Markets: The Case of International REITs." *Journal of International Money and Finance* 31:7, 1867–1889.

Cauchie, Séverine, and Martin Hoesli. 2006. "Further Evidence of the Integration of Securitized Real Estate and Financial Assets." *Journal of Property Research* 23:1, 1–38.

Chikolwa, Bwembya. 2011. "Investigating the Capital Structure of A-REITs." *Journal of Real Estate Literature* 19:2, 391–411.

Deloitte Touche Tohmatsu (Deloitte China). 2012. "China Real Estate Investment Handbook: The Details that Make a Difference." http://www.deloitte.com/view/en_CN/cn/ind/re/c795525c67b06310VgnVCM3000001c56f00aRCRD.htm.

Deqing, Diane Li, and Kenneth Yung. 2007. "REIT Returns: Between the Pacific and the Atlantic." *Review of Accounting and Finance* 6:4, 353–369.

Devos, Erik, Seow-Eng Ong, and Andrew Spieler. 2007. "Analyst Activity and Firm Value: Evidence from the REIT Sector." *Journal of Real Estate Finance and Economics* 35:1, 333–356.

Edelstein, Robert, Wenlan Qian, and Desmond Tsang. 2011. "How Do Institutional Factors Affect International Real Estate Returns?" *Journal of Real Estate Finance and Economics* 43:1, 130–151.

Eichholtz, Piet, Nils Gugler, and Nils Kok. 2011. "Transparency, Integration, and the Cost of International Real Estate Investments." *Journal of Real Estate Finance and Economics* 43:1, 152–173.

EPRA. 2012. "Monthly Statistical Bulletin: December." http://www.epra.com/research-and-indices/research/.

Fama, Eugene, and Kenneth French. 1992. "The Cross-Section of Expected Stock Returns." *Journal of Finance* 47:2, 427–465.

Forbes, Kristin, and Roberto Rigobon. 2002. "No Contagion, Only Interdependence: Measuring Stock Market Comovements." *Journal of Finance* 57:5, 2223–2261.

Gyamfi-Yeboah, Frank, David Ling, and Andy Naranjo. 2012. "Information, Uncertainty, and Behavioral Effects: Evidence from Abnormal Returns around Real Estate Investment Trust Earnings Announcements." *Journal of International Money and Finance* 31:7, 1930–1952.

Hamelink, Foort, and Martin Hoesli. 2004. "What Factors Determine International Real Estate Security Returns?" *Real Estate Economics* 32:3, 437–462.

Hoesli, Martin, and Elias Oikarinen. 2012. "Are REITs Real Estate? Evidence from International Sector Level Data." *Journal of International Money and Finance* 31:7, 1823–1850.

Hudgins, Michael. 2010. "Brave New Worlds: Revisiting the Strategic Case for Global REITs." New York: J. P. Morgan Asset Management.

Hutchings, William. 2012. "A REIT in Spain Could Help Reduce the Pain." *Financial News*, June 8. http://www.efinancialnews.com/story/2012-2006-08/reit-property-help-spain-crisis.

Jacobius, Arleen. 2006. "CalPERS First to Form in-House International REIT Index Fund." *Pensions & Investments* 34:11, 2, 87.

Jones Lang LeSalle. 2012. "Real Estate Transparency; Back on Track (Global Real Estate Transparency Index)." http://www.joneslanglasalle.com/Transparency.

Kroencke, Tim, and Felix Schindler. 2012. "International Diversification with Securitized Real Estate and the Veiling Glare from Currency Risk." *Journal of International Money and Finance* 31:7, 1851–1866.

La Porta, Rafael, Florencio Lopez-De-Silanes, Andrei Shleifer, and Robert W. Vishny. 1997. "Legal Determinants of External Finance." *Journal of Finance* 52:3, 1131–1150.

La Porta, Rafael, Florencio Lopez-De-Silanes, Andrei Shleifer, and Robert W. Vishny. 1998. "Law and Finance." *Journal of Political Economy* 106:6, 1113–1155.

La Porta, Rafael, Florencio Lopez-De-Silanes, Andrei Shleifer, and Robert W. Vishny. 2002. "Investor Protection and Corporate Valuation." *Journal of Finance* 57:3, 1147–1170.

Lecomte, Patrick, and Joseph Ooi. 2013. "Corporate Governance and Performance of Externally Managed Singapore REITs." *Journal of Real Estate Finance and Economics* 46:4, 664–684

Liow, Kim Hiang. 2008. "Financial Crisis and Asian Real Estate Securities Market Interdependence: Some Additional Evidence." *Journal of Property Research* 25:2, 127–155.

Liow, Kim Hiang. 2010. "Integration among USA, UK, Japanese and Australian Securitized Real Estate Markets: An Empirical Exploration." *Journal of Property Research* 27:4, 289–308.

Liow, Kim Hiang, and Wei Chen. 2013. "Is There Volatility Convergence in Asia-Pacific Securitized Real Estate Markets?" *Journal of Real Estate Finance and Economics* 47:2, 370–390

Liu, Jing, Geoffrey Loudon, and George Milunovich. 2012. "Linkages between International REITs: The Role of Economic Factors." *Journal of Property Investment and Finance* 30:5, 473–492.

Lu, Chiuling, Yiuman Tse, and Michael Williams. 2013. "Returns Transmission, Value at Risk, and Diversification Benefits in International REITs: Evidence from the Financial Crisis." *Review of Quantitative Finance and Accounting* 40:2, 293–318.

Newell, Graeme, and Wu Yue. 2010. "The Development and Performance of REITs in Hong Kong." *Pacific Rim Property Research Journal* 16:2, 190–206.

Nikbakht, Ehsan. 2011. "Performance of Real Estate Investments and Spillover Effect of Financial Markets 2000–2009." *Financial Decisions* 23:2, 1–11.

Niskanen, Jaakko, and Heidi Falkenbach. 2010. "REITs and Correlations with Other Asset Classes: A European Perspective." *Journal of Real Estate Portfolio Management* 16:3, 227–239.

Ong, Seow-Eng, Joseph Ooi, and Yuichiro Kawaguichi. 2011. "Seasoned Equity Issuance by Japan and Singapore REITs." *Journal of Real Estate Finance and Economics* 43:1, 205–220.

Ooi, Joseph, Seow-Eng Ong, and Poh-Har Neo. 2011. "The Wealth Effects of Property Acquisitions: Evidence from Japanese and Singaporean REITs." *Real Estate Economics* 39:3, 487–505.

Pham, Anh Khoi. 2011. "The Significance and Performance of South Korean REITs in a Mixed Asset Portfolio." *Journal of Real Estate Literature* 19:2, 373–390.

Pham, Anh Khoi. 2012. "The Dynamics of Returns and Volatility in the Emerging and Developed Asian REIT Markets." *Journal of Real Estate Literature* 20:1, 79–96.

Pica, Angela. 2001. "Asia-Pacific REITs: Building Trust through Better REIT Governance." The CFA Institute, Asia-Pacific Office. http://www.cfainstitute.org/learning/products/publications/ccb/Pages/ccb.v2011.n4.1.aspx.

Pirolo, Alessia. 2014. "New REITs in Ireland Gain Interest From Investors" *Wall Street Journal (Online), February 04.*

Quek, Michael, and Seow-Eng Ong. 2008. "Securitizing China Real Estate: A Tale of Two China-Centric REITs." *Journal of Property Investment & Finance* 26:3, 247–274.

Rajan, Raghuram, and Luigi Zingales. 1995. "What Do We Know about Capital Structure? Some Evidence from International Data." *Journal of Finance* 50:5, 1421–1460.

Rehring, Christian. 2012. "Real Estate in a Mixed-Asset Portfolio: The Role of the Investment Horizon." *Real Estate Economics* 40:1, 65–95.

Ryan, Laura. 2011. "Nowhere to Hide: An Analysis of Investment Opportunities in Listed Property Markets during Financial Market Crises." *Journal of Property Research* 28:2, 97–131.

Schindler, Felix. 2011. "Market Efficiency and Return Predictability in the Emerging Securitized Real Estate Markets." *Journal of Real Estate Literature* 19:1, 111–150.

Schulte, Kai-Magnus, Tobias Dechant, and Wolfgang Schaefers. 2011. "Systematic Risk Factors in European Real Estate Equities." *Journal of European Real Estate Research* 4:3, 185–224.

Serrano, Camilo, and Martin Hoesli. 2010. "Are Securitized Real Estate Returns More Predictable than Stock Returns?" *Journal of Real Estate Finance and Economics* 41:2, 170–192.

UBS Global Asset Management (UK) Ltd. "Real Estate—All You Need to Know." August. http://www.ubs.com/global/en/asset_management/gre/luxembourg/real_estate_funds/research/_jcr_content/par/teaserbox_86dd/teaser_7a65.1651121193.file/dGV4dD0vY29udGVudC9kYW0vdWJzL2dsb2JhbC9hc3NldF9tYW5hZ2VtZW50L2dyZS9yZWFsLWVzdGF0ZS1hbGwteW91LW5lZWQtdG8ta25vdy5wZGY=/real-estate-all-you-need-to-know.pdf.

Whiting, Dominic. 2007. *Playing the REITs Game: Asia's New Real Estate Investment Trusts*. Singapore: John Wiley & Sons.

Worzala, Elaine, and C. F. Sirmans. 2003. "Investing in International Real Estate Stocks: A Review of the Literature." *Urban Studies* 40:5/6, 1115–1149.

Xu, Pisun, and Jian Yang. 2011."U.S. Monetary Policy Surprises and International Securitized Real Estate Markets." *Journal of Real Estate Finance and Economics* 43:4, 459–490.

"Yale Endowment Earns 4.7percent Investment Return." 2012. *Yale News*, September 27. http://news.yale.edu/2012/09/27/yale-endowment-earns-47-investment-return.

Yunus, Nafeesa. 2009. "Increasing Convergence between U.S. and International Securitized Property Markets: Evidence Based on Cointegration Tests." *Real Estate Economics* 37:3, 383–411.

Yunus, Nafeesa, and Peggy Swanson. 2007. "Modeling Linkages between US and Asia-Pacific Securitized Property Markets." *Journal of Property Research* 24:2, 95–122.

Zhou, Jian. 2012. "Multiscale Analysis of International Linkages of REIT Returns and Volatilities." *Journal of Real Estate Finance and Economics* 45:4, 1062–1087.

Zhou, Jian. 2013. "Extreme Risk Spillover among International REIT Markets." *Applied Financial Economics* 23:2, 91–103.

13

REITs: Capital Structure

ZHONGHUA WU
Associate Professor, Tibor and Sheila Hollo Research Fellow,
Florida International University

Introduction

Capital structure refers to the mixture of debt and equity that a firm uses to finance its operations. The firm's decisions on which types of financial claims to issue and how much capital to raise determine its capital structure over time. Typical financial claims issued by public firms include seasoned equity offerings (SEOs), long-term debt including public offerings, and short-term debt such as bank lines of credit.

Capital structure affects a firm's operations and its investment activities. Inappropriate use of debt may introduce distortions in investments of a firm. For instance, managers of a highly leveraged firm may prefer to invest in only high-risk projects in order to maximize shareholders' value. This can be detrimental to the debt-holders because they face higher bankruptcy costs, while not being compensated for the additional risks. This is the so-called *asset substitution problem*. Thus, a firm's risks and performance are closely related to its capital structure. A goal of financial managers is to determine the optimal financial policies to facilitate the firm's operations. Moreover, the financial managers should secure the least expensive capital available for the firm.

Capital structure is one of the most studied areas in finance. From the perspectives of both practitioners and academics, many interesting and important questions relate to a firm's capital structure. For example, researchers are interested in examining what determines a firm's debt-to-total-asset ratio, also called the *leverage ratio*. Does a firm target a long-term leverage ratio? What influence do financial decisions such as SEOs, public debt, and bank debt have on the firm? Do firms time their security issuances based on capital market conditions? How do financing policies influence investment activities and performance of a firm? Understanding these questions is important to help investors make sound investment decisions.

Studying capital structure and the related issues is essential to understanding REITs' operations and performance for several reasons. First, REITs are capital-intensive firms, buying and holding large commercial properties. Due to the 90 percent dividend payout requirement in the United States, REITs have limited internal funds available for their operations. According to Ott, Riddiough, and Yi (2005), retained earnings fund only 7 percent of REIT investments compared with 70 percent for non-REIT firms. Thus, REITs must frequently go to external capital markets to raise capital, which makes financing a crucial component in REITs' management and operations. Second, the REIT industry has grown dramatically and also engaged in consolidation over the past few decades. During this period, most REITs grew in size through acquisitions and investments. Securing flexible financing and managing financial liquidity are vital for REITs to grow and succeed in such a competitive environment.

The literature on REIT capital structure has grown substantially over the past decade. Studies can be classified into three main groups. First, one line of research examines the determinants of the overall leverage ratio of REITs (Feng, Ghosh, and Sirmans 2007). Second, other studies such as Brown and Riddiough (2003) investigate the factors influencing security issuance decisions of REITs. Some more recent studies examine how REITs manage financial liquidity, including cash and bank lines of credit policies, to facilitate their operations (Ooi, Wong, and Ong 2012).

This chapter provides an overview of REIT capital structure based on recent research. The remainder of the chapter is organized as following. The next section provides some basic theories related to capital structure and is followed by a discussion of the relevant empirical evidence from recent research. This discussion helps to answer important questions on REIT capital structure. The chapter ends by providing a summary and conclusions about REIT capital structure.

Theories of Capital Structure

This section begins by examining several theories involving a firm's capital structure. These theories consist of partial equilibrium theories and industry equilibrium theories.

PARTIAL EQUILIBRIUM THEORIES

Two major types of theories focus on the determinants of capital structure: partial equilibrium theories and industry equilibrium theories. The partial equilibrium theories assume each firm operates in isolation from other industry peers. Each firm makes capital structure decisions on its own. The three most popular theories of capital structure—trade-off, pecking order, and market timing—are all based on partial equilibrium models. In contrast, industrial equilibrium theories consider the interactions among industry peers and study how their financial decisions influence a firm's leverage ratio.

Trade-off Theory

Trade-off theory, the first theory developed about capital structure, is based on benefits and costs associated with using debt. The main benefit is the marginal tax shield and the main cost is the marginal bankruptcy cost. A typical firm faces a trade-off between these two. Everything else equal, more debt means a reduced tax burden because interest payments are tax deductible. However, when a firm issues more debt, its potential bankruptcy cost could increase. Thus, the theory posits that an optimal mix of debt and equity exists in a firm's capital structure. The benefit of using debt is weighted against the bankruptcy cost of financial distress. A natural extension is that if an optimal mix of debt and equity exists, a firm should adjust its financial policies to maintain the optimal leverage ratio in the long run. Its leverage ratio may deviate from the optimal level temporarily.

Trade-off theory is straightforward and offers important insights. Not surprisingly, many studies provide supporting evidence to the theory. For example, survey evidence by Graham and Harvey (2001) shows that 81 percent of the financial managers in their study report engaging in target leverage behavior. However, the theory also has limitations. For example, not all public firms pay taxes at the firm level. Others contend that trade-off theory cannot explain some observed patterns of capital structure. Alternative explanations appear in the literature such as pecking order theory and market timing theory.

Pecking Order Theory

Myers (1984) and Myers and Majluf (1984) propose a pecking order theory of capital structure. They contend that firms have a pecking order when making security issuance decisions. That is, a firm prefers to use internal funds from retained earnings to finance its operations, and then debt and finally equity. This implies that equity is the last resort for a firm to raise capital. The main argument of the theory is based on information asymmetry between managers of the firm (insiders) and its investors (outsiders). Myers and Majluf claim a firm's managers possess private information about the true firm value. However, outside investors cannot observe the same amount of information as managers do. Therefore, investors suspect that managers choose to issue equity only when the firm is overvalued. Consequently, investors rationally discount equity offering prices. Managers understand the potential discounting from investors, so they issue equity when internal capital and debt options are not viable.

Market Timing Theory

More recently, Baker and Wurgler (2002) propose market-timing theory. The theory states that firms time their equity issuances based on capital market conditions. When a firm's share price is high, managers are more likely to issue equity to maximize shareholder value. In contrast, when the share price is low, the managers may repurchase shares. Baker and Wurgler maintain that a firm's capital structure is a cumulative outcome of its past attempts to time the equity market. Baker, Greenwood, and Wurgler (2003, 284) extend market-timing theory to debt issuances. They define market timing as "raising finance in whatever form is currently available at the lowest-risk adjusted risk."

Industry Equilibrium Theories

Besides the three major partial equilibrium theories, industry equilibrium theories propose that the equilibrium outcome in competitive industries determines a firm's capital structure. For example, Maksimovic and Zechner (1991) suggest that in a competitive industry financial decisions of each firm may influence the decisions of other firms, resulting in capital structure variation within an industry. Moreover, Shleifer and Vishny (1992) consider the impact of asset liquidation value on a firm's capital structure in an industry equilibrium model. They extend Williamson's (1988) idea that financing those assets is easier with high liquidation values. Shleifer and Vishny conclude that the leverage of other firms in its industry influences a firm's optimal leverage.

REIT Capital Structure

Studies on capital structure typically exclude REITs from their data sets because researchers consider REITs as regulated firms. However, REIT capital structure is an important research topic because of several unique features of the firms. A few controversial and intriguing views persist about REIT capital structure.

First, REITs do not pay taxes at the corporate level, so no obvious tax benefit results from using debt. This excludes the tax-based considerations for issuing debt. Howe and Shilling (1988) contend that REITs could have a 100 percent equity capital structure because they may find issuing debt more expensive compared with non-REIT firms that receive the tax benefit of debt. However, Jaffe (1991) contends that the tax benefit is only one factor explaining leverage, and there are other rationales explaining why REITs use debt. The issuance costs of debt for small firms may be lower than the costs of equity. Also, REITs may have higher debt capacity relative to other firms, which facilitates issuing debt.

Second, with the 90 percent dividend payout requirement, REITs are considered cash constrained. As Hardin, Highfield, Hill, and Kelly (2009) note, REIT cash holdings are about 1.57 percent of total assets, compared to 18.48 percent for the non-REIT public firms. Because REITs often have to go to the external capital markets to raise equity, pecking order or information asymmetry-based theory seems to be less relevant. However, the issue of whether information asymmetry matters for REITs is still unsettled. Some contend that valuing REIT assets is difficult because commercial properties are heterogeneous, complex, and illiquid (Harrison, Panasian, and Seiler 2011b). Others claim that REIT assets are relatively easier to value because they have limited investment in human capital and fewer growth options (Feng et al. 2007). Hence, pecking order theory is not necessarily irrelevant for REITs.

Third, Jensen (1986) proposes an agency-based free cash flow hypothesis. Internal funds in excess of those needed for positive net present value (NPV) projects, or free cash flow, could erode shareholder wealth. Managers may use free cash flow for their benefit, which differs from that of the shareholders. In the REIT context, based on the 90 percent dividend payout requirement, the implication is that managers of REITs cannot hold much cash. Thus, the free cash flow problem is not an issue for REITs. However, the agency conflicts from free cash flow still matter for REITs. The 90 percent dividend payout requirement is based on taxable income. REITs have a large amount of a non-cash flow item from depreciation. Consequently, REIT managers can accumulate free cash flow for their own benefit rather than that of shareholders.

Finally, most of the assets held by REITs are tangible and not firm-specific. The bankruptcy costs for REITs are relatively low because selling the assets to other investors is not difficult. Based on this reasoning, REITs could issue more debt. The trade-off theory is less relevant to REITs because of low potential bankruptcy costs.

SOME STATISTICS ABOUT REIT CAPITAL STRUCTURE

Harrison et al. (2011b) examine financial data on all REITs traded on the New York Stock Exchange (NYSE), American Stock Exchange (AMEX), and NASDAQ from 1990 to 2008. The average market leverage or ratio of total book debt to the sum of book debt and the market value of equity is 48 percent. The mean of secured loan plus mortgages as a ratio of total debt is 67 percent. These ratios are higher than those of typical non-REIT firms. Based on a sample from 1990 to 2003, Brown and Marble (2007) find that REITs have a mean leverage ratio of 47.4 percent, and a secured debt ratio is 66.8 percent. However, the mean leverage of non-REIT firms over the same period is only 27.5 percent, while 33.0 percent of the total debt is secured.

Other studies present a similar mean leverage for equity REITs. Based on data of equity REITs from 1997 to 2007, Ghosh, Giambona, Harding, and Sirmans (2011) show that the mean leverage of REITs is 43 percent, which is slightly lower than the 48 percent in Harrison et al. (2011b). Ghosh et al. show that hotel REITs have the highest mean leverage at 50 percent followed by residential REITs at 47 percent, and then retail REITs with 44 percent. Office REITs and industrial REITs have lower mean leverage of 41 percent and 31 percent, respectively.

Based on equity REIT data from 1986 to 2003, Ooi et al. (2010) find that interest is the largest expense item for most of equity REITs. Specifically, the interest expense in their sample ranges from 30 to 70 percent of the total expenses of REITs. This is consistent with the notion that REITs are capital-intensive firms and rely on external debt markets to provide funding for investment and acquisitions.

To show the evolution of REIT capital structure over time, Hardin and Wu (2010) report different financial sources for equity REITs from 1992 to 2003. The bank debt borrowed by REITs in the sample increased significantly. The total bank debt in 1992 was $329 million, while the amount grew to $13.4 billion in 2003. The mortgage debt borrowed by REITs also increased but at much slower pace over the same period. REITs borrowed $911 million in mortgages in 1992, but the amount was $1.7 billion in 2003. SEOs and public debt offerings also increased significantly, but they varied with capital market conditions and different growth periods of REITs. For instance, during the boom of 1997–1998, REITs issued $20 billion of equity and more than $10 billion of public debt each year.

Based on these financing patterns, Hardin and Wu (2010) claim that REIT capital structure evolves through at least three stages. The first stage includes using SEOs and secured single-asset liabilities such as mortgages. The second stage features a dramatic growth in using revolving bank credit lines, much of which are unsecured. The third stage includes using arm's length, unsecured public debt. During this evolution of REIT capital structure, banks play an important role and banking relationships improve the overall capital acquisition process of REITs.

Empirical Findings on REIT Leverage and Security Issuance Decisions

Two sets of empirical studies concern REIT leverage and security issuance decisions. One focuses on what determines the REIT leverage ratio. Typically, researchers use a panel data regression to identify factors influencing the REIT leverage ratio. Another set of studies examines the forces driving REIT security issuance decisions. Researchers use either a market reaction study on security announcement or a discrete choice model (multinomial logit model) to examine the factors influencing security issuance decisions.

EARLY RESEARCH ON REIT CAPITAL STRUCTURE

The early research focuses on the signaling effects of bank debt or security offerings. Howe and Shilling (1988) document a positive market reaction to short-term debt, an insignificant market reaction to long-term bonds, and a negative stock price reaction to equity issuances. They maintain that firms with better credit quality choose to issue short-term debt in order to send a positive signal to the market about their credit quality. Elayan, Meyer, and Li (2004), who extend this original research, contend the positive market reactions to newly issued and expanded bank loan commitments suggest that the market interprets the issuance of bank debt as a positive signal about REITs' true equity value.

MAJOR DETERMINANTS OF REIT LEVERAGE RATIOS

This section begins by reviewing the results of various partial equilibrium studies to identify the determinants of REIT leverage ratios. It then examines evidence involving industrial equilibrium-based studies.

Partial Equilibrium Studies

Based on a panel data set of REITs from 1990 to 2008, Harrison et al. (2011b) conduct a comprehensive analysis of the determinants of REIT leverage ratios. They find a positive relationship between asset tangibility, measured as the ratio of net property investments to total assets and firm size, and market leverage. The results show an inverse relationship between growth opportunities, measured by a firm's market-to-book ratios, and the leverage ratio.

Harrison et al. (2011b) also find that operational and financing characteristics play a role in explaining the REIT leverage ratio. Specifically, REITs with large bank lines of credit available have lower leverage ratios, which is not surprising because available lines of credit provide off-balance-sheet credit to firms. Further, REITs that draw down a higher percentage of their available credit lines have higher leverage ratios. These REITs are likely cash constrained and need to borrow more from the capital markets. Finally, REITs concentrating on regional mall and manufactured homes appear to use more debt, while REITs focusing on self-storage assets tend to use less leverage.

Ghosh et al. (2011) examine the effects of corporate governance on REIT capital structure. They examine whether managerial incentives, monitoring mechanisms, and managerial entrenchment influence leverage ratio of REITs. Based on a panel data set from 136 equity REITs during the period 1997–2007, the results show REITs with entrenched chief executive officers (CEOs) use less leverage and shorter maturity debt. The authors contend this is consistent with the empire building behaviors of managers who act in their own interest. These managers prefer lower leverage in order to control for liquidity risk and they choose short maturity debt to enhance their compensation and reputation.

Hardin and Wu (2010) examine the impact of banking relationships on REIT capital structure. Using a sample from 1992 to 2003, they find that REITs with banking relationships have lower leverage and use less secured debt. These findings support the hypothesis that bank relationships influence REIT capital structure, and firm leverage is positively related to the secured debt ratio.

Based on a REIT sample from 1991 to 2003, Feng et al. (2007) find REITs with high historical market-to-book ratios have persistently high leverage ratios. Given that researchers often use the market-to-book ratio as a proxy for a firm's growth opportunities, they conclude that REITs with high market-to-book ratios tend to issue debt to finance their growth. The positive relationship between historic market-to-book and leverage ratios is inconsistent with the results from non-REIT firms. The authors contend that this finding is likely due to the special regulatory environment of REITs.

Industrial Equilibrium-based Studies

Giambona, Harding, and Sirmans (2008) examine the Shleifer-Vishny hypothesis in the REIT context. The hypothesis states asset liquidation values affect firm leverage and the choice of debt maturity. Using panel data from 1997 to 2003, Giambona et al. find REITs with the most liquid assets use more leverage and longer debt maturities. In contrast, REITs with fewer liquid assets use less leverage and short maturities. Hence, the results are consistent with the hypothesis. REITs with substantial growth opportunities, as proxied by the market-to-book ratio, use less debt and with short maturity.

Another industry equilibrium-based study is Ertugrul and Giambona (2011), which links a REIT's competitive position within its property type such as office or retail to its capital structure. They find that a REIT's volatility of operating performance relative to the median of its segment peers is an important determinant of its leverage ratio. A REIT's leverage ratio also depends on the median leverage ratio in its property segment. Moreover, the leverage ratio is related to a REIT's status as an incumbent and its role as a leader in the property segment. In summary, industry competition appears to have some influence on REIT leverage ratios.

DO REITS TIME CAPITAL STRUCTURE DECISIONS BASED ON MARKET CONDITIONS?

Using 1,994 financing events including equity offerings, debt offerings, equity repurchases, and debt retirement of REITs between 1986 and 2003, Ooi et al. (2010) examine whether capital market conditions influence marginal financing decisions. The results show a strong correlation between capital market conditions and security issuance choices of REITs. REITs tend to issue or retire securities based on time-varying costs of debt and equity. Specifically, REITs issue equity when their stock prices are high and issue debt when the risk premium for long-term debt is low. The market timing behavior is also reflected in REIT capital reduction decisions. These findings suggest REITs time their security offerings in terms of when and what type of securities to issue or reduce. Thus, Ooi et al. provide strong evidence supporting market-timing theory.

Boudry, Kallberg, and Liu (2010) examine how traditional capital structure theories can explain the security issuance decisions of REITs. Their security issuance data are from 96 REITs between 1997 and 2006, which include 834 issuances of common equity, private debt, public debt, and preferred equity. Their findings support market-timing theory. The results based on a multinomial logit model show that REITs are more likely to issue equity when their price-to-net asset value (NAV) ratios are high, suggesting REITs issue equity when the cost of equity capital is relatively lower in the public market than in the private market. Moreover, consistent with market-timing theory, REITs are more likely to issue equity after experiencing large price increases.

Instead of focusing on security issuance decisions, Harrison et al. (2011b) examine the impact of market timing behavior based on the overall leverage ratio of REITs. Following Boudry et al. (2010), they include the ratio of price-to-NAV in the leverage regression. The results show the ratio is inversely related to REIT leverage, indicating REITs are more likely to issue equity when their stocks are highly valued. Also, a negative relationship exists between REIT leverage and the capital appreciation in their stock values over the previous 12 months. This implies REITs are more likely to issue equity when market conditions are favorable. Finally, REIT debt usage is inversely related to the market interest rate, as proxied by the yield on 10-year Treasury notes. These findings provide supporting evidence to market timing theory.

DO REITS EXHIBIT LEVERAGE TARGET BEHAVIOR?

Trade-off theory suggests an optimal leverage ratio for firms. Firms issue financing claims to offset any deviation from targeted leverage ratios in the long run. However, market-timing theory implies that leverage targeting is of little importance when financial managers actively time the capital markets. Thus, whether REITs target the leverage ratio is an empirical issue.

Brown and Riddiough (2003) focus on public debt offering data to examine leverage target behavior of REITs. REITs issuing public debt tend to target the leverage ratio. This is mainly driven by a desire of REITs to maintain a minimum investment grade credit rating. Specifically, during the year of issuing securities, the leverage ratio of REITs that issue public debt moves back toward the level that leads to a minimum investment-grade credit rating. Moreover, this study documents three sources of evidence that are consistent with leverage target behavior: (1) REITs issuing public debt have credit ratings that cluster just above the minimum investment-grade credit rating; (2) issuing junk bonds is extremely expensive for REITs; and (3) a positive relationship exists between debt maturity and the bond's offer spread.

Using a more complete sample on both capital raising and capital reduction activities, Ooi et al. (2010) examine the role of target leverage on the marginal financing decisions of REITs. Their main conclusion is that target leverage behavior plays a secondary role relative to market timing behavior in the financing decisions of REITs. However, most REITs adjust their leverage ratio to the target debt level in the long run. Specifically, while equity offerings take REITs away from target leverage ratios, most REITs are engaged in a partial adjustment process toward the target debt level. Moreover, overleveraged REITs often retire debt in order to reduce leverage, while underleveraged REITs are likely to increase their use of debt.

Boudry et al. (2010) also provide support for trade-off theory. Using REIT financial security issuance data, they find REITs are less likely to issue debt when proxies for expected bankruptcy cost are high. The authors measure expected bankruptcy cost as the difference of the average interest rate of a REIT's debt over the rate on BBB debt. Thus, this finding is consistent with trade-off theory.

Another prediction of trade-off theory is that a firm's leverage ratio tends to be low when the market's default risk is high. By examining the determinants of REIT leverage, Harrison et al. (2011b) find evidence supporting trade-off theory. They find a positive relationship between the market's default risk spread and REIT leverage ratio. Moreover, higher firm-specific yield spreads reduce REIT leverage ratios. Finally, they document that a high cash yield, as measured by the net operating income-to-net property investment ratio, is associated with a high leverage ratio.

DO REIT DATA SUPPORT PECKING ORDER THEORY?

Consistent with the theoretical predictions, most REIT studies do not find evidence supporting pecking order theory. As Harrison et al. (2011b) contend, if pecking order theory is relevant to REITs, those with greater uncertainty should signal to the market by increasing the leverage ratio. They use two variables to measure information opacity of REITs. One is the dispersion of reported funds from operations (FFO) from National Association of Real Estate Investment Trust (NAREIT) benchmark guidelines. The other is the presence of split bond ratings. Neither measure influences the leverage ratio. Moreover, if firms prefer to issue debt over equity as pecking order theory suggests, REITs with a dividend payout ratio higher than the 90 percent threshold should issue more debt and use less equity. In contrast, they find REITs with higher payout ratios have lower market leverage ratios, which is inconsistent with pecking order theory.

Boudry et al. (2010) use financial security issuance data to test the relevance of pecking order theory to REITs. They show that REITs with a dividend payout ratio more than 90 percent are two times more likely to raise equity capital than public debt. They contend that the evidence is inconsistent with pecking order theory, which suggests firms should use debt first.

The REIT literature contains an exception. Using a panel data set from the period 1991–2003, Feng et al. (2007) examine how historical market-to-book ratios influence levels or changes in aggregate leverage of REITs. Their evidence reveals that firms with high historical market-to-book ratios have relatively high leverage ratios. The positive relationship between the leverage and market-to-book ratios is consistent with pecking order theory.

In summary, strong evidence supports market-timing theory, which means REITs time their equity or debt issuances based on the market conditions (Boudry et al. 2010; Harrison et al. 2011b; Ooi et al. 2010). Yet, several studies provide solid evidence consistent with trade-off theory (Brown and Riddiough 2003; Ooi et al. 2010) although it tends to play a secondary role in REIT capital structure. Finally, pecking order theory gets little support based on REIT data.

HOW DO REITS MANAGE LIABILITY STRUCTURE?

Instead of examining the overall leverage ratio, Brown and Riddiough (2003) conduct a detailed analysis on REITs' liability structure. Secured debt, public unsecured debt, and common stock are distinguished based on seniority of financial claims. Their study provides insights on how REITs manage liability structure and issue financial claims to facilitate investment. Proceeds from REIT equity offerings are more likely to fund investment. Managers typically use the proceeds from public debt offers to reconfigure a firm's liability structure. When REITs issue public debt or equity to fund investment, the amount of the offerings is larger than that of other use-of-proceeds categories. Accessing capital is easier when the purpose of the offerings is for investment as opposed to reconfiguring liability structure.

Brown and Riddiough (2003) also use a probit model to examine the likelihood that a REIT issues public debt relative to equity. The results show the pre-offer liability structure affects the issuance of financing choice. That is, REITs with higher leverage are less likely to issue debt. More importantly, REITs with a higher pre-offer level of secured debt are more likely to issue equity. Those with more unsecured debt issue more public debt. Higher credit quality REITs tend to issue longer-term bonds. REITs that have never issued public debt are unlikely to issue it in the near future. Finally, Brown and Riddiough claim a bifurcation in REIT liability structure. Some firms use secured debt and equity to finance their operations, whereas other REITs have a more complex capital structure with various types of secured and unsecured debt.

Recent Research on REIT Liquidity Management

As capital-intensive firms, REITs often go to the external markets to raise capital. REITs also need to secure financial liquidity in order to take quick actions in the acquisition market so that they can grow and succeed. Thus, the financial health of REITs largely depends on their ability to access the financial slack or liquid capital when they need it. Recently, researchers have investigated the liquidity management of REITs, which includes cash holding and bank line of credit policy.

WHY DO REITS HOLD SO LITTLE CASH?

According to Hardin et al. (2009), REITs hold cash and cash equivalents of about 1.57 percent of their total assets, compared to the percentage of 18.48 percent documented for non-REIT public firms. The rationale for REITs having so little cash holdings merits study. One explanation is that REITs have to pay 90 percent of taxable income via dividends as required by the tax code. Thus, REITs are cash constrained. However, Hardin et al. maintain this is not the whole story. REITs can retain more cash if they desire. Because depreciation is a large non-cash item, the amount of taxable income is usually much lower than the true cash flow available for many REITs. In fact, most REITs pay out more dividends than the amount required by the minimum 90 percent of funds from operations. Several studies document that the average dividends-to- funds from operation ratio is 50 to 65 percent (Bradley, Capozza, and Seguin 1998), which implies REIT managers choose not to hold as much as cash they could.

In the finance literature, a free cash problem occurs when managers retain earnings and deploy them in ways that benefit themselves instead of increasing shareholders' wealth. Jensen (1986) is the seminal paper to raise the issue. One way to control the free cash problem is to pay out more dividends to shareholders in order to reduce the resources under managers' control.

Hardin et al. (2009), who examine the determinants of REIT cash holdings, contend their findings are consistent with Jensen (1986). REIT cash holdings are negatively related to funds from operations, leverage, and credit line access and use. However, cash holdings are positively related to the cost of external finance and growth opportunities. REITs reduce their cash holdings in order to reduce the agency cost problem so that the firms can gain better access to the external capital market in the future.

RESEARCH ON USING BANK LINES OF CREDIT BY REITS

This section consists of two parts. The first part examines the impact of bank credit lines on REIT capital structure and the second part focuses on bank credit lines and REIT operations.

Impact of Bank Credit Lines on REIT Capital Structure

A *bank line of credit*, also called *loan commitment* or *revolving credit line*, is a prearranged, legally binding loan contract allowing firms to borrow from the credit facility when they need capital. Unlike equity or public debt offerings, which usually take time in the security issuance process, bank lines of credit provide access to financial liquidity so that firms can act quickly to make investment or acquisitions. Because of these features, bank lines of credit have become an important capital source for industrial firms (Sufi 2009). Given that the industry experienced rapid growth and REITs had to rely heavily on financial liquidity to make property acquisitions (Riddiough and Wu 2009), REITs have increasingly used bank lines of credit to fund their operations since the 1990s. Consequently, using bank lines of credit by REITS has been the subject of more research.

Hardin and Wu (2010) study the effect of bank debt usage and banking relationships on REIT capital structure. Using a data set compiled from different sources, they document a dramatic increase in the use of bank debt by REITs over the period 1992–2003. They claim that using bank debt for liquid capital and development of banking relationships became an industry norm for REITs. During the same period, REITs reduced their reliance on mortgages and raised more capital from public capital markets.

Another finding from Hardin and Wu (2010) is that REITs with banking relationships are more likely to obtain long-term debt ratings and subsequently issue public debt. Also, REITs with banking relationships tend to use less secured debt and have lower leverage. These results suggest banks play an important role in the evolution of REIT capital structure. Banking relationships facilitate REITs gaining access to the public debt markets. With development of banking relationships, finding that REITs have shifted from traditional mortgage financing to bank debt and public capital market financing is not surprising.

Brown and Riddiough (2003) question why REITs use debt to finance the ownership of real estate assets. Because no obvious tax advantage exists to using debt for REITs, trade-off theory implies REITs should employ little or no debt. Extending Jaffe

(1991), Hardin and Wu (2010) contend that one important reason for REITs to use bank debt is to provide near-term financial flexibility in order to fund operations and investment.

Bank debt also influences REIT cash retention policy. Based on a REIT sample from 1990 to 2003, Riddiough and Wu (2009) examine the interaction between bank line of credit usage and cash retention policy. The results show a negative relationship between bank line of credit usage and both cash holdings and retained cash flow of REITs. Retained cash flow is measured as available cash flow minus dividend payout. Most REITs pay more dividends than the required minimum level and dividend payouts display considerable inertia over time. These results suggest REITs use bank lines of credit to relax cash constraints in the short term and smooth variation of available cash flow.

Using a data set from 1990 to 2008, An, Hardin, and Wu (2010) study the influence of information asymmetry on REITs' choice between cash and credit lines. Using analyst forecast error and dispersion, REITs with more severe information asymmetry problems are less likely to use bank credit lines. The results suggest that information asymmetry plays an important role in corporate liquidity management.

Bank Credit Lines and REIT Operation

Because bank lines of credit allow firms to borrow from the facilities quickly, they function like financial slack or cash reserves. Thus, bank lines of credit provide insurance or credit protection to firms during capital market downturns. However, using bank lines of credit has limitations. To control for credit risks, many banks specify materially adverse change (MAC) clauses in the loan contracts, through which banks can revoke certain terms of the credit lines. Sufi (2009) documents that, if firms violate a covenant, then banks reduce the availability of their unused credit lines by 30 percent on average. Bank lines of credit are not necessarily liquidity substitutes for all firms.

Ooi et al. (2010) examine the question: Can bank lines protect financially constrained REITs against a credit crisis? They use a sample of 275 publicly traded REITs from 1992 to 2007. The authors obtain the data for used lines of credit or the amount drawn down and the unused portion from the SNL REIT database. The individual REITs' quarterly (10-Q) and annual (10-K) filings supplement the credit line data. The evidence at both the broad market and firm levels shows bank lines of credit help REITs gain access to liquid capital during a credit crunch, which supports the insurance hypothesis. REITs use more loan commitments than spot loans in tight capital markets. When a firm's creditworthiness decreases, the firm exhibits greater reliance on bank credit lines. However, the insurance benefit is qualified for smaller and risky firms. For these REITs, either they cannot establish a credit line or they fail to expand their existing one during a crisis when the firms need liquid capital the most. Even if these REITs expand the existing credit lines, some restrictions exist on drawing down debt from established credit lines.

Harrison et al. (2011a) use a sample of equity REITs between 1990 and 2009 to examine the relationship between REIT credit line availability and subsequent operating profitability. If banks enjoy economies of scale in information acquisition and lending decisions serve as an effective signal to the capital markets, a positive relationship should exist between credit line usage and firm performance. Indeed, they find that the total credit line-financial liquidity ratio is positively related to operating performance measures. The *credit line-financial liquidity ratio* is the ratio of the total available credit line to itself plus cash. Furthermore, enhanced liquidity has a strong effect on profitability for those REITs considered being capital-constrained. These findings provide evidence that better access to bank credit lines improves profitability of REITs.

Other Related Topics in REIT Capital Structure

This section examines the issue of whether collateral affects capital structure and debt capacity. It also investigates whether REIT capital structure affects firm investment.

DOES COLLATERAL AFFECT CAPITAL STRUCTURE AND DEBT CAPACITY?

Given that most REIT assets are tangible, an interesting question is whether collateral influences REITs' capital structure and debt capacity. In their investigation on the determinants of the REIT leverage ratio, Harrison et al. (2011b) find that asset tangibility is positively related to leverage. This finding is consistent with the notion that real assets provide good quality collateral to lenders and help increase debt capacity of the firm. However, because this is not the focus of their study, they do not discuss any specific theory regarding the result.

Hardin and Wu (2010) find that REITs with banking relationships have a lower secured debt ratio and use less leverage. Leverage is positively related to the amount of secured debt. This finding is robust across different measures of the secured debt ratio. They argue this finding is consistent with the theory in Brown and Marble (2007), which posits that the asset substitution problem increases when firms secure more debt. In other words, if a firm uses more secured debt, the managers are likely to use higher leverage to pursue high-risk projects.

Using a panel data set of REITs from 1992 to 2010, Giambona, Mello, and Riddiough (2012) conduct a theoretical and empirical analysis on how firms use collateral to issue financing claims to fund investment. They consider two types of firms based on collateral quality. The theory suggests that firms with better quality collateral tend to pledge it to finance new investment with unsecured debt. Lower-quality firms use more secured debt. Because better quality firms should maintain a strong balance sheet in order to separate themselves from lesser quality firms, they use less leverage. The authors use the 1998 Russian crisis to establish a causal link. They find that higher quality residential REITs moved to the secured debt market during the Russian crisis to raise the average revealed quality of the firm. The results are consistent with the model predications. Overall, asset tangibility appears to help REITs increase their debt capacity. However, high credit-quality REITs use less secured debt in their liability structure.

IMPACT OF REIT FINANCIAL POLICIES ON INVESTMENT

REIT capital structure should affect firm investment. The question is how this channel works. Riddiough and Wu (2009) examine the relationship between REIT investment and liquidity management. Based on data from 1990 to 2003, they find that bank line capacity, incremental credit line usage, and retained cash all significantly influence firm investment. When REIT investment increases, credit line usage also rises. However, cash retention policy is unrelated to investment. To examine the effect of financial constraints on investment, Riddiough and Wu split the full sample into more and less financially constrained subsamples. The results show that both credit line capacity and usage have a stronger effect on investment in more constrained firms. These results suggest that REITs use credit lines to relax cash constraints and accelerate investment, especially for those that are more constrained.

Based on data from Real Capital Analytics, Case (2013) points out that REITs tended to be net sellers during the market peak of 2006–2007, which is considered a preferred period for asset divestiture. REITs were net buyers before and after the market peak. In contrast, unlisted property companies often sell properties before or after the market peak. Case maintains that this different pattern can be attributed to the difference in the sources of capital for REITs and non-REIT property companies. Unlisted property companies raise capital mainly through private equity and debt. REITs have better access to public capital markets for equity and debt financing, which allows them to take advantage of the better acquisition opportunities.

MacKinnon (2011) examines whether REITs have an advantage over other entities when the credit market is tight. Because REITs have better access to the public capital markets, they should have a built-in advantage in times of constrained credit through the ability to raise capital via seasoned equity or unsecured bond issues. MacKinnon documents that, while REITs issued less capital in 2008 relative to 2006–2007, the total amount raised significantly increased in 2009. Specifically, more than $20 billion in SEOs occurred in that year, which is more than in any year since 2002.

According to MacKinnon (2011), if the capital markets perceive REITs as having an advantage over other entities during the credit crunch, their premiums to NAV, a measure for the gap between public and private market pricing of real estate assets, should be higher. Using data on REIT returns, private real estate returns, and leverage ratio, MacKinnon investigates whether premiums vary systemically with credit market conditions. His findings are consistent with the hypothesis. NAV premiums are significantly higher when the credit markets are tighter. However, a lag effect appears to exist. REIT prices are most affected by credit conditions three quarters earlier. This is not surprising given that the REIT market is considered relatively inefficient and investors' reactions to the tighter credit conditions may be delayed.

Summary and Conclusions

During the past decade, growing research has appeared on REIT capital structure and related issues. This chapter has discussed different topics in this area including determinants of the REIT leverage ratio, financial security issuance decisions, liquidity management, and the effects of capital structure on investment and operations. Given the influence from the financial crisis of 2008–2009 on the real estate sector, researchers are likely to conduct more studies in this area. Although research documents that REITs have become increasingly integrated into the stock market, many important questions remain to be answered. Examples are how capital structure of REITs will continue to evolve and how capital structure will play a role in the transition process when the REIT industry continues to consolidate. In summary, REIT capital structure is likely to continue to be a topic of interest for both practitioners and academics in the future.

Discussion Questions

1. Identify several unique characteristics of REITs and discuss how they make REIT capital structure a worthwhile topic to research.
2. Identify which capital structure theories (trade-off theory, pecking order theory, and market timing theory) the REIT data support.
3. Identify several major determinants that affect REIT capital structure.
4. Discuss how a REIT's capital structure influences its investment activities and operations.
5. Explain why REITs hold so little cash.
6. Discuss the evolution of REIT capital structure over the past two decades.

References

An, Heng, William Hardin III, and Zhonghua Wu. 2010. "Information Asymmetry and Corporate Liquidity Management: Evidence from Real Estate Investment Trusts." *Journal of Real Estate Finance and Economics* 45:3, 678–704.

Baker, Malcolm, and Jeffery Wurgler. 2002. "Market Timing and Capital Structure." *Journal of Finance* 57:1, 1–32.

Baker, Malcolm, Robin Greenwood, and Jeffery Wurgler. 2003. "The Maturity of Debt Issues and Predictable Variation in Bond Returns." *Journal of Financial Economics* 70:2, 261–291.

Boudry, Walter I., Jarl G. Kallberg, and Crocker H. Liu. 2010. "An Analysis of REIT Security Issuance Decisions." *Real Estate Economics* 38:1, 91–120.

Bradley, Michael, Dennis R. Capozza, and Paul J. Seguin. 1998. "Dividend Policy and Cash Flow Uncertainty." *Real Estate Economics* 26:3, 556–580.

Brown, David T., and Hugh Marble. 2007. "Secured Debt Financing and Leverage: Theory and Evidence." Working Paper, University of Florida.

Brown, David T., and Timothy J. Riddiough. 2003. "Financing Choice and Liability Structure of Real Estate Investment Trusts." *Real Estate Economics* 31:3, 313–346.

Case, Brad. 2013. "Real Estate Investment Trusts." In H. Kent Baker and Greg Filbeck, eds., *Alternative Investments—Instruments, Performance, Benchmarks, and Strategies*, 119–141. Hoboken, NJ: John Wiley & Sons.

Elayan, Fayez A., Thomas O. Meyer, and Jingyu Li. 2004. "Creditworthiness or Management Signal? An Empirical Investigation of Loan Commitments Obtained by Non-taxable Firms." *Journal of Real Estate Finance and Economics* 28:1, 59–79.

Ertugrul, Mine, and Erasmo Giambona. 2011. "Property Segment and REIT Capital Structure." *Journal of Real Estate Finance and Economics* 43:4, 505–526.

Feng, Zhilan, Chinmoy Ghosh, and C. F. Sirmans. 2007. "On the Capital Structure of Real Estate Investment Trusts." *Journal of Real Estate Finance and Economics* 34:1, 81–105.

Ghosh, Chinmoy, Erasmo Giambona, John P. Harding, and C. F. Sirmans. 2011. "How Entrenchment, Incentives and Governance Influence REIT Capital Structure." *Journal of Real Estate Finance and Economics* 43: 1, 39–72.

Giambona, Erasmo, John P. Harding, and C. F. Sirmans. 2008. "Explaining the Variation in REIT Capital Structure: The Role of Asset Liquidation Value." *Real Estate Economics* 36:1, 111–137.

Giambona, Erasmo, Antonio Mello, and Timothy Riddiough. 2012. "Collateral and the Limits of Debt Capacity: Theory and Evidence." Working Paper, University of Amsterdam.

Graham, John R., and Campbell R. Harvey. 2001. "The Theory and Practice of Corporate Finance: Evidence from the Field." *Journal of Financial Economics* 60:2–3, 187–243.

Hardin, William G., III, and Zhonghua Wu. 2010. "Banking Relationships and REIT Capital Structure." *Real Estate Economics* 38:2, 257–284.

Hardin, William G., Michael J. Highfield, Matthew D. Hill, and J. H. Wayne Kelly. 2009. "The Determinants of REIT Cash Holdings." *Journal of Real Estate Finance and Economics* 39:1, 39–57.

Harrison, David, Kimberly F. Luchtenberg, and Michael J. Seiler. 2011a. "REIT Performance of Lines of Credit of REITs." *Journal of Real Estate Portfolio Management* 17:1, 1–14.

Harrison, David, Christine A. Panasian, and Michael J. Seiler. 2011b. "Further Evidence on the Capital Structure of REITs." *Real Estate Economics* 39:1, 133–166.

Howe, John S., and James D. Shilling. 1988. "Capital Structure Theory and REIT Securities Offerings." *Journal of Finance* 43:4, 401–407.

Jaffe, Jeffery F. 1991. "Taxes and the Capital Structure of Partnerships, REITs, and Related Entities." *Journal of Finance* 46:1, 401–407.

Jensen, Michael C. 1986. "Agency Costs of Free Cash Flow, Corporate Finance, and Takeovers." *American Economic Review* 76:2, 323–329.

MacKinnon, Greg. 2011. "Do REITs Have an Advantage When Credit Is Tight?" *Journal of Real Estate Portfolio Management* 17:1, 15–25.

Maksimovic, Vojislav, and Josef J. Zechner. 1991. "Debt, Agency Costs and Industry Equilibrium." *Journal of Finance* 46:5, 1619–1643.

Myers, Stewart C. 1984. "The Capital Structure Puzzle." *Journal of Finance* 39:2, 575–592.

Myers, Stewart C., and Nicholas S. Majluf. 1984. "Corporate Financing and Investment Decisions When Firms Have Information That Investors Do Not Have." *Journal of Financial Economics* 13:2, 187–221.

Ooi, Joseph T. L., Seow-Eng Ong, and Lin Li. 2010. "An Analysis of the Financing Decisions of REITs: The Role of Market Timing and Target Leverage." *Journal of Real Estate Finance and Economics* 40:2, 130–160.

Ott, Steven H., Timothy J. Riddiough, and Ha-chin Yi. 2005. "Finance, Investment, and Investment Performance: Evidence from the REIT Sector." *Real Estate Economics* 33:1, 203–235.

Riddiough, Timothy J., and Zhonghua Wu. 2009. "Financial Constraints, Liquidity Management and Investment." *Real Estate Economics* 37:2, 447–481.

Shleifer, Andrei, and Robert W. Vishny. 1992. "Liquidation Values and Debt Capacity: A Market Equilibrium Approach." *Journal of Finance* 47:4, 1343–1366.

Sufi, Amir. 2009. "Bank Lines of Credit in Corporate Finance: An Empirical Analysis." *Review of Financial Studies* 22:3, 1057–1088.

Williamson, Oliver E. 1988. "Corporate Finance and Corporate Governance." *Journal of Finance* 43:3, 567–592.

14

Real Estate Operating Companies

PETER ZABIEREK
Chief Executive Officer, Presima, Inc.

Introduction

Hudson-Wilson, Fabozzi, and Gordon (2003) divide real estate for institutional investors into a two-by-two matrix: debt versus equity on one axis and public versus private on the other. These quadrants—private equity, private debt, public equity, and public debt—comprise the real estate investment universe. Table 14.1 presents these quadrants.

Real estate investment has historically focused on the largest of the four quadrants—private commercial real estate equity held as individual assets or in commingled vehicles. Before tradable securities and the availability of broader time series starting in the early 1990s, investors placed less emphasis on indirect property investments or public equity including real estate securities (Hines 2001). This market moved from an afterthought in the early 1990s to a legitimate asset class. Public equity is a complement to if not a substitute for direct real estate in a multi-asset class portfolio. Many impediments to real estate investment trust (REIT) conversion no longer exist in the United States, making it more flexible and attractive to owners, operators, and investors. REITs have spread to markets including Australia, the United Kingdom, Japan, Hong Kong, Singapore, and many countries in Europe.

REIT research is so prolific that Hoesli and Oikarinen (2012) include real estate operating companies (REOCs) in a group labeled as REITs. Many in the investment community consider REOCs with REITs as real estate securities or listed REITs.

The chapter compares REOCs to REITs in terms of dividends, liquidity, and leverage. REOCs generally have lower dividend yields and lower liquidity, but not always higher leverage. U.S. REOC to REIT conversions increase equity market capitalization (cap) by 2 to 4 percent, and even more when a high level of tax-exempt ownership of the company exists. Dividend levels generally increase upon REIT conversion. Outside of the United States, the impact of the REIT structure on firm value is less clear.

The chapter then covers REOC valuation approaches with net asset value (NAV), discounted cash flow (DCF), and cash flow multiples emerging as the most common metrics. In the market environment, REOCs have higher systematic risk and greater

Table 14.1 **Four Quadrant Investment Market**

	Public	*Private*
Debt	Commercial mortgage-backed securities (CMBS), listed company unsecured debt	Directly issued whole loans or commercial mortgages held in funds and/or commingled vehicles
Equity	REITs and REOCs	Real estate equity, held as individual assets or in commingled vehicles

Note: This table characterizes the real estate investment universe with a two-by-two matrix. The resulting four quadrants are public debt, public equity, private debt, and private equity.

Source: Hudson-Wilson et al. (2003).

volatility. They outperform REITs in rising markets and underperform them in falling ones. From a diversification perspective, given the similarities in assets, REOCs and REITs perform roughly the same in a multi-asset class portfolio.

What Are REOCs?

The literature contains various definitions of REOCs (Evans and Evans 2007; Friedman, Harris, and Diskin 2009; Schäfers and Shulte 2012). The following definition encapsulates those views. A *REOC* is a publicly traded real estate company that is listed on a major exchange that is not otherwise restricted structurally in the type of real estate business it conducts and has not elected REIT status. REOC profits come from leasing and sale of portfolio properties, project development, management of real estate, and the provision of corresponding services. According to Linneman (2011), neither REITs nor REOCs need be listed companies. The decision whether to be a REIT or a REOC primarily involves taxes, whereas the decision to be public mainly concerns access to capital.

REOCs are companies that operate in countries without REIT legislation, or choose not to elect REIT status. In the United States, Hilton Hotels was the first REOC, formed in 1947. In Japan, after the separation of the real estate division from the Mitsui Company, Mitsui Fudosan Co., Ltd. was formed in 1941. The listing of this REOC came in 1949, 52 years before the first Japanese REIT went public in 2001. Mitsui Fudosan is the third largest REOC in the world. In Hong Kong, the second largest global REOC is Sun Hung Kai Properties. It became public in 1972 and listed on the Hong Kong Stock Exchange long before Hong Kong REITs came into existence in 2006.

Table 14.2 shows the top 10 largest REOCs globally. Size is determined by total equity market capitalization. Most of the large REOCs are domiciled outside the United States, with the top 10 all in Asia, particularly in Japan. Therefore, location strongly influences REOC performance and characteristics, making comparisons difficult and necessitating control for geography and capital markets to carry out any comparative market analysis.

Table 14.2 **Top 10 REOCs in the World**

Rank	*Name*	*Country*	*Equity Market Cap ($billion USD)*
1	Mitsubishi Estate Co Ltd	Japan	44.75
2	Sun Hung Kai Properties Ltd	Hong Kong	37.87
3	Mitsui Fudosan Co Ltd	Japan	30.63
4	Wharf Holdings Ltd	Hong Kong	26.59
5	Sumitomo Realty & Development Co	Japan	23.52
6	Hong Kong Land Holdings Ltd	Singapore	17.50
7	Hang Lung Properties Ltd	Hong Kong	17.41
8	Henderson Land Development Co Ltd	Hong Kong	17.40
9	CapitaLand Ltd	Singapore	12.08
10	Global Logistic Properties Ltd	Singapore	10.61

Note: This table presents the largest REOCs in the world, ranked by equity market capitalization. The table shows that these are very large global companies and that much of the global REOC exposure is in Asia.

Source: FTSE (2013) and Bloomberg (2013).

Structural Differences between REITs and REOCs

This section begins by discussing the similarities between REITs and REOCs and then reviews the general structural differences between the two organizational forms. REITs and REOCs are similar in that management is centralized, with directors entrusted with protecting shareholder interests. Shareholders can vote on business matters including election of directors. Schäfers and Schulte (2012) identify these structural differences.

Structural differences exist between a REIT and a REOC. REITs are a product of each country's financial legislation. REITs must satisfy various requirements including dividend payouts. In contrast, Delcoure and Dickens (2004) describe REOCs as having fewer restrictions than REITs. REOCs do not have to pay specific dividend levels, involve no minimum restriction on the number of owners, and do not place limits on ownership concentration. REOCs can also invest in any assets and derive income from any investment. Outside management is not required to conduct specific tasks. By contrast, REITs trade favorable tax treatment for operating restrictions.

A difference between REITs and REOCs involves organizational control. REOCs have no restrictions on organizational control. REIT rules require a minimum number of shareholders, with no block holding a large number of shares.

Another difference is taxation. REOC shareholders face double taxation. REOC taxation is the same as a standard corporation. In contrast, a REIT is not taxed at the firm level. According to Linneman (2011), becoming a REIT is a tax status election. In the United States, dividends paid by REITs are taxed as ordinary income and do not receive a preferential lower rate.

Table 14.3 **Organization Structure Similarities and Differences between REOCs and REITs**

Characteristic	*REOCs*	*REITs*
Management	Centralized; directors protect shareholder interests	Same as REOCs
Voting rights of shareholders	Shareholders have a right to vote on certain matters affecting the company, including the election of directors or trustees	Same as REOCs
Organizational control	No restriction on the number of shareholders or how many can own a certain percentage of shares	Minimum number of shareholders, with limitations on how few can own a certain amount of the company
Taxation	Subject to double taxation at the firm and at the shareholder level. Can use tax loss carry forwards for three years	In most countries, not taxed at the firm level if company meets certain requirements
Dividend policy	No requirements. Management is free to determine the best use of income	Must distribute ≥ 90 percent +/− of taxable income as dividends
Restrictions on business	No specific restrictions	Must derive ≥ 75 percent +/− of income from real estate. Restrictions on certain asset classes and development

Note: This table highlights the similarities and differences between REOCs and REITs. The key differences are in the areas of organizational control, taxation, and dividend policy.

A third difference involves dividend policy. A REIT is required to pay out at least 90 percent +/− of its taxable income as a dividend. Payouts of more than 100 percent of taxable income are possible because depreciation is a non-cash expense. This dividend requirement means that REITs are highly dependent on returning to capital markets. REOCs can retain earnings and accumulate cash.

A fourth difference concerns restrictions on business. In many countries, REITs cannot engage in certain activities that are considered more risky such as development, or beyond property or mortgage income such as offering brokerage or other real estate services. Table 14.3 summarizes the key structural differences between REOCs and REITs.

Global Differences in REITs

Table 14.4 compares four REIT structures across the globe. A main area of dissimilarity relates to management. Three of these four countries—the United States, Germany, and

Table 14.4 **A Comparison of Global REIT Structures**

Country	*Australia*	*Germany*	*Japan*	*United States*
Internal/ External	Internal or External	Internal or External	External	Internal or External
Shareholders	No special regulatory or legal requirements	Initial free float ≥ 25 percent, ≥ 15 percent after No direct shareholder > 10 percent ownership Equity ≥ €15m	Capitalization ≥ 100 million yen	≥ 100 Largest 5 shareholders ≥ 50 percent No restriction on foreign shareholders
Real estate investments	> 60 percent of revenue from rent	≥ 75 percent of earnings and investments in real estate No residential property built before January 1, 2007	≥ 70 percent of assets	≥ 75 percent in real estate ≥ 95 percent of income from real estate ≤ 25 percent in securities of taxable REIT ≤ 10 percent ownership of another stock
Overseas Investment	Yes	Yes	Yes	Yes
Development	Yes	Restricted	No	Yes
Trading	NA	≤ 50 percent of portfolio over five years	NA	NA
Gearing limit	No restrictions; but the interest that can be deductible is capped	55 percent LTV	No restrictions	No restrictions
Payout	100 percent of taxable income after depreciation	> 90 percent of profit and half of realized disposal gains	> 90 percent of annual net income	> 90 percent of taxable income after depreciation
Closed ended	Yes	Yes	Yes	Yes
REIT Type	Trust	Corporate	Trust or corporate. All publicly traded corporate	Corporate

Table 14.4 **continued**

Country	*Australia*	*Germany*	*Japan*	*United States*
Listed/ Unlisted	Both	Listed	Both	Both
Tax transparency	Yes	Yes	Yes	Yes

Note: This table compares REIT structures around the globe. It highlights the similarities and differences of the REIT regimes in areas such as shareholders requirements, eligible investments, and gearing limits.

Source: UBS (2012).

Australia—allow both internal and external management. *Internal management* is where the management company sits within the REIT while *external management* is where a third party manages the REIT. Japan is the only country on this list that requires external management. This largely occurs because of the influence of the REITs' sponsors who want to continue to collect fees on the management of the REIT. U.S. and other investors express a preference for internal management, ascribing higher valuations where managers have an investment in the firm. Other important differences include the level of restriction on development, overseas investment, leverage, and payout levels. Bloomfield and Greenberg (2011) highlight the advantages of REITs, including no entity level tax even for publicly traded REITs and the ability to attract tax-exempt and foreign investors.

Advantages and Disadvantages of REOCs

Choosing the REOC form of organization has numerous advantages. These benefits include using debt, growth potential, ability to time the market, fewer restrictions on the investor base, more permissible activities, and flexibility in times of distress.

BENEFITS OF USING DEBT

The major advantages of using debt are the deductibility of interest and the reduction of free cash flow, which lowers agency costs (Graham 2000). REOCs can take advantage of these benefits. REITs do not pay corporate income taxes and benefit from interest deductibility. REIT payout requirements minimize free cash flow as compared with REOCs resulting in lower agency costs. REITs must compete for capital with REOCs in the debt capital markets. Therefore, the after-tax cost of using debt is lower for REOCs than for REITs given these considerations (Chan, Erickson, and Wang 2003).

GROWTH POTENTIAL

Unlike REITs, REOCs have no distribution requirements and are not limited to a maximum percentage of income from capital gains. These conditions facilitate the growth of the company through retained earnings. In contrast, REITs rely more on external capital to grow. The after-tax costs of issuing debt are higher for REITs. Issuing equity dilutes existing shareholders and therefore can depress stock prices. According to Chan et al. (2003) and Clark, Hackemann, Mesmin, Roche, and Road (2009), a key cost of electing REIT status is limiting future growth. The inability to use internal capital or retained earnings to facilitate growth translates into a major cost to REITs. All else equal, REOCs have an advantage in this regard.

ABILITY TO TIME THE MARKET

As real estate follows cycles, investors want to buy at the bottom and sell at the top. A management team's ability to take advantage of these cycles is a key to long-term value creation. Further, if a company forecasts major distress ahead in the market, it may choose to liquidate its portfolio or at least those in markets or product types that are most at risk. Because REITs in either properties or mortgages have restrictions on capital gains as proportions of income, REOCs are in a better position to time the market.

FEWER RESTRICTIONS ON THE INVESTOR BASE

REOCs often eschew REIT election because of the restrictions on the investor base. Many real estate companies started as family businesses where insiders are reluctant to give up control. Family members or trusts have substantial ownership of large Hong Kong REOCs such as Sun Hung Kai and Henderson Land. Studwell (2007) asserts that a small handful of families controls the economies of Hong Kong and much of Southeast Asia. Among their interests are investments in property including listed REOCs.

MORE PERMISSIBLE ACTIVITIES

Two major advantages of REOCs are being able to invest internationally in all property types and to vertically integrate a listed property company. Although not all REIT regimes restrict these activities, the impact on organizational form is considerable and tilts the balance to REOCs.

MORE FLEXIBILITY IN TIMES OF DISTRESS

The global financial crisis, which began in 2007 and hit its depths in 2009, severely tested all asset classes, including global real estate securities. That period provided an opportunity to see how listed property companies, both REITs and REOCs, performed operationally. These times had extreme property market and equity market distress. Until 2008, a criticism of REITs was that as capital-intensive businesses, they had to pay out a large portion of their earnings in dividends, leaving little financial flexibility.

Various researchers document REIT activities at the height of the credit crisis in December 2008 (Adornato and Anderson 2009; Case, Hardin, and Wu 2012; Lee, Chiang, and Lin 2012). REITs successfully lobbied for retention of cash and stock dividends through 2009 to meet income distribution requirements. REITs could pay up to 90 percent of dividends in shares instead of cash. In December 2009 under Revenue Procedure

2010–12, this rule extended until December 2011. REIT heavyweights Vornado Realty Trust and Simon Property Group chose to pay quarterly dividends partially in stock in 2009, shifting back to cash in 2010 as the crisis subsided. Cousins Properties and General Growth Properties were the last REITs continuing to pay dividends in both cash and stock (Juge 2011). There were 27 REIT issuances of stock and cash dividends in 2009 and seven in 2010. The REIT structure is flexible in responding to distress. A firm faces less necessity to consider REOC status out of concern for a lack of cash flow flexibility.

Damodaran, John, and Liu (1997) study changes in the real estate industry among organizational forms, including REITs and REOCs. They conduct their study just as the modern REIT era was taking shape and before the late 1990s real estate recession. The authors document the associated changes in profitability, free cash flow, debt, dividends, and investment policies. Troubled or distressed firms move to a more flexible organizational structure, with subsequent reductions in dividends, improvements in performance, and increases in asset sales and investments. Healthy non-distressed firms that move to a tighter structure have larger free cash flows before the change. They increase dividends, reduce free cash flows, and improve profitability after the change.

Firms consider taxes when making organizational changes. The choices have notable effects on stock prices. Organizational changes are followed by increased equity value and improved earnings for non-distressed firms moving to a tighter structure and troubled firms moving to a looser structure. The increase is more dramatic for the latter group. Non-distressed firms that move to a looser structure lag both of these groups in terms of stock price and earnings performance.

Firms are motivated to change to a looser organizational form to take advantage of the greater flexibility and to a tighter structure for the tax benefits. In the United States, the Tax Reform Act of 1986 simplified REITs, allowing them to be internally advised and managed. The 2008 REIT Investment and Diversification Act (RIDEA) allows REITs to buy and sell assets more efficiently, increasing the size of taxable REIT subsidiaries. Healthcare REITs can use taxable subsidiaries in the same manner as hotel REITs.

Defining the REOC Investment Universe

The REOC market is a subset of the global real estate securities market. Estimates on the size of the global real estate securities market vary widely for two reasons. First, global investors have differing opinions on what is a real estate security. Second, the size depends on geographies. Investors in some countries might consider homebuilders to be real estate securities, whereas others might consider them to be a separate asset class. Some consider only developed markets while others include emerging markets in the global market.

Block (2011) estimates that as of December 31, 2010, REITs accounted for 51 percent of the global real estate securities market, leaving 49 percent as REOCs. Block bases this estimate on CBRE Clarion free-float equity market capitalization data. According to CBRE data at the end of 2010, there were 492 REOCs with a total market capitalization of $1.0 trillion and a free float of $581 billion. FTSE (2013) provides a smaller estimate of the REOC market.

The FTSE European Public Real Estate Association/National Association of Real Estate Investment Trusts (EPRA/NAREIT) Global Developed Index is one of the most popular analytical benchmarks for active investment managers. According to FTSE (2013, 3), the index series "is designed to represent general trends in eligible listed real estate stocks worldwide. Relevant real estate activities are defined as the ownership, trading and development of income-producing real estate." It is the reference index for a large amount of passive and exchange traded fund (ETF) money. This index defines the market as property-dedicated professional investors use it. A subset of the FTSE EPRA/NAREIT Global Developed Index, the FTSE EPRA/NAREIT Global Developed Non-REIT Index is considered to be the global REOC Index.

The difference between the CBRE and the FTSE estimate probably does not result from timing, but is more likely due to how analysts define the market. The fact that the FTSE index has a somewhat narrower scope explains why its total market capitalization is smaller than CBRE's estimate. At the end of the first quarter of 2013, REITs comprise 67.5 percent of the market capitalization of global real estate securities. REOCs comprise the remaining 32.5 percent, from the FTSE global index with a free float of $386 billion.

Figure 14.1 shows the mix of REITs and REOCs within the market capitalization of each country's publicly traded real estate stocks. In the United States, virtually 100 percent of the real estate public equity market is in REITs and it is 80 percent in the United Kingdom. In Europe, the ratio is 50 percent. Japan has less than 40 percent of real estate equity in REITs, while in China, REOCs account for virtually all of the market. The REOC investment universe is compared with those companies that are in the FTSE/EPRA NAREIT Global Non-REIT Index. Other firms that are in real estate but not considered to be REOCs are homebuilders or other similar companies. Instead, the focus is on what many market participants consider as the investment universe. Another advantage to defining the universe this way is that it allows comparable performance and risk analysis, given REIT- and REOC-specific indexes.

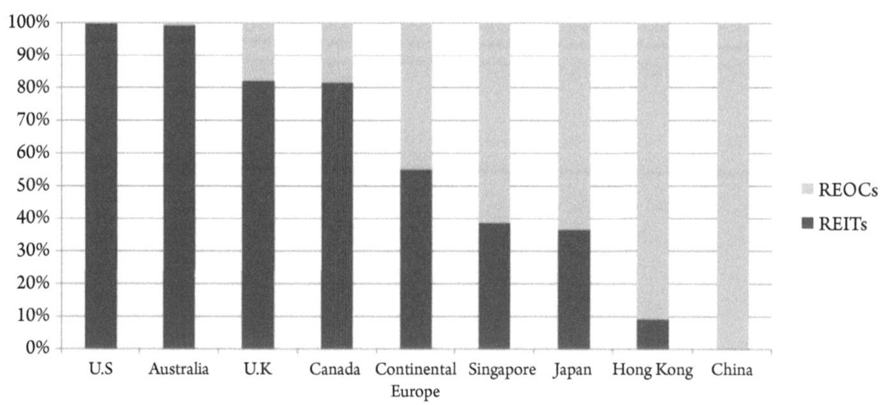

Figure 14.1 REITs and REOCs by Region. This figure shows the vast differences in REIT concentrations in various countries. The United States has the highest percentage of companies choosing the REIT format, while Hong Kong has the lowest amongst countries with REIT legislation.

REOC Characteristics

With respect to financial metrics, the key differences between REOCs and REITs involve leverage and dividend yield. Liquidity can also vary between the two forms.

LEVERAGE

Niskanen and Falkenbach (2013) examine capital structure decisions of REOCs and REITs. Their work concludes that the tax-neutral REITs in Europe are much less levered than their taxed REOC counterparts. Along with tax neutrality, a further potential reason for the structurally less monitored REOCs' higher leverage could be an attempt to mitigate the potential agency costs with additional debt. Although European REOCs are more highly levered than their REIT counterparts, this is not true in all regions.

Table 14.5 presents debt-to-equity ratios for the largest REOCs, ranked by lowest leverage (gearing) to highest. In Hong Kong debt-to-equity ratios are low. Singapore and China-focused REOCs have moderate leverage, while Canadian, European, and Japanese REOCs have the highest leverage. REOCs such as Forest City, where leverage at more than 200 percent is higher than at U.S. REIT counterparts, makes this "largest" list. U.S. REIT leverage is typically at 100 percent, or an equal proportion of debt and equity. In summary, REOCs can take on more leverage but they do not always do so.

Table 14.5 **Debt-to-Equity Levels of Largest REOCs ($000)**

Company Name	*Country*	*Debt*	*Equity*	*Debt-to-Equity (%)*
Hysan Development	Hong Kong	766,502	7,798,808	10
Sino Land Company Limited	Hong Kong	1,287,947	11,654,057	11
Cheung Kong Holdings Limited	Hong Kong	6,205,682	44,317,103	14
Swire Properties Limited	Hong Kong	4,026,810	24,933,684	16
Hong Kong Land Holdings Limited	Hong Kong	4,255,500	26,184,400	16
Sun Hung Kai Properties Limited	Hong Kong	9,187,552	45,245,333	20
Swire Pacific Limited	Hong Kong	6,585,772	32,168,808	20
Henderson Land Development	Hong Kong	6,159,751	27,081,205	23
MTR Corporation Limited	Hong Kong	4,441,348	18,640,656	24
Hang Lung Properties Limited	Hong Kong	3,836,507	15,995,510	24
Wharf (Holdings) Limited	Hong Kong	9,601,590	33,145,740	29

continued

Table 14.5 **continued**

Company Name	*Country*	*Debt*	*Equity*	*Debt-to-Equity (%)*
Hang Lung Group Limited	Hong Kong	4,856,918	16,722,790	29
Kerry Properties Limited	Hong Kong	4,197,626	10,883,248	39
City Developments Limited	Singapore	3,776,070	7,577,812	50
Global Logistic Properties Limited	Singapore	4,175,896	8,308,227	50
New World Development	Hong Kong	11,436,598	20,374,471	56
China Overseas Land and Investment	Hong Kong/ China	7,691,314	11,296,506	68
China Resources Land Limited	Hong Kong/ China	6,825,466	9,869,921	69
CapitaLand Limited	Singapore	11,607,546	15,916,654	73
Brookfield Office Properties Inc.	Canada	11,763,000	12,964,000	91
IMMOFINANZ Group	Europe	7,112,136	7,345,697	97
Mitsubishi Estate Co., Ltd.	Japan	20,760,874	15,276,795	136
Mitsui Fudosan Company Limited	Japan	21,184,252	13,108,187	162

Note: This table shows that although REOCs do not have any specific leverage limits, many choose to maintain very low leverage levels. The Hong Kong companies, in particular, have very low debt-to-equity levels.

Source: SNL Financial (2013).

DIVIDEND YIELDS

The next issue is dividends. Figure 14.2 compares REOC and REIT dividend yields for the three broad regions of the universe: Asia, Europe, and North America (i.e., the United States and Canada). Due to their minimum distribution requirement and cash flow-oriented business models, REITs have historically offered higher dividend yields than REOCs. This yield advantage is more pronounced in Europe, given the number of smaller REITs that have high yields. Given the current sour tone in the European property markets, these yields are at risk of being reduced.

LIQUIDITY

Stocks with higher equity market capitalizations enjoy liquidity, which leads to greater equity prices. Given the presence of many small- to mid-cap stocks in the REOC/REIT universe, liquidity has become a popular research topic in recent years. Niskanen, Rouhento, and Falkenbach (2011) and Niskanen and Falkenbach (2012) compare the liquidity of

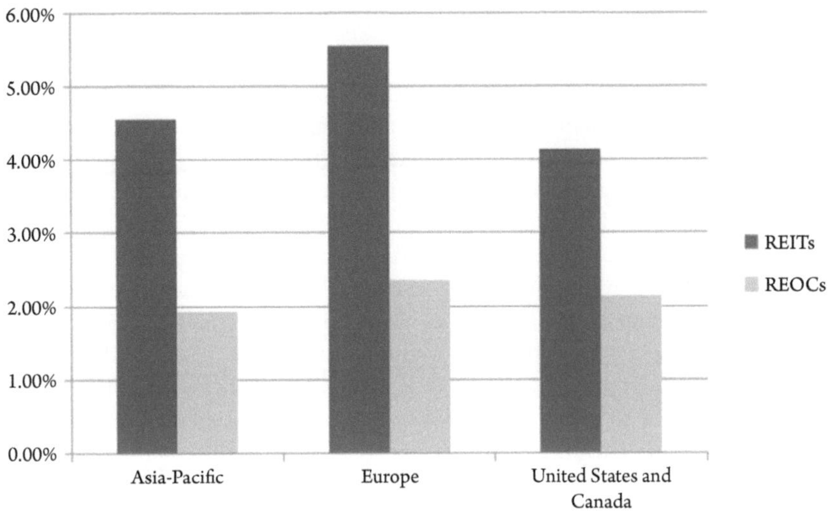

Figure 14.2 Dividend Yield of REITs and REOCs. This figure shows that REITS have higher dividend yields that their REOC counterparts. This is mainly due to REIT payout requirements.

European REITs and REOCs. They find that REITs are significantly more liquid than REOCs. The increased liquidity is likely because of restrictions on concentrated ownership in REITs, including the five-or-fifty (5/50) rule. In the United States, a private REIT needs to have at least 100 unrelated holders. Furthermore, pursuant to the "5/50 rule" no more than 50 percent of the ownership of a REIT may be held by five or fewer individuals, which as defined in the Tax Code to include certain tax-exempt entities.

Brounen, Eichholtz, and Ling (2009) document market capitalization, retail share ownership, and dividend yield as drivers of liquidity across markets. The larger, more yield-focused stocks including REITs with higher market capitalization enjoy greater liquidity. Retail share ownership varies stock-to-stock and country-to-country, and does not necessarily favor REITs over REOCs. Liquidity is more closely tied to free float than total equity. Higher levels of free float, which REITs have, naturally lead to higher levels of liquidity. By comparison, lower free float is a characteristic of REOCs. Greater block ownership for REOCs makes them less preferred to investors, all else equal. *Free float* is the percentage of outstanding equity not held by insiders and can be freely traded on the open market. Because REOCs generally have higher levels of insider ownership, they have lower free float than REITs.

Block (2011) compares the capitalization and free float capitalization of REOCs and REITs. At the end of the fourth quarter of 2010, REOCs had a market capitalization of $1.02 trillion compared to $0.68 trillion for REITs. The free-float capitalization of REOCs was $0.58 trillion, or 57 percent of the market value of equity. For REITs, the free-float capitalization was $0.61 trillion or an 89 percent ratio. This difference helps explain Brounen and de Koning (2012) and Niskanen and Falkenbach (2012) for Europe. Because North America and Asia have similar REOC and REIT structures, the results are also likely to apply in these regions.

Impact on Firm Value

Recent headlines suggest that REOC-to-REIT conversions can be very profitable for shareholders given the evidence of stock price jumps upon announcement of such a conversion. A prominent REOC-to-REIT conversion is that of American Tower (AMT) in 2011. AMT is the leading owner of mobile-communication transmission towers, which moved to become a REIT soon after exhausting its tax-loss assets (Santoli 2012). Upon conversion, American Tower became the second-largest publicly traded U.S. REIT. The stock gained 14.7 percent during the second half of 2011 after it started the conversion process, outperforming the market. Ryman Hospitality Properties announced its REIT conversion plan in 2012. From the time of announcement to approval by its shareholders, the stock price increased 12 percent (Lee 2009). The stock price of Equinix nearly doubled during 2012 as the equity analyst community predicted that a REIT conversion was in the offing (Faughnder 2012).

Many property companies elect to be REOCs. The question, considering the REIT's tax benefits, is why. Apparently, certain costs prevent some firms from adopting this organizational form (Chan et al. 2003). Gyourko and Sinai (1999) assess these trade-offs between tax benefits and costs of external fundraising for U.S. REITs. They conducted their study at a time when the REIT structure had come under increasing scrutiny given the depressed state of the real estate equity and debt markets. Three factors—two positive and one negative—drive the cost-benefit trade-off of electing REIT status relative to a REOC.

The first and most obvious benefit of the REIT structure is the tax shield provided against corporate income tax. The value of this benefit is complicated by REITs having to pay out higher dividends to its shareholders. In the United States, REIT dividend tax rates are higher than the capital gains tax rates. In 2013, the highest federal capital gains and dividend tax rate was 20 percent. REIT dividends are taxed as ordinary income with a highest federal tax rate of 39.6 percent. The maximum corporate income tax rate is 35 percent, although depreciation and interest shields are available. A REOC has a double tax rate of 55 percent. The REOC has flexibility to reduce its corporate tax rate and state taxation reduces the differential. Nevertheless, a major tax benefit remains.

The second positive factor where REITs offer an advantage over the REOC structure is from the transaction cost savings from not having to engage in intense tax minimizing strategies used by taxable firms. Companies converting to REIT status often cite this benefit. For example, Gaylord Entertainment (2012), when announcing its name change and conversion, referred to the leaner and more efficient cost structure associated with a REIT.

The third factor is a disadvantage for REITs and therefore favors REOCs. The primary cost of the REIT structure results from having to raise external capital. If REITs could retain earnings like REOCs, this would reduce the need to raise equity and debt in public and private capital markets. The net benefits of the REIT conversion structure are between 2 and 5 percent of industry equity market capitalization. The benefits are larger for firms with lower payout ratios. Firms achieve the high estimate of 5 percent when the share of tax-exempt and deferred investment in REITs increases to 40 percent, the fraction occurring in the broader equity market. Tax-exempt investors enjoy the value that is created by lower corporate tax rates, while facing no taxation on dividends.

Nadauld (2010) examines agency issues and the choice of organizational form for real estate securities. This study extends the issue of the REOC versus REIT choice almost another decade beyond Gyourko and Sinai (1999) and covers international real estate securities. Investors value international REITs at a discount to REOCs from 1992 to 2006 before the global financial crisis, a result opposite to what might be expected.

REIT valuation does not have any statistical association with measures of home-country investor protection. REITs and REOCs exhibit statistically similar returns. The valuation of international REOCs versus REITs involves corporate governance. Environments that foster increased protection for minority shareholders have higher firm valuations. REITs have an advantage over REOCs in this regard. The agency costs of dominating controlling shareholders lead to lower valuations for REOCs.

Surprisingly, Nadauld (2010) finds that the market valued REITs at a discount to REOCs during the 1992 to 2006 time frame. One explanation is that inferior properties go into a REIT. Managers are less likely to adopt REIT status if they have more valuable properties. Firms are less likely to become a REIT when a high level of inside ownership exists. Another explanation is that REITs were considered more risky. The lower the Tobin's Q, the higher is the likelihood that a company will become a REIT. The ratio Tobin's Q is calculated by dividing the market value of a company by the replacement value of the book equity. Equivalently, REITs have higher book-to-market ratios and are more risky value stocks relative to REOCs. Note that after the financial crisis, many of these international REIT discounts reduced or reversed.

Studwell (2007) documents the reasons behind the reputational challenges of REITs in Hong Kong. Governance issues affect the REITs brand in the marketplace and help explain valuation discounts at certain times in the region. The observations are REIT listings that began in Southeast Asia in 2005 subsequent to the formation of K. S. Li's Prosperity REIT. According to Studwell (2007, 172), "The game here was for tycoons to sell low-grade property assets into new corporate entities, back-load the debt repayments of the purchaser and list them with the story that dividends in year one would be a guide to future earnings." This low-grade asset and financial engineering blueprint led to copycat listings that followed a similar path in the market. The stocks would spike upon an initial public offering and steadily decline as investors realized what they had bought. The market is now less tolerant of these types of listings, but some investors still recall these events. This partly explains the discounts to NAV. Selecting the REOC or REIT form remains a highly individualistic process. The selection depends on company variances in ownership structure, tax loss status, market environment, and the REIT regime.

REOC Valuation

REOCs differ from REITs in various ways. With a higher focus on growth versus income, fewer restrictions on leverage, and greater retained earnings, the valuation approach of REOCs must differ from that for REITs. Further complicating matters is the global nature of the REOC universe, where valuation drivers and methodologies differ widely. This section suggests a general approach to valuing REOCs and provides details on geographic differences.

REOC valuation approaches include equity market price versus private market value (price to NAV), DCF, cash flow multiples, and implied cap rate. A main valuation metric is NAV, which determines the underlying value of the holdings of a REOC. In the DCF valuation, free cash flow is discounted by an appropriate discount rate. The result is the present value of free cash flows. Another approach is to apply a cash flow multiple. Analysts use funds from operations (FFO) or adjusted FFO (AFFO) forecasts to arrive at an intrinsic value for the firm's current performance. This approach is appropriate for a REOC with high levels of income-producing property. Analysts also use forward dividend yields or dividend discount models (DDM) for REOCs with high proportions of income-producing properties.

While real estate fundamentals are the key drivers of REOC share prices,the various markets focus on some different drivers. Bank of America Merrill Lynch (2013) lists the following value drivers for the Asia property stocks.

- *Japan.* Vacancy rates in Tokyo's five central wards are a key driver for the sector. Others include real estate transaction activity, bank lending to the real estate sector, and foreign exchange rates through yen depreciation.
- *Hong Kong.* Key drivers of REOC shares are macro growth, interest and exchange rates, government policies, sales at property development projects, operating performance and earnings, and rentals.
- *China.* Key drivers are housing policy and monthly contracted sales performance.
- *Singapore.* REOCs in Singapore trade in tandem with the residential market. Residential transaction volumes pricing trends appear to be the strongest drivers. As the sector's exposure to China has increased, the stock performance is correlated with the performance of China developers.
- *Australia.* Apart from the performance of the underlying property markets, drivers include interest rates, economic growth, and sentiment.

REOCs in the Market Environment

How do REOCs perform in the market environment? Delcoure and Dickens (2004) conclude that REOCs, with their higher agency costs, have higher betas than REITs. REOC systematic risk is sensitive to financial leverage. REOCs have a higher capacity for leverage, greater retained earnings, and a lower dividend payout ratio relative to REITs. Analysts expect REOCs to perform more like growth than value stocks and view REITs as the latter. REOCs are expected to have higher levels of systematic risk (beta) along with higher volatility. REOCs perform better than REITs in an up market and underperform in a down market. This section explores the validity of these theories.

PERFORMANCE IN BULL AND BEAR MARKETS

The years in the stock market leading up to the financial crisis provide an opportunity to explore how REOCs perform relative to REITs and other asset classes in a variety of market environments. Five distinct bull and bear markets occurred between 2006 and

2013. FTSE has created separate indexes for global REOC and REIT shares (Simontacchi and Stoschek 2011), and data for both go back to March 31, 2006.

- *Phase 1.* From March 31, 2006, through February 2007, a major bull market occurred.
- *Phase 2.* From February 2007 to March 2009, global real estate securities peaked and subsequently fell dramatically during the financial crisis. In this bear market, the market lost 70 percent of its value.
- *Phase 3.* From March 2009 through July 2011, the market enjoyed a major rebound. Global real estate securities rose more than 100 percent.
- *Phase 4.* From late July 2011 to early October 2011, a brief bear retrenchment occurred.
- *Phase 5.* From October 2011 to the first quarter of 2013, the market experienced a notable upswing, mostly driven by very loose monetary policy around the globe. Since its bottom in October 2011 to March 31, 2013, the global real estate securities market was up more than 50 percent.

Table 14.6 shows how global REOCs and REITs performed relative to each other from 2006 to 2013. In the first phase, REOCs outperformed REITs in a strong market for stocks and real estate. In the second phase during the global financial crisis REOCs did not underperform REITs. Global REOCs and REITs fell by equal amounts, about 70 percent. Also surprising were the performance results in the wake of the global financial crisis. In the two-year-plus bull market that followed the debt crisis, global REITs outperformed dramatically. The lower dividend, growth-oriented stocks might be expected to outperform over that time, but they did not. These results are consistent with REITs being more risky value stocks and REOCs relatively less risky growth ones. In the most recent phase growth outperforms value, consistent with the overall market. During phase 4, the brief correction around the U.S. credit rating downgrade by Standard & Poor's in summer 2011, REOCs were down 28 percent while REITs decreased only 20 percent. In the bull market run that followed, REOCs outperformed REITs on a total return basis by about 13 percent. Overall, REOCs and REITs posted very similar returns of 4.07 percent and 3.26 percent, respectively, between 2006 and 2013.

Other potential explanations help to clarify the results. REOC and REIT indexes differ not only in the companies' organizational structure but also in geography. Because Japan is such a large property market and has a high percentage of REOCs, it represents more than 40 percent of the REOC index. Its country weight is far less than 10 percent in the global REIT index. The performance of the yen and Japanese equity markets strongly influence the REOC index performance. Controlling for these variables is appropriate.

Table 14.7 compares REITs and REOCs during the five phases, focusing on the Japanese market. Controls are included for currency and capital markets. The table compares average returns of the largest three Japan REOCs and REITs over nearly identical timeframes. The only difference is the availability of more data because the first phase extends backwards to June 30, 2005. The backward expansion allows another nine months of bull market data.

Table 14.6 **Global REOCs versus REITs: March 31, 2006 to March 31, 2013**

Phase	*Dates*	*Months*	*Type*	*Description*	*Total Return*		*REOC*
					REOC (%)	*REIT (%)*	*Premium (%)*
1	March 31, 2006 to February 23, 2007	11	Bull	Pre-GFC run up	45.3	34.7	10.7
2	February 23, 2007 to March 9, 2009	25	Bear	Global financial crisis	−69.8	−72.4	2.6
3	March 9, 2009 to July 26, 2011	28	Bull	Post GFC upswing	144.6	198.6	−54.1
4	July 26, 2011 to October 4, 2011	2	Bear	Correction	−27.5	−19.5	−8.0
5	October 4, 2011 to March 31, 2013	18	Bull	Bull market	61.0	48.1	12.8
Annualized return					4.07	3.26	0.8

Note: This table shows that on a global basis, the REOC market did not always perform as expected relative to REITs over various bull and bear markets. Table 14.7 shows that after controlling for geography, the results are much more intuitive.

Source: Bloomberg LLC (2013).

Table 14.7 **Big Three Japan REOCs versus Big Three JREITs: March 31, 2006 to March 31, 2013**

Phase	*Dates*	*Months*	*Type*	*Description*	*REOC (%)*	*REIT (%)*	*Premium (%)*
1	June 30, 2005 to February 23, 2007	20	Bull	Pre-GFC run up	247.6	67.9	179.7
2	February 23, 2007 to March 9, 2009	25	Bear	Global financial crisis	−79.0	−60.9	−18.1
3	March 9, 2009 to July 26, 2011	28	Bull	Post GFC upswing	93.7	40.4	53.3
4	July 26, 2011 to October 4, 2011	2	Bear	Correction	−17.3	3.9	−21.2
5	October 4, 2011 to March 31, 2013	18	Bull	Bull market	127.6	85.4	42.2

Note: This table shows that when isolating the REOC and REIT markets to one country, the results become more intuitive. The higher-beta REOCs perform better in "up" markets, while the lower-beta REITs perform better in "down" markets.

Source: Bloomberg (2013).

After controlling for currency and capital markets the findings are consistent with Japanese REOCs having higher levels of systematic risk. Japanese REOCs outperform in up markets and underperform in down markets.

RISK AND RETURN PERFORMANCE

Volatility is expected to be higher with REOCs. The volatility results as of March 2013 suggest that global REOCs are more volatile than REITs. The rolling 36-month annual standard deviation of returns is 23.5 percent for global REOCs and 14.6 percent for the global REITs (FTSE EPRA/NAREIT 2013).

Table 14.8 summarizes correlations of REOCs and REITs with other securities. Global bonds performance is the JPM Global Aggregate Bond Index and equities is the MSCI Daily TR World Index. The performance covers the first quarter of 2010 to that of 2013. The results show that over that relatively short time frame, both REOCs and REITs are highly correlated at 78 percent and 89 percent, respectively, with global equities. This evidence suggests that as the index is constructed, these baskets of stocks provide some diversification relative to a pure global equities portfolio. However, the high correlations between traded securities including real estate temper this conclusion.

Table 14.8 **Correlations: Global REOCs, REITs, Bonds, and Equities**

Index	*FTSE/EPRA NAREIT Developed Non-REITs*	*FTSE/EPRA NAREIT Developed REITs*	*JPM Global Aggregate Bond Index*	*MSCI Daily TR World Index*
FTSE/EPRA NAREIT Developed Non-REITs	1.00	0.71	0.25	0.78
FTSE/EPRA NAREIT Developed REITs	0.71	1.00	0.21	0.89
JPM Global Aggregate Bond Index	0.25	0.21	1.00	0.16
MSCI Daily TR World Index	0.78	0.89	0.16	1.00

Note: This table shows that REOCs and REITs have a correlation coefficient of 0.71, which is lower than each of the markets' correlation to the global equity market (MSCI World Index). Both REITs and REOCs have a fairly low correlation to global bonds.

Source: Bloomberg (2013).

Lee (2009) provides evidence that the correlations of real estate stocks with equities fall over longer periods. Real estate stocks eventually perform more like private real estate than stocks or bonds.

Both global REOCs and global REITs have a very low correlation with global bonds. The 2010–2013 correlations are 25 percent and 20 percent, respectively. The correlation between global REOCs and REITs is 71 percent. Although this is high, the correlation could be higher by controlling the indexes for geographical differences.

Summary and Conclusions

Listed real estate companies can choose to be REOCs or REITs. Although not legally defined, a REOC is a listed company that specializes in real estate and has not or cannot elect REIT status. REIT rules have become more accommodative, but REOCs still retain advantages over REITs. These advantages include benefits of using debt, growth potential, market timing, fewer restrictions on the investor base, more permissible activities, and flexibility in times of distress. By contrast, REITs receive favorable tax treatment. They pay no corporate income tax, but they are restricted from holding retained earnings and must make dividend payouts taxed at higher ordinary rates in the United States.

The REOC market is extensive. Equity free float is at least $400 billion at the end of the first quarter of 2013. REOCs generally have lower dividend levels in all parts of the world. Although they have fewer leverage restrictions than REITs, REOCs are not always more highly levered. For example, Hong Kong REOCs have very low leverage levels. As for liquidity, given the lack of restrictions such as the five-or-fifty rule, REOCs have higher levels of insider ownership and lower levels of free float. All else equal, REOCs are less liquid.

Converting from a REOC to REIT in the United States increases equity market capitalization by 2 to 4 percent. This percentage increases in countries having a high level of tax-exempt ownership. Outside of the United States, the impact of the REIT structure on firm value is less clear. Until the financial crisis, REITs traded at a discount to REOCs. This might be explained by lower quality assets put into REITs by their REOC sponsors. The most common measures to value REOCs are NAV, DCF, and cash flow multiples. In the market environment, after controlling for currency and capital markets, REOCs have higher systematic risk and volatility. They outperform REITs in up markets and underperform in down markets. From a diversification perspective, given the similarities in assets, REOCs and REITs perform about the same in a multi-asset class portfolio. Finally, over a market cycle, REOCs and REITs provide roughly similar returns.

Discussion Questions

1. Define a REOC.
2. Identify and discuss the key structural differences between a REOC and a REIT.
3. List the main advantages and disadvantages of choosing the REOC form.
4. How do firms choose between the two organizational forms—REOC or REIT?
5. Identify and discuss the key valuation metrics for REOCs.
6. Explain how REOCs perform in the market environment.

References

Adornato, Paul E., and Richard C. Anderson. 2009. *REIT Dividends: Serious Soul-Searching Ahead!* New York: BMO Capital Markets Corp.

Bank of America Merrill Lynch. 2013. *Pan Asian Real Estate: A Primer*. New York: Bank of America Merrill Lynch.

Block, Ralph L. 2011. *Investing in REITs: Real Estate Investment Trusts*. New York: Bloomberg Press.

Bloomberg LLC. 2013. http://www.bloomberg.com.

Bloomfield, Micah W., and Mayer Greenberg. 2011. *REITs: Overview*. New York: Thomson Reuters Practical Law Company, Inc.

Brounen, Dirk, and Sjoerd de Koning. 2012. "50 Years of Real Estate Investment Trusts: An International Examination of the Rise and Performance of REITs." *Journal of Real Estate Literature* 20:2, 197–223.

Brounen, Dirk, Piet Eichholtz, and David Ling. 2009. "The Liquidity of Property Shares: An International Comparison." *Real Estate Economics* 37:3, 413–445.

Case, Bradford, William G. Hardin, III, and Zhonghua Wu. 2012. "REIT Dividend Policies and Dividend Announcement Effects during the 2008–2009 Liquidity Crisis." *Real Estate Economics* 40:3, 387–421.

Chan, Su Han, John Erickson, and Ko Wang. 2003. *Real Estate Investment Trusts: Structure, Performance, and Investment Opportunities*. New York: Oxford University Press.

Clark, Simon, Tim Hackemann, Olivier Mesmin, Matthias Roche, and Tom Road. 2009. "Progress on REIT Regimes in Europe." In Graeme Newell and Karen Sieracki, eds., *Global Trends in Real Estate Finance*, 34–45. New York: Blackwell Publishing.

Cohen & Steers. 2013. *Introduction to Real Estate Securities*. New York: Cohen & Steers, Inc. http://www.cohenandsteers.com/insights/read/introduction-to-real-estate-securities.

Damodaran, Aswath, Kose John, and Crocker H. Liu. 1997. "The Determinants of Organization Form Changes: Evidence and Implications from Real Estate." *Journal of Financial Economics* 45:1, 169–192.

Delcoure, Natalya, and Ross Norman Dickens. 2004. "REIT and REOC Systematic Risk Sensitivity." *Journal of Real Estate Research* 26:3, 237–254.

Evans, Denise L., and O. William Evans. 2007. *The Complete Real Estate Encyclopedia*. New York: McGraw-Hill Companies, Inc.

Faughnder, Ryan. 2012. "Equinix Jumps after Board Approves Conversion to REIT." September 13. http://www.bloomberg.com.

Friedman, Jack P., Jack C. Harris, and Barry A. Diskin. 2009. *Real Estate Handbook*. Hauppauge, NY: Barron's Educational Series, Inc.

FTSE. 2013. *Ground Rules for the Management of the FTSE EPRA/NAREIT Global Real Estate Index Series Version 5.3*. http://www.ftse.com/Indices.

FTSE EPRA/NAREIT. 2013. *Global Real Estate Index Series–Monthly Statistical Bulletin*. http://www.ftse.com/Indices.

Gaylord Entertainment. 2012. *Gaylord Entertainment Announces Organizational Structure of Newly Created Ryman Hospitality Properties, Inc.* Press Release. http://www.gaylord.com.

Graham, John R. 2000. "How Big Are the Tax Benefits of Debt?" *Journal of Finance* 55:5, 1901–1941.

Gyourko, Joseph, and Todd Sinai. 1999. "The REIT Vehicle: Its Value Today and in the Future." *Journal of Real Estate Research* 18:2, 355–375.

Hines, Mary Alice. 2001. *Investing in International Real Estate*. Westport, CT: Quorum Books.

Hoesli, Martin, and Elias Oikarinen. 2012. "Are REITs Real Estate? Evidence from International Sector Level Data." *Journal of International Money and Finance* 31:7, 1823–1850.

Hudson-Wilson, Susan, Frank J. Fabozzi, and Jacques N. Gordon. 2003. "Why Real Estate? An Expanding Role for Institutional Investors." *Journal of Portfolio Management* 29:5, 12–25.

Juge, Elizabeth. 2011. "2010 REIT Cash, Stock Dividends." *SNL Data Dispatch*. Charlottesville, CA: SNL.

Lee, Ming-Long, Kevin C. H. Chiang, and Chia-Wei Lin. 2012. "REIT Stock Dividends: The Policy and Intra–Industry Wealth Effects." *Journal of Property Investment and Finance* 30:6, 563–582.

Linneman, Peter. 2011. *Real Estate Finance and Investments*. 3rd edn. Philadelphia: Linneman Associates.

Nadauld, Taylor D. 2010. "Essays in Real Estate Finance." PhD dissertation. Department of Finance, School of Business, Ohio State University.

Niskanen, Jaakko, and Heidi Falkenbach. 2010. "REITs and Correlations with Other Asset Classes: A European Perspective." *Journal of Real Estate Portfolio Management* 16:3, 227–239.

Niskanen, Jaakko, and Heidi Falkenbach. 2012. "Liquidity of European Real Estate Equities: REITs and REOCs." *International Journal of Strategic Property Management* 16:2, 173–187.

Niskanen, Jaakko, and Heidi Falkenbach. 2013. "European Listed Real Estate: The Capital Structure Perspective." *Nordic Journal of Surveying and Real Estate Research* 9:1, 76–97.

Niskanen, Jaakko, Jussi Rouhento, and Heidi Falkenbach. 2011. "European Real Estate Equities: Ownership Structure and Value of the Firm." *Journal of European Real Estate Research* 3:2, 131–143.

Santoli, Michael. 2012. "Changing Their Stripes." *Barron's*, May 19. http://online.barrons.com/article/SB50001424053111904571704577406161684395748.html.

Schäfers, Wolfgang, and Kai-Magnus Schulte. 2012. "REOCs and REITs." In Tobias Just and Wolfgang Maennig, eds., *Understanding German Real Estate Markets*, 331–348. Berlin and Heidelberg: Springer Verlag.

Simontacchi, Stefano, and Uwe Stoschek. 2011. *Guide to Global Real Estate Investment Trusts*. Amsterdam: Kluwer Law International.

SNL Financial. 2013. http://www.snl.com.

Lee, Stephen. 2009. "The Big Picture." *IPE Real Estate Magazine*, January/February: 26–27.

Studwell, Joe. 2007. *Asian Godfathers: Money and Power in Hong Kong and South East Asia*. New York: Profile Books.

UBS. 2013. *Global Real Estate Analyzer and 2013 Outlook*. Hong Kong: UBS Securities Asia Limited.

Answers to Discussion Questions

Chapter 2 Diversification Benefits of Real Estate

1. Discuss how the diversification benefits of real estate relative to other asset classes have changed over time.

   From a DCC-GARCH model of time variation, during the 1990s the correlation between listed equity real estate and stocks declined from 0.69 to 0.30, indicating that the diversification benefits of real estate increased sharply. From October 2001, when the S&P 500 and other broad market indexes first included REITs, to the onset of the 2008–2009 liquidity crisis, the correlation between real estate and stocks increased to 0.59. During the crisis and its aftermath the correlation spiked to as high as 0.79.

   A Markov regime switching model, however, suggests that correlations can be viewed as shifting among four different regimes: (1) a "normal" state with a REIT-stock correlation of 0.65; (2) a "REIT premium" state with a REIT-stock correlation of 0.48; (3) a "dream" state with a low REIT-stock correlation of 0.28; and (4) a "nightmare" state with a REIT-stock correlation of 0.81.

   Diversification benefits depend not only on correlations but also on relative risk-adjusted returns as measured by the Sharpe ratio. Listed equity real estate in the United States has historically provided risk-adjusted returns to provide diversification benefits even during periods of relatively high correlation with other assets.
2. What effect does the investor's horizon have on the diversification benefits of real estate?

   Correlations are typically measured using monthly returns primarily because such data are available for many assets over long historical periods. Yet, return characteristics based on one-month returns are inappropriate for investors with longer horizons. Within the stock market, correlations over longer investment horizons are higher than over one-month horizons, implying that long-horizon investors benefit less from sector diversification. The REIT-stock correlation, however, declines over longer horizons with a downward-sloping term structure of correlations. Diversification benefits of real estate are stronger for investors with longer investment horizons than monthly returns data indicate. Factors driving share prices in other parts of the stock market may affect short-term REIT returns. Yet, the real estate market cycle, not the stock market cycle, drives long-term REIT returns.

3. What problems arise when evaluating the benefits of diversifying between public and private real estate, and what conclusions can be drawn?

   Because properties are illiquid and heterogeneous, returns to private real estate investments are extraordinarily difficult to measure. Even when returns are measured using actual market prices from property transactions, return measurements suffer from two deficiencies. The first is *illiquidity lag* because at least two quarters are needed before information that affects property values can be revealed in completed transactions. The second is the smoothing of *aggregation bias*, because transactions must be aggregated over relatively long periods in order to have enough data to estimate returns. More commonly, returns are measured using appraised values. In this case, return measurements suffer from two added deficiencies. The first is *stale data* because two additional quarters are needed before information revealed by completed transactions becomes incorporated into appraisals. The second encompasses *appraisal smoothing*. Appraisers suffer from the behavioral bias known as *anchoring* or the tendency to place undue weight on previous values rather than on new information and *sample selection* because most properties are not appraised during a given quarter.

   The effects of stale data, appraisal smoothing, and selection reduce the measured but not the true volatility of private real estate, which appears to offer greater diversification benefits than it really does. No reason exists to believe that the true volatility of private real estate should be less than the volatility of public real estate. The effects of illiquidity lag and stale data are to generate a measured but not a true *temporal diversification* benefit, which arises because real estate returns have a low correlation with their own values lagged by two or four quarters.

4. Identify the benefits of diversifying among different real estate investment strategies.

   The measured benefits from diversifying between the core, value-added, and opportunistic real estate investment strategies are very slight. This is probably because return measurement problems are common to all three private real estate strategies and correlated across them. Decomposing the total returns of each strategy into income and capital appreciation components suggests differences between the core and opportunistic strategies but not between core and value-added strategies. Moreover, the correlations between income-only and appreciation-only returns are lower than the correlations among total returns. Thus, there may be benefits to diversifying by investment strategy although such benefits appear weak in existing return measurements.

5. Discuss whether diversification between property types, internationally or geographically provides greater benefits.

   Return correlations among geographic regions of the U.S. real estate market are relatively high, suggesting only slight benefits of within-country regional diversification. Property markets may be segmented into other geographic areas, such as central business district versus suburban office markets, but reliable data are unavailable. Existing studies suggest that property type diversification is much more beneficial than in-country geographic diversification. International diversification seems to offer very low return correlations, and therefore very substantial diversification opportunities. Risk-adjusted returns are different across countries. As a result, only two countries and one region (Asia) offer diversification benefits to a U.S. real estate portfolio.

Chapter 3 International Real Estate Markets

1. Provide the arguments for and against investing in international real estate.

   International real estate investment is any portfolio or strategy that includes real estate from different countries. Geographic diversification can reduce country-specific risk. However, investors need to balance this benefit against various costs, notably currency risks, unstable correlations between markets, and institutional constraints including laws and taxes that undermine real estate performance and liquidity.
2. Discuss the validity of the statement "international real estate investment requires skills in both real estate and foreign exchange markets"?

   The statement is true if the foreign exchange market is volatile and currency risk is not or cannot be hedged. For instance, during the period 2007–2012, the yen appreciated by 50.2 percent against the dollar. From the perspective of U.S. investors, even though the average real estate return in Japan was almost zero, the dollar return would be 9 percent annually. In contrast, the pound dropped against the dollar by 19 percent during the same period, which made the U.K.'s real estate return less attractive from U.S. investors' perspective. These examples reinforce the importance of managing currency risk in international real estate investment.
3. Based on the 17 countries and cities examined in this chapter, discuss whether their domestic (DRE) and international (IRE) real estate markets deliver similar performance in terms of average returns, volatilities, and correlations.

   DRE and IRE markets do not have similar average returns and volatilities. During 2007–2012, most DRE markets show positive returns in local currency but most IRE markets have negative returns in U.S. dollars. The return differences are as high as 31.6 percent. The volatility of most IRE markets fall within a range of 20 to 40 percent as an annual standard deviation, which is substantially higher than that of the DRE markets. However, correlations reflect greater consistency. A majority of the countries and cities show positive correlations between their DRE and IRE returns. Only five pairs of DRE and IRE markets exhibit negative correlations.
4. Identify the institutional barriers to investing in foreign real estate markets.

   Institutional barriers can come in two forms: tangible and intangible. Tangible barriers refer to explicit trading costs such as capital gain taxes, stamp duties, agency commissions, and legal charges that international investors have to pay when trading occurs. Intangible barriers include the system of property rights, accounting and reporting standards, access to mortgage loans, information transparency, market characteristics, and regulation or policy on real estate ownership and REIT investment. Because tangible and intangible barriers can vary substantially, international investors should take them into account in assessing the risk-return characteristics of a foreign real estate market.

Chapter 4 Strategy: Seeking Alpha Opportunities and Managing Risks in Global Markets

1. Discuss whether real estate investing strategy is simple or complex.

   Although real estate investing strategy may seem to be easy, simple, and straightforward, investing in real estate is complex, daunting, and nuanced, involving numerous strategy questions. To realize superior risk-adjusted returns or alpha, investors must be very skilled and pursue strategies that diverge from the market norms. Alpha-seeking property investing strategies may embrace more active rather than passive styles plus investing in different places. Such initiatives are characterized more by complexity than simplicity. Because pursuing opportunities in search of alpha returns involves more risk, the resulting strategies necessarily are more complex than simple.
2. Explain why investors should consider investing outside of their home country.

   Increasingly investors are either explicitly or implicitly global in their investing outlook. The global rationale is both offensive and defensive. The offensive objective of global property investing is that extraordinary opportunities exist beyond one's hometown and native country. If investors do not venture beyond their local territory, they will miss out on extraordinarily rewarding property investing involvements. The defensive motivation for global property investing is the consideration that when domestic property involvements are in a downward phase of the cycle, properties in other places may be performing more positively. By investing globally, investors achieve the diversification benefit of reduced volatility in their overall performance in ways that could not be obtained locally.
3. Identify the major challenges to investing in real estate on a global basis.

   As daunting as real estate investing can be to implement in a place in which investors are familiar, it is made much more difficult in places unfamiliar to these investors. Consequently, effective real estate investing must be strategic in its approach. Because of the rapid change in real estate markets and the financing process, what was good enough in the past may not be good enough in the future.

   Given the accelerating pace of change, few individuals, companies, and investing programs are as adaptable today as they will need to be in the future. Investors, especially those with real estate involvements, face the challenge to adapt and adopt new strategies. This means the emphasis must be on recognizing change, its implications for traditional practices determining what may be threatened, identifying opportunities for differentiation, and developing innovative approaches. The adaptability style with its resilient, innovative, and reinventive attributes is more often alien than familiar to the character of property involvement.

   Viewing real estate as the platform or stage on which life and the culture of a place are lived and experienced is essential to effective investments. Even though not readily associated with real estate investing, understanding the culture of those who would procure, purchase or transacts is a precondition to effective property involvement. If investors do not understand the culture and integrate that understanding into their investing, they may not profitably and effectively realize desired rewards of the property involvement.

4. Discuss how market structure and relative market efficiency influence investing strategy.

   The less efficient nature of real estate markets leads to greater rewards for superior expertise and to greater adverse consequences for miscalculation. In an inefficient market, superior competence and expertise are more rewarded, while miscalculations are more severely penalized. Thus, the greater the market inefficiency, the greater is the reward for expertise and the greater the penalty for miscalculation.

   The character, maturity, and efficiency of real estate markets are defined by the relative levels of such influential factors as:

   - Transparency and accountability
   - Quality and availability of information
   - Competency, tools, and resources of professional services providers specializing in assisting and representing tenants
   - Capital markets functions and maturity
   - Occupiers' managerial sophistication and prioritization of the corporate real estate function
   - Level and quality of scholarly and commercial research
   - Academic societies' providing forums for the creation and dissemination of knowledge by sponsoring journals publishing scholarly research, and organizing meetings of thought leaders promoting knowledge.

   These factors vary considerably among markets, reflecting the differing character, maturity, and efficiency of those markets. Emerging markets inherently are more inefficient than established markets, so a greater likelihood exists of a transaction occurring at prices that diverge from what knowledgeable, informed, and sophisticated professionals would conclude represent fair value.

5. Identify how investors can access different profit centers through five primary real estate categories of activity.

   Investors access different profit centers through five primary real estate categories of activity:

   - *Investors.* Business properties, residential rental properties, retail and warehouse properties, diversified and other property portfolios, and mortgage portfolios.
   - *Development firms.* Homebuilders, commercial property developers, engineering and construction firms, cement companies, building steel manufacturers and suppliers, building materials suppliers and furniture, fixture and decorations suppliers.
   - *Service firms.* Hospitality related firms, healthcare and senior living services firms, brokers, agents, property managers and other business space service providers, serviced apartment and other residential service providers, property and place related information and software providers.
   - *Property resource firms.* Corporations without a real estate business model, but derive a substantial portion of their firm value from their land holdings. The ideal situation that the land value exceeds the firm value as an operating business, thereby capturing hidden real estate value.
   - *Place strategy firms.* Firms creating substantial value through a strategic use of place and space.

6. Discuss how the level of real estate professionalism of a place influences investing strategy.

   The level of real estate professionalism influences how real estate professionals implement investing strategy and therefore investment performance. Factors leading to and reflecting higher levels of real estate professionalism are education programs, books, professional associations and designations, career guidance and resources, and licensing. The less developed status of real estate professionalism in emerging markets reflects the status of all of these elements. Professional standards mirror the development status of that place: more advanced economies have higher levels of real estate professionalism than in emerging economies. One consequence of real estate professionalism differences is the greater prospect divergent outcomes at the transaction level. Lesser levels of corporate real estate professionalism are conducive to property owners realizing alpha performance. Another consequence is the greater prospect of miscalculation–at both the individual and company level and also by multiple companies. This can result in market dislocation or excess construction leading to surplus supply inventory, in excess of demand, that diminishes the value of all properties in that market.

Chapter 5 Mortgage Markets: The United States

1. What benefits did the housing finance system of the 1990s bring to housing consumers?

   The housing finance system delivered a wide range of choices of mortgage products including the widespread availability of pre-payable 30-year fixed rate mortgages at competitive interest rates. This long-term fixed product benefits consumers because it allows them to refinance if rates fall and insulates them from increasing rates if they rise. The system delivered deep and highly liquid markets for mortgage-backed securities.. This allowed the system to fund tens of millions of small mortgage loans originated through diverse channels to idiosyncratic borrowers and collateral. Nonbanks and global investors looked past these diverse channels and idiosyncratic borrowers and collateral because of explicit and implicit government backing. The system began using statistical scoring models that allowed borrowers to get access to credit that previously would have been denied.
2. What federal laws have had the most impact on the structure, conduct, and performance of the housing system?

   Three types of laws have had a major impact on the housing system. The first type of laws established explicit and federal backstops of the market and the specific institutions that delivered them. These include the Federal Home Loan Banks, Fannie Mae, Freddie Mac, FHA, Ginnie Mae, and VA. These institutions created many of the products, underwriting standards, and forms borrowers encounter when applying for and obtaining loans today. The second type of laws is aimed at protecting consumers, banning discrimination in lending, and encouraging lenders to serve underserved markets. The third type of laws deregulated the financial system and paved the way for excessive risk taking.
3. What factors contributed to excessive mortgage risk-taking in the 2000s?

Factors contributing to excessive mortgage risk-taking in the 2000s included the following:

- Access to the asset backed securities market, which supplied subprime and most Alt-A credit and which federal regulators supervised and regulated much more lightly than deposit-taking institutions.
- Widespread belief that pricing models did not need to take into account a national house price decline.
- Failure to regulate the widespread availability of risky mortgage products underwritten to loose standards and limited documentation.
- Failure to appreciate the degree to which risks were being layered until falling home prices and dismal loan performance exposed the extent of these risks.
- Low capital reserves at Fannie Mae and Freddie Mac and high leverage at investment banks and off-balance sheets special investment vehicles.

A debate exists over the degree to which the Community Reinvestment Act played a role but the weight of evidence suggests it did not play much if any.

4. What debates are likely to shape the future of the U.S. housing finance system?

   The future of the housing finance system is likely to be shaped by:

   - How the federal mortgage market backstops are reformed
   - How regulatory reforms affect credit availability, pricing, and safety and soundness, including consumer protections, capital requirements of issuers, and affirmative obligations to meet underserved needs
   - How mortgage underwriting and pricing are set to withstand economic and housing market stresses
   - How acceptable risk is defined and regulated
   - How much leverage consumers are allowed when mortgage borrowing.

Chapter 6 Mortgage Markets: International

1. Identify a popular indicator to measure the size of a country's mortgage market and its key determinants.

   A widely used indicator for the size of the mortgage market is the ratio of mortgage debt outstanding (MDO) to gross domestic product (GDP). Based on a sample of 27 countries the level of development measured by per capita GDP is a key determinant of the MOD-to-GDP ratio. The income variable explains more than 40 percent of the variation in the MDO-to-GDP ratio, implying that the depth and the width of financial systems are positively correlated with the level of economic development. Other market and institutional factors influence the size of the mortgage market including the composition of the mortgage loan products, tax breaks for mortgage lending, and other government regulations and interventions in the mortgage market.
2. Identify two main funding methods for mortgage lending and discuss the pros and cons of each.

Deposit-based and capital-market-based funding mechanisms are two primary funding methods. In a deposit-based model, banks mobilize funds through short-term deposits, originate loans, service them, and manage risks. This model is called the *originate-to-hold model* because the lenders hold the mortgages until borrowers fully repay the principal and interest. Because the lenders keep the mortgage loans on their balance sheets, they have an incentive to apply caution in assessing loan applications and to modify the terms as required by a fall in house prices. The scope of lending is limited by the ability to raise funds and is subject to interest rate risk from the term structure mismatch between deposits and mortgage loans.

The capital-market-based model consists of a primary market for loan origination and a secondary market with securitization or issuance of covered bonds. In the securitization or *originate-to-distribute* (OTD) *model*, the originators sell the mortgages to a third party. The third party packages them into securities backed by the cash flow from the repayment of the loans, selling the MBS to capital market investors. The originators have weak incentives to conduct careful assessment of the creditworthiness of the borrowers because they transfer the credit risk by selling the mortgages to a third party. Because the investors who purchase MBS have sufficient information about the quality of the underlying mortgages, credit enhancement such as a guarantee on the repayment of principal and interest may be needed.

3. Discuss the general characteristics of ARMs and FRMs in terms of their impact on the housing market outcome.

   ARMs offer more affordable options for financing home purchases because they carry lower interest rates than FRMs. FRMs are funded from the wholesale capital market and have a scale advantage over deposit-based funding. Countries with FRM-dominated mortgage markets are likely to have larger market size and those with ARM-dominated mortgage markets are likely to have higher homeownership rates, other things being equal.

4. Identify the criteria that can be used to gauge how well a country's mortgage finance system is functioning.

   The criteria that can be used to gauge how well a country's mortgage finance system is functioning include (1) accessibility to mortgage credit, (2) risk appetite in managing mortgage interest rate risk, and (3) risk appetite in managing mortgage credit risk. Table 6.4 provides specific sub-indicators for each and a classification of difference countries in terms of the extents of these criteria.

Chapter 7 Development of the Market for Mortgage-Backed Securities

1. How does the standard mortgage meet those needs in comparison with the instrument mortgage of several hundred years ago?

   A mortgage is a loan that is secured by real property. Today's typical homebuyer expects to make an initial down payment but seeks to obtain a loan for a substantial portion of the cost of the real estate, often 80 percent or more. A loan of such size could easily be more than an entire year's worth of income for a typical borrower.

Hence, a borrower needs an extended period to pay off the loan. Additionally, although some borrowers might be willing to accept the uncertainty represented by a variable rate of interest, many prefer a fixed rate of interest. A standard United States mortgage provides a fixed rate of interest for a fully amortizing loan of up to 30 years. In contrast, mortgage loans of the 1930s and earlier often provided a variable rate of interest, were not amortizing, and had a nominal maturity in the range of three to five years.

2. What is a MBS?

   A MBS is any financial product where the income used to provide payments for that financial product is derived from a portfolio of mortgages. Early examples of such financial products were simple pass through securities with clearly defined priorities for distributing payments made by mortgage borrowers to specific classes of investors. The subsequent development of other products, such as collateralized mortgage obligations (CMOs), provides a wider range of choices for potential investors.

3. Describe both the political and economic factors that have contributed to the development of the MBS market.

   The U.S. federal government has a long history of efforts to extend opportunities for homeownership to a broader class of citizens. Efforts to develop an active MBS market were clearly part of this initiative. The very first public offering of a MBS was by an agency (Fannie Mae) that the federal government created. Moreover, despite a subsequent and meaningful development of private sectors counterparts, public offerings by government entities have continued to play a dominant role in total volume of offerings. Government standards for specific forms of mortgages that are eligible for specific financial products have also played an important role for a substantial portion of the total MBS market.

4. To what extent, and in what specific ways, has the MBS market allowed for greater separation of the traditional functions of originating mortgages and investing in mortgages?

   Before the development of an active MBS market, institutions that expected to hold those mortgages to maturity or until a given borrower either defaulted or paid off in full underwrote the vast majority of home loans. Hence, the functions of mortgage underwriting and investing, while conceptually distinct, were nevertheless essentially joined. An institution wanting to compete for mortgage business needed to develop expertise with respect to both functions. During an era in which competition for originations generally required a local presence, the essential linkage between origination and investment led to recurring financial crises. The most severe of these crises was the Great Depression of the 1930s. However, for the narrower mortgage market, the eventual collapse of the U.S. S&L industry in the 1980s also had a devastating effect. The separation of underwriting and investing that is permitted by the MBS market has not brought an end to financial crises in general. Nevertheless, the risk is no longer as great that a local economic problem will effectively shut down the local mortgage market.

5. Identify economic advantages for homebuyers that have resulted from the development of the MBS market.

   An individual mortgage is not easily tradable because the property securing the mortgage and the mortgagor who is liable for the mortgage are unique. Because they are unique, a potential buyer of a mortgage must expend resources to investigate each property and each buyer. In contrast, one share of the common stock of Microsoft is the same as every other share of Microsoft. Thus, shares are fungible such that the observed price for one share is the same for every other share. This is not the case for mortgages because every loan is distinct. In theory, the initial Ginnie/Freddie/Fannie MBS created tradable mortgages because a federal government agency guaranteed or insured the underlying loans. Thus, an investor need not know anything about the underlying loans when buying a share of a Ginnie/Freddie/Fannie MBS. This fungibility of mortgages meant that more buyers were interested in investing in mortgages and could do so at lower search cost. This reduction in cost ultimately meant lower required yields for mortgages. The ultimate winners in this process are homeowners who could now borrow at lower cost. This putatively lower cost to home buyers was historically used to justify government incursions into the MBS market.

6. Discuss whether the empirical evidence indicates that securitization has been beneficial for home buyers.

 The broad empirical question is whether any MBS led to a lower cost of housing finance and an increase in homeownership. The narrower question is whether government backed MBS led to a lower cost of housing finance and an increase in homeownership. The evidence is mixed on these questions. Regarding homeownership during the period 1960–2002, the rate of homeownership in the United States was stable at around 64 percent. This period encompassed the time when the major federal government-sponsored initiatives in the MBS market including the first Ginnie Mae MBS, and the subsequent first MBS sponsored by Freddie and Fannie. The period also witnessed the creation of the first CMOs (all backed by Ginnie/Fannie/Freddie MBS). Government-sponsored MBS programs appear not to have increased the rate of U.S. homeownership. The implication is whatever economic gains derived from creating government-sponsored MBS were not passed on to homeowners. However, beginning in 2002 and ending with roughly 2006, the rate of homeownership increased from 64 to about 68 percent. During this period, the private label MBS market flourished. An implication is that, to the extent that the MBS market reduced the cost and increased the rate of homeownership, it was the initiative of a non-government-sponsored MBS that did so. The dwindling of the private label MBS market and a coincident decline in the rate of homeownership in the United States started in 2007.

Chapter 8 Prepayment and Default Risk

1. Identify which modeling technique assumes only optimal termination execution and explain why this is the case.

 Structural models assume only optimal termination. Structural models estimate termination endogenously so that only interest rates and home prices enter into a borrower's decision to terminate a loan.

2. Explain why a borrower would not immediately default upon the realization of negative equity.

Besides observing current interest rates and home prices, a borrower considers expectations of future interest rate and home prices levels when making a decision to default. As an example, a borrower who expects interest rates and home prices to increase over a short horizon is unlikely to default today.

3. Discuss why the absence of arbitrage is important for mortgage pricing.

   If a contract is not balanced and the value of the mortgage is different from the amount of the loan, then either the lender or the borrower holds a position of greater value. When a contract is not balanced at origination, a borrower's optimal strategy is immediate prepayment or default when the first mortgage payment is due. Immediate termination then prevents a structural model solution to the mortgage-pricing problem. Introducing both points and insurance into a mortgage contract prevents arbitrage and satisfies the balancing condition at origination.

4. Explain why a reduced form model is appealing for estimating mortgage termination.

   A reduced form model estimates termination exogenously using empirical termination data. The model allows explanatory flexibility whereby the modeler identifies variables describing the loan or borrower characteristics that influence termination behavior. Because termination is often observed to occur at suboptimal points in time, a reduced form model projects some level of suboptimal termination provided these instances exist in the data used to estimate the model.

Chapter 9 Commercial Mortgages and Commercial Mortgage-Backed Securities

1. Explain how the sources of financing for commercial real estate evolved over time.

   Until the Industrial Revolution, most commercial real estate was farmland. Landed gentry controlled large estates. In the United States, the government owned new lands that were sold to private landowners at low prices. As prices increased and urbanization and industrialization occurred, a need for debt financing began. This was originally satisfied by mortgage banking correspondents, who sold their originated mortgages to large financial institutions. The issuance of mortgage bonds occurred in the 1920s, but failed in the Great Depression. The commercial mortgage market was moribund until the end of World War II. Banks and insurance companies provided most commercial mortgage financing until the 1970s, when pension funds, prompted by Employee Retirement Income Security Act (ERISA), and offshore investors became active. The first MBS for income properties were GSE-backed multifamily securities. The first private-issue CMBS products were offered in the mid-1980s, but the market was thin until after the S&L crisis in the early 1990s, when the Resolution Trust Corporation (RTC) began issuing securities backed by the commercial mortgage assets of failed S&Ls. The growth of private-issue CMBS products continued until the financial crisis of 2007–2010, when high default rates caused retrenchment. Since the crisis, GSEs, multifamily, and insurance company products have been the most resurgent sectors. The banks remain dominant but have been slow in recovery, while the CMBS market is showing signs of renewed life.

2. Indicate how commercial mortgages differ from residential mortgages.
   Commercial and residential mortgages differ in the following ways:

   - Commercial mortgage loans are usually balloon loans and many of them have payments of interest only (IO) or have IO periods.
   - Prepayment is usually restricted in commercial mortgages through lock outs, prepayment penalties, yield maintenance, and *defeasance*, which is a provision that voids a bond or loan when the borrower sets aside cash or bonds sufficient enough to service the borrower's debt.
   - Commercial mortgages usually have higher default risk than prime residential mortgages.
   - To limit lender risk, commercial mortgage loans relative to residential have lower loan-to-value (LTV) ratios, higher debt service coverage ratios (DSCR), requirements to hold reserves for capital expenses, property taxes and insurance, recourse clauses or personal guarantee requirements.
   - Commercial mortgages typically have much higher spreads than residential mortgages.

3. Identify the major factors influencing commercial mortgage default.
   The major default risk factors include the health of property cash flow, equity position, loan size, volatility of collateral value, change in market interest rate, legal environment, strength of the macro economy, local commercial real estate and economic conditions, and underwriting prudence.
4. Describe how the senior-subordinate structure works in CMBS.
   CMBS tranches have varying credit qualities from AAA, AA (senior tranche), to BB, B (subordinated), and unrated (first loss). Cash flows of CMBS tranches come from the monthly mortgage payment of the underlying commercial mortgage pool. According to the cash flow distribution rule, any return of principal generated by amortization, prepayment, and default is allocated to the highest-rated tranche first and then the lower-rated tranches in a waterfall structure. Subordinated tranches will not receive any principal payback until the senior tranches are retired. Meanwhile for default loss distribution, any losses that arise from a loan default are charged against the principal balance of the lowest rated tranche that is outstanding or first-loss piece. This is referred to as the *reverse waterfall structure*. Finally, in some structures any interest received from outstanding principal is paid proportionately to all tranches. Given the cash flow distribution rules, senior CMBS tranches are protected by the subordinated tranches from default risk. Subordinated tranches act as default buffers for senior tranches.
5. Give four examples of changes in the CMBS market after the recent financial crisis.
   Overall, new CMBS issuances (CMBS 2.0) have more conservative underwriting and intend to have more transparency. Specific examples include but not limit to:

   - CMBS 2.0 deals have simpler deal structure including fewer bond classes and fewer loans in the pool.
   - CMBS 2.0 has more conservative LTV and DSCR ratios.
   - Loan amortization is generally expected and full or partial IOs are limited in the pool; fewer loans with B-notes or mezzanine debt are allowed in the pool.

- CMBS 2.0 has stricter CMBS loan and deal covenants, such as more stringent cash management, expanded representation and warranties of the loan pools, and more strictly enforced recourse carve-out guarantees.

Chapter 10 The Subprime Mortgage Crisis

1. Explain whether the pursuit of higher homeownership rates contributed to the housing bubble and burst.

   The pursuit of high homeownership rates contributed to the housing bubble and subsequent burst. This pursuit involved the Department of Housing and Urban Development (HUD) encouraging high LTV lending, requiring banks to meet a particular quota of loans in specific areas, and organizations such as Fannie Mae taking up the cause of securitizing mortgages. This created incentive structures that caused banks to lend to people who would otherwise not qualify for a loan. Such actions later led to a housing bubble as borrowers bought houses with these loans. Many borrowers knew they could not afford to pay off the loans resulting in defaults. As a result, these houses went back onto the market resulting in the decline in housing prices. Eventually, the housing bubble burst.
2. Discuss how the federal government contributed to the subprime mortgage crisis.

   The federal government's actions within the marketplace through its pursuit of high homeownership rates led to the subprime crisis. The government through its many agencies such as HUD promoted high LTV lending, no documentation (no-doc) loans, and subprime lending. This increased the amount of subprime mortgages in the marketplace resulting in various instability issues. Additionally, government-sponsored enterprises, namely, Fannie Mae and Freddie Mac, securitized these mortgages. The end result was the growth in housing prices and the inevitable bust of the housing bubble.
3. Discuss whether the government should encourage mortgages with LTVs greater than 90 percent or credit scores, such as FICO, below 660.

   The government should not encourage high LTV lending, which led to subprime lending. The government's initial pursuit of this practice eventually contributed to the downfall of the financial sector in 2008. Various edicts of HUD and the Federal Housing Finance Agency (FHFA) led to increased lending to subprime borrowers. When those borrowers realized they could not afford to pay off the loan, they defaulted. By encouraging high LTV and subprime lending, the government contributed to the financial crisis and subsequent recession.
4. Explain the involvement of non-bank lenders and HUD in the subprime crisis.

   Until the start of the financial crisis, HUD encouraged low down payment, high LTV lending among financial institutions. HUD also encouraged no-doc or "stated-income" lending in order to promote homeownership. Non-bank financial entities such as New Century Financial pursued a policy of creating mortgages in order to securitize them. These factors ultimately resulted in toxic assets being securitized and then placed into the securities markets.
5. Discuss the contribution of CDOs in the subprime crisis.

CDOs contributed to the subprime crisis mostly due to their content and structure. Before the financial crisis, many CDOs involved MBS containing mortgages belonging to subprime borrowers. The structure of CDOs often consisted of tranches, which the credit rating agencies gave overly high ratings. When the housing bubble burst, CDOs collapsed in value harming all of the tranches by reducing their value.

Chapter 11 REITs: Structure and Performance

1. Discuss the reasons for the apparent lack of a contemporaneous link between the performance of REITs and the performance of the underlying real asset market.

   The consensus is that REITs and underlying real estate share a long-run relationship, but this relationship is much weaker in the short run. The most obvious explanation of this is that REITs are publicly traded stocks and as such they are likely to impound much more forward-looking information than measures of the underlying real estate returns. This difference may be most extreme for appraisal-based real estate returns. There is an inherent backward looking nature of the appraisals that make up such returns. This would explain the appearance of a long-run relationship, but in the short run a weak linkage occurs between the two. A less obvious explanation is that measures of underlying real estate returns are not very effective. The underlying real estate contains heterogeneous assets that trade in illiquid markets. This makes accurate measurement of the underlying real estate returns very difficult. Each methodology such as appraisals, hedonic regressions, and repeat sales models has empirical limitations. So the true relationship may be stronger than observed simply because of using a poor proxy for the underlying returns.
2. Explain why REITs may not require as strong a corporate governance structure as typical corporations.

   Corporate governance systems are designed to prevent management from engaging in activities that are harmful to shareholders, such as investing in bad projects (over-investment) or consuming perquisites. This is more likely to occur when the firm has excess cash flow with which management could engage in these activities. This is likely to be less of an issue for REITs than for regular corporations because REITs have limited free cash flow. The dividend distribution requirements imposed on REITs limit the amount of free cash flow. If management wants to engage in over-investment or perquisite consumption, it would need to fund this using external capital and the capital markets are unlikely to fund such activities.
3. Discuss why institutional investors hold an increasing percentage of REIT shares.

   Several factors contribute to the increased institutional ownership levels of REITs, but they do not completely explain the observed relationship. First, the level of institutional ownership in all equities has, on average, increased through time. Markets have become more institutional through time and REITs as part of the general stock market have experienced this trend. Second, the relaxation of the five or fewer rule in 1994 removed a barrier that limited institutional ownership. To the extent that this was a barrier to institutions, removing it would have a positive impact on ownership levels. This explains the rapid increase in ownership in the mid-1990s. Third, the size of an average REIT has grown dramatically through time. Because firm size has a positive impact on institutional ownership, this would also help explain a portion of the increased ownership levels.

4. Compare the historical performance of REITs with mid-cap equities and riskless bonds.

   Both REITs and mid-cap equities have higher mean returns and standard deviations than riskless bonds. In terms of means and variances, REITs and mid-cap equities appear similar and have experienced a high correlation over the past two decades. REITs had higher Sharpe ratios than riskless bonds in the mid-1990s and late 2000s, but they were similar during other periods. Comparing REITs to mid-cap equities, mid-cap equities have higher Sharpe ratios except for the mid-to-late 2000s where REITs outperformed.

Chapter 12 REITs: International Dimensions

1. Which international REIT markets are as developed as the U.S. market?

   Australian REITs are the only international market that is nearly as developed as the United States. While The Netherlands passed legislation allowing for REITs just a few years after Australia, its markets have not developed at the same pace. The Asian REITs (Singapore, Japan, and China) were formed during the first decade of the twenty-first century.

2. Why are I-REITs attractive to both domestic and global investors?

   Empirical evidence indicates that REITs sometimes simulate the returns of the underlying physical property. Because property returns are tied to the local economic environment and the national economy, this allows for a more pure exposure to a given country's economic environment. This contrasts with equity where most large companies with sufficient liquidity receive a substantial portion of their revenue from non-domestic sources. A more domestic-minded investor may want additional diversification benefits by adding international assets. Because REITs follow the underlying property (or comparable local property), asset diversification benefits exist. For an investor who is already holding international assets, particularly international equity, adding international REITs offers more direct exposure to economies of interest, while adding another asset type to enhance the portfolio's risk-return ratio.

3. What are the primary growth factors for I-REITs?

   I-REITs are likely to grow because of their introduction and expansion worldwide and limited holdings. In Europe, REIT markets are still in the developing stages, with many countries launching programs and funds for investing in REITs. Also, the global financial crisis left many countries in the region looking for ways to increase investment interest in commercial property. REIT structures are a natural choice to accomplish this goal. For instance, both Germany and Spain may revise their current laws to encourage the growth of their REIT markets and Ireland is introducing REIT legislation. As Asia and Latin America continue to grow, the amount of investable property in these regions is also likely to grow. This should fuel continued long-term growth in the I-REIT markets. The current amount of global investable property held by REITs is low (5 to 10 percent) of the total stock of commercial real estate. The growth potential for international REITs has a high ceiling before competition from new REITs entering the market, or by growth of those existing drives up property prices to potentially unprofitable levels.

4. How large is the public real estate market as compared to the total investable property worldwide?

   For every hundred dollars invested worldwide, eight dollars are allocated to the public real estate markets. This is consistent with various public reports that the total securitized portion of investable real estate is only between 5 and 10 percent. The breakdown in real estate is currently skewed toward Europe and North America, with about 70 percent of the investable property contained in these two locations. The remaining 30 percent is in Australia and other Asian countries. The anticipated growth of Asian cities, particularly in China, India, and Southeast Asia, is likely to lead to an increase in both supply and demand for investable property in Asia and global investors. This may lead to additional securitization of property. Hence, the aggregate size of the REIT markets is likely to grow considerably.

5. What are the empirical research findings on the correlation of I-REITs with other major asset classes?

   The empirical research findings on the correlation between I-REITs and other types of assets are mixed. Assuming the performance of I-REITs from different regions is in line with that of other assets, asset managers may pay less attention to diversification. No need exists to diversify across international markets. In the event of increased correlation overtime, the risk-reward ratio of a globally diversified real estate portfolio will be jeopardized. The exact degree of correlation among assets is important in finding an optimal portfolio where the overall risk should be minimized and return maximized.

Chapter 13 REITs: Capital Structure

1. Identify several unique characteristics of REITs and discuss how they make REIT capital structure a worthwhile topic to research.

   REITs do not pay taxes at the corporate level, so no obvious tax benefit accrues from using debt. This excludes the tax-based considerations for issuing debt. However, REITs still use much debt in their capital structure. Thus, why REITs use debt given no tax benefit is puzzling. With the 90 percent dividend payout requirement, REITs must go to the external capital markets frequently to raise equity. Some argue that pecking order or information asymmetry-based theory seems to be less relevant for REITs. By contrast, others contend that valuing REIT assets is difficult. Thus, information asymmetry and pecking order theory are still relevant to REITs. Some researchers believe that managers of REITs cannot hold much cash and thus the free cash flow problem is not an issue to REITs. Yet, others claim that agency conflicts from free cash flow still matter to REITs. Because the 90 percent dividend payout requirement is based on taxable income and REITs have a large amount of depreciation, REIT managers can accumulate free cash flow for their own benefit. Most of the assets held by REITs are not firm-specific, tangible assets. Thus, the bankruptcy costs for REITs are relatively low. Some contend REITs should issue more debt and trade-off theory may be less relevant to REITs due to low potential bankruptcy costs.

2. Identify which capital structure theories (trade-off theory, pecking order theory, and market timing theory) the REIT data support.

   Strong evidence supports the market timing theory, which suggests REITs time their equity or debt issuances based on the market conditions. Several studies provide evidence consistent with trade-off theory while trade-off theory tends to play a secondary role in REIT financial structure. Little empirical evidence supports pecking order theory.

3. Identify several major determinants that affect REIT capital structure.

   Asset tangibility and firm size are positively related to the REIT's debt-to-asset ratio, while profitability and growth opportunities are inversely related. REITs with large bank lines of credit available or REITs that draw down a lower percentage of available credit lines have a lower debt-to-asset ratio. REITs with entrenched chief executive officers use less leverage and shorter maturity debt. REITs with banking relationships have lower debt-to-asset ratios. REITs with the most liquid assets use more debt. A REIT's volatility of operating performance relative to the median volatility of operating performance of its segment peers is an important determinant of its debt-to-asset ratio. In short, industry competition influences a REIT's debt-to-asset ratio.

4. Discuss how a REIT's capital structure influences its investment activities and operations.

   Bank line capacity, incremental credit line usage, and retained cash all significantly influence firm investment. Moreover, both credit line capacity and usage have a stronger effect on investment in the more constrained firms than in the less constrained firms. These results suggest REITs use credit lines to relax cash constraints and accelerate investment, especially for those more constrained REITs. REITs were net sellers during the market peak (2006–2007) and were net buyers before and after the market peak. In contrast, unlisted property companies often sell properties before or after the market peak. Compared with unlisted property companies, REITs have better access to public capital markets for equity and debt financing, which allows them to take advantage of the better acquisition opportunities. Bank lines of credit helped REITs gain access to liquid capital during a credit crunch. There is a positive relationship between the total credit line-financial liquidity ratio and operating performance measures. Furthermore, enhanced liquidity has a strong effect on profitability for those REITs considered being capital constrained.

5. Explain why REITs hold so little cash.

   Although REITs must pay 90 percent of taxable income via dividends as required by the tax code, they can retain more cash if they desire. Because depreciation is a large non-cash item, the amount of taxable income is usually much lower than the true cash flow available for many REITs. REIT cash holdings are negatively related to funds from operations, leverage, and credit line access and use. However, cash holdings are positively related to the cost of external finance and growth opportunities. REITs lower their cash holdings in order to reduce the agency cost problem so that the firms can gain better access to the external capital market in the future.

6. Discuss the evolution of REIT capital structure over the past two decades.

REIT capital structure has evolved through at least three stages. The first stage uses secondary offerings and secured single-asset liabilities such as mortgages. The second stage features dramatic growth using revolving bank credit lines, many of which are unsecured. The third stage uses arm's length, unsecured public debt. During this evolution of REIT capital structure, banks clearly play an important role and banking relationships improve the overall capital acquisition process of REITs.

Chapter 14 Real Estate Operating Companies

1. Define a REOC.

   A *REOC* is a publicly traded company that is listed on a major exchange, specializes in real estate investments, is not legally defined, is not otherwise restricted structurally in the type of real estate business it conducts, and has not elected REIT status.
2. Identify and discuss the key structural differences between a REOC and a REIT.

   The key structural differences between a REOC and a REIT involve organizational control, taxation, dividend policy, and restrictions on business. REOCs have no restrictions on organizational control. In most countries, REIT rules require a minimum number of shareholders with no block holding a large number of shares. REOC shareholders face double taxation. REOC taxation is the same as a standard corporation. In contrast, a REIT is not taxed at the firm level. A REIT is required to pay out at least 90 percent of its taxable income in dividends. This dividend requirement means that REITs are highly dependent on returning to capital markets to fund their businesses. REOCs can retain earnings and accumulate cash. REITs cannot engage in certain activities that are considered more risky such as development or beyond the scope of property or mortgage income, such as offering brokerage or other real estate services. REOCs have no such restrictions.
3. List the main advantages and disadvantages of choosing the REOC form.

   The main advantages of REOCs involve: (1) benefits from using debt, (2) more growth potential, (3) greater ability to time the market, (4) fewer restrictions on the investor base, (5) more permissible activities, and (6) greater flexibility in times of distress. The key disadvantages are: (1) double taxation and (2) higher transaction costs from engaging in tax minimizing strategies.
4. How do firms choose between the two organizational forms—REOC or REIT?

   REOCs offer flexibility in changing organizational structure. Because REITs have payout and ownership restrictions, they choose assets with limited risk of fluctuation in returns. Troubled distressed firms move to a more flexible organizational structure, with subsequent reductions in dividends, improvements in performance, and increases in asset sales and investments. By contrast, healthy non-distressed firms that move to a tighter structure have larger free cash flows before the change. They increase dividends, reduce free cash flows, and improve profitability after the change. REOCs are generally more flexible than REITs.

5. Identify and discuss the key valuation metrics for REOCs.

   Four key metrics are available for valuing REOCs:

   - *Net asset value (NAV).* This approach determines the underlying value of the holdings of a REOC.
   - *Discounted cash flow (DCF).* In the DCF valuation, free cash flow to equity is discounted using the cost of equity. Analysts ordinarily use funds from operations (FFO) or adjusted FFO (AFFO).
   - *Cash flow multiples.* For REOCs with high levels of income-producing property, analysts use a cash flow multiple approach.
   - *Forward dividend yields/discount dividend models.* Analysts usually use forward dividend yields or dividend discount models (DDM) for REOCs with high proportions of income-producing properties.

5. Explain how REOCs perform in the market environment.

   The following summarizes how REOCs perform in the market environment. After controlling for currency and capital markets, REOCs have higher systematic risk than REITs and exhibit greater volatility. REOCs outperform REITs in up markets and underperform in down markets. From a diversification perspective and given the similarities in assets, REOCs and REITs perform about the same in a multi-asset class portfolio. Over a market cycle, REOCs and REITs achieve similar returns.

Index

N

www.ingramcontent.com/pod-product-compliance
Ingram Content Group UK Ltd.
Pitfield, Milton Keynes, MK11 3LW, UK
UKHW041434160926
475595UK00019B/16

9 780199 993277